Herbicidal Warfare

Herbicidal Warfare

The RANCH HAND Project in Vietnam

By
Paul Frederick Cecil

PRAEGER

PRAEGER SPECIAL STUDIES • PRAEGER SCIENTIFIC

New York • Westport, Connecticut • London

Library of Congress Cataloging-in-Publication Data

Cecil, Paul Frederick.
  Herbicidal warfare.

  Bibliography: p.
  Includes index.
  1. Operation Ranch Hand.   2. Vietnamese Conflict, 1961-
1975—Chemical warfare.   3. Herbicides—War use.
I. Title.
DX559.8.C5C43   1986   959.704'38   85-30779
ISBN 0-275-92007-0 (alk. paper)

Library of Congress Catalog Card Number: 85-30779
ISBN: 0-275-92007-0

First published in 1986

Praeger Publishers, 521 Fifth Avenue, New York, NY 10175
A division of Greenwood Press, Inc.

Printed in the United States of America

The paper used in this book complies with the Permanent
Paper Standard issued by the National Information Standards
Organization (Z39.48-1984).

10 9 8 7 6 5 4 3 2 1

Contents

RANCH HAND UNIT INSIGNIA

Designed in 1962 by Captain Allen Kidd and Lieutenant John Hodgin, the insignia symbolized various aspects of the RANCH HAND organization. The red lettering on a yellow circle represented the close association of the unit with the Republic of Vietnam, the national colors of which were red and yellow. The brown stripe across a green field depicted a defoliation swath through a forest. The silver caligraphy in the center of the stripe was the Chinese character for the word "purple," the code name for the first primary herbicide used by RANCH HAND in Vietnam, and the color of the scarves worn by the unit members.

In Memory of Comrades
Who Wore the Purple Scarf

Staff Sergeant Milo B. Coghill
Captain Fergus C. Groves II
Captain Robert D. Larson
Captain Roy R. Kubley
Major Lloyd F. Walker
Captain Harvey Mulhouser
Captain Howard L. Barden
Airman First Class Ronald K. Miyazaki
Captain Thomas E. Davie
Lieutenant Colonel Everett E. Foster
Major Allan J. Sterns
Major Donald T. Stienbrunner
Staff Sergeant Irvin G. Weyandt
Sergeant Le Tan Bo, RVNAF
Captain William B. Mahone
Captain Virgil K. Kelly, Jr.
Technical Sergeant Jacklin M. Boatwright
Technical Sergeant Harold C. Cook
Lieutenant Colonel Emmett Rucker, Jr.
Major James L. Shanks
Sergeant Herbert E. Schmidt
First Lieutenant Charles M. Deas
Master Sergeant Donald L. Dunn
Technical Sergeant Clyde W. Hanson
First Lieutenant Richard W. O'Keefe
Lieutenant Colonel Daniel H. Tate
Captain Joseph B. Chalk

And of a Commander, Roommate, and Friend
Lieutenant Colonel Merle D. Turner

List of Photographs

All photographs are from the RANCH HAND Collection, Texas A & M University Archives, College Station, Texas.

List of Maps

List of Charts

Preface

At the time of this writing, more than a decade has passed since the last RANCH HAND mission in Vietnam. The realities of new ground-to-air defensive weapons make it unlikely that such a role will again be attempted, even if chemical warfare is used on future battlefields. The 1,247 men who returned from duty with RANCH HAND have gone their own ways—most are retired or separated from the Air Force, some having attained high rank, at least five becoming flag officers. Annually, near the anniversary of the organizational date for the 12th Air Commando Squadron, a number of these "RANCHERS" meet for three days of partying, reminiscing, and paying tribute to the men who did not come home. Each year they get grayer and the tall tales get taller. As one veteran put it, "We have to tell lies, the truth is just too unbelievable."

Like most veterans of Vietnam, these men returned to no celebrations or speeches of welcome, no banquets or parades; but because their program had been associated in the media with "chemical warfare," RANCH HAND veterans were even more a pariah than most Vietnam returnees. The unique aspects of their episode in the history of aerial warfare were buried under the adverse publicity of the controversies over ecological warfare and the use of one particular herbicide. At the reunions, the men and their wives jokingly wear tee-shirts emblazoned with phrases like "I married Agent Orange," "Retired Tree Killer," and "Have defoliant, will travel." Underlying the humorous attire, however, is a sense of frustration, born of the belief that the American public has never realized that the program saved many lives. Beyond that is a bitterness that their accomplishments have been transformed into something unclean and indecent. The RANCH HAND veterans are as eager as anyone else for the facts about herbicide effects to be fully determined, but they also want the truth told concerning the job done in Vietnam by the men who wore the purple scarves.

At the urging of several fellow RANCH HAND veterans, this work attempts to describe the RANCH HAND mission and the controversies that surrounded it. There is a sameness and repetition of events from year to year because that is the way the war was. Very little is said about the upper-level political and military decisions that guided RANCH HAND because most of that material remains classified, or locked in the memories of individuals who choose not to discuss it. In any case, it makes slight difference; the men of RANCH HAND knew little of the policymaking, or even of the controversies among scientists and politicians. Men in combat are concerned primarily with staying alive, alleviating the discomforts of heat, filth, and "jock itch," and getting letters from home; anything else is unimportant. These men did not heed the headlines of stateside newspapers or scholarly journals, nor the bombasts of military leaders citing records in body counts or bombs dropped. The drive to excel at what they did was the drive of professionals to do the best possible job, to finish the task, to get the war over so all could go home.

Research into the available records and into the memories of fellow veterans has resurrected painful images better left buried. Time and nature seem to help ex-warriors recall only good times and humorous incidents, which may explain why war is so glamorous and heroic in later prose; but serious scholarship exposes the unpleasantries, misery, and terror of reality. Furthermore, since I served with RANCH HAND, to the difficulty of describing the events is added the burden of reliving them. Personal and emotional biases assume a major role, and it becomes almost impossible to remain clinical. It is hoped that some sense of what RANCH HAND really was will come from these pages. More importantly, perhaps this work will encourage further scholarly studies of the processes by which the political and military decisions concerning herbicidal warfare were reached, and of the overall issue of environmental alteration as an element of military tactics and strategy.

A serious problem in dealing with a topic of such recent military import and continuing controversy is the difficulty of gaining access to classified materials. The task has been made much easier by the cooperation of the Office of the Secretary of the Air Force, Office of Air Force History, and staff of the Albert F. Simpson Historical Research Center at Maxwell Air Force Base, Alabama. Especial thanks must go also to the personnel of the Air University Library and the Inter-Library Loan Office of the Texas A&M University Library for their patient help. To Professors Roger A. Beaumont, Larry D. Hill, Arnold P. Krammer, and Martin V. Melosi, of Texas A&M University, go my deepest appreciation for the long hours they spent correcting my drafts and providing invaluable suggestions. In particular, I must express my gratitude to Professor William P. Snyder for his friendship and steadying hand during moments of crisis. Most importantly, I thank my wife, Barbara, and my children for tolerating my periods of frustration and for the many sacrifices they made so this work could be completed; they are more joyful than I that it is finally done. Finally, I owe a debt that cannot be paid to the hundreds of RANCHERS who helped provide the information for this work. Only they will understand the depths of my feelings when I end with the traditional toast:

TO THE RANCH!

Map 1: South Vietnamese provinces and separate city administrative areas, 1967.

Boundary and location representations approximate

Separate City Administrative Areas	
Hue	Da Nang
Dalat	Cam Ranh
Saigon	Vung Tau

Source: author.

Map 2: Corps Tactical Zone boundaries, South Vietnam.

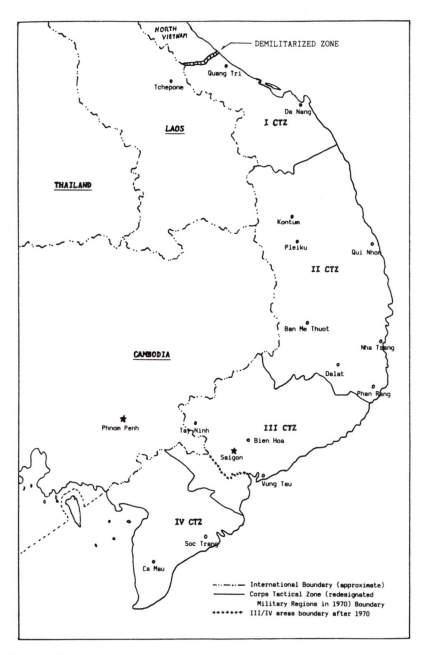

Source: author.

An Introduction to
Indirect Warfare

On a warm summer day in 1980 an aging Air Force transport plane gently
settled onto the runway at Wright-Patterson Air Force Base (AFB), Ohio, for
the last time. The 23-year-old aircraft, nicknamed "Patches" in honor of the
repairs caused by almost 600 hits by enemy ground fire in Vietnam, was on its
way to permanent display in the Air Force Aviation Museum, retired after
10,000 hours flying time. Patches (officially carried on the Air Force inventory
as C-123K serial number 56-4362) was more than just a relic of the United States'
longest war; it was a reminder of one of the most controversial operations in the
history of the United States Air Force (USAF)—chemical defoliation of forests
and destruction of crops—and a tribute to the over 1,200 volunteers who
serviced and flew the chemical spray planes during the operation's nine-year
history.[1]

Flying unarmed, obsolescent aircraft at slow speed and tree-top level,
these volunteers, under the code name "Operation RANCH HAND," attacked
the enemy's environment again and again, while being shot at and hit by
ground fire more frequently than any other Air Force unit in the Vietnam
War.[2] Almost from the beginning of this operation, requests from field
commanders for herbicide missions far exceeded the capacity of the organization, despite repeated expansion of the unit. At the same time, criticism of
these attacks on the environment also multiplied, both from within the United
States and from around the world. American officials denied that chemical
application in Vietnam violated international agreements concerning the rules
of warfare, and they disputed claims that the herbicides used either were
permanently damaging to the environment or were hazardous to human
beings. Nevertheless, by 1971 internal and external political pressures on the
US government were so intense that it became necessary to cancel the entire

RANCH HAND program. Thus ended a combat organization dedicated solely to the purpose of conducting war upon the environment—to attacking plants instead of people. Created in secrecy and disbanded in controversy, this specialized warfare unit occupies a unique place in aviation history.

The story of environmental warfare, however, did not end with the deactivation of the defoliation units in Vietnam. During the mid-1970s, while the dispute over the extent and permanence of damage to the Vietnamese ecology declined to a matter of scholarly debate, a new controversy arose. With increasing numbers of veterans of the Vietnam War claiming serious health and genetic damage from exposure to one of the primary herbicides, the "Agent Orange" issue caught the public eye to a far greater extent than had the previous critiques and postmortems by the scientific and academic communities.[3]

The topic of chemical warfare was also kept before the public by allegations of Soviet activities, including reports of the use of noxious gases and toxic sprays by Soviet troops against Afghan insurgents. Rumors of the use of a new, third-generation chemical weapon, so-called "Yellow Rain," by communist forces against the Hmong tribesmen of Laos and other Southeast Asian opposition attracted the attention of the press and American congressmen. Previously assailed for its gas/herbicide policies in Vietnam, in the 1980s the United States played the role of the accuser in the realm of chemical/biological warfare and counterguerrilla tactics.[4]

Chemical/biological warfare, however, is not a recent development. Indeed, chemical weapons predate the use of bullet and bomb, themselves normally dependent on a chemical reaction as propellant or exploder, or both. One of the earliest recorded uses of chemical warfare appeared in the Peloponnesian War, when the Spartans burned wood, saturated with pitch and sulphur, under the city walls of Plataea in 428 B.C. to create choking, poisonous chemical fumes. This tactic also was used in 424 B.C. at the siege of Belium. Ironically, this crude chemical warfare surfaced again in the same area 2,300 years later when burning sulphur fumes were used against guerrilla-occupied caves during the Greek Civil War. The use of burning sulphur also was suggested by Lord Admiral Dundonald (Admiral Sir Thomas Cochrane) in 1855 as a method of reducing Sebastopol during the Crimean War. A committee of the Palmerston government in Great Britain rejected this proposal on the basis that the effects would be "so horrible that no honorable combatant could use the means required to produce them." The contestants in World War I apparently were less appalled by the potential results; in the autumn of 1914 the British Admiralty gave serious consideration to clouds of sulphur dioxide fumes as an offensive weapon.[5]

Throwing diseased bodies into water wells or over the walls of besieged cities was another frequent tactic of the ancients which continued into the twentieth century; German troops allegedly poisoned wells in the Somme area during the retreat to the Hindenburg Line in February 1917. An earlier example of this form of warfare occurred in 1763 when the British provided Indians near Fort Pitt in the Ohio Territory with blankets contaminated with smallpox, thus decimating an unwary foe that lacked immunity. The same tactic was used during the American Revolution, this time by Americans against British troops.[6] In the general view of "total war," not all warfare involves direct attack against the enemy armed forces. Military units can be appreciably weakened or exposed through assaults on their supporting elements, including the civil population and the environment. Destruction of housing, forced relocations of populations, destruction of food supplies, elimination of concealment and forest sanctuary, and driving the enemy into inhospitable terrain unsuitable to agricultural support constitute what has become known as environmental warfare. Again, this aspect of war is not a recent phenonenon; in 146 B.C., after defeating the Carthaginians, the Romans leveled their enemy's city and sowed the site with salt to sterilize the soil.[7]

More familiar to Americans as an example of "total war" is General William T. Sherman's march across Georgia during the American Civil War, which cut a 50- to 60-mile-wide swath of destruction through the heart of the Confederacy. Accused of practicing unjustifiable excesses, Sherman's campaign against the property and resources of the South was later recognized as "conceived as a substitute for further human slaughter." Sheridan's Valley Campaign, on the other hand, was distinctly a defensive measure designed to eliminate the Shenandoah Valley as an invasion route for Southern forces by systematic destruction of all supplies useful to a foraging invader.[8]

In the Indian Wars that followed the reunification of the American states, the Army successfully employed environmental warfare to counter the "hit-and-run" tactics of the plains Indians. Civilian destruction of buffalo herds upon which the tribes were almost totally dependent was applauded by the Army, and aided materially in forcing the tribes onto reservations, where they were more easily controlled. Destruction of food supplies and starvation of hostile belligerents—"whether armed or not"—also was the stated policy of General J. Franklin Bell in the Batangas Campaign during the Philippine Insurrection following the Spanish-American War.[9]

The activities of total war, however, were not extended to include modern chemistry until the twentieth century. Widespread apprehension of chemicals as weapons was evident in the attempts to restrict their use during the Hague Peace Conference of 1899 and the subsequent Congress of 1907, although the wording of the pledges mentioned only poisons and poisonous weapons specifically. The idea of filling shells with lethal chemicals had surfaced a half century earlier, but it was not until the First World War that the concept found widespread application.[10] First to use chemical weapons were the

French. In August 1914 French soldiers fired rifle-launched cartridges filled with ethylbromacetate, an irritating, slightly suffocating, but nontoxic, agent. The small amount of liquid held by the 26-millimeter cartridge (approximately 19 cubic centimeters) had little effect on the enemy. By early 1915 both French and Germans had modified standard artillery shells into improvised chemical weapons, still using irritant agents. Much more effective was the April 1915 German attack using cylinder-dispensed chlorine gas against French Territorials and the 45th (Algerian) Division occupying the line at Ypres. Despite more than two months' warning of the impending attack, the French were unprepared and their front line was broken; the Germans were equally surprised by the extent of their success and failed to exploit the breakthrough. Estimates of respiratory casualties from this initial use of lethal gas range from 7,000 to 20,000.[11]

Following the Ypres attack, chemical weapons proliferated rapidly. Phosgene, mustard gas, diphenyl-cyanarsin, and ethylcholoarsine were among the approximately 40 harassing, percutaneous, and respiratory casualty agents developed by the warring powers. War departments were flooded with suggestions for new chemical weapons, many of which were more innovative than practical. An example of the former was the proposal received by the British Board of Ordnance and Fortifications for filling a bomb with snuff. The suggestion was to explode the "snuff bomb" so that "the enemy would be convulsed with sneezing, and in this period of paroxysm it would be possible to creep up on him and capture him in the throes of the convulsion."[12]

Research in chemical delivery systems produced such new weapons as chemical hand grenades, emplaced gas cylinders, Livens Projectors, various artillery projectiles, and several sizes of trench mortars, including one of the most effective new weapons designed for chemical warfare, the widely copied British four-inch Stokes mortar. Although both sides experimented with the idea, an aerially delivered gas weapon was not developed, and by 1917 the gas artillery shell was the major means of chemical attack. In spite of equally frantic development of protective devices to counter chemical attacks, by the end of the war gas casualties totaled nearly 1.3 million men, with more than 91,000 fatalities.[13]

On the other hand, environmental damage on the Continent during the war was mainly incidental to the combat of the times. Trench warfare and widespread use of massed artillery damaged the ecology in the immediate vicinity of the fronts, but areas remote from fixed lines of battle suffered little damage. The major exception was the 1917 "Alberich" program to make the German position between Arras and Soissons more defensible by withdrawing to the Siegfried Line. In five weeks, German clearance and demolition turned the region into a totally desolate wasteland, unable to support more than marginal occupation (when they advanced, the Allies were forced first to rebuild the basic structures of support in the devastated area). While this maneuver temporarily relieved pressure on the German armies and helped prolong the war, it obviously did not lead to German victory. Environmental warfare continued as a defensive, rather than offensive, weapon.[14]

The interwar years were a period of research and review of the lessons of World War I. Although widely disliked, chemical warfare had become a standard weapon that few doubted would be used again in future conflicts. In the United States, the Chemical Warfare Service was made a permanent part of the military establishment by the National Defense Act of 1920, and Army scientists searched for the ultimate chemical weapon. Not all aspects of this chemical research were negative; the quest for weapons led to the discovery of new means for ridding storage areas of insects and rodents. At the same time, chemical experimentation was given new impetus by unsubstantiated reports of the use of chemical weapons by both sides in the Russian Civil War, by British forces on police duties in the Middle East and the northwestern frontier of India, and by Spanish and French troops in the Moroccan wars.[15]

The 1920s also saw a renewal of the movement to prohibit the use of chemical and biological warfare, despite the recent example of World War I where all the major powers of Europe had reneged on prewar promises to respect the ban agreed to at the Hague in 1899. The United States had been one of the few nations to refuse to ratify this treaty, expressing the belief that it would not be adhered to once war broke out, a view vindicated by subsequent events. Even so, in the 1919 Versailles Treaty the victorious Allies inserted a provision outlawing "the use of asphyxiating, poisonous, or other gases and all analogeous liquids, materials or devices." For various reasons the United States again was not a signatory, but in later agreements resulting from the Washington Conference on the Limitation of Armaments in 1922, the US delegation was responsible for insertion of a prohibition against the use of chemical agents in war. This treaty was approved by the Senate and ratified by President Harding on 9 June 1923, although a subsequent dispute over the provisions pertaining to submarines caused the French to reject the treaty, making it nonbinding on all parties.[16]

During a Washington meeting of Central American states in 1923, and in the Fifth International Conference of American States in 1924 in Santiago, Chile, resolutions were passed denouncing gas warfare. Chemicals in war also were the subject of the Geneva Protocol of 1925, again at the instigation of the US delegation. Although the Senate had accepted the Washington Treaty provisions without a dissenting vote in 1923, the 1925 Protocol aroused widespread opposition. Anti-Protocol Senators succeeded in bottling up the agreement in committee, where it remained until recalled by President Truman more than two decades later, in 1947, leaving the United States as the only major government not to ratify the Geneva Protocol. Despite support in some military circles for a chemical ban, Brigadier General Amos A. Fries, Chief of Chemical Warfare from 1920 to 1929, successfully lobbied against treaty restriction on chemical weapons. The lean appropriations available to the War Department in the interwar period, however, restrained the Chemical Service from any major program of weapons development.[17]

In the early 1930s, chemical weapons were rumored to have been used during civil strife in northern China, but the first authenticated use of chemical warfare since World War I did not occur until 1935-36, during the Italo-Abyssinian campaign in Ethiopia. Fearing that the Italian front might be broken, the Italian commander used S81 bombers to rout attacking columns of Ethiopians by spraying them with yperite, a powdered mustard agent that burned and blistered on contact. Italian aircraft also dropped grenades containing lachrymatory gas, an eye irritant, on Ethiopian troops and camps, and swaths of yperite were sprayed during Italian advances to protect flanks and prevent ambushes.[18]

Newspaper communiqués from the Spanish Civil War were another source of vivid, but unsubstantiated, reports of chemical warfare. Most stories, however, appeared to have been designed to arouse international support for one side or another. On the other hand, the Japanese reportedly made extensive use of chemical bombs, artillery shells, and toxic candles against the Chinese from 1937 to the end of World War II. The Japanese tactic of combining harassing gases with conventional firepower proved especially effective. Unlike the Italians, the Japanese apparently did not use aerochemical sprays.[19]

The use of spray tanks on aircraft was not unique to the Italians. American agriculturalists were among the first to recognize the advantages of an airborne delivery system. Although one report gives 1918 as the first time cotton fields were dusted with poison from an aircraft, firm data support the initial experiment as having occurred in Ohio under the direction of the Department of Agriculture and the Army Air Service on 3 August 1921. Using a modified Air Service Curtis JN-6 aircraft and powdered arsenate of lead, the experiment near Troy, Ohio, resulted in a successful kill of 99 percent of sphinx caterpillars infesting a grove of catalpa. Further tests using de Havilland DH-4Bs during the following two years confirmed the worth of aerial dusting in controlling malaria-carrying mosquitoes.[20]

From agricultural dusting to aerochemical warfare was only a short step, and in the early 1930s the Army Air Corps began testing air-delivered chemical munitions. After experiments with a modified O-1E observation plane at Langley Field in 1932, evaluators concluded that spraying liquid chemicals was superior in extent of distribution of chemical and result compared to bursting gas bombs. In November a subcommittee to the Chemical Warfare Technical Committee was formed to consider requirements for dispersion of gas from airplanes and to recommend developments in chemical bombs and spray tanks.[21]

Due to budgetary restraints, testing of airborne chemical warfare proceeded slowly during the next few years. In 1934 the 13th Attack Squadron from Kelly Field conducted chemical exercises against ground troops stationed at Fort Crockett, Texas. Two years later, Langley Field's 37th Attack Squadron was ordered to develop and test tactics for airborne chemical attacks on airdromes, but lack of chemical supplies hampered realistic training. A 1937 memorandum pointed out that students at the advanced school for attack aviation were allotted only ten pounds of chemical spray per day of training under the then-current Day of Supply allocation—which meant that each student flew only one spray mission during his entire advanced training course. This allowance, moreover, was under review for further reduction.[22]

As a substitute for chemical gases, A-17 attack planes sprayed limewater from their 250-gallon wing tanks during the 1937 General Headquarters Air Force maneuvers. Ground elements apparently were indifferent to attacks with limewater, in contrast to the lessons learned when a 10 percent solution of irritant gas was used during exercises. Of more concern than the lack of realism in training exercises was the inadequate allocation of combat chemical stocks for future theaters of operations. The authorized 30-day supply in 1937 was sufficient for only 1½ days of normal combat operations per attack aircraft. This shortage seemed particularly critical because operations planners expected that "chemical spray undoubtedly will be used [in the next war] against enemy airdromes, troop concentrations, supply dumps and to interdict or canalize enemy ground movements by neutralization of ground areas."[23]

American planners were not the only ones to expect widespread employment of gas weapons in a future war. In November 1936 the British government announced that gas masks would be provided everyone in the United Kingdom; by the Munich crisis, over 30 million masks had been issued. New facilities for manufacturing phosgene, lewisite, and mustard gas were built by the major world powers, and former World War I plants, such as those at the Edgewood Arsenal in the United States, were reopened. Scientists in numerous laboratories worked long hours to discover new, more deadly gases. The British chemical warfare research establishment at Porton Down came up with a special wrinkle of their own, a triply powerful variant of mustard gas that was very effective when sprayed from high altitude.[24]

Fortunately, when another world war came, chemical weaponry did not play the major role foreseen by its advocates, despite heavy stockpiling of war gases by all the major belligerents. Frequently stored within the battle zone, chemical weapons remained an instrument of deterrence—a check against potential enemy chemical attack. Luckily, no nation took the first deadly step. With the exception of the previously cited Japanese chemical use in China, the few isolated incidents that took place in Poland, in the Crimea, and on some Pacific islands appeared to have been either accidents or unsanctioned acts by junior officers.[25]

In place of chemical warfare, World War II saw an increase in deliberate attacks upon the environment in the battle zones. Holland, for example, planned to stop a German invasion by a series of inundations of low-lying areas. Subsequent massive flooding in 1940 caused long-term environmental damage to the Dutch countryside, but failed to significantly delay the Wehrmacht advance. Equally futile were Soviet attempts to fire the forests of Finland with "phosphor bombs" in revenge for the Finns' alliance with Hitler in 1941. Soviet armies also practiced environmental warfare in their retreat from the Ukraine; pursuing German soldiers passed through a wasteland of burning villages and destroyed crops. Stalin's order that everything useful be removed or destroyed was climaxed by the blasting of the Dnieper Dam.[26]

This scorched earth tactic was reversed when the Soviets launched their offensive against the Germans in northern Norway in 1944. As they withdrew, the German forces carried out a program of systematic destruction of every man-made structure, including chopping down fences and dynamiting building foundations after the superstructures were burned. In a 23,000-square-mile area only a few churches were spared, forcing the Soviets to be totally self-sufficient in the harshness of this northernmost European region. This tactic, while effective, required a considerable time period and extensive manpower. In spite of this, the Germans did not yield to the temptation to resort to chemical warfare, perhaps because of the vulnerability of their fatherland to retaliation.[27]

The possibility was everpresent, however, that some country might use its chemical stockpiles, particularly if its homeland was relatively secure from attack. This possibility came perilously close to fruition during the later stages of the Pacific campaign. By late 1944 heavy US losses due to the Japanese practice of resisting to the death caused the War Department to consider using poison gas to assault heavily fortified islands, such as Iwo Jima. The Pacific area commander, Admiral Chester Nimitz, opposed the idea, later explaining: "I decided the United States should not be the first to violate the Geneva Convention."[28] Army Chief of Staff General George C. Marshall, in contrast, favored using gas in the Pacific, particularly after heavy casualties on Iwo Jima convinced him of its need in the forthcoming, much larger assault on Okinawa. Marshall was not concerned as to justification, but only whether chemical warfare would get results without such terrible US losses. This position was a reflection of the attitude of a wide segment of the American press and public throughout the war. Marshall was supported by the Joint Chiefs of Staff (JCS), who approved a plan for gas attacks on the Japanese-held islands. President Franklin D. Roosevelt, however, rejected US-initiated poison gas attacks for any reason, receiving strong backing from British

Prime Minister Winston Churchill and his military advisors, who feared it could provoke German gas assaults against England.[29]

Not all chemical weapons were proscribed during World War II. In particular, incendiary devices of many kinds were widely used by both sides, including various firebombs—oil, gasoline, inflammable metal, and chemical—designed to start massive conflagrations, the most famous of which were the Dresden attack of February and the Tokyo "firestorm" of March 1945. Portable and tank-mounted flamethrowers were used against bunkers and entrenched enemy troops. Also employed were white phosphorous munitions and the newly invented jellied gasoline, called "napalm," the latter especially effective in destroying vegetation concealing the mouths of caves where last-ditch Japanese defenders made their stand on Pacific islands.[30]

In Great Britain, the Air Ministry planned long-range bomber attacks in 1940 against German cultivated crops and coniferous forests, using "pellet" incendiaries. Coupled with prospects for a poor central-European harvest, these attacks were aimed at aggravating food shortages, disrupting military and industrial activities, and hurting German morale. Following the fall of France in June, British air attacks against canals, transportation, and forests were shifted to targets directly involved with the threat of invasion of England. Nevertheless, the attack on crops was considered sufficiently vital to remain on the list of approved operations.[31]

By late July forests were back on the list of targets to be struck during suitable weather. The Air Staff also asked for authority to use "pellets" to start fires in the heath lands of western Germany in the hope of "adding to the demoralizing and psychological effects of our operations." The shortage of long-range bomber aircraft and an overabundance of primary targets, however, apparently caused the Air Staff to reconsider the worth of attacks on the ecology. Subsequent Air Ministry letters discussed only towns and transportation as "morale" targets, without reference to either crops or forests. By 1943 both British and US operations analysts agreed that there were "no promising targets" in the target class labeled "food," and forests were not even listed as a distinct category in the Anglo-American target committee's report.[32]

Like Great Britain, the United States also considered practicing indirect warfare through attacks on enemy vegetation and crops. At the urging of several scientists in 1941, Secretary of War Henry L. Stimson asked the National Academy of Sciences (NAS) to investigate the potential for biological warfare. The subsequent report of the academy committee led to the creation of the War Research Service in February 1942, under the direction of George W. Merck, President of a large chemical company. With the approval of President Roosevelt, this civilian agency was attached to the Federal Security Agency and made responsible for all aspects of biological warfare, including the use of antiplant chemicals. In November 1942 the War Department established test laboratories and pilot facilities at Camp Detrick, Maryland.

Thirteen chemical warfare plants were constructed throughout the United States during the war, including the huge Pine Bluff Arsenal in Arkansas, begun five days before Pearl Harbor, and the 20,000-acre Rocky Mountain Arsenal near Denver, Colorado. Dugway Proving Ground, a quarter-million-acre site near the Great Salt Lake Desert in Utah, became one of the largest chemical warfare test areas in the world. In 1944 the entire program was combined and placed under the supervision of the Army's Chemical Warfare Service. Merck became special consultant to the Secretary of War and Chairman of the US Biological Warfare Committee.[33]

One of the many ideas investigated by the War Research Service was the use of synthetic growth-regulators as weedkillers when applied in toxic doses, a concept that first occurred in the 1930s to E. J. Kraus, Head of the Botany Department of the University of Chicago. During the war, Kraus suggested to a NAS committee that these toxic properties might be practical for the limitation or destruction of crops. Further tests by Kraus and John W. Mitchell at the University of Chicago led to an Army contract in 1943 for the work already done. The report that resulted caused the War Department in January 1944 to make herbicide research part of the work of the Biological Research and Testing Center at Camp Detrick. By the war's end, this agency had synthesized and tested almost 1,100 defoliant substances.[34]

Field tests of inorganic defoliants in aerosol form in Florida produced mixed results. Although defoliation trials in the Chasshowitzka Swamp near Bayport caused some leaf drop, the Army Air Forces (AAF) Evaluation Board concluded that the length of time for significant defoliation to occur confined the tactic to "long range objects only" and therefore lacked tactical application. The same conclusion was applied to the marking of bomb lines by aerial chemical sprays. In August-September 1944 tests to defoliate and then burn tropical forests were conducted near the Marathon Emergency Airstrip on an island 48 miles east-northeast of Key West. These experiments were also unsatisfactory; "oil bombs," drop-tanks filled with napalm, and other incendiaries dropped after defoliation resulted in only limited burns of short duration. On the other hand, the evaluation board suggested,

> The most important tactical application indicated for the use of ammonium thiocyanate and zinc chloride ... is for the purpose of killing, or extensively damaging food crops, established for the support of isolated Japanese units on certain islands in the Pacific.[35]

The report apparently referred to Japanese-held islands bypassed during US advances in the central and southwest Pacific, such as Wake Island.

Following additional trials in the Florida Everglades in 1945, the Army recommended that ammonium thiocyanate be used in the Pacific theater, rather than explosives, to deny the Japanese concealment offered by tropical vegetation. The recommendation was rejected due to the similarity of the agent's name with cyanide, a widely known poison. Ranking government officials were concerned that using this particular chemical compound would lead to the accusation that the United States was conducting poison-gas warfare; however, no other adequate agent was immediately available for use. "Only the rapid ending of the war," Merck later declared, "prevented field trials in an active theater of synthetic agents that would, without injury to human or animal life, affect the growing crops and make them useless." When Japan surrendered, an entire shipload of crop destruction agents was en route to the B-29 bomber bases in the Marianas Islands, and plans had been made for "an attack on the main islands of Japan early in 1946, calculated to destroy some 30% of the total rice crop."[36]

Despite predictions of military theorists during the 1920s, chemical warfare had not dominated the field of battle in the subsequent major war. The reasons why chemical weapons were not used were varied and complex—in some instances, perhaps no more than a question of time and circumstance. Yet there was little doubt that World War II research into chemical/biological weaponry had provided the basis for future exploitation in this field. Kraus's suggestions for the use of growth-regulators as plant destroyers would find widespread future application, first in agriculture and then by the military.

2

Mosquito Sprays and Weedkillers: Another Kind of Chemical War

Failure of the World War II combatants to make use of the chemical weapons at hand did not deter scientists from developing new, more deadly compounds. Even as victorious Allied soldiers were dumping thousands of tons of captured chemical weapons into the Atlantic, Baltic, and Pacific Oceans, laboratories in Great Britain, the USSR, and the United States were reviewing captured documents and samples to discover the chemical secrets of German and Japanese science. The end of the war did not mean an end to the chemical/biological weapons race, only a reduction in the overall effort.[1]

Not all of the results of wartime research disappeared into the recesses of government secrecy and "Cold War" competition. Ironically, some chemicals that the US government hesitated to apply in war were soon widely accepted in peacetime agriculture. Even while military herbicide tests remained secret, parallel experiments on common weed control were openly published and generated public excitement. In particular, the herbicide 2,4-dichloro-phenoxyacetate (2,4-D) demonstrated great specificity and gave dramatic results from only small application quantities. In 1945 the first weedkiller using 2,4-D (American Chemical Paint Company's "Weedone") was put on the market, and within a year US production of 2,4-D had climbed to 5,466,000 pounds.[2]

Although the chemistry of herbicidal effect was not immediately clear to biologists, fears of toxicological danger to animal and human life were put to rest at the 1945 North Central States Weed Control Conference. John Mitchell reported that application of double doses of 2,4-D to pastures had no ill effect on grazing animals, and feeding pure 2,4-D for three months to a cow with a nursing calf harmed neither. More dramatically, Professor Kraus revealed to the conferees that he had ingested a half-gram of pure 2,4-D daily for three weeks without effect. This demonstration of the apparent safety of systemic herbicides, together with Secretary of War Robert Patterson's end-of-war order that wartime-developed scientific data not involving vital military security be published "promptly and fully," stimulated geometric growth in the agricultural chemical industry.[3]

Another chemical practice that gained general acceptance during the war was the aerial application of insecticides to control various insects in combat zones. As American forces expanded tropical operations, insect-transmitted diseases accounted for more casualties than did enemy bullets and bombs, for example, Army Air Forces in the Pacific theater lost more man-days to mosquito-borne disease alone than to any other cause. In the Milne Bay area in January 1943, conditions were so bad that one bombardment squadron and two fighter groups were withdrawn "because of the high incidence of malaria among flying personnel of these units." Ground combat personnel were even more vulnerable to diseases such as dengue, filariasis, and fly-borne dysentery, in addition to the ever-present malaria.[4]

Although aerial spraying for mosquito control began in 1922, practical control was not possible until discovery of the insecticidal properties of dichloro-diphenyl-trichloroethane (DDT) by a Swiss scientist in 1939. Faced with staggering disease casualties in the Pacific, the AAF Tactical Center, in cooperation with the Department of Agriculture Laboratory at Orlando, Florida, and scientists from the Bureau of Entomology and Plant Quarantine, initiated a program to develop the equipment and tactics for dissemination of DDT by combat aircraft. In the United States, successful tests using single-engine Cub (L-4) aircraft were completed in October 1943 and high-speed tests using a twin-engine A-20 medium bomber with modified M-10 and M-33 chemical smoke tanks followed in December.[5]

The first combat zone mosquito control flights were made by an L-4B aircraft near the Markham River in New Guinea in February 1944; the control agent, however, was Paris Green dust, rather than DDT. Further combat area tests, using both dust and liquid insecticides, indicated light aircraft were useful but limited in capability. More effective was the B-25 "Mitchell" medium bomber, equipped with the E-1B Chemical Warfare Service smoke tank. Several B-25s in formation could spray a small beachhead in only 30 seconds, each dumping its 195 gallon load during a single pass. Using a 10 percent DDT solution diluted with fuel oil, a minimum reduction of 90 percent in adult and larval mosquito populations could be achieved. Such treatments usually persisted for at least five days, suppressing disease casualties for four or five weeks. Since this spray equipment did not appreciably replace aircraft armaments, the same plane could release DDT over the landing zone and then immediately strafe and bomb in support of the beachhead. Beachhead spraying was used during the Morotai, Palau, Iwo Jima, and Okinawa landings.[6]

Responding to demands for more extensive insecticide spraying, in March 1945 the Fifth Air Force modified four C-47 transports for aerial spray, using 330-gallon B-24 bomb-bay fuel tanks. In formation, these four aircraft covered nearly five square miles with insecticide in a single sweep. The Southwest Pacific Area Air Evaluation Board conducted a study of the various solutions to the insect spraying problem, and in a postwar report suggested that "even more effective results would have been obtained had a special unit been developed for this purpose."[7]

Headquarters, AAF, had already recognized the need for a new organization. Consideration, however, had to be given to possible effects of insecticides on the ecology and wildlife, a factor of lesser priority during combat. In November 1944 a Committee of Insect and Rodent Control was created to supervise and coordinate the methodology of insecticide application. Authority to approve insecticide projects was transferred to Headquarters, Continental Air Forces, and in September 1945, IX Troop Carrier Command was ordered to form a special aerial spray unit.[8]

On 22 April 1946 the AAF Insect Control Unit was activated as Squadron "D," 303d AAF Base Unit, Greenville Army Air Base, South Carolina, and attached to the 434th Troop Carrier Group (TCG), Third Air Force. Authorized three C-47 and three L-5 aircraft, the unit's first task was to spray the Huntsville Arsenal in Alabama. Most of the time, however, was spent in developing tactics and techniques for effective aerial delivery of insecticides. By the end of the 1946 insect season, the unit had flown only 15 spray missions. In October the squadron was disbanded and the peacetime experience evaluated for effectiveness. In its short initial existence, the Insect Control Unit had set a pattern; the procedures and flight patterns used 20 years later in Southeast Asia would vary little from those developed by this prototype organization.[9]

In 1947 the United States Air Force became a separate service, under the newly created Department of Defense (DOD). Among other duties, the Air Force was assigned responsibility for insecticide spraying of all Army and Air Force installations. To meet this responsibility the DDT aerial spray unit was reactivated for the 1947 insect season, again at Greenville AFB, South Carolina, but this time as a flight of the Headquarters Squadron, Ninth Air Force. The elimination of separate squadron status had been recommended following the 1946 experience. Using C-47 aircraft only, the 8 pilots, 3 entomologists, and 13 maintenance men of the DDT flight completed 28 missions in 1947.[10]

The 1947 organizational arrangements again proved unsatisfactory, and in January 1948 the DDT flight was transferred from Greenville to Langley AFB, Virginia. The primary advantage of the move was that Langley was the Headquarters of Tactical Air Command (TAC), the major agency responsible for directing spray missions. Here the DDT unit remained, although frequently shifted from one organization to another within the base structure. No actual spray unit existed per se, only a set of manpower allocations to be used at the whim of the possessing organization. Despite requests from the air surgeon and overseas commands, TAC Headquarters opposed establishing a separate organization for insect control in the continental United States, where a less than six-month spraying season existed. The air surgeon's arguments that a permanent organization was needed in order to retain specialized personnel and to perform research and development for future wartime missions were rejected.[11]

The stalemate continued until war broke out in Korea in 1950, when it quickly became obvious that insect-transmitted diseases would reach epidemic levels unless vigorous control measures were immediately instituted in the combat zone. Although the air staff initially considered sending the Langley flight to the Far East on temporary duty, the eventual solution was to activate a new organization in Japan, the 1st Epidemiological Flight, led by a former commander of the Langley unit, Major William M. Wilson. Using three C-46 transport aircraft from the 437th Troop Carrier Wing at Brady Field, Japan, and four L-5 liaison planes borrowed from the Army, the Fifth Air Force spray flight became a major element in the preventive medicine campaign in Korea.[12]

The lack of peacetime research and preparation in spray operations was reflected in the medical flight's jury-rigged equipment. The C-46s were prepared for insecticide work by installing two 450-gallon long-range auxiliary gasoline tanks, normally used by four-engine C-54 transports, in the belly compartment. Two fuel pressure pumps forced the insecticide through perforated pipes clamped to the underside of the horizontal stabilizers, creating a crude but effective dispersal apparatus. When the Army L-5s proved uneconomical and unsafe as insecticide aircraft, four World War II T-6 "Texan" training planes, being used as forward control aircraft, were obtained from Far East Air Forces Headquarters and modified by bolting a 110-gallon aluminum tank under the fuselage between the main landing gear. Chemical dispensing was accomplished through a simple "open/shut" electrical valve and a gravity feed/venturi system. Although this primitive mechanism provided satisfactory spray patterns, the aircraft load factor* and resultant control sluggishness made flight with a full insecticide tank extremely dangerous. A more acceptable light aircraft for spraying was eventually found when the Army and Air Force ordered a number of Canadian-built de Havilland "Beavers," subsequently designated the L-20. In the meantime, the achivements of the 1st Epidemiological Flight, despite equipment handicaps, led to the activation of a second

---

*The T-6 was not intended to carry a load such as imposed by the tank of insecticide, and the location of this weight, needed to allow the tank to clear the runway while on the ground, caused an extremely far-forward center of gravity, making the aircraft both overweight and very unstable.

spray flight for Korea (the 5th) and creation of a spray unit for the European/ North African area (the 4th Epidemiological Flight).[13]

In spite of the success of these overseas organizations, the urgings of the air surgeon, and Army threats to form its own insecticide units, Tactical Air Command still refused to establish a permanent unit based in the United States. Instead, manpower spaces for what had become known as the Special Aerial Spray Flight (SASF) were transferred with monotonous regularity. Between 1950 and 1960 the manning slots went from TAC's Headquarters Squadron to the 47th Air Base Group (ABG), to the 4430th ABG, to the 405th ABG, to the 4405th Operations Squadron, to the 4500th Support Squadron, to the 4500th Operations Squadron. Although many of these transfers were little more than paper reorganizations, administrative continuity was disrupted and no provision was made for retaining trained, specialized personnel.[14]

Compounding the problem was the opposition of commercial aviation interests to any military spray organization. By the mid-1950s agricultural chemical application had become big business, and nearly one-fourth of the over 90 million acres treated annually was serviced from the air. The growing civilian spray industry saw the vast government lands as a potential servicing bonanza. Government assurances that the SASF would be used only to spray military installations and during certain emergencies declared by the Public Health Service did not mollify industry spokesmen. These spokesmen were also critical of the SASF's lack of expertise, pointing out that aerial chemical application was a highly specialized field.[15]

The USAF engineer, arguing for a permanent military spray organization, also emphasized that untrained personnel could damage wildlife and the ecology. This danger was increasingly likely as demand for spray missions multiplied and targets became more varied. The Air Force engineer's concern was justified. Between 1945 and 1960 almost 1,200 missions would be flown to treat 69 different government facilities. Although most flights were in support of the mosquito control program, a significant number of them were made to cope with unusual problems and natural disasters. Targets of the TAC unit included floods in Kansas, grasshoppers in Nebraska, black flies in Maine, and flies feeding on massive fishkills caused by "red tides" in Florida. The spray flight also was used to reduce the number of insects in maneuver areas during large-scale military exercises, to fight fire ants and white-fringed beetles in Georgia, and to suppress equine encephalitis in New Jersey and New Mexico. Various special test missions were flown in cooperation with the Canadian government and the United States Department of Agriculture. Despite this record, after 15 years the Special Aerial Spray Flight remained an orphan organization, often misused and frequently misunderstood. Renewed interest in the late 1950s in chemical herbicides as a military weapon, however, held the promise of a new mission for the SASF.[16]

When World War II ended, research in chemical warfare, like most military research and development (R&D), was cut back. Atomic weapons, for a time, seemed to promise an end to warfare through the threat of total annihilation. The Chemical Corps' budget, reduced to an average of only $35 million a year, could support only minimal project continuation. Defoliation research at Fort Detrick was confined to screening potential defoliation agents for military use and conducting limited developmental studies on the most promising defoliants. Of 12,000 compounds examined, only 700 later underwent field and greenhouse tests. In 1950 even this minimum effort was ended when the Chemical Corps Technical Committee cancelled the project; the only antiplant research still underway was a minor program involving anticrop warfare.[17]

In the meantime, outbreaks of limited war had punctured the dream of an atomic-enforced permanent peace. In Malaya in 1948 insurgents began a 14-year attempt to overthrow the British-supported Federation government. Using hit-and-run guerrilla tactics and roadside ambushes, the terrorists initially had the advantage over local security forces. By 1953, however, the British Army was winning the jungle war. One British tactic set a precedent for future use of herbicides by the military. Stocks of the n-butyl ester of 2,4,5-trichlorophenoxyacetate (2,4,5-T) were kept available in Malaya to eradicate possible outbreaks of an obligate parasite of rubber, Dothidella ulei. The British Army used this chemical as a defoliant to thin the jungle cover along communications routes to reduce ambushes. Helicopter-dropped chemicals also were used to attack aborigine "cultivations" from the air as part of the food control program—food denial to the terrorists was later described by the general officer commanding in Malaya as one of the "decisive weapons in anti-guerrilla warfare." British forces, however, eventually abandoned crop destruction from the air as part of the program, when it became apparent that it was counterproductive in the long run; air-delivered chemicals did not discriminate between foodstuffs destined for terrorist use and those belonging to the local populace, thereby alienating those whom the British were attempting to defend. The roadside defoliation program in Malaya was restricted to surface spraying due to lack of airlift, and was too limited to permit adequate evaluation of its effectiveness. Even so, the positive aspects of the British experience in Malaya would form the basis for future American involvement in herbicidal warfare in Southeast Asia.[18]

The events in Malaya had virtually no effect in Korea; there was little use of chemical warfare in the peninsular conflict, with the exception of previously cited epidemiological efforts. Allegations by the Chinese communists and other propaganda groups that the United States dropped gas bombs and used chemical artillery shells in 1951 and 1952 were not substantiated by reliable evidence. On the other hand, US forces did engage in environmental warfare by attacking enemy food production and supplies. Only a month before the 1953 armistice, Fifth Air Force fighter-bombers destroyed several North Korean irrigation dams to damage communications and inundate a major portion of their rice-growing areas. Earlier, American aircraft attacked enemy food stocks by using napalm bombs on caches of enemy rice in light straw bags. Air Force General Earle E. Partridge requested an operations analysis of this napalm tactic to determine if this method of food destruction was effective; Partridge suggested that chemicals might be used to spray North Korean rice paddies instead. It appears that the general's suggestion was not acted upon, although a civilian witness at a congressional hearing almost twenty years later claimed,

> There was some use of defoliants in the waning days of the Korean war. Very minor use, but I saw a film which detailed some of the damage done in the last year of the war in Korea, so that precedent had already been set years before.

No evidence to support this statement was submitted.[19]

Although defoliation research by the Chemical Corps had been reduced, the Air Force continued testing aerial delivery systems in the early 1950s, including experiments with C-47s, B-26 medium bombers, and B-17 heavy bombers. American scientists at Fort Detrick had determined that the best vegetation control chemicals available were mixtures of the butyl esters of 2,4-D and 2,4,5-T; in 1952 the Air Force purchased a supply of these chemicals for possible use in a newly developed, high-volume, anticrop system known as the MC-1 "Hourglass" system. Secretly designed and built by the Hayes Aircraft Corporation, the primary component of the MC-1 system was an insulated 1,000-gallon tank that could be installed in the bomb bays of B-29 and B-50 heavy bombers, or in the cargo compartment of C-119 transports, allowing these aircraft to be quickly and easily turned into spray planes. The Korean War ended before the system was used, and the equipment and chemicals were placed in storage.[20]

Testing at Fort Detrick also continued on the World War II idea of using chemical agents on vegetation to mark targets and detect camouflage. A series of trials were completed in 1954. One compound tested (tributyl phosphate) produced a discernible mark in less than 30 minutes, and the results of another (3-amino 1,2,4-triazole) could be seen for more than three months after initial application. Lack of funding, however, curtailed further investigation and by 1957 research had been reduced to "only a token effort" in crop destruction. Budget cuts for fiscal year 1958 forced the total anticrop warfare staff to be cut from 125 to 12. Although slight budgetary increases by 1961 allowed increased manning to 16 professionals, only one individual was specifically assigned to research anticrop chemicals.[21]

Ironically, as military funding and research declined, chemical vegetation control in the civilian sector expanded rapidly. Production of 2,4-D, first publicly tested in 1945, climbed to 14 million pounds by 1950 and 36 million pounds by 1960. Production of 2,4,5-T, insignificant in 1950, reached nearly 10 million pounds in 1960, while production of all herbicides exceeded 75 million pounds. The chemical industry rushed to develop new herbicides that were more effective, more selective, and less hazardous than compounds previously used. Chemicals such as picloram, bromacil, cacodylic acid, and paraquat became widely used in agriculture and forestry, and to control vegetation along roads and power lines. Sales of herbicides rose from $2 million in 1950 to more than $129 million in 1959, when US farmers alone treated 53 million acres.[22]

The year 1959 also saw the first large-scale attempt at airborne military defoliation. Camp Drum, New York, had a serious vegetation control problem. Extensive tree coverage, predominantly sugar maples, was blocking observation of artillery shellbursts in a four-square-mile area of the firing range, but the trees could not be cleared by normal means because of the sizable number of unexploded shells in the area. Chemical defoliation from the air appeared the best solution, and the task was assigned to the Biological Warfare Laboratories at Fort Detrick. Military funds for defoliation were not available, so the job was complicated by restriction to the use of on-hand materials.[23]

By June all available materials had arrived at Camp Drum. The experimental spray apparatus from Fort Detrick was designed for use on an H-19 helicopter, but the only aircraft available was an H-21, so the equipment was modified on site. The only chemicals available for the operation were from the 1952 Air Force stocks, which later had been declared surplus and transferred to the Department of Agriculture at Beltsville, Maryland. This supply consisted of approximately 1,000 gallons each of pure butyl 2,4-D and butyl 2,4,5-T, a fortunate circumstance since these chemicals were ideal for the task at hand. The two chemicals were mixed in a one-to-one ratio, and the mixture was sprayed over the artillery area during 15 flights in an eight-day period. Despite the handicaps presented by jury-rigged equipment, pilots untrained for aerial spray operation, and application of the chemical six to eight weeks later than would have been ideal, the project was a complete success—visibility was improved by 100 percent and the vegetation "kill" was still effective two years later—although it also raised a number of questions about the future of military vegetation control.[24]

The Biological Warfare Laboratories was not the only organization attempting to "make do" by using surplus equipment. Because the C-47 aircraft were being phased out of the Air Force in the late 1950s, the Special Aerial Spray Flight had to find a new spray aircraft. At the suggestion of Captain Carl Marshall, Officer-in-Charge (OIC) of the SASF, the Fairchild-built C-123B "Provider" was selected as a potential replacement. This high-wing, twin-engine assault transport had been originally designed as a glider and its rugged airframe would later prove its worth in Vietnam. The excellent low-speed maneuverability of the aircraft suited SASF's needs exactly, and the high-mounted wings allowed convenient positioning of wing spray-booms. More importantly, the large cargo compartment and load capacity of the C-123 offered the advantage of carrying either a liquid-dispensing system as in the C-47 or a dry chemical dispersal system as in the L-20, thus offering a replacement for both aircraft. In either case, a much larger amount of insecticide could be carried, a need long recognized by SASF crews. Lack of funds, however, meant that SASF personnel would have to design and fabricate the C-123 spray system themselves, rather than have it done by an outside contractor.[25]

After surveying various equipment in military stocks, Captain Marshall discovered the 1,000-gallon Hourglass tanks and pumps in the classified storage facility at Ogden, Utah. A check with potential insecticide "customers" indicated that the one-gallon-per-acre capacity of the pumps would more than adequately meet any foreseen SASF requirements. Coincidentally, the weight of the Hourglass system when filled with chemicals almost exactly equalled the C-123's maximum cargo weight allowable. Marshall managed to get several of the chemical tanks declassified and shipped to Langley for installation and evaluation. The pairing of equipment and aircraft appeared to be ideal. Yet even as arrangements were being made to procure two more C-123s for spray modification, messages were being exchanged between the Republic of Vietnam (RVN) and the United States that would drastically affect the role of the spray-equipped C-123 and US chemical warfare policies.[26]

3

Defoliation Comes to Vietnam

After World War II France reimposed colonial government on the associated states of Indochina, despite the objections of many Americans who felt that this act violated wartime pronouncements concerning the rights of self-determination of peoples. The United States, however, was busy disbanding its wartime military forces, and in the press of other postwar matters, nothing was done. Within Indochina the French presence was actively opposed by several nationalistic groups, and full-scale guerrilla war broke out in 1946 in the region known as Vietnam, under the insurgent leadership of the *Vietnam Doc-Lap Dong Minh Hoi* (Revolutionary League for the Independence of Vietnam, popularly contracted to Vietminh). Grudging American toleration of the French position gradually changed to acceptance, and in 1950 the United States began providing active military and economic support to the French regime in Indochina. By 1954, 78 percent of France's Indochina War costs were being met by US aid, and Americans were directly assisting French forces through a Military Assistance Advisory Group (MAAG) in Saigon and on-scene maintenance support of US-loaned aircraft.[1]

Following defeat of the French forces at Dien Bien Phu in 1954, the French and Vietminh signed the Geneva Protocols, which required a phased French withdrawal from northern Vietnam, stabilization of local military forces, temporary division of Indochina into four states (including separation of North and South Vietnam), and creation of an International Control Commission (ICC) to oversee compliance. The accords did not require withdrawal of the 342-man MAAG. Neither the United States nor the new government of South Vietnam, which had been granted full independence by France six weeks earlier, was signatory to the Geneva accords, a fact later cited by the Saigon government as partial justification for its abrogation of the agreements. When France withdrew military assistance from the southern armed forces, the South Vietnamese government requested help from the United States, and on 12 February 1955 the American advisory group assumed responsibility for training the South Vietnamese Army.[2]

During 1956 the French-sponsored Bao Dai government in the south was replaced by a new regime entitling itself the Republic of Vietnam, under the leadership of a northern-born Catholic politician, Ngo Dinh Diem. When the new government refused to participate in the general elections called for in the Final Declaration of the Geneva Conference, sporadic fighting broke out between government forces and various insurgent groups collectively known as the Viet Cong (VC), a pejorative term coined by the South Vietnamese government. Inevitably, American advisors came under attack. On 22 October 1957, the Military Assistance Advisory Group headquarters and the United States Information Services (USIS) facility in Saigon were damaged by terrorist bombs, injuring several Americans. Frequent ambushes along public highways and the national railroad made travel increasingly dangerous for foreigners and Vietnamese alike. By 1959 Viet Cong forces were strong enough to make unit attacks. In an assault on the Vietnamese Air Base at Bien Hoa on 8 July, two American advisors, a major and a master sergeant, were killed.[3]

As a result of the increasing terrorism, the South Vietnamese government appealed to President Dwight Eisenhower for additional military aid. In partial response, the size of the advisory group was doubled in early 1960. Later, after Vietnamese Air Force (VNAF) Commander Colonel Nguyen Xuan Vinh grounded his only fighter squadron's decrepit World War II Navy F8Fs as unsafe, the United States replaced them with 25 more modern, but still obsolete, AD-6 aircraft. The US also agreed to modernize Vietnamese military air transportation and surveilance capabilities. When the first of 11 H-34 helicopters were delivered to the VNAF in December 1960, these force changes were cited by the International Control Commission as violations of the provisions of the Geneva Protocols prohibiting upgrading of local military forces. The charges were rejected by the South Vietnamese and US governments on the basis that neither had signed the 1954 accords and that their actions were necessary to counter violations supported by the North Vietnamese government. By the end of the year, over 900 American advisors were in South Vietnam, including US Army Special Forces teams engaged in counterinsurgency training.[4]

The situation in Indochina continued to deteriorate in 1961. Shortly after taking office, President John F. Kennedy announced that Soviet transport aircraft had been repeatedly seen supporting insurgent forces in Laos. At about the same time, the North Vietnamese government in Hanoi announced formation of the *Mat-Tran dan-toc giaiphone* (National Front for the Liberation of South Vietnam, or NLF), with the avowed purpose of overthrowing the existing South Vietnamese government. In May 1961 Vice-President Lyndon

B. Johnson was sent to Saigon by President Kennedy to consult with Vietnamese President Diem about future American assistance. One result of this consultation was establishment of a joint United States/Vietnamese Combat Development and Test Center (CDTC) in Vietnam, under direction of the Defense Department's Advanced Research Projects Agency (ARPA). The CDTC was formed to develop new counterinsurgency methods and weapons, and one of its first tasks was to evaluate the use of herbicides to destroy concealing tropical vegetation and enemy food supplies (Project AGILE). At the same time, Air Force Chief of Staff General Curtis E. LeMay ordered activation of the 4400th Combat Crew Training Squadron (CCTS) at Eglin AFB, Florida, to train US airmen for counterguerrilla warfare units, code named JUNGLE JIM.[5]

The joint center was established in Saigon within a month, and by the following month equipment and personnel were already arriving for the first herbicide tests, designated Task 2 and Task 20. Task 2 was designed to determine the feasibility of destroying a guerrilla food staple, manioc (tapioca), while Task 20 evaluated the ability of various defoliants to increase forest area visibility. Task 2 was later expanded to include sweet potatoes and rice, when an accidental spraying revealed their chemical susceptibility. Because men and equipment had to be rushed to Vietnam to take advantage of the growing season, which would end in September or October, much of the equipment used in the initial tests was "what was available," rather than "what was ideal."[6]

Dr. James W. Brown, a veteran of 17 years in plant growth-regulating chemical research, was selected to direct the project. Brown, Deputy Chief of the Crops Division at the Army's Chemical Warfare Center at Fort Detrick, was assisted by a second scientist on temporary loan from the Crops Division, initially William B. Johnson and later Lester Boyer. To train Vietnamese pilots in spray techniques and to act as advisor for air operations, the US Air Force sent Captain Mario C. Cadori on temporary duty from an assignment in Korea. Cadori was a former member of the Special Aerial Spray Flight at Langley. Two noncommissioned officers, Technical Sergeant Leon O. Roe, from Langley AFB, and Sergeant James McIntosh, US Marine Corps, were assigned to install and check out the spray equipment.[7]

Commercial aerial spray equipment in the United States was usually mounted on light aircraft, such as the PA-18, AgCat, or Steerman World War II trainer. These aircraft, however, were unsuitable for operation in a combat environment and limited in the amount of chemical that could be carried. Instead, it was decided to equip several available military aircraft with spray equipment originally designed for other purposes. Eventually the test project obtained two Aero 14-B spray tanks, on loan from the Marine Corps, for use on an AD-6 fighter aircraft; one surplus C-47 aircraft insecticide spray system from the Langley spray flight, to be subsequently retained by the VNAF; two

HIDAL (Helicopter Insecticide Dispersal Apparatus, Liquid) spray assemblies, loaned for use on H-34 helicopters; and one "Buffalo" turbine sprayer for roadside defoliation from the ground. Aircraft and aircrews for the tests were furnished by the VNAF. The Vietnamese government was responsible for selecting test sites, compensating property owners for any damages, and providing security for test areas.[8]

Three chemicals were selected for aerial applications—dinoxol, trinoxol, and "concentrate 48." These chemicals were all commercial preparations in regular concentrates of 40 percent or less active ingredients. Dinoxol was a 50/50 mixture of the butoxyethanol esters of 2,4-D and 2,4,5-T, with two pounds of each chemical per gallon of solution. Trinoxol consisted of four pounds of 2,4,5-T per gallon and concentrate 48 had three pounds of ethyl ester of 2,4-D per gallon. Concentrate 48 was a water-dilutable herbicide used in the United States for spraying coniferous species, while the other mixtures were oil-based herbicides. Small amounts of 15 other chemicals were available for micro-tests on individual plants, but were not used due to a lack of time.[9]

One of the difficulties facing the defoliation evaluators was a scarcity of information concerning vegetation species in South Vietnam. Dr. Brown, responding to a January 1960 inquiry regarding vegetation control in Southeast Asia, had suggested that a herbicide mixture containing both 2,4-D and 2,4,5-T might be most effective in a forest of unknown species, drawing his conclusion from incomplete results of earlier experiments in Louisiana. In reports on the 1961 Vietnam tests, Brown again called attention to the many unknown species of vegetation in Asia, recalling an earlier trip to Singapore in which three scientists made 14,000 collections in six months, of which only 50 could be classified as to genus.[10]

To further complicate the Vietnam project, terrorist activity and lack of security made on-site observations almost impossible. Most test areas were limited to inspection from the air, a very unsatisfactory method. Only the initial tests in the Dak To area were checked by ground teams, and even they were not inspected until two months after spray application, due to closure of the Kontum airfield and VC activity in the area. When the observations were finally made on 11 October, local woodcutters and farmers had partially destroyed the results by removing much of the affected vegetation.[11]

The project was also hampered by slow delivery of spray system components and a lack of cooperation among Air Force MAAG members. Not until the US task advisor refused to take responsibility for mission safety did MAAG personnel accept the need for mandatory special flight instruction for VNAF spray pilots. The first spray test did not take place until 10 August, although Dr. Brown and the test personnel arrived in Vietnam on 17 July. The original schedule called for this test to be made with the C-47 insecticide system, but since the HIDAL-rig mounted on an H-34 helicopter was the first system finally ready, it was used to make initial chemical tests on roadside vegetation and cultivated manioc in the Dak To area. Crops were again sprayed on 11 August, including an accidental spraying of rice and several other foodstuffs. However, vibration of spray-booms in flight caused fuselage cracks on the H-34, and the HIDAL equipment had to be grounded, pending receipt of a modification kit.[12]

After another two-week delay, the first C-47 spray mission was flown on 24 August. The following day the only AD-6 mission was flown, using the sole operational 14-B spray tank. Ironically, the latter test, using dinoxol against mangrove trees, yielded one of the most effective results of the test series. Despite heroic efforts by the Marine maintenance technician, numerous malfunctions prevented further tests with this system. The C-47 flew five more spray missions in September and October, although hampered by frequent pump and valve malfunctions. On 18 September the "Buffalo" turbine was tested on vegetation near the Vietnamese Army headquarters and housing area at Saigon, the only test in which it was possible for ground teams to frequently check chemical effects. Aerial inspection of the other test areas continued during September and October, revealing mixed and inconclusive results. To the surprise of the test observers, one of the most impressive effects occurred on the accidentally sprayed rice crop near Kontum, which was so severely damaged that its expected yield was cut by 90 percent.[13]

In October 1961 Brown accompanied presidential advisors General Maxwell Taylor and Walt W. Rostow on an aerial inspection of the herbicide test areas. Despite the limited test results available at that time, Dr. Brown suggested that chemicals potentially "could provide a means of doing some jobs more efficiently than can otherwise be done," noting that "no one appreciates food or visibility more than those deprived of it."[14] The Vietnamese government also urged adoption of a herbicide program. President Diem was particularly anxious that a food denial program be set in motion against VC havens in the highlands, and showed his interest in the herbicide evaluations by personally selecting some of the test areas. South Vietnamese officials were so certain that the chemical program would play a key role in the control of the countryside that they classified the test program data *Toi Mat* (Top Secret), even though the United States considered a "Secret" classification adequate.[15] Brown recommended to the Taylor/Rostow party, and in later reports, that if the operation were expanded, the SASF from Langley be used.[16]

Prior to mid-1961, the Langley unit's mission had remained basically unchanged—aerial dispensing of insecticides at government facilities within the continental United States. SASF manning consisted of an OIC, 4 pilots, 1 entomologist, 1 assistant entomologist, 1 clerk, and 20 maintenance personnel. Two C-123 aircraft were on hand for pilot checkout and suitability testing, while three C-47s and two L-20s were retained for normal spray operations.[17]

In July several telephone calls were received by the SASF concerning the spray capabilites of various aircraft, including one from Dr. Brown. Brown, in particular, expressed interest in the C-119, one of the aircraft for which the Hourglass system was originally designed. Captain Marshall, OIC of the Langley flight, pointed out that the C-119s had been phased out of the inventory, but that the SASF's newly acquired C-123s were capable of the same mission. Subsequent telephone inquiries and rumors made it clear that the SASF was being considered for some type of spray operation in Southeast Asia. (When asked, Captain Marshall recommended Captain Cadori's assignment for the Vietnam tests.) On 13 July 1961, a Headquarters USAF secret message alerted TAC to be prepared to deploy six C-123s for a jungle defoliation test program in the Far East.[18]

Three months later, after lengthy discussions in Washington, President Kennedy approved sending units from the newly created Air Force Special Air Warfare Center (SWAC) at Eglin AFB to assist the Vietnamese Air Force. Detachment 2A of the 4400th CCTS would provide transition and combat training for Vietnamese aircrews, while VNAF capability would be augmented by three companies of Army H-21 helicopters, a squadron of Air Force C-123 transports, and the loan of 30 T-28 training aircraft. This deployment, under the overall code name FARM GATE, was authorized in response to a dramatic increase in Viet Cong attacks against transportation systems around Saigon and to President Diem's urgent appeal for help.[19]

Meanwhile the American Embassy in Saigon informed the secretary of state on 7 October of a MAAG request for temporary assignment of six C-119 or C-123 aircraft and four H-34 helicopters for a defoliant spraying program. Although the helicopters would have to be reported to the ICC on arrival in Vietnam, Ambassador Frederick E. Nolting, Jr., suggested that the fixed-wing aircraft carry civilian markings and their crews wear "civvies" to preclude overt violation of Protocol 23 of the Geneva Accords; this tactic already had been discussed with the Canadian delegation to the ICC on a "hypothetical case basis."[20] Nolting warned against advance publicity in view of possible North Vietnamese charges of germ warfare. The State Department, on the other hand, took the view that since the aircraft were obviously American and would be flown by USAF pilots, it would be best if the South Vietnamese announced that they had asked for the program and that it was under their control and direction. Secretary of State Dean Rusk particularly wanted the Cambodian government kept fully informed of the program, avoidance of the Cambodian border area by defoliation missions, and pre-mission public assurances to Vietnamese citizens of the defensive nature of the chemicals and their lack of harmful effects on animals and humans.[21]

Pending presidential approval of the project, Tactical Air Command was ordered on 9 November to prepare six C-123s from Pope AFB, North Carolina, as spray aircraft. Using spare MC-1 tanks from Langley, the aircraft were quickly modified at Olmstead AFB, Pennsylvania. Besides removing unnecessary equipment, a special engine oil replenishment system and extra plumbing to permit the 1,000-gallon chemical tank to be used as a fuel tank were installed for the trans-Pacific ferry flight; modification was completed by 25 November. Then the six C-123s were returned to Pope for installation of the cockpit armor plating originally delivered with the aircraft; however, after years of laying in storage, the presumably useless plating had been salvaged and sold for scrap. Because permission for the overseas movement already had been received, maintenance personnel at Pope worked through Thanksgiving Day fabricating and fitting new armor plating to allow the C-123s to depart on schedule the following day.[22]

In the meantime, SASF's aircraft were transferred to flyable storage, except the two C-123s undergoing insecticide modification at the Middleton, Pennsylvania, depot. To augment SASF personnel, 51 volunteers with C-123 experience (9 pilots, 2 navigators, and 40 maintenance personnel) were selected from the Air Transport Wing at Pope. Although they could not be told anything about the mission, it clearly involved duty in Vietnam, and the volunteers were required to sign statements promising not to reveal where they were going or what they were doing when they got there. (Mail was to be received through a box number in the Philippines.)[23]

Another five pilots and four navigators were assigned to supplement the ferry crews on the exhausting trans-Pacific crossing and then return to Pope. The C-123 had no autopilot or long-range navigation equipment, and at least two overwater legs were more than 15 hours long; the extra crewmembers would provide for a relief pilot and a navigator aboard each aircraft (normal complement was two pilots and a flight mechanic, with a navigator only on the lead aircraft of a formation). Accompanying the smaller planes were two huge C-124 "Globemaster" transports carrying maintenance personnel, en route support equipment, and supplies for 120 days sustained field operations. To avoid publicity, the deployment was included by supplement in the operations plan for FARM GATE. A separate operations order using the code name RANCH HAND was not published until after the unit's arrival in the Philippines.[24]

The six C-123s left Pope on 28 November 1961 on a nonstop flight to Travis AFB, California—a flight plan deliberately selected because it would exceed the distance of the longest overwater leg en route to Vietnam. Not only would this flight test the long-range capabilities of the modified aircraft, but it would give the aircrews badly needed cruise control data for planning the overwater legs; there had been no time to verify the chemical tank and external wing-tank fuel system performance, there were no engine oil quantity gauges, and existing planning data probably were not applicable. Bad weather at Travis and a malfunctioning wing-tank on one plane forced the mission to divert to George AFB, California. The trip experience indicated, however, that the aircraft were capable of safely flying the overwater legs (a satisfactory engine oil level was maintained by the crude, but effective, method of hand pumping a gallon of oil to each engine at the end of each hour of flying).[25]

The trans-Pacific portion of the deployment appeared to be off to a bad start on the first day when the number two aircraft aborted back to Travis due to severe icing, escorted by the number three aircraft (it had earlier been decided that as a cross-check of navigation and a matter of safety, the aircraft would fly in pairs on the overwater legs). The unit was reunited in Hawaii the following day, and the remainder of the overseas trip was without serious incident as the planes island-hopped from Hawaii to Johnson Island to Wake to Guam and finally to Clark Air Base in the Philippines. The oil replenishment system proved its real worth on the final leg when the lead aircraft developed an oil leak on one engine three hours after leaving Guam; the crew was able to keep the engine running and continue to Clark, arriving five days and eight hours after leaving the United States. Two days later, a typhoon forced the weary crews to temporarily leave Clark for Kadena Air Base, Okinawa.[26]

The influx of US air units into Southeast Asia during late 1961 created the need for a new command structure in the area. On 15 November, Thirteenth Air Force activated the 2d Advanced Echelon (ADVON) at Saigon, Vietnam, under command of the former Thirteenth Air Force Vice-Commander, Brigadier General Rollen H. Anthis. This intermediate-level headquarters controlled three numbered detachments in Vietnam and one in Thailand; Anthis wore a second "hat" as Chief, Air Force Section, MAAG, insuring continuity of effort. When it reached the Philippines, the spray unit, now designated Tactical Air Force Transport Squadron, Provisional One, also was assigned to 2d ADVON (the unwieldy new unit title was hardly improved by the official acronym—TAC AF Transron Prov 1).[27]

The spray planes remained at Clark Air Base for the next month, awaiting final approval for their participation in Vietnamese operations. In addition to political reasons, the delay was also a matter of logistics. Some chemicals for the food denial tests by the Vietnamese already had been airlifted to Vietnam, but the bulk of the military herbicides purchased for the defoliation program were coming by sea—a one-month voyage. Since this shipment left the United States two weeks after the spray aircraft, adequate chemical stocks were not expected in Vietnam until early January.[28]

The waiting period gave the Langley pilots some much needed time to begin training the Pope volunteers in spray tactics, using a Philippines Air Force overwater gunnery range off the coast of Luzon. Unfortunately, the training was unrealistic; no spray was dispensed since spray-booms would not be installed until arrival in Vietnam, and low-level overwater flight did not approximate tree-top flying. The training did, however, begin development of the close crew coordination that was so vital in this especially hazardous type of flying.[29]

In the meantime, Dr. Brown, who had returned to the United States on 14 November, was again placed in charge of the resumed herbicide test program in Vietnam. On 4 December 1961, Brown and Charles E. Minarik, Chief of the Crops Division at Fort Detrick, met in Washington, DC, with William Godel, Deputy Director of the Advanced Research Projects Agency. Godel informed Brown that on recommendation of the State and Defense Departments the operation had been approved and that Brown had final operational authority over all tests. As the direct representative of the secretary of defense, he would outrank all military personnel, including the Chief of the Military Assistance Advisory Group. Brown was also made personally responsible for approving the wording of pre-mission warning leaflets, which would be dropped in the test areas, and instructed to assure that food supplies were available to replace destroyed crops before beginning crop denial operations. Tests were to be coordinated to allow the Vietnamese military to exploit any resulting advantages. Brown was also authorized to use napalm in defoliated-foliage burning experiments and ordered to "be ignorant of all other technical matters" if questioned by "friendly authorities" about biological anticrop or antipersonnel agents. Inquiries were to be redirected to the Chief, MAAG.[30]

Godel's instructions reflected the US government's sensitivity to the propaganda potential of the herbicide operation. Already, on 6 November, Radio Hanoi had attacked the South Vietnamese government for using "poison gas" against rice crops near Tay Ninh, reporting the chemical caused a number of people to become ill. Despite the Top Secret classification given the earlier tests, captured VC documents indicated the guerrillas were well aware of defoliant plans and planned propaganda exploitation of them.[31]

The United States was also concerned about the reaction of other Southeast Asian nations, particularly Cambodia. In order to avoid any misunderstandings, State Department messages regularly warned Nolting and the Vietnam Task Force to avoid defoliant operations near the Vietnam/Cambodian border, and to ensure that the Cambodian government was informed well in advance of herbicide missions. All agencies were to downplay the US role in herbicide operations as much as possible.[32]

In compliance with these directions, Headquarters, Pacific Air Forces (PACAF), messaged Fifth Air Force to park the deploying spray planes in relatively inaccessible areas at en route bases, and if the press asked about them to reply that the aircraft were on a classified mission that could not be discussed. On the other hand, Ambassador Nolting's earlier suggestion of civilian aircraft markings and civilian clothing for aircrews was rejected. In a memorandum for President Kennedy, Deputy Secretary of Defense Roswell Gilpatric pointed out that the nature of the aircraft employed prevented any disguise of its US military lineage. The same reasoning applied to use of Vietnamese markings and covert aircrews, although FARM GATE aircraft did enter Vietnam wearing red and yellow VNAF insignia.[33]

Dr. Brown returned to Vietnam in December. The October proposal of the Chief, MAAG, had been for a three phase program. Phase I was crop destruction, Phase II involved jungle defoliation of the VC main base area north of Saigon known as area "D," and Phase III was selective defoliation of certain roads and border areas to increase transportation security and reduce Viet Cong reinforcement and resupply. Although an initial cost estimate for this proposal was $75 million, Brown believed that the contemplated areas could be done for much less, basing his figures on a computed cost of $1.7 million per 100 square miles. The discrepancy became academic when the Commander-in-Chief, Pacific (CINCPAC), restricted the program to lines of communication targets radiating north and northeast out of Saigon. Highest priority was recommended for Route 15 to Vung Tau and Route 1 to Phan Rang, priority two was given Route 14 to Ban Me Thout and Route 20 to Dalat, and third priority was assigned to the national railroad right of way to Phan Rang. Although Brown urged that the C-123s' entry into Vietnam be expedited, political considerations forced him to begin the tests using a Vietnamese C-47 aircraft and the "Buffalo" ground turbine. Targets were selected along the portion of Route 15 between Bien Hoa and the former French coastal resort area of Cap St. Jacques, renamed Vung Tau.[34]

Finally, on 6 January 1962, the Joint Chiefs of Staff authorized CINCPAC to begin using American-manned C-123 aircraft to carry out operations to defoliate selected strips along Route 15. At 0500 hours the following morning, Tactical Air Force Transport Squadron, Provisional One (which would be more commonly referred to by the project code name, RANCH HAND), was ordered to deploy three aircraft to Tan Son Nhut airport at Saigon, without delay. The RANCH HAND aircrews, who had been impatiently waiting for over a month, were airborne at 0900 hours and arrived in Vietnam at 1630 hours. Two days later stevedores began unloading the first sea-lifted shipments of military herbicides at the port of Saigon.[35]

More than a decade earlier, the French Foreign Legion had laboriously cleared roadside vegetation by hand, in an unsuccessful attempt to halt ambushes of their military convoys.[36] Now another foreign military power sought the same goal, but with a new military weapon—chemical herbicides. The resulting operation would be one of the most controversial missions in the short history of the United States Air Force.

4

Development of the Herbicide Program

The transfer of three of the six spray planes to Saigon on 7 January took place under strict security conditions. Publicly the aircraft were part of the MULE TRAIN airlift support unit (346th Troop Carrier Squadron), but on arrival at Tan Son Nhut airport they did not join the other C-123s; instead, the spray planes were placed on the closely guarded Vietnamese Air Force security parking ramp reserved for President Diem's special fighter squadron. Since news media personnel were prohibited in this area, it was hoped that this would prevent any publicity concerning American participation in the chemical mission. The commander of the security ramp—and of the special "anti-coup" VNAF squadron—was a highly experienced combat veteran, Lieutenant Colonel Nguyen Cao Ky. This important figure in the history of the Republic of Vietnam, famed for his black flying suits, pearl-handled pistols, and violet-colored scarf, would be closely associated with the RANCH HAND organization throughout its service in Vietnam.[1]

Operational headquarters for the spray unit was also located in the security area, while the enlisted personnel initially were quartered in a hastily erected "tent city" on the Saigon airport. Water and bathing facilities were in short supply, a problem compounded when most of the Americans fell prey to intestinal diseases, commonly referred to as the "GIs" or "Ho Chi Minh's revenge." Security for the aircraft was provided by armed VNAF guards; but after a morning preflight discovery that all planes had been sabotaged by cutting control cable turnbuckles, and a later incident in which a Vietnamese guard was discovered at 0500 hours with his throat cut, US ground crewmen began guarding their own aircraft at night, in addition to their normal daily workload. These were temporary inconveniences, however, since it was optimistically hoped that the RANCH HAND crews would finish their mission and return to the United States within 90 days (the PACAF deployment order to Saigon specified the unit's return to the Philippines after approximately eight sorties). The RANCH HAND officers were left on their own to find housing in local hotels. Several of them, with cynical confidence that "short" temporary duty (TDY) always lasts longer than planned for by higher headquarters, eventually rented some former French villas in town.[2]

Dr. Brown had been impatiently waiting for the RANCH HAND detachment after his earlier unsuccessful attempts to expedite their arrival, and gave the spray crews little time to get settled into their new surroundings. While photo reconnaissance missions were being flown over the target areas, RANCH HAND pilots held a series of coordination meetings with Vietnamese officials and VNAF pilots on 8-9 January. The Vietnamese indicated that they needed three days to psychologically prepare the population in the test areas, using leaflet drops, so it was agreed that the spray planes would fly familiarization missions on the 10-11 January, with operational sorties beginning on the twelfth. By the 14 January, 11 orientation, 1 survey, and 6 defoliation sorties had been flown against roadside targets along the Bien Hoa-Vung Tau highway (Route 15), an area chosen for its variation in terrain and vegetation types. During the following ten days, RANCH HAND aircraft sprayed selected areas along the highway with a military herbicide, code named "Purple," consisting of a 50:50 mixture of 2,4-D and 2,4,5-T. (The code name came from the four-inch colored bands painted around the outside of the 55-gallon shipping drums to help servicing personnel identify the chemical contents.) The main objective of this series of tests was to determine whether defoliation was militarily feasible and effective. Most missions were flown by single USAF aircraft, although a formation of two aircraft was used on several targets requiring a swath wider than 300 feet.[3]

At the same time, Vietnamese helicopters and a C-47 aircraft were being used to spray other crop and jungle targets with various trial chemicals. Included in the VNAF crop tests was a well-known chemical, cacodylic acid (code named "Blue"), which had recently shown excellent defoliant properties when experimentally applied at low application rates to American cotton fields. Also under evaluation was the use of fire as a clearing weapon. Burning tests of chemical-dried vegetation were conducted near the Army of the Republic of Vietnam (ARVN) headquarters area and at the Saigon Navy Yard.[4]

Following the initial series of test missions, spraying was discontinued to allow the chemical time to affect the vegetation. Preliminary evaluations indicated that additional tests were needed, especially on vegetation types more common to the water-logged southern coastal areas of Vietnam. Dr. Brown recommended, however, that all further operational testing be held in abeyance until the end of the dry season in South Vietnam because he felt that climatic conditions and nearly dormant vegetation during this period prevented an accurate assessment of the results of chemical defoliation.[5]

A delay in operations was also needed to permit recalibration of the spray equipment to compensate for the higher viscosity of the new military herbicides. Even with the Hourglass pumps running at maximum output (150 gallons per minute), application rates of less than one gallon per acre were all that could be achieved, an amount insufficient to significantly affect any but the most sensitive forest plants. Application by Vietnamese H-34s was even less satisfactory, with the helicopters required to make two spray passes over each target just to achieve the minimal one gallon per acre. As Dr. Brown feared, State and Defense Department officials viewing these inadequate spray results from the air during brief visits to Vietnam were not impressed and the project was in danger of being cancelled. Ironically, within two weeks a total of 112 Viet Cong surrendered in An Xuyan Province, primarily as a result of the Thoi Binh district chief's decision to allow defoliation and crop destruction tests in his area. The detainees reported that defoliants were quite effective and they surrendered in the belief that "their crops and source of food would be cut off."[6]

RANCH HAND crews, unfamiliar with the weather and terrain of South Vietnam, welcomed the break in operational missions as an opportunity for familiarization flights and badly needed spray training missions. Not only were the Pope volunteers new to spray procedures, but even the experienced Langley pilots were finding that combat defoliation did not always fit the patterns of the insecticide missions of the past. For over a decade SASF supervisors had unsuccessfully lobbied for a permanent peacetime organization to develop future operational tactics and doctrine. Now they were being forced to learn these lessons in the combat area even as the missions were flown—sometimes at great cost. On 2 February 1962, the United States Air Force lost its first combat aircraft in Vietnam when one of the RANCH HAND C-123s (aircraft number 56-4370) crashed in a heavily forested area during a low-level mission near Vung Tau (target RH-8 along Route 15), destroying the aircraft and killing all three crew members. The fiercely burning wreckage prevented an exact determination of the cause of the crash, but failure of the fire to spread through the surrounding unsprayed trees and brush provided Dr. Brown with "indisputable evidence" that Vietnamese forests would not normally burn. Even as services were held for the dead, one of the spare spray aircraft and crews at Clark Air Base was ordered to Saigon as a replacement, and the detachment prepared to resume regular defoliation testing. The initial 90-day TDY for Captain Marshall and most of the other RANCH HAND personnel was extended for an additional 90 days.[7]

Despite Dr. Brown's recommendation to await the next vegetation growing season, a set of new test targets was approved by the Joint Chiefs of Staff for defoliation in February and March 1962. These target areas, located near Saigon and on the Ca Mau peninsula, were selected to provide data on foliage types encountered along lines of communication in the sea-level, rice-growing areas of the country. This second series of test missions was completed in less time than originally planned. RANCH HAND crews were certain that the concept had been proven worthwhile, and while CDTC personnel were studying the results of the second test series, the remaining aircraft and crewmen were brought to Saigon from Clark Air Base in anticipation of going into a full-scale spray operation.[8]

Ranking officers in Vietnam and the United States, however, were not satisfied with the test results. Perhaps anticipating more dramatic effects, inspecting officers disappointedly reported that while some leaves fell, "visibility was not substantially improved." A briefing paper prepared for the Secretary of Defense stated "COMUSMACV [Commander, United States Military Assistance Command, Vietnam] concluded that no results of military significance have been achieved as a result of defoliant operations."[9] In response the Department of Defense directed ARPA to send a team of experts, headed by Brigadier General Fred J. Delmore, Commanding General of the Research and Development Command of the Army Chemical Corps, to review and evaluate the entire defoliation program. The team was charged with determining herbicide effectiveness, assessing vertical and horizontal visibility improvement through defoliation, and recommending program changes to exploit this new weapon.[10]

Part of the reason for the on-again/off-again life of the herbicide program was the continuing US intra-governmental debate on the relative merits of the project. A number of State Department officials, in particular Roger Hilsman, head of the Bureau of Intelligence and Research and, later, Assistant Secretary of State for Far Eastern Affairs, strongly opposed the use of herbicides for any reason in Vietnam. "Defoliation was just too reminiscent of gas warfare," Hilsman later wrote. "It would cost us international political support, and the Viet Cong would use it to good propaganda advantage as an example of Americans making war on the peasants."[11] Secretary of State Rusk agreed that the project would be an object of intense communist propaganda, but felt that a "carefully controlled" program would be "of substantial assistance" in defeating the Viet Cong. Rusk joined the majority of government officials in supporting a continued program.[12]

The question of how to publicize the herbicide missions also affected program decisions. Army experiments with techniques for stripping jungle foliage had been first publicized in the release of censored transcripts of March 1961 testimony before the House Defense Appropriations Subcommittee of Congress by Major General Marshall Stubbs, the Army's chief chemical officer, and Dr. Riley D. Housewright, scientific director of the Army's Biological Laboratories. The tactic was down-played by Housewright's statement that existing chemicals took two to three days to strip wooded areas, which was "too long." Other testimony indicated that no chemical agents were known that would clear substantial areas satisfactorily. These revelations caused little comment and were overshadowed by testimony concerning Soviet advances in bacteriological and radiological warfare techniques.[13]

The arrival of the RANCH HAND unit in Vietnam in January 1962, however, created more stir in the news media, particularly after Vietnamese officials reported this new program would "improve the country's economy by permitting freer communication" as well as "facilitate the Vietnamese Army's task of keeping avenues of communication free of Viet Cong harassments."[14] When the Vietnamese government later announced that "defoliant chemicals would also be sprayed on Viet Cong plantations of manioc and sweet potatoes in the highlands," the United States admitted the Route 15 defoliation missions, but indicated a reluctance to join in any plans for attacks on crops.[15] The Viet Cong further publicized the early missions by spreading reports of "American plans to cut a swath of devastation through the countryside" with chemicals. Orders were issued to local cadres to use troops in "nests" of rifles and machine guns to fire on spray aircraft and the people were warned that the defoliation "powder" would have an ill effect on them. Soviet propagandists accused the United States of taking part in biological warfare.[16]

In the meantime, Tactical Air Force Transport Squadron, Provisional One, faced a problem that would recur throughout the entire history of the RANCH HAND operation—Air Force officers at intermediate command levels did not fully comprehend the spray mission, a mission essentially dedicated to support of the ground forces. Not only did these flights require specialized training and pilot proficiency, but the climatological limitations for effective chemical application restricted sorties to the early morning hours. Systemic herbicides could not be sprayed at air temperatures in excess of 85 degrees Fahrenheit (29.4 degrees Celsius) or when wind surface winds exceeded 8 to 10 knots—precluding spray sorties in South Vietnam after approximately 1030 hours during most of the year. Higher daytime temperatures caused the fine droplets of herbicide to rise instead of descend, negating effective chemical application. Senior officers, however, saw only that transport aircraft were sitting on the ramp, not being utilized, while flight and ground personnel spent their afternoons and evenings touring Saigon, playing cards, or "just soaking up the rays" (suntanning).[17]

The high visibility maintained by the RANCH HAND volunteers did not help their cause. Not only did their rented quarters soon become famous for their parties, but crewmembers adopted black Vietnamese-style berets with Vietnamese rank insignia as their headgear, instead of the authorized broad-brimmed campaign hats. This was particularly objectionable to some Special Forces advisors, who wore authorized green berets.[18]

Over strenuous objections from RANCH HAND officers, the unit was directed to remove the spray equipment from three of the five aircraft when the second test series was completed in March. Although the provisional squadron did not have loadmasters, these three aircraft, manned by RANCH HAND crews, became a fulltime part of the MULE TRAIN logistics mission, also operating out of Tan Son Nhut airport. It was while on a logistics support mission that the second RANCH HAND aircraft was lost. Assigned to deliver supplies to a small airstrip near Hue, the aircrew commanded by Captain Harry Overman landed at the wrong airfield (Hipp Khanh) and crashed while attempting to take off again from the too short field, damaging the aircraft beyond repair. Fortunately, the crew escaped without injury, other than to their pride. The spray unit was now down to four operational aircraft.[19]

From the time of its arrival in the Philippines, the RANCH HAND commander had complained that the unit was not organized or manned to function administratively as an independent squadron for an extended period. Squadron command (other than the commander himself), administration, heavy maintenance, and supply elements did not exist. Captain Marshall remained continuously in hot water with higher headquarters over late or nonsubmitted reports and other administrative details. Apparently as a result of these complaints and the operational loss of one-third of its aircraft, General Anthis downgraded the RANCH HAND unit from squadron status and placed it under operational control of the MULE TRAIN commander.[20]

By mid-April only two pilots remained spray qualified and requalification of the other pilots was precluded by 2d ADVON minimum altitude restrictions that prevented the necessary low-level missions. A total of 210,000 gallons of military herbicides was on hand and General Delmar recommended resuming spray operations until the herbicide was consumed. Delmar's recommendation was rejected, and because the number of spray planes appeared excessive for any foreseeable need, on 25 April USAF authorized PACAF to return two RANCH HAND aircraft to the United States. Since replacement TDY aircrews were on the way, the aircraft would leave when the new crews arrived.[21]

At the request of the State Department, one of the returning spray planes was diverted through the Middle East, with stops in Afganistan and Iran. A serious locust plague threatened crops in these two countries and their governments had appealed for United States help. Accompanied by a C-124 Globemaster transport to carry extra equipment, supplies, and maintenance personnel, C-123B serial number 56-4362 left Saigon on 2 May 1962 for Teheran. Immediately after arriving in Iran, the spray aircraft began its attacks in the heavily infested area along the Arhandab and Dori Rivers. Under the direction of US air attachés at Teheran and Kubel, Captain Charles Hagerty's crew sprayed over 17,000 acres in the two countries with insecticide between 10 May and 2 June, bringing the locust plague under control. The crew then continued through Europe and across the Atlantic, rejoining the Pacific-route returnees at Langley AFB, Virginia, on 10 June 1962—the first and only C-123 to make an around-the-world flight.[22]

The returned RANCH HAND aircrews were given little time to rest. On 14 June the aircraft were redeployed to Eglin AFB, Florida to participate in a 30-day test spray operation on Range C-52A. In the meantime, General Delmore's evaluation of 21 targets in 11 target areas found the herbicide used in Vietnam to be 70 percent effective when evaluated from the air and 60 percent effective when evaluated from the ground. Although this represented a significant increase in combat visibility, the evaluation team concluded that additional effectiveness could be achieved by modifying the delivery equipment to increase application rates per acre and to increase droplet size to minimize herbicide loss due to drift off target. As an interim fix, the team recommended a minor modification to the spray pump motor that would allow it to deliver approximately 1½ gallons per acre. This volume would permit delivery of the minimum requirement of three gallons per acre of chemical if the aircraft made two passes over each target. Modification of the "Teejet" nozzles and reduction of the number of nozzles per wing-boom from 42 to 35 were expected to increase the droplet size to 300 microns, thus minimizing drift. The Florida range sorties were to test these proposals. Delmore's team suggested a permanent solution in the form of a whole new system of pumps and plumbing, which would have a flow rate of at least three gallons per acre, and installation of a third spray-boom under the tail of the aircraft. For unhampered equipment evaluation, it was recommended that initial test flights be conducted in the United States and Thailand, rather than in the combat zone.[23]

Delmore's report did little to increase COMUSMACV's enthusiasm for the defoliation project, although both the Vietnamese government and the country team urged program continuation. The two spray aircraft still in Vietnam remained under the command of Captain Marshall, who had been extended for a third consecutive 90-day TDY when the other original members returned home in May. Defoliation capability was maintained, but spray activities remained at a standstill during the summer. The two-plane flight continued to fly logistics missions in support of the MULE TRAIN task and to train the replacement crews in spray tactics and procedures by flying low-level "dry" runs (no herbicide was carried or dispensed).[24]

In August 1962, President Kennedy approved defoliation of a few selected targets along canals and communications routes in the Ca Mau peninsula, an area of increasing VC infiltration. Based on the successful Florida tests, the spray planes were modified to achieve a 1½ gallon per acre dispensing rate, and in anticipation of the new defoliation program, the RANCH HAND unit was authorized to increase to three aircraft and crews. One of the returned aircraft and crews was again deployed to Vietnam, arriving in September in time to take part in the Ca Mau project. Between 3 September and 11 October, six canal target areas were attacked, with missions flown almost daily. The flat target terrain presented the RANCH HAND crews with no new problems, although some enemy ground fire was received. Since spray aircraft were the only ones flying sustained low-level flights, VC antiaircraft gunners apparently were inexperienced and the ground fire was ineffective. None of the hits caused serious aircraft damage or injury to crewmembers.[25]

Following completion of the Ca Mau targets, defoliation activities again came to a halt. A number of survey missions were flown to check on effects of the spring tests, and another round of training missions was started to familiarize two more replacement crews with the latest techniques, two of the three RANCH HAND crews having completed their 120-day TDYs. Captain Marshall also rotated home, replaced by Captain Mike Devlin, an original "RANCHER" returning for a second tour. (Devlin's apartment at 62 Tran Hung Dao would be the informal RANCH HAND headquarters during the entire period of the operation from Saigon airport.) Marshall returned to the TAC Special Aerial Spray Flight at Langley, which subsequently became responsible for training RANCH HAND replacements in addition to its domestic insecticide mission.

In December defoliation missions were ordered against road targets in a mountain pass south of Qui Nhon. The modifications in equipment and procedures had proven effective in the Ca Mau canal defoliations, with 90 to 95 percent improved visibility, and higher headquarters now endorsed the herbicide program. At the conclusion of the Qui Nhon project, however, spraying was once more stopped until the systemic herbicides again became more effective with the beginning of the growing season in May. During 1962 1 RANCH HAND aircraft had flown a total of only 60 defoliation missions while dispensing 49,240 gallons of herbicide over 20.1 square miles, but it appeared that this new weapons concept had finally found political and military acceptance.[26]

Crop destruction missions also gained a degree of acceptance during 1962. Although the United States had publicly rejected Vietnamese announcements of plans to attack enemy food crops, some senior Defense and State Department officials had privately endorsed a food denial program as part of the defoliation concept from the beginning. The South Vietnamese government regularly sought approval of a proposal to use VNAF H-34s and aircrews, together with American herbicides and technical assistance, to attack enemy cultivations in selected areas. President Diem's request for a trial program was supported by Ambassador Nolting, the Country Team, and General Paul D. Harkins, Military Assistance Command, Vietnam (MACV) Commander. Opposition to the program was strong in the State Department, again from the assistant secretary for Far Eastern affairs in particular, on the basis that "the underfed people of South East [sic] Asia would never understand this act by a country with surplus food."[27] Because food shortages in the highland areas already appeared to be handicapping the Viet Cong, "CINCPAC considered crop destruction a promising and singular weapon," and urged approval of a pilot program.[28] On 3 October, after extensive reviews by Defense and State Department officials and the personal involvement of President Kennedy, crop destruction was accepted in principle and a limited food denial project was approved for War Zone D and Thua Thien Province (for individual province locations, see Map 1). Final approval authority for individual missions was delegated to the assistant secretary of state for Far

Eastern affairs and the Department of Defense, jointly. The first crop missions were flown by the VNAF on 21-23 November and succeeded in destroying a large quantity of rice; by year's end, 750 acres of crops had been destroyed.[29]

During the dry season between January and May 1963, the RANCH HAND commitment again reverted to primary support of the MULE TRAIN logistics mission, under control of the newly activated 315th Troop Carrier Group. RANCH HAND crews took part in aerial troop drops, in addition to more routine missions delivering ammunition, general cargo, and personnel. Two of the three C-123s were modified with special radio receiving equipment and flew 65 sorties testing the British three point Tactical Air Positioning System (TAPS), an electronic aircraft navigational aid that had recently been installed in Vietnam. To warn of enemy air attack against South Vietnam, ground radar facilities also had been established to provide an air-to-air intercept capability. RANCH HAND aircraft flew a number of missions, including low-level flights, acting as simulated enemy targets for Ground Controlled Intercept radar operator and F-102 interceptor pilot training. Survey flights over previously sprayed targets and potential target areas also continued during this period.[30]

An indication of the effectiveness of the earlier herbicide missions was the increasingly strident tone of communist antiherbicide propaganda. Radio Hanoi broadcasts in English to Europe and Asia claimed that hundreds of persons had been "affected by noxious chemicals," becoming "blind," "unconscious," and suffering "swollen bodies." Colonel Ha Van Lau, Head of the Liaison Mission of the Vietnam People's Army High Command, sent a message to Indian Ambassador R. Goburdhun, Chairman of the ICC, accusing the United States of violating international law and the Geneva agreements by its "barbarous" acts. Local cadres spread the word among villagers that the chemicals were deadly to both people and their animals, an act that sometimes backfired when it caused panic among the rural population. To counter VC propaganda that the herbicide project was a terror program designed to force the peasants into strategic hamlets, South Vietnamese officials conducted demonstrations of the chemicals in the villages, including applying herbicide mixtures to their skin to prove its harmlessness. The United States' answer to the communist propaganda barrage was to hold briefings for the press in March on all aspects of the defoliation operations in South Vietnam and to encourage widespread publicity of the spray unit, a policy change Assistant Secretary of State Hilsman had been advocating since his March 1962 trip to Vietnam.[31]

Following a high level review of the entire herbicide program, a joint State/Defense Department message was sent to Saigon on 7 May 1963 delegating authority to initiate defoliation operations jointly to the American ambassador and COMUSMACV; approval for crop destruction remained in Washington, as before. Guidelines provided that defoliation missions should be few in number, remote from populated areas (except in special circumstances), used where terrain and vegetation favored use of herbicides, and used only when hand cutting and burning were impracticable. The first target approved under the new system was a canal complex in the Ca Mau peninsula, similar to those attacked the previous September.[32]

In mid-May a new crisis over the use of herbicides threatened when rumors began to circulate in the Cambodian capital, Phnom Penh, that food imported from the border province of Svay Rieng had been contaminated by defoliant spray drifting across the border. Cambodian Agricultural Ministry officials cancelled a previously scheduled trip with United States Agency for International Development (USAID) personnel to the border area, and pointedly reminded American officials that Cambodian Prime Minister Sihanouk planned to visit Svay Rieng the following week. In return, the American Embassy reminded the Cambodian Foreign Office of the *aide-memoire* of 15 January 1962 in which the United States had assured the Cambodians that herbicides would be used "in such a manner and at such a distance from the frontier as to ensure that they do not enter Cambodia."[33] The embassy also pointed out that the nearest defoliation and crop destruction had been "34 and 114 miles respectively from the nearest point on the Cambodian border and conducted in February and on November 21-23, 1962, respectively."[34] The distances and time period made it highly unlikely that these operations could have affected the Cambodian crops, raising the possibility that the rumors were either part of a local campaign against the use of "noxious chemicals" or started to provide leverage during negotiations for increased American aid to Cambodia.[35]

The embassy in Saigon had made an error, however, when they reported the crop destruction data. Apparently American officials had not been kept informed that crop target 2-2, site of the February sprayings, was again under attack. Using backpack equipment, Vietnamese soldiers sprayed scattered crop fields in Thua Thien Province during the period 7 May to 17 June 1963; 67 hectares of crops were destroyed. Even so, the error did not invalidate American claims of innocence in the Cambodian allegations; the Thua Thien site was more than 100 miles from Svay Rieng. The coincidence of the accusations coming just after resumption of herbicide operations lent credence to the theory that it was merely part of the continuing communist propaganda campaign in Southeast Asia.[36]

On 6 June, RANCH HAND aircraft began defoliation of the newly approved target 20-9 complex, along the Cua Lon and Cua Bo De Rivers in An Xuyan Province, a task similar to the attacks the previous September. The target was completed in only eight sorties, although light ground fire was encountered. Three weeks later a second target was approved by Saigon officials, involving 11 subtargets along the Da Nhim electrical power line running from near Dalat to Bien Hoa, some of which was in extremely rugged country. Vietnamese H-34 helicopters were used to help spray sections deemed unsuitable for C-123 sorties, beginning on 15 July. Despite problems with adverse weather, the project was completed on schedule without incident, using 19 C-123 sorties, during 3-27 July. To counter enemy propaganda, several journalists were invited to accompany the air mission. Despite these successes, the RANCH HAND operation once more was being considered for withdrawal from Vietnam, this time by a team from MACV, due to political pressures and the seasonal aspects of the defoliation program.[37]

In the meantime, the spray planes again responded to an appeal for help from outside the war zone. A plague of "Bombay" locusts was devastating crops in the vicinity of Lopburi, Thailand, and the Thai government requested assistance through the State Department to prevent a possible national disaster. A RANCH HAND C-123 was immediately dispatched to Thailand on 30 August and was joined by a second aircraft nine days later. Flying 17 sorties, the two planes saved more than 80,000 acres of farm crops from destruction, and earned the gratitude of the Thai people. On 16 September the versatile crews returned to Vietnam to resume their defoliation mission.[38]

While RANCH HAND attacked locusts, the MACV study once more confirmed the effectiveness of herbicides as a military weapon, reserving its criticisms for the "lengthy and involved" target approval system. "Military and political administrative procedures ... hinder and, at times, deny the tactical utilization of chemical herbicidal operations to maximum advantage," the report stated. Although the nature of the weapon required prompt response to requests, delays of six months or more occurred between initial identification of targets and final approval for attack. The study recommended further decentralization of approval authority for herbicide operations and a follow-up system to evaluate targets that had been sprayed.[39]

In September, four more projects were scheduled for defoliation—a strategically important canal south of Ca Mau, a VC base camp area in War Zone D (the heavy jungle area north of Saigon), and two lesser targets. Sixty-five sorties were flown during October and November against the four targets, with 34 sorties occurring during one 14-day "maximum effort." Aircrews noted an increasing amount of enemy resistance, and a number of hits were taken.[40]

Prior to 1963, ground fire presented little problem for the RANCH HAND crews. Either the few targets were in government-controlled areas or government troops were used to secure the area during defoliation. Active insurgent forces were relatively few in number and usually unskilled in firing on aircraft. By late 1963, however, local recruitment and increased infiltration from the north drastically changed the situation; many areas were no longer government controlled, especially around the Ca Mau peninsula. Previously secure areas were now contested by the Viet Cong, and guerrilla units had obtained newer, heavier weapons. Vietnamese Army forces formerly used for spray area occupation now were needed for more urgent tasks, even as defoliation became a more important factor to the ground commander and the number of target requests soared.[41]

One answer to these changes was fighter escort—sending a flight of fighter planes along with the spray aircraft to try to protect them. The effectiveness of this tactic, however, was limited by the restrictive rules of engagement then in effect and by the lack of sufficient fighter aircraft in Vietnam. Fighter aircraft were allowed to attack only in defense of rescue operations or after the spray planes had been fired on. The retaliatory nature of this limitation did little to discourage enemy gunners, although the presence of the fighter cover provided a measure of emotional comfort to the spray crews. In the list of mission priorities for the fighters, RANCH HAND escort ranked near the bottom.[42]

Another suggestion to counter ground fire involved night spray missions—a suggestion reportedly made by an officer at a higher headquarters, which also helps explain the antipathy toward staff officers held by former RANCH HAND members. A collateral purpose of the proposal was to increase effectiveness of the herbicide by taking advantage of the lower temperatures and wind speeds at night. The first night mission was flown on 8 December, using another aircraft above and to the right of the spray plane to drop high-intensity parachute flares so the low-level pilots could see the terrain. The mission was successful, but the flares also silhouetted the spray planes for enemy gunners. Two nights later another mission was flown on the same target, this time using moonlight only. The pilots reported that tree-top visibility was poor, though better than with flares, and the planes averaged only two hits, despite heavy ground fire. Instead of the smoke grenade usually used to mark enemy ground fire positions for the fighters, a flare pistol with parachute flare proved successful. Night spray missions, however, required targets with flat terrain, long straight runs, and good visibility conditions, criteria seldom met in Vietnam. More importantly, night time fighter support was marginal and the chances of survival and rescue if downed at night were considerably reduced. RANCH HAND discontinued the tactic.[43]

The end of 1963 found the defoliation program still not firmly established and ground fire presenting an increasing hazard; spray tactics and procedures were in a state of flux as the aircrews sought to counter the enemy threat. Most of the year had been spent on tasks other than defoliation—only 107 sorties were flown to defoliate 33.7 square miles of vegetation. Vietnamese-conducted crop destruction projects had been even more limited—destroying a mere 197.5 acres.[44] With the end of the growing season, the herbicide unit prepared once more to turn to the less hazardous, but more tedious, task of resupply.

5

The Developing War

The use of herbicides in Vietnam was not intended as a complete answer to the problems of jungle warfare. A 1962 "Talking Paper" prepared for a meeting between the president of the United States and the chairman of the Joint Chiefs of Staff concluded,

> Certainly some of the projects we are implementing are outright R&D [i.e., experimental] efforts such as the defoliation project and bear all the earmarks of gimmicks that cannot and will not win the war in South Vietnam.[1]

The use of such "gimmicks," however, was designed to demonstrate the depth of the US commitment to Vietnam—a means of emphasizing that the United States would not allow unanswered aggression in South Vietnam and Southeast Asia. Like the tank and the airplane in World War I, herbicides were an unknown and untried weapon of war, but during 1964 the program would go beyond the gimmick stage and give indications of widespread applicability in future conflicts.

The American role in Vietnam at the beginning of 1964, however, was uncertain. The number of US "advisors" had peaked at 16,732 in October 1963, and the withdrawal of 1,000 of them beginning in December seemed to confirm official statements that the Vietnamese Army had become an effective force, requiring only logistical support and limited technical advice in the future. The murder of President Diem and his brother in Saigon in November, followed by President Kennedy's assassination only a few weeks later, however, cast a shadow of uncertainty over what course the war would take and what roles the new leadership would play. The weakness of the fragmented, unstable South Vietnamese government was quickly exposed in February 1964 when the Viet Cong inflicted a major defeat on ARVN forces in Tay Ninh Province, prompting American officials to again consider a major escalation of US involvement.[2]

Meanwhile, the onset of the dry season in January saw the RANCH HAND detachment once more tasked with the mundane missions of logistical support as part of MULE TRAIN and flying test sorties for the TAPS project. Unlike the previous year, however, the dry season did not cause the herbicide program to be completely shelved. In addition to several January survey flights to evaluate previous targets and to map proposed new ones, four defoliation sorties were flown against the target abandoned in December. The following month, 16 more spray sorties were flown against a new target, a large canal at the tip of the Ca Mau peninsula. In an unusual joint maneuver, small Vietnamese patrol boats provided area security during the spray runs; only light ground fire was received and no serious damage resulted.[3]

The situation changed drastically in March and April. Several new targets on the Ca Mau peninsula were too far inland for the Navy to secure, and the Vietnamese government could no longer make ground forces available for this purpose. Moderate enemy small-arms fire was encountered. Hits on the spray planes averaged four per mission, causing damage to various electrical and hydraulic systems. Twice, when landing gear were shot up, emergency landings were made. One problem with these southern target areas was the open water areas and open fields between tree lines, which gave the enemy relatively clear zones to track and fire on the low-flying aircraft. Furthermore, insurgent forces in the peninsula had been significantly strengthened in manpower and weapons. Viet Cong boasts that they were strong enough to take any town at any time were corroborated when they overran the district capital of Kien Long on 12 April.[4]

Thus, when a four-target river complex south of the city of Quan Long (Ca Mau) was assigned in mid-April, RANCH HAND crews decided to use a recently developed "pop-up" tactic, plus target rotation, to reduce their vulnerability, particularly since some of the targets were in an area that had been VC controlled for almost four years. The pop-up procedure consisted of an approach to the objective "on the deck" (20 feet or less above the terrain), then climbing suddenly to the 150 foot spray altitude at the last minute, giving the enemy little time to aim and fire. Between targets the aircraft would again drop to minimum altitude. Target rotation involved changing the target schedule on a daily, random basis, rather than completing all runs against one target before moving on to the next, as in the past. It was hoped that this procedure would preclude VC anticipation of the next day's target and prevent enemy concentration of heavy weapons along the logical spray paths.[5]

The change in tactics failed to help; spray planes continued to suffer three to five hits daily, although without serious damage until a mission on 30 April. Attacking a canal target early that day, a two-ship flight encountered what looked like mortar airbursts and very heavy .50-caliber machine-gun fire from both sides of the canal. Caught in this cross fire, the lead aircraft was hit 14 times and the copilot was wounded. Aircraft repairmen later counted 40 shrapnel holes in the skin of the plane. Damaged engine instruments forced the pilot to shut down the right engine and make an emergency landing at Soc Trang. The crew was picked up by the second aircraft and returned to Saigon. Spray crews put part of the blame for the successful ambush on the Army's Psychological Warfare (psywar) Unit, which had dropped 450,000 leaflets in the area warning of the forthcoming defoliation—a standard procedure. MACV temporarily suspended further defoliation missions pending reevaluation of tactics.[6]

As a result of the subsequent MACV study, a new policy required scheduling a primary and an alternate target for each mission. Thus, if the pilots encountered a "hot" target, they could break off and change to one that might be less active. Schedulers were also told to avoid scheduling sorties against the same target complex on more than two consecutive days.[7]

While all this was going on, another significant change was made— RANCH HAND changed from a temporary duty unit to a permanent organization. In April the first two permanent change of station (PCS) pilots arrived, Captains Wilbur I. Robinson and Tony T. Tellez. Because this first PCS crew did not include a fight mechanic, a volunteer was obtained from the C-123 logistics support squadron, recently redesignated as the 309th Troop Carrier Squadron (Assault). Future replacement crews, scheduled to arrive in August and September, were to include flight mechanics. Transfers also left the detachment without a navigator, and again it had to turn to the troop carrier squadron for a volunteer.[8]

On 19 May RANCH HAND returned to defoliation, this time in a supposedly secure area along a canal west of Tan Hiep. All three planes possessed by the unit were used, and runs during the first two days met only sporadic ground fire. On the third day, heavy fire from directly ahead caused the spray run to be discontinued, since the C-123 had no armor plating in front of the cockpit. The decision was made to return for a fourth straight day, but with fighter prestrike against the area of heavy ground fire. The prestrike was to be timed to take place just before the spray planes' arrival. Unfortunately, lack of coordination caused the fighters to miss their target by two miles and the RANCH HAND aircraft were heavily hit—number one losing its hydraulic system and number three having both the spray pump and a generator knocked out; however, all safely landed at Saigon.[9] The need to avoid repeated, consecutive runs over the same target area had again been violently emphasized.

While MACV selected new targets in the Delta area, RANCH HAND twice moved north to Da Nang to defoliate lines of communication between Vietnamese army posts along the rugged Vietnam-Laos border area of I Corps Tactical Zone (CTZ) (see Map 2). Thorough coordination with the host base enabled the spray unit to change bases and be prepared for operations in only one day. Using a fast-loading procedure that cut turnaround time to approximately ten minutes, three "lifts" (herbicide sorties) per aircraft could be made in only three hours; targets planned for two or three days of operations were finished in a single morning. The unit commander credited this rapid completion for minimizing enemy reaction and reposition of forces; only four hits were taken during 26 sorties.[10]

Yet even without strong enemy opposition, these northern sorties were particularly hazardous. Defoliation in a "mountain" area required a different technique than the "flat-land" runs in the Delta. The experience gained from the December 1962 Qui Nhon pass and July 1963 Da Nhim power line projects proved invaluable. To increase maneuverability, gross weight was reduced by decreasing fuel loads to the absolute minimum consistent with safety. Extra care was taken in flight planning to ensure that spray runs were made in the direction of the downhill slope—low airspeed and high power setting left little margin for error or battle damage recovery if the run was made over rising terrain. Even under ideal conditions, the single-engine rate of climb capability (one engine shut down and the propeller fully feathered) was less than 100 feet per minute. Equally important, the violent turns necessary to follow the winding roads and trails through the narrow mountain valleys required extraordinary crew coordination and precise aircraft control—the 110-foot wingspan of the C-123, when combined with tree-covered hillsides and steep turns, could quickly reduce terrain clearance to zero in the hands of a careless crew.[11]

By July 1964 the RANCH HAND flight was again at Saigon and facing a return to their old nemesis south of Quan Long. The spray planes had been driven from this target in April, before they could make a second application of herbicide, and the 1½ gallon per acre initial application had been ineffective; the entire target complex would have to be resprayed. RANCH HAND crews anticipated heavy enemy resistance. The government had lost control of most of the Ca Mau peninsula and the Viet Cong were equipped with increasingly more and better antiaircraft weapons. To give some badly needed protection to the vulnerable flight mechanic, his position at the spray console in the rear fuselage was modified by enclosing it in a four-foot-per-side, open-topped box made of two half-inch-thick sheets of Doron armor plating—adequate to stop most small arms projectiles and pieces of shrapnel.[12]

When spraying was resumed the expected enemy reaction occurred and hits were taken on all missions, including a 16 July attack in which the two-ship flight received 14 hits each. In retaliation for the heavy fire received on these An Xuyen Province targets, a new tactic was tried on 17 July. A decoy C-123 was used to draw ground fire, exposing VC antiaircraft positions; then, four VNAF and eight USAF fighters attacked the revealed sites with general-purpose and fragmentation bombs, napalm, and 20-millimeter cannon fire, setting off two secondary explosions. Normally, heavy escort of this type was not available to RANCH HAND; fighter planes were in limited number, and defoliation escort had the lowest priority; however, it was hoped that this example might cause enemy gunners to think twice before exposing their positions by firing on future RANCH HAND missions. Operations against the An Xuyen target complex were finally completed on 22 July.[13]

Less than a week later, RANCH HAND made international headlines when the Cambodian Minister for Foreign Affairs, Huot Sambath, charged the governments of South Vietnam and the United States with conducting chemical warfare against Cambodian territory. In a letter to the president of the United Nations Security Council, he alleged that Vietnamese planes sprayed several Cambodian villages in the Dandaungpich region of Ratanakiri Province with "poisonous yellow powder" between 13 and 23 July. The attacks were reported to have caused the deaths of 76 persons and some domestic animals.[14] The French-language press in Phnom Penh amplified the charges, claiming that the "powder" caused "syndromes of fatal gastroenteritis" among the people of six villages.[15] The Hanoi and Liberation Front Radios took up the refrain, reinstituting their campaigns against chemical spraying. The radio broadcasts also claimed that spraying in Ca Mau on 7-8 July resulted in local protests and "mass meetings" to demand indemnities from the Saigon government.[16]

The Cambodian charges appeared to parallel those of the Pathet Lao, which a month earlier had accused the United States of poisoning both people and oxen in Cammon Province by sending "a plane to spray poisonous chemicals."[17] Ratanakiri Province was a primary infiltration route for VC supplies and reinforcements, lying adjacent to the South Vietnamese central highlands, opposite Kontum and Pleiku. The Vietnamese Foreign Minister, Pham Huy Quat, denied the Cambodian charges, suggesting that if poisonings had taken place, they had been at the instigation of Viet Cong terrorists attempting to damage relations between South Vietnam and its neighboring countries.[18] An investigation by the American Embassy at Saigon indicated that neither South Vietnam nor the United States had conducted any herbicide operations in the three Vietnamese provinces nearest Ratanakiri during the period in question. Furthermore, none of the herbicides used by the RANCH HAND organization were dispensed in powder form. The Department of State recommended that the Vietnamese government ask for a United Nations medical team investigation, although it was earlier pointed out that this kind of request might serve to dignify the charge.[19] The Cambodian government rejected the idea of an outside investigation by either the United Nations or the International Red Cross. Instead, they continued to claim violation of Cambodian territory, including fresh charges that two South Vietnamese planes spread toxic powder over the Bost Touk region on 11 August. The inhabitants reportedly became ill when they ate contaminated vegetables. The validity of these 1964 chemical warfare charges by Cambodia, like those of 1963, were never independently verified.[20]

The acceptance of defoliation as a viable tactic of warfare, earlier indicated by the arrival of permanent duty aircrews, was further confirmed on 30 July 1964, when RANCH HAND was designated as Detachment 1, 315th Troop Carrier Group (DET 1, 315 TCG), a part of the PACAF mission forces. Parking and operations for RANCH HAND remained in the VNAF security compound at Tan Son Nhut airport, and the crews maintained their separate identity from the other C-123 personnel, humorously referred to as "trash haulers."[21]

More important than the title change were the modifications being made to the equipment. During 1963-64, tests at Range C-52A, Eglin AFB, Florida, and on the calibration grid at Pran Buri, Thailand, indicated that higher rates of application (2.5 to 3.0 gallons per acre) were needed to provide more complete and long-lasting defoliation. This rate was achieved in early 1964 by making two passes over each target area, but only at the cost of increased exposure to enemy antiaircraft fire. The 1963 PACAF-proposed solution for a quick-removable spray module capable of delivering up to three gallons per acre was still under development and testing. As an interim measure, however, a "quick-fix" modification was achieved in August 1964 by locally installing two 20-horsepower pumps in the existing MC-1 system. Together with some changes in the plumbing, these pumps were capable of delivering a flow of 430 gallons per minute of Purple, adequate to deposit 3 gallons per acre over a 240-foot-wide swath. Between August and November other modifications were made to the aircraft, primarily at the suggestion of the RANCH HAND crews, including stripping the aircraft of unnecessary equipment to lighten it, installing a workable frequency modulation (FM) radio to provide direct communication with ground units and forward air controllers, and installation of Doron armor "half-moon" cut-outs in front of the instrument panels to provide limited "head-on" protection for the cockpit area.[22]

The C-123 had proved itself a tough, dependable aircraft, capable of absorbing considerable punishment. Originally designed in 1945 as the XCG-20, a "powered glider," the C-123 retained the heavy-duty glider structure in the fuselage and empennage, including a tow-ring attachment point in the nose section, giving it a simple, but very strong, airframe. Control systems were dual cabled for safety, and the engine-nacelle fuel tanks had self-sealing bladders; the nacelle section containing the fuel tank was mounted on bomb shackles and could be electrically jettisoned in an emergency. Power was provided by two extremely reliable 2,500-horsepower Pratt and Whitney R-2800-99W engines. Purchased as an assault transport in 1951, the Air Force authorized the Fairchild-Hiller Aircraft Company to produce 398 "B" models of the C-123 "Provider."[23]

Compared with the modern USAF century-series jet fighters, the C-123 appeared outdated and ungainly. The Air Force planned to retire the Provider, declared obsolescent in 1956, from the active inventory in 1961. Yet at the peak of American involvement in Vietnam nearly ten years later, four full squadrons of cargo C-123s and the oversize squadron of spray-modified C-123s were still actively engaged in combat. Pilots assigned to RANCH HAND and the other C-123 units initially looked down their noses at the snub-nosed, high-winged transport. (A C-123 instructor pilot best described the special qualities of the relationship between the ungainly assault transport and modern Air Force pilots when he said: "Flying the one-twenty-three is a lot like playing with yourself—it's a hell of a lot of fun, but you're ashamed to admit that you do it.") The aircraft, however, matched the exact needs of the Vietnam theater, and of RANCH HAND in particular. Their missions required a close match of man and machine; performance had to be sensed, not judged by reference to complex instruments. Herbicide sorties, especially, were a throwback to the 1920s—to the days of barnstorming and "seat-of-the-pants" flying.[24]

As a temporary organization, RANCH HAND crews had tested and proven the tactics of herbicidal warfare. In two and one-half years, RANCH HAND aircraft had flown more than 800 total sorties, using over 300 spray sorties to dispense more than 250,000 gallons of chemicals over 80,000 acres. Never equipped with more than three operational aircraft and crews at any one time, the unit developed the defoliation concept at a cost of two aircraft and three crewmen, in addition to a number of wounded. Tactics and procedures still had room for refinement and modification, but the organization had demonstrated itself capable of meeting an increased demand for herbicide missions—43 percent of all defoliation to date was accomplished in the four months preceeding redesignation as a separate detachment within the Troop Carrier Group.[25] By mid-July 1964 the days of flying support and "make-do" sorties just to keep busy appeared a thing of the past; defoliation as a weapon was no longer experimental.

The changes taking place in the chemical operation in Vietnam, however, were overshadowed by two events—an American election and an attack on US Navy vessels in Asian waters. In the United States 1964 was a presidential election year, and Vietnam occupied a key place in the rhetoric of the various candidates. The frontrunner for the Republican Party nomination caused an uproar when he reportedly proposed using low-yield atomic weapons to defoliate forests along South Vietnam's borders to expose enemy supply lines. It did little good for a Los Angeles spokesman for Senator Barry Goldwater to point out that the candidate was merely saying such plans had been studied. Nor could Goldwater explain that he was referring to the 1950 Fifth Air Force contingency plan; as a reserve Air Force general officer he was privy to the information, but this information remained classified Top Secret, preventing further disclosure.[26]

Public opinion was further influenced when the Tonkin Gulf incident took place in August. The supposedly unprovoked attack on US vessels apparently well offshore in international waters caused both the public and Congress to support expanded United States involvement in Southeast Asia with almost no dissent.[27] Newsmen had little time to comment on, or even notice, the organizational realignment of an insignificant three-plane unit.

Even as the redesignation was taking place, however, it was obvious to RANCH HAND officers that the unit would soon have a new responsibility, replacing the VNAF as the primary agency for attacking the enemy subsistence system. Destruction of enemy crops, frequently referred to by the more acceptable term "food denial," was an outgrowth of the original Project AGILE Task 2 tests in 1961. Until 1964 the program was exclusively a VNAF mission; the Vietnamese used five HIDAL spray units mounted on H-34 helicopters to spray various targets with relative inefficiency. Final approval authority over specific targets was a joint responsibility of top officials in the US Department of State and the South Vietnamese government, operating under a well-defined set of criteria. VNAF field officers, however, sometimes failed to get permission before destroying crops in areas of marginal VC control (probably out of frustration due to the complex and time-consuming approval system, as noted in the 1963 herbicide evaluation). Delays and poor results also resulted from inexperienced pilots, equipment failures, and lack of motivation on the part of the aircrews—the H-34 helicopter being especially vulnerable to small-arms ground fire.[28]

As a result of the VNAF problems and the findings of the 1963 investigation, approval procedures for both crop and defoliation missions were simplified. Following delegation in 1963 of approval authority for defoliation targets to the American ambassador in Saigon and to COMUSMACV, responsibility for hand-spray defoliation was further decentralized to the ARVN division level in January 1964 (this did not apply to hand spraying of crops). Ambassador Henry Cabot Lodge, who replaced Nolting in August 1963, had requested authority to conduct crop destruction missions throughout Vietnam on the same basis as defoliation. Pending action on his original request, on 3 January Lodge asked for limited authority for a single area within War Zone D. The ambassador assured the State Department that: "As a general practice I intend to insist that every request for crop destruction be signed by either Gen. Don, Gen. Kim, Gen. Minh or the Prime Minister before I affix my signature."[29] Secretary of State Rusk approved the second request on 12 January, and asked Lodge to submit a list of other areas under Viet Cong domination where he and General Harkins (COMUSMACV) believed crop destruction was "necessary and justified." In February a list of 12 areas outside South Vietnamese control was submitted (see Map 3), and in March Lodge and Harkins were authorized to conduct crop destruction in these areas without further reference to Washington; acting jointly with the US officials would be a "responsible top-level GVN [Government of Vietnam] military or civilian authority," usually Lieutenant General Nguyen Khanh, then-President

Map 3: Photocopy of the original secret map showing the 12 Viet Cong-occupied areas recommended for crop destruction by American Ambassador Henry Cabot Lodge in a classified telegram from Saigon to the State Department (Embassy Telegram 1543, 12 February 1964.)

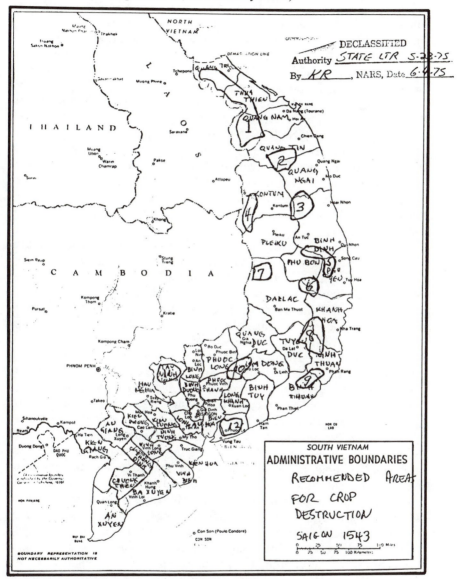

Source: National Security File, Countries, Vietnam, Box 2, vol. 4, Cables, item 56e. Lyndon Baines Johnson Presidential Library, Austin, Texas.

of the ruling Revolutionary Council.[30] Each operation, however, had to be reported to Washington, and attacks were to be preceded by psywar and civic action preparations. Relief and compensation procedures were to be used to help affected civilians. The ambassador's authority was further expanded on 29 July to "all chemical crop destruction operations in Vietnam," but targets still required the personal approval of "one senior GVN official, i.e., Khanh, Khiem, or Vice Premier." Secretary Rusk warned General Maxwell Taylor, who had replaced Lodge as ambassador on 1 July, that "crop destruction remains [a] matter of serious political concern here and political aspects must be given careful consideration by Saigon before approval [of] each operation."[31]

Although the VNAF's July-August crop spray missions in Binh Thuan Province achieved an 80 percent crop destruction level, Taylor was dissatisfied with overall results. RANCH HAND was directed to assume part of the crop mission responsibility under the FARM GATE concept, that is, using mixed USAF/VNAF aircrews. To provide for the increased workload, an additional spray-modified C-123 was requested from TAC. Thus, just as defoliation finally gained military acceptance and project requests were escalating rapidly, RANCH HAND found itself committed to a more hazardous and also more controversial task.[32]

The crop mission forced RANCH HAND to once again develop a new set of procedures and tactics. VNAF-developed procedures did not help; they applied to helicopters, not to fixed-wing aircraft. American domestic spray experience, civilian and military, had even less application to crop destruction than it did to defoliation. Nor were the recent hard-won defoliation tactics totally compatible with crop missions. Defoliation runs were usually flown on a single heading, with occasionally one or two fairly easy turns. Herbicide normally was dispensed in one continuous spray—nearly 1,000 gallons during a 14-kilometer (8.7-mile) run of about 4½-minute duration. Even lines-of-communication targets in the mountains, requiring more violent maneuvering, were commonly sprayed with a continuous run. Defoliation aircraft flew in a tight echelon formation, like the last three fingers of a hand, angled away from the direction of planned turns, with all aircraft spraying on and off at the same time, as directed by the leader. Including initial descent to low-level and post-target climbout, exposure to most enemy weapons usually was only eight to ten minutes (to the aircrews it always seemed considerably longer).[33]

Crop destruction was different. Enemy cultivations were primarily of the "slash-and-burn" type—small, scattered openings in the forest surrounding enemy fixed locations, such as base camps, logistics centers, and staging points, and along infiltration routes. Targets were assigned by specifying a "target box"—a set of coordinates outlining a relatively unpopulated area not under government control—in which cultivated crops were grown by the VC or their sympathizers. Extensive planning and coordination were needed to destroy these cultivations just prior to harvest when it was too late to replant, but after the enemy had invested a maximum amount of effort in raising them.

Timing was critical. Crop missions in extensive target areas, such as mountain valleys, were flown in a loose modified "V" formation, much like the middle three fingers of a hand, with lead in the center spraying crop up the middle of the valley and number two and number three spraying on either side, zigzagging up and down the valley walls to catch individual cultivated areas clinging to the slopes. Each aircraft turned its spray on and off individually as the target required. On more isolated highlands targets, one spray plane often remained at a higher altitude to provide directions from one plot to another, while the other aircraft did the spraying. The planes exchanged roles back and forth until all were out of herbicide or all targets within the box had been covered. Occasionally, the aircraft followed each other, one behind the other, diving down, dipping into the jungle to release bursts of chemicals into clearings, and roaring back into the sky, like some gigantic, disconnected amusement park roller coaster. Exposure to enemy weapons while on crop missions could be as long as 45 minutes.

Coordination between the pilots in each plane was extremely critical. The left-seat pilot flew the aircraft, maintained vertical and horizontal position in relation to the other aircraft, spotted targets, held the proper spray altitude, and turned the spray on and off with a switch mounted on the control yoke. The right-seat pilot controlled the power, monitored all engine and flight instruments, kept the airspeed within limits, maintained fore-and-aft spacing vis-à-vis the other aircraft, helped spot targets, and followed up on the control yoke. In a sense, the two pilots had to operate as one individual with four hands and four eyes; each had to anticipate the other's actions and the reactions of the aircraft, each had to be prepared to take over instantly if the other was hit. While low-level flight is inherently dangerous, in such situations it was even more so.

RANCH HAND had to consider another factor in planning for the crop destruction program—vigorous enemy reaction. Because these targets were vital to the enemy war effort, they would be strongly defended. By the nature of the target locations, large numbers of personnel and weapons would be available to act in this defense. The terrain surrounding most crop targets favored the defender and often forced the attacker into obvious routes of assault, along which the defense could concentrate its weapons. Restrictions on the rules of engagement that required preattack warning by psywar units, and the short vulnerability period of crops to efficient attack, narrowly defined the time when particular targets could be struck, thus allowing further concentration of enemy defenses. RANCH HAND anticipated that crop missions would meet more ground fire than defoliation had; this anticipation soon became reality.

The American spray unit began its first crop attacks on 3 October 1964 in southwest Phuoc Long Province, a food-raising region adjacent to a major enemy base camp area in War Zone D. The target area was titled "Project 2-14" and code named "Big Patch." Missions were flown using a modified mixed-crew concept—each US-manned aircraft carried a Vietnamese observer. Both the C-123s and their escorting A-1E fighters bore Vietnamese insignia. On 3-6 and 12-13 October, RANCH HAND aircraft returned again and again to the target box, despite heavy resistance. By the time Big Patch was completed, the C-123s had been hit 40 times.[34]

October also saw the beginning of defoliation attacks on Project 20-36, a VC "safe haven" known as "Go Cong." Safe havens were insurgent-controlled areas of Vietnam bordering Cambodia and Laos that had been selected for their natural defenses; they provided secure areas for guerrilla forces to train and reorganize, terminals for logistics resupply and reinforcement arriving through neutral territory, jumping-off points for forays against government units, and refuge for Viet Cong units fleeing GVN counterattacks. The areas were so heavily held that South Vietnamese ground forces usually could not or would not enter them, leaving aerial attack as the only method of government action. Defoliation opened these safe havens to airborne observation and attack.[35]

In November a second crop target was assigned to RANCH HAND. Fifteen sorties were flown between 28 November and 4 December against Project 2-19 in Phuoc Thanh Province. Aptly named "Hot Spot," the target box provided very heavy ground fire from automatic weapons. Spray formations were hit 50 times, including one mission in which an aircraft received battle damage to the left engine, which burst into flames. When engine shutdown and use of the engine fire extinguisher failed to put out the fire, the crew was forced to jettison the nacelle fuel tank for fear that it would explode. The aircraft made an emergency recovery to Bien Hoa airfield and landed with the engine still burning fiercely.[36]

The success of the RANCH HAND assault on the Phuoc Thanh rice was indicated by a VC province committee report that Hot Spot attacks destroyed enough rice to feed VC troops in the area for two years. Overall, 15,039 acres of crops were sprayed during 1964, with over 40 percent of this during the final three months, after the United States began flying crop missions. RANCH HAND sorties for the year increased to 363—spray sorties accounted for 273—and total defoliation amounted to 99.5 square miles. Herbicide consumption rose to 218,510 gallons. More indicative of the increasing use of herbicides as weapons was the utilization rate for the RANCH HAND aircraft, which averaged only 48 percent for the year, but shot up to 92 percent for the final four months of the period. The arrival of the fourth spray-modified aircraft in December gave the unit some much needed additional capacity to meet the increasing demand. The fourth plane also provided some relief for the maintenance personnel responsible for repairing battle damage; the current rate of hits was in excess of one every other sortie, and maintenance crews were sometimes hard pressed to get enough aircraft ready for the next mission.[37]

Much needed relief was also on the way in the form of more aircrews. Conversion to one-year duty tours under the permanent unit concept, instead of the previous 90-day TDYs, plus the increasing workload and more hazardous missions, meant that a spare crew was needed to provide flexibility to cover days off, rest and recuperation (R&R) leaves, and convalescence periods for wounded crewmembers. In his July End-of-Tour Report, Captain Eugene D. Stammer had recommended that a fourth aircraft and a fifth aircrew be added. The departing commander's suggestions were more than accepted—the December aircraft arrival was followed in January by not one, but two additional crews.[38]

Other changes were in store for the aerial spray organization. In mid-year PACAF had begun considering replacing Purple herbicide with a less expensive 2,4-D/2,4,5-T mixture, code named herbicide "Orange." This chemical, however, would not be available in Vietnam until early 1965. More immediately, in December 2d Air Division changed the rules of engagement for RANCH HAND fighter escort, requiring that all defoliation projects permit free strike zones, rather than return fire only. This change would allow development of offensive fighter tactics designed to counter and reduce the increasing ground fire RANCH HAND was facing.[39]

At the beginning of 1964 the herbicide concept was merely a small adjunct of questionable value to the US effort in Vietnam. By the end of the year the RANCH HAND mission was not only accepted by the military, but eagerly sought after, with sortie demands exceeding capacity. While not all questions had been answered, or all problems solved, the foundation for continued development had been laid. Western public comment had been negligible, and the outburst of scientific and lay criticism of the herbicide program was still in the future; 1964 had been a year of development and preparation for continued growth.

6

Boi Loi Woods to
Ho Chi Minh Trail

The overt American role in Vietnam changed during 1965. Instead of primarily training and supplying the South Vietnamese armed forces, with only a limited combat role for a few "advisors," the United States committed itself to direct combat participation on a major scale. The basis for this change had been laid by the August 1964 North Vietnamese "attacks" on the destroyers *Maddox* and *Turner Joy,* and by the subsequent Tonkin Gulf Resolution giving President Johnson virtually a free hand in Vietnam. When the inability of the ARVN to protect supporting US forces was exposed by a major mortar attack on Bien Hoa Air Base in November 1964 and an assault on the US compound at Pleiku in February 1965, Johnson ordered the deployment of ground combat forces to Vietnam to guard American lives and property. Less than two months later, the Pentagon authorized these "guards" to use combat patrols. Additional increases in US strength eventually would total more than 100,000 men by the end of 1965 and lead to increasingly larger ground battles, mainly against North Vietnamese regulars.[1]

Operationally these changes had little immediate influence on the RANCH HAND organization since it had been directly involved in combat from the beginning. Effectively, however, the influx of United States combat units meant a dramatic increase in defoliation mission requests as American field commanders discovered the dangers in the heavy Southeast Asian vegetation and the advantages of chemically "opened" jungles. Moreover, when interrogation of Viet Cong prisoners and defectors suggested that crop destruction had significantly affected enemy logistics, demands for these projects also mounted. Reportedly, in late 1964 food had become so scarce in the central highlands and War Zones C and D that VC forces had to "live largely on food grown by their own production units."[2] Food procurement activities absorbed "over one-third of the manpower and up to 50 percent of the time of many Viet Cong units." Aerial spraying also was claimed to have caused relocation of enemy camps and units because many VC soldiers believed the spray was "dangerous to their health."[3]

While RANCH HAND targets in early 1965 were being selected to further exploit the problems of the Viet Cong, the first order of business in January was to finish a project begun the previous October. The main transportation links between Saigon and the important central port city of Nha Trang, Highway 1 and the national railway, had both been rendered hazardous to travel by guerrilla ambushes. To improve communications security, RANCH HAND was ordered to defoliate 18 of the most densely overgrown areas where the VC operated along these routes (Project 20-32/33). The limited number of spray aircraft and frequent diversions to higher-priority targets delayed completion of all areas until 29 January. The change in RANCH HAND's status, however, was reflected in the fact that while January spray missions were almost nonexistent in previous years, the January 1965 expenditure on Project 20-32/33 alone was 40 sorties and 36,600 gallons of chemical. To the relief of the aircrews, only two hits were received on these 40 sorties, but the unit was not so fortunate during the other January task.[4]

For over seven years, the primary guerrilla headquarters and staging area for the Saigon region was in a dense forest 26 miles northwest of Saigon, known as the Boi Loi Woods. The enemy had turned this area into a stronghold of trenches, caves, and tunnels that could not be seen from the air and which was almost impregnable from the ground. Past efforts to drive the VC out by bombing or ground assaults had been failures. American and Vietnamese planners hoped to clear a 7 by 14-kilometer section of these woods by defoliation followed by firebombing, both deemed essential for a successful ground assault. Reports of numerous machine-gun emplacements and an estimated 4,000 VC in the area caused 2d Air Division to authorize fighter prestrikes for the first time in the III Corps area. Defoliation planes also would be supported by rescue helicopters and additional fighter escort.[5]

The attack on the Boi Loi Woods, code named "Operation Sherwood Forest" (Project 20-46), began on 19 January with two days of intense bombing; A-1Es and A-1Hs dropped 800 tons of bombs in 139 sorties. The spray planes started their portion of the project on 21 January and continued for 16 of the next 29 days (nonspraying days were due primarily to weather). RANCH HAND aircraft dispensed 78,800 gallons of herbicide during 102 sorties, supported by 256 fighter and 32 helicopter sorties. Despite the use of a large share of the fighter resources in South Vietnam on this single project, defoliation aircraft were hit by ground fire 79 times and had three crewmen wounded, one seriously.[6]

This unprecedented aerial effort was unsuccessful. The Viet Cong had withdrawn the bulk of their forces as the attack began, leaving only small units to provide ground security, gather intelligence, and man antiaircraft weapons. Forty days later, after giving the vegetation time to react to the defoliant and to dry, American leaflet drops warned noncombatants to leave the area. C-123 transports from the 309th Air Commando Squadron (ACS) then dropped improvised firebombs on the area in hopes of starting a "fire storm." Each C-123 "bomber" (another first for the obsolescent assault transport) dropped four wooden pallets, each containing four 55-gallon drums of diesel fuel with a Mk-6 flare in the center as an igniter. To help intensify the fires, the "bombers" were followed by A-1Es and B-57s dropping "incendijel" and incendiaries. At first fires were seen to blaze encouragingly, but the rising heat triggered a rain storm over the target and by the next day all fires were out. The hoped-for denuding of the woods did not occur, although failure of the plan was not due to the defoliants; their use did improve vertical visibility and the insurgents were denied use of the Boi Loi Woods for a short period. What the failure of the plan indicated was that permanent denial of an area to the enemy through chemical agents alone was not possible.[7]

While 2nd Air Division waited for the Boi Loi Woods to dry out, the RANCH HAND unit moved on to other targets. Supply ships moving up the main shipping channel to the port at Saigon were receiving increasing harassment from riverbank snipers, and there had been attempts to mine the channel. Improved visibility along the river would facilitate aerial patrols and increase security. Beginning on 1 March, 42 sorties were flown to defoliate portions of the banks of the Saigon River from the capitol city to the South China Sea (Project 20-21). Apparently the enemy was not prepared to seriously defend this area, only two aircraft were hit by ground fire. To test its effectiveness, some of the newly procured Orange herbicide was used for the first time during the later stages of the river project; most of the 27,000 gallons of chemical used, however, was the standard defoliant, Purple.[8]

On 8 March the 315th TCG was redesignated the 315th Air Commando Group (ACG), and RANCH HAND became a flight of the 309th Air Commando Squadron, rather than a separate detachment within the group. As at Langley, the spray unit was now known as the Special Aerial Spray Flight. The change made no difference in RANCH HAND operations; the four aircraft and six crews remained separate from the squadron's 16 "trash haulers" and their crews.[9]

The remainder of March and April was spent attacking the "rice bowl of the northern coast," the An Lao Valley of Binh Dinh Province. Designated Project 2-18 and code named "Yankee," this series of targets was one of the most politically sensitive attacked to date. Not only was the planned coverage of 6,500 hectares "twice as large as any previous crop destruction effort," but because civilians in the target areas might not be able to escape after their crops were destroyed, approval would violate previously established guidelines for crop projects.[10] From the beginning there had been concern in Washington that the real reason the Saigon government wanted a crop destruction program was to force segments of the population to move to government controlled areas, more than to attack Viet Cong supplies. For this reason the United States limited approval of crop destruction to remote areas with sparse civilian population, and required an active civic action program to provide relief and resettlement to affected civilians. Binh Dinh Province in 1965, however, was heavily populated and contained large VC forces. A significant portion of the civilian population either opposed or was indifferent to the Saigon government, although not necessarily supportive of the Viet Cong. The narrow, government-controlled area along the coast was not capable of handling large numbers of refugees, if they appeared. Even so, Ambassador Taylor sanctioned crop destruction in the An Lao Valley, citing the gravity of the situation and the imminent maturity of the crops.[11]

Taylor's decision was questioned by the State Department, which expressed concern about possible adverse civilian reaction in the area and potential widespread international criticism. The American Embassy was asked for a review of local reactions to previous crop destruction actions. The issue was further complicated on 22 March when a MACV press conference admitted the use of irritant gases in Vietnam. The resultant furor in Washington caused the State Department to suggest that "while 'gas' uproar is running its course," the Binh Dinh operation should be "reduced in visibility" if it could be done without causing problems with the ARVN, which hoped to regain control of the province after the herbicide attacks. Despite contrary denials, it was clear the Vietnamese expected the Binh Dinh project to force local inhabitants to move to government-dominated areas.[12]

Again, on 25 March, the State Department warned Saigon that "publicity should be avoided as far as possible."[13] The American Embassy advised Washington that spray aircraft would operate out of Nha Trang and Qui Nhon, and would spray only the "least conspicuous area," remaining prepared to interrupt spraying if "any adverse reaction [was] observed." In the meantime target area 7 was cancelled, since harvesting had already taken place, and, in an apparent change of the ambassador's mind, target area 5 was deleted because of its proximity to populated areas.[14] On 26 March, when Vietnamese observers scheduled to fly on RANCH HAND aircraft failed to appear, more sorties were cancelled. Overall, these various delays and changes in the operation destroyed its potential effectiveness, since many areas were at least partially harvested by this time.[15] To replace the original program, a limited operation was authorized in a remote section of the province. Secretary Rusk expressed hope that this reduced project would be ignored by the press, as they had ignored crop destruction in the past. American officials in Saigon were told to keep the entire operation "low key" and to let the Vietnamese government speak first if the press found out.[16]

Although some Binh Dinh crops were destroyed, much rice was harvested, including four million pounds in target areas 5 and 6 alone. The American Embassy reported that no refugees had emerged from areas sprayed on 1-2

April, despite leaflet drops, loudspeaker broadcasts, and reconnaissance by armed helicopters. When the project ended on 18 April, only 37 sorties had been flown, dispensing 27,300 gallons of chemicals. Some consolation for the limited success of the operation came from the lack of enemy resistance—spray planes were hit only nine times.[17]

The low level of enemy response in March and April did not last much longer. A portent of the future was suggested in aerial photographs taken in South Vietnam in April—for the first time, VC antiaircraft weapons larger than machine guns were noted. Photographs showed a four-gun 37-millimeter position 20 kilometers south of Tam Ky in Quang Tin Province, while a three-gun position of the same type was located 25 kilometers to the southwest.[18]

Meanwhile, planning for the largest defoliation project to date had been completed. Operation "Swamp Fox" (Project 20-44) was intended to open up areas in Bac Lieu, Ba Xuyen, and Vinh Dinh Provinces virtually immune from government attack for several years. Viet Cong forces operated extensive supply and training facilities in these coastal areas. Supplied by shallow-draft sampans, they were central in the maintenance of insurgent control in the Mekong Delta. Using USAF A-1E prestrike and close air support against suspected automatic weapons positions, defoliation started on 30 April 1965. Unlike the previous two projects, ground fire was extremely heavy. By late May 84 sorties had been hit 124 times and five crewmembers wounded. The climax came on 25 May when a spray plane was badly damaged during its run and had difficulty climbing out of danger after it lost one engine. The accompanying C-123 immediately moved in between the stricken plane and the tree tops, deliberately absorbing enemy fire to protect the other aircraft's remaining engine. The second aircraft also was heavily damaged, forcing the spray operator to manually dump the heavy load of herbicide. Both aircraft eventually safely reached an emergency airfield. Although the target was only 70 percent completed, 2d Air Division temporarily suspended defoliation pending re-evaluation by the MACV intelligence division.[19]

While no spray aircraft had been lost since 1962, PACAF was concerned for defoliation aircrew safety in light of increasingly effective enemy resistance. The question was whether the results justified the risks. The resultant MACV evaluation endorsed continued defoliation, but recommended increased fighter support. The ideal aircraft to escort the C-123s was the A-1, because of its comparable speed, ability to carry a wide variety of weapons, and long loiter time. A-1s, however, were in short supply. USAF-manned FARM GATE A-1Es at Bien Hoa were used primarily for training VNAF pilots; only 20 of the 68 Bien Hoa sorties each day were available for nontraining use, and these were usually needed for ground support missions. Both training and ground support had priority over escort duties. At the same time, the value of VNAF-manned fighter support was suspect. Not only did the language differences hamper effective communication and coordination, but RANCH HAND personnel doubted the reliability and discipline of the VNAF pilots. The situation was not helped by the "expressed reservations by the VNAF Director of the AOC [Air Operations Center]" (which directed fighter operations) concerning using VNAF fighters for escort. The Special Aerial Spray Flight regarded use of VNAF A-1s for support as "undesirable."[20]

Two other factors affected support planning for herbicide sorties—incompatible weather minimums and unrealistic escort requirement projections. Defoliation aircraft could operate with ceilings as low as 300 feet and visibility of only 2 miles, although with some risk, while escorting fighters were required to have at least 3,000 feet and 3 miles over flatlands, and 4,000 and 4 in the mountains. Since herbicides were best applied during the growing season, which was also the rainy season, suitable operating conditions for fighters could be expected only 20 percent of the time, according to a SASF study. The same report also concluded each RANCH HAND mission would need eight fighters for on-target support and four additional fighters for pre- and poststrikes on enemy gun positions. Using these assumptions, the study estimated that the next scheduled project, a crop complex in Kontum Province, would require 128 C-123 sorties, 64 forward air controller (FAC) sorties, 128 medical evacuation sorties, and 1,530 fighter sorties.[21] This projection was far beyond the existing fighter capacity in Vietnam at the time. Even after the war effort was later expanded, this unrealistic level of support per mission was achieved in only a few isolated, exceptional instances. It is hard, however, to fault these impractical demands by RANCH HAND planners who at the time were facing increasing numbers of enemy guns while flying slow, unarmed aircraft at low-level.

Adding to the confusion over fighter support was the debate within RANCH HAND itself over just how the available fighters should be used. One faction felt surprise was essential in reducing enemy ground fire, and argued that fighter prestrike only alerted the enemy; they therefore felt that fighters should hold at a distance from the target area until after spray aircraft began their run. A second faction held that herbicide operations could not be concealed due to approval criteria, restricted application factors, and the lack of secure communications within Vietnamese channels used to get approval of targets, free-fire zones, and support. This faction claimed VC agents learned of daily mission orders even before the SASF did, and that such security leaks made little difference anyway, since once the project was begun, it was obvious where subsequent runs would be made. Thus, they argued, surprise was impossible and emphasis should be placed on measures to keep the enemy's heads down—the "he can't shoot if he's ducking" theory.[22] This debate over methodology continues, unresolved, at reunions of RANCH HAND veterans, more than a decade later.

During MACV's re-evaluation of the defoliation concept, RANCH HAND again reverted to hauling cargo alongside the other 309th aircraft. In addition to routine logistical sorties, in June SASF aircraft participated in a "rice lift" to supply the population around Ban Me Thout (Lac Giao) in the central highlands, which the Viet Cong had almost totally isolated. In July the spray crews returned to their herbicide tasks, with 40 sorties against crop targets in Binh Dinh and Kontum Provinces (Project 2-23). August saw a reduction to only 24 sorties; long delays in approval of new targets sometimes left the unit with only a single active project. Change was again in the air, however, and MACV was making plans for a significant increase in the herbicide operation. The restrictions limiting crop destruction to remote, unpopulated areas were eased in August by Washington, allowing the targeting of more populated areas where shortages of local food supplies were already causing the VC difficulties. A further alteration came in September when authority for defoliation by ground-based power equipment was delegated to Corps level.[23] Essentially, only aerial defoliation still required joint approval by the ambassador and COMUSMACV.

To meet the increased workload caused by the relaxed criteria, the aircraft authorization and manning of the SASF again were increased, this time by three aircraft, nine pilots, five navigators, and five flight mechanics, almost doubling the size of the unit. The new crews received C-123 transition training at Eglin AFB Auxiliary Field No. 9 (Hurlburt Field), Florida, and spray training in Virginia from the reformed Langley AFB insecticide unit. After spray modification at the Fairchild-Hiller plant at Crestview, Florida, the additional aircraft were ferried to Vietnam by the newly trained crews, arriving on 13 November 1965. Meanwhile, USAF Headquarters recognized the unique configuration of the spray-modified transports by redesignating them as UC-123Bs.[24]

During August and September crop and defoliation targets in Kontum, Binh Dinh, Khanh Hoa, Tay Ninh, and Bien Hoa Provinces were attacked; 67 sorties took only sporadic ground fire. On 20 October the spray flight, now commanded by Major Russell E. Mohney, launched a major operation (Project 2-28) against War Zone D, a Viet Cong stronghold northeast of Bien Hoa that had resisted all efforts at government control since before World War II. For the first time, RANCH HAND aircraft were supported by newly arrived F-100 and A-4 jet fighter-bombers, in addition to the propeller-driven A-1s. Through frequent and reliable association, the F-100s would eventually become RANCH HAND's favorite close-support aircraft. Over the next two months, 163 sorties sprayed 137,650 gallons of chemicals on the triple-canopy forest covering a concentration of bunkers, base camps, and trails in Zone D. The proximity of this area to fighter support from Bien Hoa Air Base made it an ideal alternate target when spray missions had to cancel other targets due to weather or enemy activity.[25] During the next five years, War Zone D became one of the most defoliated sections of Vietnam.

Arrival of the additional aircraft gave SASF the capacity to work several projects simultaneously, even when one or more planes were out of commission from battle damage. This added flexibility meant that 18 sorties could be used in late November to defoliate river banks along the Oriental River (Project 20-58), without neglecting the War Zone D project. In December two long-term projects in Kien Hoa (20-55) and Phuoc Tuy (20-68) Provinces were started at the same time. Enemy ground fire remained a significant hazard, with 34 hits recorded on the Oriental River sorties and a mounting toll of hits from the other targets. A single four-ship attack on a Delta target in Kien Hoa on 19 December added nine hits to the total during a four-minute run; the aircrews reported the use of rifle grenades as a crude, but impressive, substitute for antiaircraft guns. Almost half the aircrew members assigned to RANCH HAND in December 1965 had been wounded at least once and their aircraft had a total of nearly 800 hits; one of the older planes, nicknamed the "Leper Colony," had been hit 230 times and its occupants had earned eight Purple Heart medals.[26]

To counter the increase in hits, particularly in the cockpit area, RANCH HAND crew members began using flying helmets equipped with a clear visor that could be lowered to protect the eyes. Used in place of the standard radio headset while on the spray run, the helmet, together with a flak jacket, offered pilots and navigators extra protection from flying shrapnel and glass. Twice in December this protection allowed crews to complete runs despite cockpit damage, although it did not prevent them from receiving minor wounds. Some extra-cautious pilots, concerned about their future ability to father children, also checked out a second flak jacket to sit on.[27]

In early November herbicide planners got an indication of future problems when, for two days, the spray planes remained on the ground due to a lack of chemical. Since mid-year the cheaper Orange herbicide had totally replaced Purple as the primary defoliant chemical; Blue herbicide was used mainly for crop targets. The increasing ability of the SASF to meet field requirements, however, caused chemical consumption to outstrip the supply system.[28] At the time, the chemical shortage was only a minor, momentary inconvenience, but soaring herbicide usage would eventually cause major procurement problems in the United States.

December found RANCH HAND flying the first herbicide sorties outside South Vietnam when they began a long-term project to expose enemy supply routes in Laos (see Map 4). This illicit transportation network, leading from North Vietnam through Laos to the Cambodian border, was known as the Ho Chi Minh Trail, and served as the primary route for supply and reinforcement of VC forces. Two spray planes were deployed to Da Nang Air Base, and the first Laotian sorties were flown on 6 December. Very mountainous terrain, bad weather, and heavy enemy resistance combined to make this target complex the most hazardous to date. Despite the difficulties, by the end of the month UC-123s from Da Nang and Bien Hoa had flown more than 40 sorties into southern Laos, defoliating almost 24 square miles of trails and roads with over 41,000 gallons of herbicide.[29]

Map 4: North Vietnamese logistics and personnel infiltration routes into South Vietnam through Laos and Cambodia, 1968.

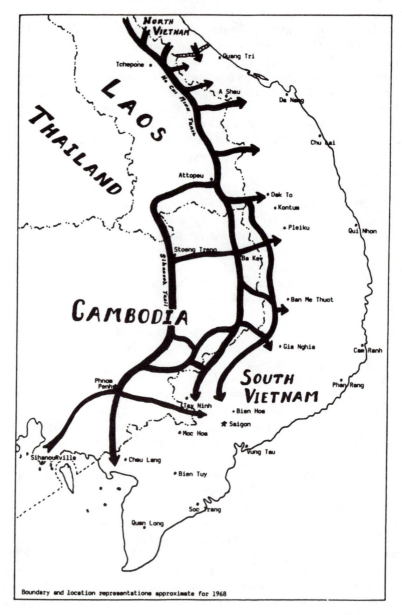

Source: Carl Berger, ed., *The United States Air Force in Southeast Asia* (Washington D.C., 1977).

During 1965 RANCH HAND also flew 897 spray sorties in Vietnam, defoliating 253 square miles of vegetation and destroying approximately 68,000 acres of crops. Although this was nearly three times the area sprayed in Vietnam the preceding year, it did not approach the 14.5 million acres treated with herbicides of one type or another in the United States during 1965. Even so, the organization began to attract the attention of the press, particularly after gaining the reputation "of being the most shot-at airmen operating over South Vietnam."[30]

Newsmen were not the only ones to notice the 309th spray flight. Air Vice-Marshal Nguyen Cao Ky, who had been Prime Minister of South Vietnam since June 1965, continued his long association with the RANCH HANDs by flying with them on target. Afterward, Premier Ky gave his violet-colored flying scarf to the aircraft commander of the spray plane, saying, "These are your colors, wear them with pride."[31] The violet scarf (whose color soon was referred to as purple since it was nearly the same shade as the faded stripe on the Purple-herbicide barrels) thus became one of the symbols of the spray organization, and was retained in spite of several later attempts to prohibit its being worn. In one instance, after General William C. Westmoreland's MACV Headquarters decreed a ban on the wearing of unauthorized uniform items by US personnel in Vietnam, a special dispensation was granted for RANCH HAND scarves after a phone call to Ky, who then called the American ambassador, who in turn called the MACV commander. Reportedly Ky threatened to close the gates of Tan Son Nhut Air Base if the spray crews were forced to remove their scarves.[32]

RANCH HAND crew members were also identifiable by a distinctive patch depicting a broad brown stripe diagonally across a green background and surrounded by a yellow circle with red lettering, "RANCH HAND VIET NAM." In the center of the brown stripe was the silver Chinese character for "Purple" (see Insignia, page vi). Designed by Captain Allen Kidd and Lieutenant John Hodgin in 1962, the insignia represented the herbicide mission and the close ties between the organization and South Vietnam.[33]

Distinct identification of RANCH HAND personnel by patch and scarf was not always advantageous. Rumors within the unit claimed that special bonuses had been offered by the Viet Cong for anyone shooting down a spray aircraft and that a reward had been offered for the capture or death of individual crew members. Spray personnel regarded these rumors more as testimony to the effectiveness of their mission than as a serious threat to their own safety. In December 1965, however, a residence occupied by RANCH HAND flight mechanics was subjected to a terrorist grenade attack; five of the six occupants were wounded. While this was not the only terrorist attack of 1965 and was, perhaps, only coincidental, it seemed to support the anti-RANCH HAND stories.[34]

The increasing enemy threat, on the ground and during missions, appeared to concern the spray personnel very little. Indeed, the aircrews seemed exhilarated by exposure to enemy fire. The low level and slow speed of the UC-123, plus the open cockpit windows and troop doors, meant that the crews could clearly hear the weapons being fired at them. When a round struck the fuselage or cockpit area, the UC-123 resounded like a garbage can struck with a baseball bat, and the ever-present rank smell of herbicide was frequently tainted with brief acid whiffs of gunpowder. Captain Paul Mitchell of Florence, Alabama, told a *New York Times* correspondent, "It's a funny thing. When we get shot at, everyone is laughing and talking [after the mission]. When we don't get shot at, people hardly say a thing."[35]

It became a tradition that new crewmembers buy champagne for the squadron at a "cherry party" the first time their plane was hit. Few newcomers lasted an entire week before having to host such affairs. Later, when the RANCH HAND organization grew to number over 100 aircrew members, four and five "cherries" sometimes occurred on the same day, leading to parties that were monumental in scope and damage to the officers' club. On these occasions the club bar sometimes ran out of champagne, and the host base commander frequently ran out of patience with RANCH HAND disregard for military courtesy and decorum. Only an occasional ill-fated crewman had the bad luck to keep his thirsty compatriots waiting to initiate him into the "Order of the Punctured Provider," although the lack of a cherry candidate did not distract from the almost daily parties, either at the club or at someone's villa. "Someone getting wounded," "No one getting wounded," "Glad to be alive," and "It's a dismal day" (for those times when the weather was too bad to fly) were also excuses for a RANCH HAND party.[36]

The constant series of parties in the tradition of aviators of previous wars perhaps provided a coping mechanism by which the crewmembers avoided thinking of the dangerous environment in which they operated. In any case, the parties did not hinder accomplishment of the mission; in December alone, an all-time high of 182 herbicide sorties was flown—more than the total for the entire first two years of operation in Vietnam. Preliminary operations plans by Seventh Air Force indicated that this record would not stand for very long. More forest-burning experiments, expanded operations in Laos, defoliation of the Demilitarized Zone (DMZ)—all were on the planners' boards for 1966, in addition to the ever-expanding, but more routine, defoliation and crop destruction missions within South Vietnam proper.[37]

7

From Flight to Squadron: More Planes, More Hits, More Problems

On 7 January 1966, RANCH HAND celebrated the beginning of its fifth year in Vietnam. Superficially, the seven aircraft of the expanded unit appeared little different from the three that arrived in 1962; they were even parked in the same area of the Saigon airport ramp. Operationally the differences were enormous—from a small experimental project in day-to-day danger of cancellation, RANCH HAND had become an integral part of the "greatest American gathering of airpower in one locality since the Korean War." By the first of the year, over 500 planes and 21,000 men of the United States Air Force were in Vietnam, in addition to other units operating over Southeast Asia from bases in Thailand and Guam. Army fixed-wing aircraft and helicopters swarmed over all parts of South Vietnam, while the Navy and Marines contributed more planes to the air armada, both from in-country bases and from several aircraft carriers in the South China Sea. American troop strength, already increased to nearly 150,000 men in 1965 and augmented by forces from Australia, New Zealand, the Philippines, Thailand, and Korea, would further expand during 1966 to reach 385,000 men.[1]

The crews of the spray planes, however, had little time to contemplate the meaning of the widening US role in Southeast Asia; they were too busy trying to keep up with the growing list of approved herbicide targets. The monthly record of 182 sorties, newly set in December, was quickly surpassed in January as 188 herbicide sorties dispensed 177,300 gallons of chemical. Besides continuing the Kien Hoa, Phuoc Tuy, and Laos projects, another forest fire experiment (Hot Tip I and Hot Tip II) was attempted in January and February. The target of 22,000 gallons of Orange defoliant was 29 square miles of heavy forest on the slopes of the Chu Pong Mountains, near the Ia Drang River Valley, southwest of Pleiku. After giving the defoliant time to take effect, Guam-based Strategic Air Command B-52s bombed the area on 11 March with M-35 incendiary cluster bombs; the heavy bombers were immediately followed by F-4 and F-100 fighter-bombers dropping napalm along the edges of the target area. On 18 March, however, a MACV briefing officer was forced to admit to Major General C. E. Hutchins that in spite of all factors being satisfactory, "the damned trees just wouldn't burn."[2]

While MACV was rediscovering the lessons of previous "forest fire" experiments, the spray planes were beginning to assume a new appearance. Heretofore, the UC-123s had retained the unpainted silver finish of the original aluminum skin, a finish marred only by red-primed patches resulting from repair of frequent enemy hits—one reporter described the effect as "the look of a beached whale all covered with measles."[3] Maintenance personnel responsible for repairing battle damage seemed to enjoy emphasizing the number of hits taken by each plane by liberally using the highly visible red primer. When ordered to stop highlighting repairs this way—it was not authorized or "military"—the sheet-metal repairmen began fixing the holes by putting on patches in the shape of playing card suits—spades, hearts, diamonds, and clubs. This practice prompted a second order to stop. At about this time, Air Force Headquarters directed the repainting of all combat aircraft in a camouflage scheme of mottled browns, greens, and yellows in irregular patterns. The perverse maintenance personnel took great delight in carefully repairing all battle damage with regulation patches, and then carefully painting the new patches in opposite colors; that is, a patch in a dark green area was painted tan, on tan it was mustard, on mustard it was green.[4]

The purpose of the new camouflage color scheme supposedly was to make aircraft harder to see, particularly when dispersed on the ground. In RANCH HAND's case the idea worked too effectively; FACs and fighters had trouble distinguishing the spray planes at low-level when they did not have their spray turned on. Eventually, the color scheme was modified again by adding a fluorescent red stripe on top of the wings of the UC-123s so the planes could be spotted more easily by their escorts.[5]

Although the tempo was picking up in all areas in 1966, Laos continued to provide an extra challenge. Before they could defoliate the Ho Chi Minh Trail, the spray crews had to find it. This involved two new tactics. When ground fire was not expected, the planes circled at 500 to 700 feet, spotting trail segments and marking them with smoke grenades. After dropping three grenades, the planes dove down and sprayed that section, flying from one marker to another before the smoke dissipated. By repeating this tactic, long stretches of the trail were gradually marked and exposed. Also frequently used was the standard mountain technique of having one aircraft at 500 feet "talk" the other aircraft along the trail as it sprayed. Again, this tactic was not used in "hot fire" areas due to the extreme exposure of the overhead aircraft.[6]

Where the trail was not at least intermittently visible from overhead, or where heavy ground fire was expected, the second new tactic consisted of short defoliation burns at 90 degrees to the suspected trail position, made every half mile or so. This allowed photo reconnaissance to map the trail and RANCH HAND then returned to defoliate the trail using time-and-distance dead-reckoning. These spray runs often revealed ingenious enemy attempts to conceal their road network. For example, in several areas lattice-work trellises overgrown with natural vegetation made living tunnels several miles in length. By February the RANCH HAND navigator at Da Nang, Captain D.B. (Pete) Spivey, was able to present Seventh Air Force with the first accurately plotted 1:125,000 scale map of the Ho Chi Minh Trail south of Tchpone, Laos.

In February the Laos defoliation project spread north of the 17th parallel, to expose segments of the infiltration route along the North Vietnamese/Laotian border. Some sorties on these northern sections of the trail were flown out of American bases at Nakom Phenom and Taklai, Thailand, with the concurrence of the Thai and Laotian governments. On at least one mission the spray planes penetrated North Vietnam to defoliate the Ban Karai Pass. Escort was provided by B-57 "Canberra" bombers to cover helicopter rescue in case a spray plane was shot down. In an unexpected role reversal, one of the bombers was downed, and the UC-123s remained overhead to relay radio instructions and help direct rescue helicopters to the site.

Throughout the next two months defoliation in Laos continued, primarily along Laotian-designated Routes 92, 922, 96, and 965 below Tchpone. Spray planes operated from both Da Nang and Tan Son Nhut, even though the distance was inconveniently long for the Saigon-based aircraft. The missions were hampered by weather since targets were isolated and forecasts uncertain. Several times spray planes flew all the way to the designated area, found both primary and secondary targets obscured by poor weather, and had to return to base with a full tank of herbicide. On one occasion, returning aircraft overflying the A Shau Valley learned that a Special Forces camp in the valley was being overrun. Knowing that VC propaganda claimed the herbicides were poisonous to human beings, the aircrews debated making spray runs around the camp in the hope that the VC soldiers might be frightened into abandoning the attack. Such a tactic, however, was questionable and unauthorized, and might hinder relief attempts already underway. Instead, one RANCH HAND aircraft remained at altitude over the valley in case it might later help in some way. While orbiting, the crew tape-recorded radio conversations of a flight of A-1 fighters attempting to relieve the camp and later rescuing one of their own downed pilots. This RANCH HAND tape later helped justify the award of the Medal of Honor to Air Force Major Bernard F. Fisher, one of the A-1 pilots, for his heroic efforts that day.[7]

When the planes could get on target, they ran into increasingly heavy antiaircraft fire as the North Vietnamese strengthened air defenses along the Laotian trail. Typical was an April mission of two spray aircraft against a road target in central Laos. Because of heavy ground cover, the lead aircraft circled at 700 feet while guiding number two along the target. Suddenly the lead plane came under heavy fire from what appeared to be a "quad-50" (four coaxially-mounted .50-caliber machine guns). The left engine was knocked out, and bullets passing through the cockpit struck the pilot's windscreen and wounded the left-seat pilot, who slumped forward. The right-seat pilot, also wounded, feathered the inoperative engine, dumped the herbicide load, and turned away from the enemy weapons fire and nearby hills; unable to climb, he managed to maintain altitude. The navigator, newly arrived in country and on a check-out flight, was wounded too, and was replaced by the instructor navigator, who directed the plane to an emergency landing at Nakhom Phanom, Thailand. Neither the instructor navigator nor flight mechanic got a scratch, and the others fortunately suffered only minor wounds.[8]

Despite heavy ground fire, including 37-millimeter weapons, the Da Nang detachment pressed the attack on various Laotian supply routes, including the so-called Sihanouk Trail section that led into Cambodia. The pace slackened in May—only 26 sorties were flown. On the fourteenth the detachment was withdrawn from Da Nang due to an unstable political situation caused by the attempted revolt of senior Vietnamese officers in I Corps and because of a temporary shortage of herbicides at the northern base. The aircraft were redeployed on 30 May. By the end of June, 220 sorties and over 200,000 gallons of herbicide had been used during 1966 to defoliate a total of 1,500 kilometers of trails and roads in Laos.[9]

Navigators as well as herbicide were in short supply, and in February a trial program without them was tested on a number of missions near Saigon. Using a preplanned TACAN (Tactical Air Navigation system) fix, the aircraft turned to target by flying a predetermined heading. This project (3-20-2-66), affectionately nick-named "Mac's Folly" for its originator, was judged a failure after six months, due to the random pattern of the resultant spray paths.[10]

Spare aircraft parts were also scarce; maintenance crews were often hard pressed to devise repairs to battle-damaged aircraft, and some maintenance "write-offs" were not exactly "by the book." In one instance, an explosive .50-caliber projectile neatly blew a hole in the main wing spar of a UC-123. After intelligence briefing officers, who earlier had refused to confirm the use of explosive .50-caliber ammunition by the Viet Cong, were shown the irrefutable evidence, the maintenance crews simply threaded the three-quarter-inch hole and screwed a plug into it. On another occasion, Captain Joe Chalk, who was later to die in an aircraft accident in Florida while teaching defoliation tactics to new crewmembers, asked permission to keep an aircraft headrest as a souvenir of a close call—during a mission Chalk had leaned over to ask the other pilot a question just as a projectile hit the headrest, blowing a large hole in its center. The request had to be refused; there were no replacements and the headrest had to be repaired and reinstalled.[11]

While not working on the planes, the ground crews, in the words of a flightline controller of the period,

> scrounged (stoled begged and borrowed) any and every thing we could find on base, that was not heavily guarded, by that I mean a guard with a loaded M-16 pointed at you, that we could use or swap to someone for something we could use.... You always would keep both eyes peeled for anything that we could use and that we could acquire one way or another.[12]

Hence the stripped frame parked in the RANCH area of a Case tractor that had disappeared from the ramp at Clark Air Base in the Philippines at the same time a RANCH HAND aircraft transited the base.[13]

The overall RANCH HAND effort continued to expand throughout the spring. In March, 163 defoliation sorties sprayed 148,450 gallons of herbicide, and the following month the sortie rate increased another 20 percent, even though maintenance crews were frequently unable to repair one day's battle damage in time for the aircraft to fly the next day. By May herbicide consumption exceeded 200,000 gallons for the first time, in spite of the temporary withdrawal from Da Nang. Recognizing the growing workload borne by only seven spray aircraft, in April COMUSMACV requested 11 more aircraft be assigned to the RANCH HAND mission.[14] These additional spray planes would also make possible a new program of area defoliation in regions of heavy enemy concentration, such as War Zones C and D and the Iron Triangle. The request coincided with the loss in June of the first RANCH HAND aircraft since 1962.

On 20 June 1966, two defoliation aircraft were spraying a multiple-pass target in Quang Tin Province in I Corps, in an area known as the Pineapple Forest. Both aircraft had received some ground fire during each of the first four passes. On the fifth pass, one plane had an engine shot out and crashed in a hedgerow at the end of a rice paddy. The pilot, Lieutenant Paul L. Clanton, was badly injured and trapped in the burning wreckage. Fortunately, the left side of the aircraft had been peeled wide open, and the other crew members, Lieutenant Steve Aigner and Staff Sergeant Elijah R. Winstead, freed Clanton through the open side. Meanwhile, the fighter escort strafed and bombed VC troops firing at the downed aircraft from a nearby tree line. Sergeant Winstead also used the crew's personal weapons to provide covering fire while the pilot was removed. Just as the fighters were down to the last of their ordnance, the other UC-123 contacted a flight of six Marine helicopters returning to Chu Lai with a Marine assault team after a fruitless mission. In the words of the RANCH HAND commander, the Marines came into the area "like John Wayne," and in less than five minutes the spray crew were on their way to safety. To prevent VC salvage of the wreckage, B-57 bombers later destroyed the downed aircraft. Lieutenant Clanton was eventually evacuated to the United States, while the others returned to duty with only minor cuts and bruises. By the end of June, total hits on RANCH HAND aircraft during 1966 had increased to 531.[15]

In July the original four spray aircraft were equipped with a modified dispenser system, known as the A/A 45Y-1. The modification included installation of new pumps capable of a 250-gallon per minute flow rate, a tail-mounted spray-boom to provide a more even spray pattern, and a 10-inch emergency dump-valve, capable of releasing the entire 1,000 gallons of herbicide in 30 seconds. The three aircraft received in 1965, and the additional aircraft being prepared for transfer to RANCH HAND, were already equipped with the improved system. Because the herbicide planes frequently flew through each other's spray, leaving an oily, vision-restricting residue on the windshields, a locally-manufactured windshield washer was also added to the planes.[16]

After repeated earlier denials, in March the United States government finally publicly admitted for the first time that Americans were directly participating in crop destruction activities. At a July press briefing, the Defense Department announced that more than 59,000 acres had been sprayed in 1966—more than the total acreage destroyed in all previous years. Spokesmen credited crop destruction as the "principal cause" of food shortages among some VC forces, but denied communist claims that "toxic gases" were used against VC-controlled fields. Military briefing officers told newsmen that the chemicals were "weed killer, the same as you buy in the hardware store at home." Increased use of the "weed killer," however, forced RANCH HAND once more to curtail sorties until the supply of herbicides caught up.[17]

The rising consumption of herbicides created problems for the Defense Department. Annual requirements for the main defoliant mixture (originally Purple and now Orange) had been doubling each year, from 50,000 gallons in 1962 to 400,000 in 1965. In 1966, however, the requirement had soared to 2.6 million gallons, and planning factors for 1967 and 1968 forecast 6 and 10 million gallons, respectively—amounts beyond the manufacturing capacity of American industry. CINCPAC suggested that herbicide requirements "were so great as to require the creation of additional production capacity." A leading chemical journal later estimated the total military requirement for Orange at four times American production capacity. Eventually, the secretary of defense directed the Army to undertake a $20 million project to construct a government-owned, contractor-operated facility to manufacture Orange herbicide. By the time the plant was scheduled for operation in 1969, however, the herbicide shortage had been solved by voluntary expansion of the chemical industry capacity and decreased military requirements.[18]

The immediate demand in 1966-67 was partially met by complementing Orange with a new defoliant, Tordon 101, developed by the Dow Chemical Company in 1965. Limited quantities of this new mixture, code named "White," had arrived in Vietnam in December 1965 for evaluation; small amounts of White also had been tested in Thailand. The mid-1966 shortages of Orange forced the use of large quantities of White by RANCH HAND before the evaluation was complete, although the new chemical was both slower acting and more expensive than Orange. Over the objections of the Department of Agriculture, which estimated it would cost American agriculture at least $70 million annually, the Department of Defense preempted all domestic production of 2,4-D and 2,4,5-T to military use under the Defense Production Act of 1950—the first total preemption of a civilian commodity since the government reallocation of nylon yarn in World War II. Only this preemption, plus rapid acceleration of White production to full capacity, prevented more than temporary shortages of herbicides in Vietnam from developing.[19]

Despite the herbicide supply problems, the arrival of three more UC-123s in August allowed the SASF to exceed 200 sorties in a month for the first time. Contributing to the high sortie rate was the beginning of area defoliation in nearby War Zone D and a return to spray operations in the Mekong Delta, under Project 4-20-1-66. Once more IV Corps provided spray crews with an opportunity for special heroics. On 31 August a three-plane flight attacked a target area 28 miles southwest of Can Tho, where two previous missions had met intense ground fire. On the third attack, the flight began taking fire while still descending to spray altitude. Shortly after the run began, the number two aircraft lost its left engine to enemy fire. The other two aircraft closed in beneath the vulnerable aircraft to protect it from further damage, although both had also been hit themselves—number three had 14 hits and its pilots were partially blinded by defoliation fluid on the windscreen. By the time the flight cleared the target area for an emergency landing at Binh Tuy, the three aircraft had taken a total of 30 hits, bringing the unit's monthly accumulation to 119.[20]

Ironically, even as the spray planes were subjected to heavier enemy ground fire, the need for their escort by fighters was questioned at higher headquarters. Shortly after the assignment of General William W. Momyer as Commander, Seventh Air Force, he ordered the discontinuance of the four flights of fighters per day that were dedicated to protection of UC-123 operations. The SASF commander, Major Ralph Dresser, immediately went to Seventh Air Force Headquarters to brief General Momyer and his Deputy for Operations, Major General Gordon Graham, on the need for fighter cover for critical RANCH HAND missions. Dresser suggested that the spray targets be classified according to threat: category A would be "hot" areas of known ground fire, which required prestrike; category B would also be "hot" targets, but could be flown without prestrike, using overhead escorts only; category C targets were in areas of unknown enemy resistance, requiring minimal escort in case heavy fire was encountered; and category D targets were historically "cold" areas of little resistance, such as the Saigon River, where escorts could be eliminated.[21]

The briefing at least partially convinced General Momyer of RANCH HAND's need for fighters, but in an effort to preserve fighter sorties for "ground force in contact" missions, the Seventh Air Force commander asked that the spray unit try using ground-alert fighters in case a need arose on B and C category targets, rather than airborne escort. The general's suggestion was tried, and proven unsatisfactory. While spraying a category C target without escort near Bien Hoa in August, a three-plane spray flight came under heavy fire, with the aircraft taking numerous .50-caliber hits; 45 minutes later the ground-alert fighters finally arrived from Bien Hoa, only 30 miles away. Faced with this evidence, General Momyer relented—and RANCH HAND again enjoyed fighter escort.[22]

The question of defoliating near the sensitive demilitarized zone also surfaced in August. During July the North Vietnamese Army (NVA) 324B Division had moved across the DMZ into Quang Tri Province. The South Vietnamese 1st Division, weakened by their rebellion two months earlier, proved no match for the NVA regulars and had to be reinforced by several battalions of the United States 3d Marine Division; eventually, the entire 3d Division was committed as a blocking force along Route 9. To expose the 324B Division camps, an area just south of the DMZ was recommended for defoliation—foliage in this mountainous areas was so dense that on one occasion a Marine relief company could not see a trapped unit's identifying smoke grenades, even though it was only 200 yards away. COMUSMACV opposed the attack, however, explaining to CINCPAC that the military requirement appeared to conflict with political considerations. Target approval was temporarily withheld.[23]

In September four more spray aircraft arrived from the United States and the Defense Department announced that the herbicide unit would be expanded into an 18-aircraft separate squadron, designated the 12th Air Commando Squadron. More areas were added to the defoliation target list, including War Zone C, the Iron Triangle area, and the previously withheld area just south of the demilitarized zone; the latter briefly caused newspaper headlines when the Department of Defense spokesman mistakenly identified the attacks as taking place within the DMZ. On 23 September another press briefing correctly reidentified the spray area as the infiltration and base camp area of the North Vietnamese 324B Division, lying between the DMZ and Route 9. Three days later, however, General William C. Westmoreland, Commander of US Forces in Vietnam, asked Washington's permission to begin defoliating a fifty-square-mile section of the DMZ itself, running from the Laotian border to the South China Sea on the south side of the Ben Hai River. Westmoreland justified his request on the need to expose North Vietnamese infiltration routes across the DMZ, since the International Control Commission had been unable to fulfill their obligation under the Geneva Accords to prevent illegal penetration of the neutralized area. The request was expanded in October to include defoliation of the northern half of the zone and adjacent routes in North Vietnam. Washington approved the attack on the southern section, but further DMZ attacks were deferred pending a MACV assessment of the political/military consequences of the initial project. In the meantime RANCH HAND was not idle; 247 sorties in September and 315 in October were flown against various targets throughout South Vietnam.[24]

Early in October the commander of the SASF received orders assigning the new squadron-to-be to the 14th Air Commando Wing (ACW) at Nha Trang. A few days later these orders were rescinded, and on 15 October 1966 the Special Aerial Spray Flight was redesignated as the 12th Air Commando Squadron and assigned to the 315th Air Commando Wing. Temporarily the organization remained at Tan Son Nhut, under the command of Major Dresser, but planning was begun for relocation of the new unit to Bien Hoa Air Base, home of the USAF 12th Tactical Fighter Wing (TFW).[25] The apparent reason for making the RANCH HAND squadron a part of the 315th, an airlift wing, was logistical—to simplify maintenance and supply support since both organizations used C-123 aircraft. The extreme differences between the two primary missions, however, would cause occasional problems between the subordinate and parent organizations.

The change in operating locations was welcomed by RANCH HAND for several reasons. Besides leaving the critically overcrowded parking ramp and air traffic pattern of the Vietnamese capital's airport, the herbicide unit was particularly interested in taking advantage of the move to establish a permanent hydrant system to supply chemicals to the aircraft. Using condemned 5,000-gallon F-6 refueling trailers joined in tandem and a system of high-pressure pumps, a "herbicide pit" was built adjacent to the south end of the new parking ramp, allowing the rapid servicing of up to four aircraft at a time with any of the three herbicides in use. This Bien Hoa bulk storage facility could hold up to 90,000 gallons of herbicide, in addition to the 55-gallon drum storage area. The new system also made it easier for the Vietnamese handlers to transfer chemicals from the shipping drums to the bulk mixing tanks. A similar, but smaller, facility was constructed at Da Nang, using nine old refueling trailers. When Bien Hoa officers inquired about possible problems from the servicing area, Major Dresser warned them that fumes from mixing and servicing herbicides probably would denude the vegetation on a small hill with a pagoda immediately south of the storage area. Similar damage had been done to trees at the Saigon airport terminal, which was located a short distance "downwind" from the RANCH HAND parking area on "Charlie" row at the airport.[26]

While RANCH HAND planned the move to Bien Hoa, the accelerated attack against targets throughout Vietnam and Laos continued. The persistent problem of herbicide shortages led to an attempt to stretch the available supply by increasing per-gallon coverage. In October a test project was begun to spray the mangrove forests along the main shipping channel to Saigon (in the Rung Sat Special Zone) with Orange herbicide at 1½ gallons per acre, half the normal flow rate. This allowed each sortie to defoliate 600 acres, instead of 300. A similar rate was applied during two missions into Project 4-20-1-66 in the Delta region. Although mangroves were highly susceptible to Orange herbicide, by November it was evident that the reduced rate was ineffective, confirming data from the previous test in Thailand.[27]

RANCH HAND was also hampered by increasingly poor weather. During the month of October, 315 aircraft reached scheduled targets, but weather conditions forced cancellation of an additional 153 sorties. The effect was particularly noticeable in I Corps, where only 78 sorties were flown. At the same time, the hit-per-sortie rate soared as the reduced number of northern flights took 55 hits. The figure was deceptive, however, since almost half of these hits were received on the eighth of the month during a single mission.[28]

The target was an area of enemy crops in three adjacent valleys immediately north of the A Shau Valley, a VC stronghold. The area was known to be well defended, and the rugged surrounding terrain made it unlikely that a UC-123 could escape the valley if an engine were lost. The importance of the target, however, outweighed the hazards, and a three-plane formation was scheduled for the attack. On descent into the first valley, heavy ground fire was met immediately and all aircraft were hit during the run. While the flight climbed back to altitude to assess damage, the escorting B-57 bombers struck the enemy weapons sites. After determining that all aircraft were still operational, the spray planes made a run through the second valley, again encountering heavy fire and receiving additional hits. When the spraying was completed, the UC-123s again climbed to altitude to check damage. Finding no serious problems, the crews decided to finish the mission by making a pass through the third valley. Intense automatic-weapons fire was encountered once more and all aircraft were hit, despite the efforts of the escorts who expended their remaining ordnance trying to protect the RANCH HAND flight. All aircraft were heavily damaged, but recovered safely to Da Nang; the three planes had been hit a total of 22 times.[29]

The major concentration of spray effort in October, however, was in the War Zone C and D areas; 206 of the 315 sorties were flown against III Corps targets. Here, too, increasing amounts of ground fire were met. The spray planes were hit 131 times in October, and on the last day of the month, RANCH HAND lost another UC-123. The mission was a routine defoliation run over the Iron Triangle, and the three-plane formation was almost halfway through the target area when they encountered automatic-weapons fire. All three aircraft were hit—Captain Roy Kubley's lead plane lost all electronics, radios, and hydraulic systems and number three had an engine shot out, but both made it back to Saigon. The number two aircraft was not so lucky. Hits in the left engine and propeller dome knocked out the engine and also prevented feathering of the propeller. It was impossible for the remaining engine to overcome the drag of the unfeathered dead engine, and the aircraft crashed into the dense jungle within seconds after being hit. Viewing the wreckage from above, Kubley thought it inconceivable "that anybody could live through it." Before losing its radios, the lead plane made an emergency call for fighter cover and rescue helicopters. Amazingly, when the two Air Force HH-43 "Huskie" helicopters arrived 25 minutes later, all three downed crewmen were found alive, suffering nothing more than cuts and bruises. At a "we survived" party at the Tan Son Nhut officers' club that night, the men of the 12th consumed over 70 bottles of California champagne, celebrating the rugged dependability of the much abused assault transport they flew. Staff Sergeant "Junior" Winstead, who had been shot down twice within six months, told reporters, "This job isn't getting dangerous, its been dangerous."[30]

The number of missions continued to increase in November, but the number of hits declined abruptly, possibly due to a concentration of sorties into "cooler" parts of War Zones C and D. Since these areas were close to Saigon, as many as 29 sorties a day were flown. For the month, RANCH HAND made 409 flights, took only 51 hits, and dispensed 384,000 gallons of herbicides. Bad weather continued to plague the spray unit, as 182 sorties were cancelled.[31]

Aside from poor weather in upper South Vietnam, heavy scheduling in III Corps was due partially to Washington's decision to again test "the feasibility of clearing a typical Southeast Asia forest by the use of fire." Although previous fire projects in "Sherwood Forest" and the Chu Pong Mountains had failed, analysts called results "inconclusive." Planning for the new operation, code named "Pink Rose," began in May 1966. Two areas in War Zone C and one area in War Zone D, squares seven kilometers on a side, were selected. The plan was to defoliate the areas prior to the end of the growing season in November, respray them at the beginning of the dry season in January, spray them again with desiccant (Blue herbicide) shortly before the burn trials, and then ignite the dried vegetation with incendiary bomblets dropped from Guam-based B-52 bombers. Targets A and B were defoliated with Orange herbicide, target C with White. Herbicide Blue application was at a normal three-gallon per acre rate on targets A and C, and with a 1½-gallon rate on target B. Eventually, 255 sorties applied 255,000 gallons of herbicide to the selected areas.[32]

Target C, 45 nautical miles northeast of Saigon, was struck first on 18 January 1967 by 30 B-52s dropping 42 M-35 incendiary cluster bombs each. The burning was ineffective; most fires spread no more than two feet from the point of ignition. On 28 January 1967, target A, 12 nautical miles southwest of An Loc, was struck by the same number of B-52s, with nearly identical results. Target B, 16 nautical miles north-northwest of Tay Ninh, was bombed on 4 April 1967 by only 15 B-52s, but the spacing was compressed to provide a bomblet density three times greater than the previous targets. The fires were slightly more effective, but the heat created a cumulus cloud that soared to over 50,000-feet altitude and dropped more than a ½ inch of rain, extinguishing the fires. In its final report, Headquarters, Seventh Air Force, "concluded that the technique of a planned forest fire using this specific method is ineffective as an operational method for clearing forest area in South Vietnam."[33] After all the time and effort, the results were remarkably similar to those of the 1944 Army Air Forces tests in Florida.[34]

In November 1966 Lieutenant Colonel Robert Dennis became commander of the 12th ACS. On the twenty-seventh of the month, Secretary of State Rusk approved the previously requested defoliation operations in the southern half of the demilitarized zone. Moving day for the RANCH HANDs came four days later, on 1 December, as the squadron finally deployed to Bien Hoa. Continuing the RANCH HAND tradition for never doing things quietly, several crewmembers decided to make a production of their departure from Saigon. After take-off, three of the planes turned and, in a maneuver previously coordinated with the control tower, made a pass across the airport at considerably less than tree-top level. To highlight the ceremony, dozens of purple smoke grenades had been taped to the tail-booms of the aircraft and arranged so that they could be fired inflight; the result was three beautiful plumes of purple smoke sprayed right through the middle of the airport. Not content with the colorful, if illegal, farewell to Tan Son Nhut, the RANCH HAND crews saved some of the smoke grenades for their arrival at Bien Hoa. A low-level, smoke-trailed pass down the main street of the base, between the officers' club and the wing headquarters, was followed by an overhead pitchout for landing, just like the fighter planes used, rather than the normal rectangular landing pattern of the staid transports.* The overhead pattern was accompanied by more smoke from the seemingly inexhaustible supply of smoke grenades. Inevitably, this spectacular arrival was followed by an equally spectacular party at the officers' club, where the spray pilots celebrated their transfer by buying champagne for the fighter pilots of the 3d Tactical Fighter Wing. Surprisingly, no senior officer was heard to criticize the antics of the spray pilots, and this unusual use of the overhead pattern continued unquestioned for the rest of the time that RANCH HAND flew out of Bien Hoa.[35]

Despite such theatrics, a full quota of missions was flown on moving day and thereafter, without interruption. Another monthly record was set in

---

*Fighter aircraft normally land by flying to a point directly over the end of the runway at 1,000 feet above the field, then abruptly bank into a descending 360-degree turn so as to roll wings level, in line with the runway, a short distance before touchdown. If in formation, the following aircraft duplicate the maneuver at three-second intervals. Larger aircraft normally use straight-in approaches or wide patterns with gentle turns, similar to civilian airliners. RANCH HAND used the overhead pattern throughout their stay in Vietnam, insisting that their planes were disguised fighters, rather than transports.

December as the squadron flew 418 sorties. The annual statistics also were far in excess of any previous years, as RANCH HAND flew 2,759 sorties, took 894 confirmed hits, and dispensed slightly more than 2.6 million gallons of herbicides. At year's end the squadron had on hand 14 of the 18 authorized aircraft and 189 of the 204 authorized personnel. The cost of herbicides alone in 1966 was $12.7 million; the estimate for 1967 was $42 million. Obviously, the new year would present a vastly expanded challenge to the spray organization.[36]

Only two things marred RANCH HAND's apparently rosy future. The move to Bien Hoa had been accompanied by a change in radio call sign. The beloved "Cowboy" radio call sign that had been used since the beginning had been replaced by "Hades," the general radio identifier for aircraft of the 315th Wing, whether spray or trash hauler. Stubbornly, the spray crews continued to use "Cowboy" in interplane communication, while regarding the call sign change as an indication that their association with the wing would not be a happy one. More ominous was the portent for the future indicated by the annual statistics. During increased operations in 1966, the unit lost their first two aircraft in four years and 22 crewmen were wounded. An expanded herbicide program in 1967 seemed likely to surpass this undesirable record.[37]

8

RANCH HAND Comes of Age:
Bureaucracy and a New Task

The move to Bien Hoa Air Base was accompanied by a subtle maturing of the spray unit. Acceptance of the herbicide mission as a viable military weapon by combat planners removed the day-to-day uncertainty that had hitherto characterized RANCH HAND. At the same time, the "seat-of-the-pants"-barnstorming-flying circus atmosphere of the early spray operation became a tradition, rather than a practice, as bureaucracy overcame innovation and paperwork displaced partying. As procedures became standardized and tasks formalized, commanders spent more time as administrators and less time as flight leaders. No longer concerned with mere survival, the expanded organization faced new problems, the biggest of which seemed to be how to deal with the spider web of organizations to which the 12th Squadron was responsible to or involved with (see Chart 1).[1]

Direct supervision of the squadron came from the 315th Air Commando Wing, headquartered at Phan Rang, apparently for no other reason than that its aircraft were the same type as the wing's airlift squadrons. The airlift orientation of the wing, however, frequently caused problems for the herbicide squadron, particularly since airlift policies appropriate to the other four squadrons did not always mesh with the spray mission. Overall policy for herbicide operations was set forth in MACV Directive 525-1, based on guidelines from the Departments of State and Defense. Final approval authority over targets belonged to COMUSMACV and the American ambassador, after consultation with the Vietnamese. Mission control over the 12th Squadron was exercised by the MACV assistant chief of staff, J-3 (Chemical Operations), but Seventh Air Force advised MACV on operational aspects and plans. The actual mission order, known as a "frag" (fragmentary order), was issued by the Tactical Air Control Center (TACC) at Saigon. TACC also provided airborne mission direction. Logistics, administrative, and heavy maintenance support

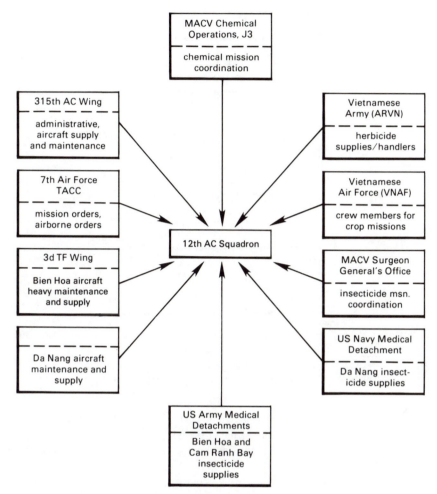

Chart 1: The maze of supply and support sources for the 12th Air Commando Squadron (RANCH HAND) in 1967.

was provided by the 3d Tactical Fighter Wing, host unit at Bien Hoa. The 366th Tactical Fighter Wing performed the same services, to a lesser degree, for the Da Nang detachment, informally referred to as the Mountain RANCH.

In the chain of command next above the 315th Wing was the 834th Air Division, again an airlift-oriented organization. All sorties of the wing, except those of the herbicide squadron, were controlled by the division's Airlift Control Center (ALCC). Because neither wing nor division were in the mission control chain of RANCH HAND, senior officers in these organizations were frequently not aware of RANCH HAND activities or special missions until briefed by the spray squadron commander. Later, when an insecticide

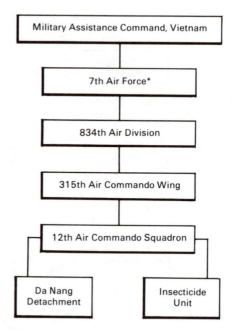

Chart 2: RANCH HAND Operational chain of command in Vietnam 1967.

*The Deputy Commander for Air, MACV, also wore a second hat as commander of the 7th Air Force. In 1967 this was Lieutenant General William W. Momyer.

spray mission was added to the squadron, operational control over this function came directly from the office of the MACV Surgeon General, again by-passing both wing and division authority. Transportation, stockpiling, accountability, and issue of herbicides were Vietnamese responsibilities, once the chemical arrived at the port in Vietnam, while malathion support for insect control was a Navy function in I Corps and an Army function elsewhere. To maintain the fiction that the crop destruction mission was controlled by the Vietnamese, the VNAF assigned a small number of enlisted men and officers to ride on the UC-123s when crop targets were scheduled.

Fortunately, the maze of command and support functions seemed to be more an irritation than a hindrance to overall mission accomplishment. By the time RANCH HAND became a squadron in 1966, the system of target identification, approval, and scheduling had been routinized. Although the approval process was plagued with inordinate delays, the number and size of previously approved spray areas had reached the point that the spray crews were no longer concerned with running short of work. Approval delays did, however, sometimes cause RANCH HAND to miss spraying a lucrative crop target at the ideal moment, just before maturity, when the enemy had expended maximum effort and it was too late to plant a replacement crop.

Even already approved targets occasionally could not be sprayed when scheduled, usually because friendly forces were in the area. Later, MACV began refusing mission clearance "because of high threat" when intelligence indicated strong enemy resistance could be expected. RANCH HAND disagreed with the latter prohibition, knowing "hot" targets frequently were flown with no enemy reaction, while "cold" targets, quiet for several missions, could suddenly erupt with ground fire. Perhaps without justification, spray crewmen had little faith in intelligence prognostications and tended to ignore this portion of mission briefings. The RANCH HAND attitude seemed to be, if they are there, they are there, and if they want to shoot, they will shoot.

This fatalism was not universal, however. One Da Nang detachment aircrew took heavy fire on a target that intelligence had classed as a "milk run, really easy"; all three cockpit occupants were wounded. Luckily, the wounds were all superficial, although one pilot had a close call when a bullet creased his head after smashing through his helmet. Following medical treatment at an intermediate base, the wounded men returned to Da Nang and joined the rest of the detachment at the officers' club to celebrate their narrow escape. While the party was at its peak, that morning's intelligence briefing officer entered the club and was immediately spotted by the over-six-foot-tall, 225-pound pilot. It was later reported at the hospital that the intelligence officer's arm was broken in two places when he slipped while being taught to dance the polka by a wounded RANCH HAND pilot.[2]

One reason for long target approval delays was the complex coordination involved. Initial requests for crop and defoliation missions usually came from province officials or field commanders, with occasional special mission requests directly from headquarters planners. RANCH HAND operations and targeting personnel met weekly with the chemical operations section at MACV to discuss these requests and schedule survey flights over proposed areas. The survey sorties were necessary to identify actual target locations and plan optimum attack routes, and were flown by single, unescorted UC-123s manned by the RANCH HAND chief or assistant chief of targeting, a copilot, a navigator from targeting, and an Army Chemical Corps officer.

Prior to 1967, survey missions usually flew 3,000 feet above the terrain, a height viewed as safe from small-arms fire. From this altitude, however, it was hard to determine the extent and maturity of crop targets. Several times missions were later flown against reported lucrative targets, supposedly containing large amounts of cultivated crops and seedbeds, only to find fields abandoned and consisting mainly of wild grass and dead stalks, thus wasting time and herbicide. The problem became even more critical as the enemy reacted to the crop destruction program by concealing cultivation. In deserted rice paddies along the coast, for example, Viet Cong replanted only one of every eight or nine paddies, leaving the appearance of disuse from 3,000 feet. In the mountains, one or two rows of crop were planted under the edge of the tree line along streams or around the edge of clearings. In cultivated fields, dead stalks of last year's crop were left standing and a new, low-standing crop carefully planted among them. Surveys from higher altitudes failed to spot these hidden cultivations.

The solution arrived at by Major Hank Good, Chief of Targeting, was to fly the survey missions at spray altitude. With permission of the RANCH HAND Commander, Lieutenant Colonel Bob Dennis, low-level survey began in early 1967 and proved highly successful. Surveys were made by flying to the target area above 3,000 feet, informing the applicable radar control site where they were and that they were going low-level, and requesting rescue assistance if they did not check back in within 30 minutes. Survey flights also protected themselves by flying at 160-knots airspeed or faster, instead of the slower spray speed. Whether because of the airspeed or because the enemy thought the single planes were airlift aircraft, few survey flights were hit by enemy ground fire.[3]

After these reconnaissance flights over the proposed area, a coordination meeting was held with the province chief, local military commanders, MACV and ARVN chemical officers, and representatives of Seventh Air Force and RANCH HAND. These meetings were normally held in the field, and details of target requests, psychological warfare requirements, intelligence data, and target peculiarities were worked out (complete agreement among the participants on either the need for a particular attack or the extent of the attack area, especially on crop targets, was not always achieved). Following the meeting, the formal written target request was prepared and forwarded to Saigon for clearance by Vietnamese and US authorities. Vietnamese coordination was provided by the Joint General Staff (JGS) 202 Committee, which included representatives from all staff elements, VNAF, and CDTC. The request then went to MACV for review by the American 203 Committee, chaired by the MACV chemical officer, with members from the Combat Operations Center, Seventh Air Force, American Embassy, MACV J-2, United States Agency for International Development, and the Political Warfare (Polwar) Advisory section. Experienced former RANCH HAND crewmembers served as liaison at MACV Headquarters, and were available to the committee for consultation. Although herbicide requests were usually initiated by the South Vietnamese, the ultimate approval authority for RANCH HAND sorties in support of the Vietnamese rested jointly with the American ambassador and COMUSMACV.

Once a particular target area—referred to as a target box—was approved, the RANCH HAND commander and his targeting officer, together with MACV staff members, determined the most effective mission dates and requested implementing orders. Target priorities were determined at MACV, but weather, fighter availability, and crop maturity also affected target completion, some large projects taking months to complete. The targeting officer determined the type of fighter support needed for the particular area, planned the individual missions, prepared necessary target charts, and drafted the order requests for submission to TACC. Orders for a week's missions were

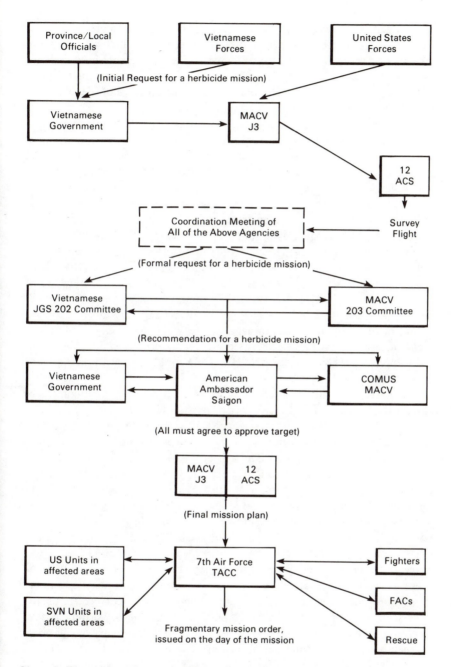

Chart 3: Flowchart of combined United States/Vietnamese herbicide target approval and directing order system in 1967.

usually sent in all at once. TACC, in turn, coordinated fighter and rescue support and issued the approved mission order the day before the mission. TACC also sent out a warning message to field forces of the impending mission. Responses to the warning message forced cancellation or modification of the spray mission if imminent operations or the presence of friendly forces in the area precluded use of heavy suppression.[4]

Two types of fire suppression area were designated in South Vietnam—"prior permission to fire" and "free fire." If RANCH HAND was operating in the former and wanted suppressive fire by the escorting fighters, the FAC had to contact his Direct Air Support Center (DASC), which then called Corps, which had to receive permission from the field forces, province chief, and district chief. Needless to say, neither fighters nor spray planes usually had fuel enough to wait for permission, even if granted. Not only was this procedure frustrating, but it frequently resulted in incomplete missions when enemy ground fire drove RANCH HAND from the target and suppressive fire could not be obtained in time to finish the run; the entire mission would have to be rescheduled and reflown. Free fire allowed herbicide crews to call for whatever assistance was available and necessary. By mid-1967 more than 300 of the 400 approved targets were in free-fire areas and RANCH HAND stopped scheduling prior-permission area targets, except when specifically ordered by higher headquarters. This selectivity presented no problems since there were more approved targets than RANCH HAND could cover with their mission capacity anyway.

Specific daily missions were known as "lifts" and were designated by alphabetical letters that were also used as part of the formation call sign; that is, the first mission from Bien Hoa each day was the "Alpha" lift, with the radio call "Hades Alpha." Individual call signs corresponded to the aircraft's position in the flight—"Hades Alpha Lead," "Alpha Two," "Alpha Three," etc. The lead navigator (and deputy lead navigator for large formations) planned the final details of the attack with the lead aircraft commander during the afternoon before the mission. If heavy suppression was planned, the lead crew usually briefed the fighter pilots involved, since heavy suppression was normally provided by fighters colocated with RANCH HAND (3d TFW F-100s at Bien Hoa and 366th TFW F-4s at Da Nang). The other spray crews were briefed immediately prior to the mission the next morning.

For each target planned, an alternate was selected, in case the primary target was cancelled or weathered out. These alternates were frequently large-scale, lower-priority area targets, such as War Zone D. Master charts of these alternate areas were marked with each burn, but primary navigational reliance was on a combination of terrain features and visible effects of the chemicals. Thus, it was desirable to have seven to ten days between adjacent defoliation runs for observable effects to begin. Diversion to an alternate target usually required coordination with TACC to get a FAC and have alert fighters launched for escort; on rare occasions the originally scheduled escort could be held on the ground or in the air until RANCH HAND reached the alternate target. The primary restraint to good fighter coverage on alternate spray targets was always the jet fighters' limited ability to loiter in the attack zone, but close coordination with fighter units, particularly the F-100 squadrons at Bien Hoa that supported several of the largest alternate target areas, kept the number of lost herbicide sorties to a minimum.[5]

Typically, show time* for the Alpha lift was 0430 hours and for the Bravo lift, 0515 hours. These early missions were planned to strike their targets at sunrise, and show times were adjusted according to the distance of the target from the launch base. Depending on aircraft availability, Alpha lift would be a large formation of 6 to 12 aircraft and Bravo, 3 or 4. After return from the first target, the Alpha crews would rebrief and relaunch at 0900 to 0930 hours to another target. This second mission could remain a large single formation (Charlie lift) or fly missions on two separate targets by splitting into Charlie and Echo lifts. Bravo lift was turned around for a second mission at approximately 0800 hours (Delta lift). The number of aircraft on later missions depended on spare availability and the amount of battle damage suffered on the first lifts. The staggered schedule was aimed at avoiding congestion on the ramp between missions; primary restriction was herbicide reservicing—only three planes could be "re-Purpled" at a time.[6]

The Da Nang detachment operated on a similar schedule, although the mountainous terrain and crop targets made it important that the crews have full daylight for the attack on the first target. Normally, all available aircraft (three or four) were flown on each mission (Hotel and India lifts). During the "good weather" season in I Corps, the Mountain RANCH was frequently augmented with additional aircraft to allow four missions instead of two, adding Juliet and Kilo lifts. Aircraft at Da Nang were exchanged with those at Bien Hoa on a regular basis to perform scheduled heavy maintenance and inspections at Bien Hoa. This did not interfere with the herbicide missions since all ferry flights were made in the afternoon, after completion of the day's work.

The move to Bien Hoa, however, caused a change in off-duty activities for RANCH HAND. While at Tan Son Nhut, most personnel above the rank of staff sergeant lived in various hotels, apartments, and villas in Saigon, several of them near "Hundred-P Alley," an infamous area named after the price of its prostitutes. Many RANCH HAND members owned motorcycles and, after a party, often held races up and down the Alley, sometimes in various states of undress, to the accompaniment of the cheers of the street's habitués. Frequent mishaps resulting from the combination of alcohol and street hazards usually visibly marked the rider with scrapes and scabs—a malady referred to as a "Honda Rash." For a reasonable price, most downtown dwellers hired fulltime cooks, cleaning women, and houseboys, putting them-

---

*The arrival time of the aircrews at the flightline.

selves in the enviable position of going to war in the morning and returning to "civilization" in the afternoon.[7]

Bien Hoa was different. Quarters were large, humid tents or un-air-conditioned, open-bay "hooches" with louvered, screened sides and concrete floors. Both were hot, dirty, and rat infested. Da Nang initially was no better, but tents eventually were replaced by concrete-block barracks. At Bien Hoa, RANCH HAND always received second-class accommodations, compared with host-unit fighter pilots. Food service was available from several base messhalls and from the clubs—a step down for those who had good cooks in Saigon. Base regulations concerning motorcycles were strict and enforced. After the initial shock wore off, RANCH HAND began a steady program of scrounging, trading, bribing, borrowing, and "midnight requisitioning" that continued unabated during the stay at Bien Hoa. The RANCH quarters in the old French compound were eventually closed in and insulated with discarded flare shipping cartons, partitioned into semiprivate cubicles, air-conditioned, and equipped with plywood-paneled lounges featuring well-stocked bars and refrigerators; most of which was accomplished outside normal military channels. Comfortable house trailers later became available for some senior officers. Large outdoor barbecue grills were built, and became the sites of regular parties centering around thick steaks obtained by further judicious trading and "exchange of favors." When missions were cancelled for the day, grills, food, and beer frequently were loaded onto several aircraft and a squadron party was held during the afternoon at one of the more secure coastal beaches.[8]

Neither the growing size of the operation nor the move to military surroundings changed the RANCH HAND irreverence toward military mores; if anything, the aircrewmen became more elitist in their attitude—assuming that they deserved preferential treatment on the ground for their efforts in the air. At RANCH HAND parties it became standard that without regard for rank or the occasion, visitors would sooner or later be greeted with a "hymn," consisting of the entire group intoning in drawn-out chorus, "him-m-m-m, him-m-m-m, fuck him-m-m-m." Even occasional female visitors received this treatment, including the Seventh Air Force commander's personal secretary. A favorite tactic of the champagne-treated cherry parties was to fire champagne corks at opportune targets while everyone screamed "ground fire," and to liberally douse visitors and hosts alike with sprays from shaken bottles of the frothy liquid.[9]

When they had no other target for their games, the herbicide crews turned on each other. Shortly after the move to Bien Hoa, Major Charley Hubbs, one of the flight commanders, became the first to acquire an air conditioner. By enclosing his portion of the hooch and running a covertly buried electrical wire to the nearby officers' club junction box (because of an electrical shortage, the base civil engineer section checked all other junction boxes to catch "electricity cheaters"), Hubbs became the envy of the squadron. Several

RANCH HANDs soon discovered that a smoke grenade dropped into the air conditioner provided suitable revenge, brightly coloring the room and its contents, including the major. From then on, Hubbs was regularly "smoked" by other officers testing the effect of the many smoke grenade colors available. Although the trick lost much of its attraction when air conditioning became more common, occasional "smokings" were reported even after the unit moved into permanent barracks at Phan Rang in 1970.[10]

Spray squadron commanders were often on the carpet for the escapades of RANCH HAND personnel, and relations with host base commanders and personnel were frequently strained by the squadron's excesses. On the whole, however, the sometimes childish activities of the purple-scarved crewmen were usually regarded with a tolerant and forgiving eye, particularly since this wild behavior seemed part of the special mystique that surrounded the unique organization. Senior officers also may have realized that men who daily faced the hazards of flying slow, unarmed aircraft at tree-top level over known enemy positions needed a release of tension.[11]

Other pilots simply regarded RANCH HAND crews as slightly insane. During debriefing following one particularly well-shot-up mission, an escorting fighter pilot stood up, carefully examined the faces of the spray crewmen, shook his head, and commented, "balls of steel." Knowing the propensity of RANCH HAND for attracting ground fire, fighter units referred to the spray crews as "magnet-asses," and the escort pilots borrowed a fishing term and called herbicide support missions "trolling," with the spray planes as bait.[12]

On at least one occasion, MACV took advantage of the attraction of spray aircraft to enemy gunners. During 1966 a large VC force moved into the U Minh Forest, but intelligence could not pinpoint its location. Well aware of enemy reaction to herbicide planes, headquarters asked RANCH HAND to act as decoy to cause the enemy to reveal himself. A flight of UC-123s was to fly over the suspected area; if it drew heavy fire, a special strike force would attack the exposed unit. The strike force, which would cover the UC-123s and attack the enemy, consisted of 2 forward air control aircraft, 2 flights of fighters, and 14 Army helicopter gunships, all waiting a short distance from the suspected enemy encampment so as not to reveal the trap. The mission went exactly as planned: RANCH HAND "trolled" for the enemy, the Viet Cong opened fire on the spray planes, and the strike force attacked the revealed positions with bombs, rockets, and machine-gun fire. The result was destruction of the enemy camp, with almost 400 VC killed and an unknown number of wounded.[13] Despite this success, acting as "bait" was not one of RANCH HAND's favorite occupations.

While herbicide pilots were deadly serious and professional during the low-level part of spray missions, they were sometimes cavalier toward other flying duties. An example was the day that "Panama," the radar control station in I Corps, called a Da Nang flight on its way to a target and gave them a coded message. Asking the radar controller to stand by, the flight leader had the spray formation change to an interplane radio frequency so that he could ask them if anyone had bothered to pick up the current code-word list at the morning briefing. Getting a negative response, the flight returned to Panama's radio frequency, and the radar controller was asked what the code words meant in plain English. After several minutes of verbal sparring as the controller tried to explain that radio security did not allow him to translate the code in the clear, the RANCH HAND pilot asked, "Well, can't you give us a hint?" After a long silence, the discouraged controller finally told the spray flight that the message cancelled their mission and ordered them to return to base, whereupon the RANCH HANDs happily turned for home, little caring that they had just compromised an entire radio-traffic system.[14] On another occasion, two officers volunteered to test fly a newly repaired aircraft. The flight progressed normally until just after landing, when it was time to fill out the flight logbook. At this point the two officers discovered that both were newly arrived in country and that neither had yet checked-out as first-pilot qualified in the aircraft—not having met before, each had assumed the other was an instructor pilot. No one had bothered to check qualifications before assigning the pilots to the flight.[15]

It was hardly surprising that such mixups could occur. The one-year Vietnam duty tour meant someone was always arriving or leaving, and was further complicated by a steady flow of people going to and coming from midtour R&R leaves, transfers to other duties, and temporary duty with the Da Nang detachment. Even before the advent of the squadron in 1966, a pipeline to provide a constant stream of replacement crews had been established: 6 weeks of transition training in Florida, 30 days of spray training in Virginia, a week at Jungle Survival School in the Philippines, 12 months of duty in Vietnam, return home. The duty tour was curtailed at the rate of one month for every 20 missions, if the individual had missions over Laos or North Vietnam. Thus, some RANCH HAND crewmen went home as much as three months early (some also extended and served more than a single tour). As the organization got bigger, the turnover increased; not only did old members need replacement, but extra personnel had to be programmed in to fill new authorizations and replace combat losses. If the new assignees had never been to basic USAF survival school, the pipeline was increased by one step—survival school at Stead AFB, in the mountains near Reno, Nevada. As a result, during the winter months incoming replacements spent several weeks learning to use snowshoes and to survive at zero degrees Fahrenheit, while on their way to a jungle war—an excellent example of rote Air Force bureaucracy.[16]

Spray training also was not above reproach for unrealistic practices. Training at Langley took place over flatlands, at light aircraft gross weight, with partial loads of water, or occasionally insecticide, in the spray tank. The crews practiced high, sweeping turns at the end of simulated runs—one particularly beautiful course reversal turn involving a 90-degree turn in one direction, immediately followed by a 270-degree turn in the opposite direction, became known as the "plumtree" turn, after Plumtree Island, Virginia, where it was practiced. In Vietnam the newcomer discovered that the terrain was seldom flat, the aircraft were almost always overloaded, and the plumtree turn was a VC gunner's dream. "One pass and get out," or if you had to reverse course, "tight, low-level turns as near to the ground as you could get" were the "real-world" answer to combat survival.[17]

The constant turn-over of personnel was not unique to RANCH HAND, it was a problem common to all units in Southeast Asia. The expansion to squadron size, however, coincided with a marked change in the type of personnel coming to the spray organization. Prior to 1967, RANCH HAND pilots and navigators were mostly young captains and lieutenants with approximately five-years flying experience—sometimes rash, frequently a little wild, always only semidisciplined. RANCH HAND commanders were senior captains, later junior majors, essentially concerned with operational matters; in actuality, they were little more than the ranking pilots of a small detachment on independent duty. Almost all the early RANCH HANDs were volunteers. The challenge of its unique mission and its reputation for hell-raising even caused several officers to pull strings to get transferred to the spray unit after they arrived in Vietnam for duty with another organization. The infrequent nonvolunteer assigned to the herbicide unit was willingly allowed to transfer out, if he requested it. For example, when a nonvolunteer captain who arrived in August 1966 took three hits on his first spray flight and two more on the second, he and another nonvolunteer asked Major Ralph Dresser, the commander at the time, for a transfer; both were immediately reassigned to an airlift squadron. During his subsequent 11 months in airlift duty, the captain picked up only two more hits, and in 1981 still believed that the transfer probably saved his life: "My decision to get out [of RANCH HAND] was the best decision I ever made—otherwise, I would probably not be around to write this."[18]

After 1967 RANCH HAND replacements were older, more experienced, and, perhaps, more cautious. First majors and then lieutenant colonels began getting cockpit assignments to spray duty; some of these older officers were experiencing their third war—having served in World War II and Korea—and several had more recent experience flying a desk than a plane. By March 1968, of 69 officers in operations, 16 were lieutenant colonels, 31 were majors, and only 5 were lieutenants. Several of them were not volunteers, but with few exceptions, they performed the mission with as much enthusiasm and dedication as their predecessors. These older officers willingly took part in the squadron parties, but were more apt to engage in restrained social drinking than in the riotous behavior of the earlier RANCH HANDs.[19]

The growth of RANCH HAND and its activation as a separate squadron also prompted a change in unit leadership. Commanders now were senior lieutenant colonels, who spent most of their time on administrative detail and in coordination meetings. The size and complexity of the operation were such that the one-year tour became a hindrance at the management level. Commanders, operations officers, maintenance officers, and senior noncommissioned officers barely became experienced with all phases of the mission before they returned to the United States. Even worse, replacements often arrived after their predecessors departed, leaving them to learn the job the hard way—sometimes repeating the mistakes of the past—and hampering continuity of effort. The damage was compounded when the rotation dates of several key personnel occurred within a short period. Again, this problem was not unique to RANCH HAND, but its effect was greater since no similar unit existed anywhere else in the Air Force; unlike other organizations in Vietnam, there was no reservoir of experienced personnel in the United States from which senior leadership could be drawn.[20]

The cockpit experience cycle reversed itself once more in late 1969 when the squadron began receiving large numbers of lieutenants newly graduated from basic pilot training (see Chapter 11). Trained in jet aircraft using high-altitude, electronically assisted navigation, these young pilots were eager and capable, but were totally inexperienced in either conventional aircraft or low-level operations and were not prepared for the demands of the RANCH HAND mission. The squadron was forced to use these inexperienced pilots in place of a second fully qualified first-pilot. The lack of two fully qualified first-pilots on spray sorties placed an inordinate and hazardous workload on the sole qualified pilot, again demonstrating higher headquarters' failure to understand the problems of the herbicide mission.[21]

Besides the changes in manning composition, activation of the 12th Air Commando Squadron in 1966 was accompanied by one other significant change. In previous wars in the tropics, the malaria-carrying mosquito had proven nearly as deadly as the enemy. The experience was repeated in Vietnam. Within the first two years of combat-force involvement, more than 10,000 Americans were rendered casualties by the bothersome insect, and in particular, by one species of mosquito-borne parasite, *Plasmodium falciparum,* which was highly resistant to traditional malarial drugs. According to a US Navy medical report, in some small units "the attack rate [of malaria] has attained the equivalent of 100% in two months" of arrival "in-country." Not only was this virulent strain of malaria sweeping Vietnam, but returning personnel were bringing it back to Guam and the United States.[22]

Even though combat area spraying had originated with World War II insecticide missions and the Vietnam spray cadre was initially drawn from the Langley insecticide flight, it was not until 1966 that USAF Headquarters decided to remodify one of the UC-123 defoliation planes to a malathion-spray configuration to help counter the anopheles mosquito, carrier of *Plasmodium falciparum.* Initial plans called for an insecticide test program in Thailand. On 14 October 1966, a 12th ACS spray plane, thoroughly washed of all herbicides and equipped with the finer-orifice nozzles needed for insecticide work, departed Saigon for Bangkok. In addition to the aircrew, the entourage included Navy Captain Richard T. Holway from the Pearl Harbor, Hawaii, medical facility; Major James R. Willman of the Army's 20th Preventive Medicine unit at Saigon; Major Claude T. Adams, an entomologist from Langley AFB, Virginia; and Major Carl T. Marshall, commander of the Langley-based insecticide spray flight, former RANCH HAND commander and technical advisor on spray operations.[23]

When the test aircraft arrived in Bangkok, it was discovered that unusually dry conditions in the selected spray area had reduced the mosquito breeding areas and the insect population was too low for accurate evaluation. The uncomplaining aircrew spent three carefree days in the Thai capital before being ordered to return to Saigon with their passengers, and an alternate test site in a supposedly secure area of Vietnam was selected for the trials. The 20th Preventive Medicine unit was made responsible for the mosquito count and "bite" tests in the designated area.[24]

Although reduction of the mosquito population would benefit the Viet Cong as well as Allied forces, apparently not everyone knew this; during one malathion test in a wide river valley, the aircraft received ground fire and took a hit in the chemical tank. Major Marshall, riding as an observer, urged that the mission be continued, but the aircrew, accustomed to defoliation missions and feeling "naked" without other spray planes and fighter cover, elected to dump the remaining load and return home. A mitigating factor was the duration of insecticide missions. Normal defoliation sorties expended their chemical in a little over four minutes, while insecticide missions could take up to two hours to spray-out.[25]

After the initial trials, little more was done until early 1967. At that time another aircraft was cleaned up and prepared for more malathion tests, again in Vietnam. Because of obvious hazards to observers spending the night in Vietnamese jungles counting mosquitoes, some test runs were made over Con Son Island, a secure island off the Mekong delta where a US Coast Guard Station and a Vietnamese government prisoner-of-war camp were located. Previously, mosquito spraying in Vietnam was accomplished by helicopters and ground-based spray equipment, but the ability of the UC-123 to cover large areas (up to 25 square miles at a time) made it the ideal vehicle for base and urban area treatment. Following the successful 1967 trials, one of the 12th ACS aircraft was ordered permanently assigned to malathion duty under the direction of the MACV Surgeon General's Office. The mission, code named "Operation Flyswatter," was supported at Bien Hoa by the Army's 20th Preventive Medicine Unit and at Da Nang by the Navy Preventive Medicine Unit located on the Marine base—truly a combined-services operation.[26]

One of the first malathion aircraft was "The Little Devil" (serial number 56-4396). This aircraft was chosen because it had not yet received the new camouflage paint treatment; however, it was soon returned to herbicide duties in favor of another aircraft. As already noted, the aircraft called "Patches" was almost sacred to the RANCH HANDs and they hoped to eventually get the aircraft transferred to the Air Force Museum. By 1967 Patches had taken well over 500 hits and the spray squadron, fearing that the venerable aircraft might be shot down, decided to designate it as the permanent insecticide spray plane on the assumption that this was the safest duty in the unit. Like the Little Devil, Patches was still uncamouflaged, which helped distinguish it from the planes involved in herbicide operations (and thus, it was hoped, help prevent the aircraft from being fired upon during its insecticide runs).[27]

The first operational UC-123 insecticide mission was flown on 6 March 1967; by the end of the month, 56,000 acres had been treated with malathion, at a rate of eight ounces per acre. Mosquito missions were preceded by psywar leaflet drops several days ahead of time telling the people not to fire on the silver aircraft and describing the benefits of its mission to the community. On the day of the spraying, a U-10 Helio-Courier "speaker" aircraft from the 5th or 9th Air Commando Squadrons usually accompanied the insecticide aircraft, orbiting overhead and broadcasting to the people that the malathion was for their own good and that it presented no threat to people, crops, or animals. The effectiveness of these precautions was reflected in the very low number of hits taken by the "bug birds." Only rarely in the four-year operation did insecticide crews receive ground fire, and then usually when spraying long-held enemy base-camp areas before major Allied ground assaults. The occasional small-arms hit taken while "debugging" American bases was only half-jokingly attributed to angry GIs routed out of bed at dawn by the roar of the spray plane making repeated passes at tent-top level.[28] Years later, when the Agent Orange controversy arose, some former GIs would mistakenly credit the insecticide aircraft with having sprayed them with herbicide.

During the remainder of 1967, 118,985 gallons of malathion was dispensed over various base areas and combat zones. Manning the aircraft were volunteers from among the regular herbicide crews; insecticide duty broke the normal routine, since the crews landed at various bases and made frequent overnight stays throughout Vietnam. Flight crews could take along their motorcycles, and it was not unusual to see the bug bird land, taxi to the terminal, drop the cargo ramp, and have a formation of Hondas come roaring out of the aircraft, as the crew, purple scarves flying, made a beeline for the nearest chow hall or base exchange. On the other hand, many herbicide crewmen were quickly bored with the long, fairly uneventful missions, uninterrupted by the excitement of fighter cover, prestrikes, or ground fire. Since the mosquito targets were transitory, precise target navigation was not required; the repeated passes back and forth over the area were quite similar to aerial spraying in the United States.[29]

Insecticide sorties in 1968 more than doubled the 1967 total, to 280 from 118, and increased again in 1969 to 390. By this time the mosquito unit had been designated a separate flight within the 12th ACS, commanded by a major, with two aircraft commanders and two uncamouflaged UC-123s. Copilots for the bug birds were selected from among the new pilots in the squadron, usually for a 30- to 45-day tour; the longer insecticide missions allowed them to accrue flying time and experience in the aircraft much more rapidly than they could on the relatively short herbicide missions. This practice became especially useful when the squadron began receiving new pilots with no conventional or multiengine experience, fresh out of flying training. Flight and aircraft commanders normally were assigned to insecticide duty for about one-half of their tour in Vietnam.[30]

The insecticide flight continued to be responsible to the MACV Surgeon General's Office, with support from both the Army and Navy. Sorties were normally blanket-fragged* through Seventh Air Force TACC; targets were sprayed every 11 days, weather permitting. This busy schedule kept at least one aircraft on the road at all times, although the targets were seldom changed. Malathion reservicing was available at Cam Ranh Bay and Da Nang, in addition to Bien Hoa.[31]

By 1970 routine malathion treatment was being applied to 14 bases and their adjacent Vietnamese cities, and the respray interval had been reduced to nine days. The insecticide chemical had the same wind and temperature limitations as herbicides, and was effective only through direct contact with mosquitoes or their larvae. Thus, the best times for spraying were just after sunrise and just before sunset, when the insects were most active. In early 1970 the Navy chemical support unit at Da Nang was replaced by the Army's 172d Preventive Medicine unit; the Army's 105th Medical Detachment continued as support unit at Cam Ranh Bay.[32]

The bug birds received an unusual assignment in May 1970. TACC directed that insecticide missions be flown over two areas south of Da Nang—Landing Zone "Baldy" and Fire Support Base "Ross." Since both were "high-threat" areas, two insecticide planes were to be used in formation and fighter escort would be provided by the 1st Marine Air Wing. After a survey flight over the first target on 21 May, the insecticide crews briefed their fighter support at Da Nang. The following day, despite the fighters' and psywar support, the two spray planes came under heavy fire shortly after beginning their first run; the mission was aborted and the flight returned to Da Nang. The number two aircraft had been hit seven times, but damage was minor. Seven days later an attempt was made to spray Ross with the same result—the

---

*Long-term mission orders covering all sorties for a specified period, rather than for a single day.

number two aircraft was hit four times before the run was abandoned. Further attempts to debug active enemy contact areas were cancelled.[33]

When the 12th ACS was deactivated in July 1970, the insecticide unit continued its mission as part of "A" Flight, 310th Tactical Airlift Squadron (TAS), with home base at Phan Rang. The remainder of the year was uneventful—the unit history noted only two exceptions. On 14 November a bug bird took a hit while innocently returning to base from a mission (hits at cruise altitude over South Vietnam were rare). The other exception occurred in December. Because insecticide corroded the bare aluminum skin of the aircraft, the planes required periodic corrosion control treatments at Kadena Air Base, Okinawa. When one of the insecticide planes came due for treatment in December, it was replaced with a camouflaged herbicide aircraft. In the hope of convincing local inhabitants of its peaceful purpose, Seventh Air Force required the painted temporary replacement to be escorted by extra psywar loudspeaker planes. The tactic was successful. During 1970 insecticide planes took only 12 hits while flying 486 sorties, dispensing 102,440 gallons of malathion.[34]

Appropriately, RANCH HAND, which had originated from the insecticide mission at Langley, finished with the same mission. After cancellation of the herbicide program in 1971 and conversion of the herbicide aircraft to airlift duties, the insecticide flight continued a limited malathion mission until it, too, was eliminated. The final RANCH HAND losses in Vietnam came in February when aircraft 56-4373 crashed while spraying Phan Rang with insecticide, killing five crewmembers. In its last year 115 malathion sorties were flown, and on 1 June 1971 aircraft 54-5577 took the last RANCH HAND hit, a single round of small-arms fire in the left spray-boom, while spraying Phan Rang. In February 1972, ten years and one month after it arrived in Vietnam, the last insecticide aircraft (appropriately the grand old lady of the spray unit, Patches) left Vietnam for contract work at Pittsburgh, Pennsylvania.[35]

The Year of Glory ...
and Death

The buildup of American forces in South Vietnam had reached 389,000 men by the beginning of 1967, and Defense Secretary McNamara already had authorized the deployment of another 80,000 men over the next 18 months.[1] The American increase had been augmented by the arrival in 1966 of more Australian and New Zealand forces and an additional Korean infantry division. American aviation had been expanded by two F-4 and one F-5 fighter squadrons, plus more AC-47 "Puff" gunships. In the United States, the antiwar movement was gaining strength as increasing numbers of young men felt themselves threatened by the draft (only 2 percent of eligibles were actually called in 1966, but this was double the previous level) and as full-color video scenes of bloodshed and agony were brought into American homes in a manner and on a scale impossible before television. American defense officials, citing intelligence estimates of heavy enemy losses, predicted a turning point in the war during spring 1967. The Vietnamese government's control over an estimated 57 percent of the population was expected to increase with a new "pacification" strategy of seizing military and political control of rural areas.[2]

The matching expansion of RANCH HAND operations in 1966—more planes, additional crews, a new primary location, increased mission requests, more intense enemy opposition—augured an expanded role for herbicides in the conflict. Thus no one was surprised when 1967 became another year of record achievements in sorties flown, herbicide dispensed, and hits taken; even so, the enlarged organization failed to keep pace with the demands of province chiefs and field force commanders, although operating at maximum capacity throughout the year. The new year also would see the squadron set an undesired record, as the intensified effort led to the loss of a record number of crew members.

Herbicide shortages continued to plague the TRAIL DUST program in 1967. The effect was most noticeable in the RANCH HAND operation, as prime users of over 90 percent of the chemicals, but it also hampered the smaller Army perimeter defense and crop destruction programs. Chemicals were the only safe method of weed and grass control in the mined, concertina-wire-strewn, perimeter-barrier areas around friendly base camps. Staff projections indicated a possible "5.5 million gallon [herbicide] deficit for FY [fiscal year] 1968." One of the causes for this pessimistic estimate appeared to be a lack of in-country herbicide accountability; it was impossible to accurately determine how much herbicide was really needed. In January CINCPAC asked for a periodic report of on-hand stocks and consumption data for herbicides, only to discover that such information was not available through USAF channels. MACV was responsible for establishing and submitting requirements to the San Antonio Air Materiel Area (SAAMA), which in turn issued the purchase request to the Defense General Supply Center, Richmond, Virginia. SAAMA also was responsible for shipping the herbicide to Southeast Asia. Once the chemicals reached Vietnam, however, off-loading, distribution, and accountability of herbicides were Vietnamese responsibilities, from the time of arrival until they were loaded aboard dispensing aircraft. Even filling the aircraft spray tank with herbicide was a Vietnamese task, although closely supervised by US personnel.[3]

To improve control of herbicide supplies, PACAF proposed that herbicides be made USAF items of supply. MACV opposed this suggestion, maintaining that the program was a VNAF operation under Vietnamese control. United States participation, MACV contended, was limited to providing the Vietnamese government with defoliant chemicals and furnishing a US squadron (the 12th) to dispense the herbicides under the FARM GATE concept. COMUSMACV called the existing program "successful from an operational and a public affairs point of view," and told CINCPAC that any improvement in supply accountability would be offset "by the disadvantage of any reduction of GVN participation." MACV also was influenced by the large amount of manpower needed to handle the chemicals. Each bottom-loaded 55-gallon shipping drum, weighing approximately 640 pounds, had to be transferred from ship, to barge, to truck, and then to refueling unit. The 20th Ordnance Storage Depot at Saigon and the 511th Ordnance Storage Depot at Da Nang administratively advised their Vietnamese counterparts, but neither unit had the manpower to replace the ARVN handlers. As a result, herbicides remained a Vietnamese supply item.[4]

In January RANCH HAND exceeded 500 sorties for the first time—totaling 554—and taxed the supply system by using 413,000 gallons of herbicide. The increased effort was paid for with 147 hits and, on the last day of the month, with the loss of an aircraft and its five-man crew; the first RANCH HAND fatalities since 1962. On 31 January a special effort was planned for the A Shau Valley, with additional aircraft moved to Da Nang from Bien Hoa. The weather, however, was too bad for the valley run and the extra aircraft returned to Bien Hoa. The three Da Nang planes went to an alternate target in Laos, about 75 miles southwest of Khe Sanh. The pilots were all highly experienced and the flight was led by Captain Roy Kubley, flight leader during the crash in the Iron Triangle the previous October. Kubley was on his second tour with RANCH HAND, and this was his 500th mission.[5]

The formation made three passes through a bowl under a low overcast. Fighter cover was provided by A-1s out of Pleiku, but no enemy fire was heard. As the lead aircraft turned in for the fourth pass, its spray came on momentarily, and then the plane snapped inverted and crashed into the trees, exploding on contact. Although no ground fire had been heard or observed, number three also was hit—a round in the prop dome caused the propeller to run away and also prevented feathering it. In most instances, the tremendous drag created by the damaged propeller would have caused this UC-123 to crash too, but the pilots managed to find a power and airspeed combination that allowed them to barely maintain altitude. In a display of outstanding airmanship, the crew nursed the stricken aircraft back through the mountains to an emergency landing at the small strip at Khe Sanh. After the large number of hits without fatal consequences in the last five years, spray crewmen had become somewhat cocky and inclined to consider themselves invulnerable. The loss of Kubley's crew and near-loss of another brought RANCH HAND back to reality.

The spray squadron held a memorial service for their comrades, but there was little time to brood over their loss. In addition to continuing activity throughout South Vietnam and along the Ho Chi Minh Trail, February marked the start of the previously authorized project to defoliate the southern half of the buffer zone created in 1954 to separate North and South Vietnam. The first missions took place on 5 February, following charges by the South Vietnamese government to the International Control Commission that NVA forces had repeatedly violated the zone to infiltrate men and supplies into the South. The South Vietnamese already had protested the inability of the ICC to adequately patrol the zone twice earlier, in September and October 1966. Defoliation of the DMZ was only part of a proposed multi-billion dollar scheme to front the blocking forces of the 3d Marine Division along Route 9 with a "'fire break' . . . of ground swept clean of vegetation and sown with barbed wire, mines, and sensors," which the press was to label the "McNamara Wall." A retired senior Marine officer later noted, "The North Vietnamese were not greatly inconvenienced."[6]

The arrival of two UC-123s in February and another in March, with the crews who brought them, helped provide the 12th ACS with some breathing room. Although RANCH HAND was authorized 27 crews, no more than 22 complete crews were ever available during the January-June reporting period. Flight crews were not the only personnel shortage; program documents allocated over 460 officers and airmen to the squadron, but actual manpower authorizations never reached half of this number. In spite of the shortage of personnel and planes, the squadron launched more than 500 sorties per month for each of the first three months.[7]

The number of hits decreased dramatically in February, to 61, but the respite was only temporary and hits totaled 157 in March. The flight crews were naturally interested in acquiring any protective equipment they could, to supplement the sparse armor paneling installed in the aircraft. In addition to standard flak vests, most crew members had helmets similar to those normally issued to jet aircraft crews, although one individual managed to come up with a vintage German flak helmet from World War II. Interest in head and face protection was stimulated by the increasing number of injuries in this area. For example, Captains Clyde Picht and John Beakley both sustained numerous wounds in the face and arms from flying glass when cockpit windshields or windows were hit during missions on 11 November and again on 1 December 1966. Dual-visor ballistic helmets provided for evaluation in February 1967 met enthusiastic acceptance.[8]

Also replaced at this time were the Air Force issue flak vests, a type developed during the Korean War. Tests by Technical Sergeant Harold C. Cook, personal equipment noncommissioned officer in charge (NCOIC), and Major Henry K. Good, flying safety officer, proved the vest vulnerable to hits from an M-14 rifle, an M-16 rifle, and a .45-caliber pistol. On the other hand, plates of ceramic armor worn by Army helicopter gunners withstood anything fired at them by the RANCH personnel. Cook and Good submitted pictures of their tests and a proposal for a ceramic vest to the Seventh Air Force Surgeon's Office. Within an unusually short time, an Air Force project officer arrived with ten experimental vests for evaluation, and RANCH HAND soon became the first Air Force unit to receive the new silicon carbide body armor. Despite the weight of the new vests, few complaints were heard, especially after the ceramic vests began proving their worth by stopping shrapnel and small arms rounds. On 13 March Staff Sergeant Donald White was flight mechanic on the number three aircraft on a valley target approximately 40 miles inland from Chu Lai. On the second pass, a 12.7-millimeter Chinese communist-made armor-piercing projectile came through the right wheel-well of the aircraft, then through the right side of the armored "flight-mech's" box, and hit Sergeant White in the left center of the chest; the spent round ended up in the left pocket of the protective vest. Brass fragments from the shell wounded White in his unprotected right arm. After treatment at the Navy hospital at Chu Lai and the Air Force hospital at Cam Ranh Bay, Sergeant White returned to Bien Hoa and completed the remaining five months of this tour, thanks to his protective vest.[9]

In April sorties dropped below 500 (499) for the only time in 1967, while hits reached the highest monthly total (164) of the year. Ironically, as sorties increased during May (610) and June (697), the number of hits went down, to

88 and 67, respectively. The high June sortie total was assisted by the arrival of 3 more UC-123s, giving the squadron 19 herbicide aircraft and 1 plane configured for insecticide.[10]

The reality of the risks they ran was emphasized once more to the RANCH HANDs on 21 May, when Captain Tom Davie, a survivor of the Iron Triangle crash, was killed in a freak incident. The mission was a routine project in Vinh Binh Province. During a banked turn that left the pilot more exposed than usual, a single shot entered the cockpit through the window, striking Davie in the neck; it was the only shot reported by any aircraft during the entire mission. The copilot, with the aid of the navigator, made an emergency landing at Binh Tuy for medical assistance; however, the pilot had been killed almost instantly. The tragedy was made more poignant because Captain Davie was flying one of his last missions—he was due to return home in only two more weeks. Davie's death led to modification of the new armor vest with a neck protector that later saved at least one other pilot's life.[11]

Enemy projectiles were not the only danger RANCH HAND crews faced. On more than one occasion, a mistimed suppression pass by an escorting fighter resulted in CBU (cluster bomb unit)* damage to spray planes. In one instance, sheet metal specialists from the 3d TFW worked alongside 12th maintenance personnel all night long to repair 104 holes in a UC-123 caused by one of their fighters. By morning the aircraft was in commission and a report to higher headquarters was avoided. On another occasion, a shaken fighter pilot responsible for damaging two spray planes with an errant pass left his apology in the form of prepaid drinks at the Bien Hoa officers' club bar for the RANCH HAND crewmembers.[12]

The spray squadron concealed these incidents from higher headquarters because they did not want to lose the use of CBU, which was considered highly effective in suppressing enemy fire. Moreover, when laid alongside the planned spray track, smoke from CBU explosions hid the UC-123s from enemy gunners on either side of the run. Again, the tactic had disadvantages when the CBU was laid improperly—several times, RANCH HAND formations flew into billowing CBU smoke and discovered the thrill of blind flying in formation at treetop level, a maneuver guaranteed to age young pilots rapidly.[13]

Another hazard to all aircraft in Vietnam, not just spray planes, was the extensive use of artillery. Several times RANCH HAND aircraft observed artillery rounds striking in the target area while they were spraying. In his end-of-tour report, Brigadier General William G. Moore, Jr., called attention to the artillery hazard, noting that aircraft were not warned of fire trajectories below 7,000 feet, although most airlift and all RANCH HAND sorties were flown below this altitude. General Moore's concern was later justified when a

---

*Antipersonnel munitions that explode on contact or at preset intervals, showering the immediate area with hundreds of projectiles.

C-7A "Caribou" transport on approach to Ha Thanh had its tail blown off by "a single artillery shell, destroying the aircraft and killing three crew members." A duplicate tragedy nearly occurred while the commander of the 12th Squadron was leading a road defoliation mission along Route 13, when a 155-millimeter round impacted between the lead and number two aircraft, damaging both with shrapnel.[14]

A danger to low-flying aircraft at any time are bird-strikes, which can have serious, even fatal, consequences; but in Vietnam RANCH HAND faced a unique hazard in the form of giant fruit bats. These were especially common in IV Corps, and on one mission into An Xuyen Province, near an area later known as "Batville," fighters scared up a flock of over 200 bats directly in front of the spray flight. Despite extensive damage to engine cowlings and wing leading-edges, all aircraft returned safely to base, but remaining missions for the day had to be cancelled. One aircraft brought back evidence of its "assailants" in the form of a bat with a five-foot wingspan and a red-furred, fox-like head, spread-eagled against the damaged nose of the plane. On another mission, the aircrew returned with the windscreen and instrument panel damaged; their trophy ended up in the cockpit with them—again a fruit bat with an almost five-foot wingspread.[15]

Even the simple act of take-off presented spray planes with a potential for disaster. The original C-123B transport was designed for a maximum take-off gross weight of 56,000 pounds. The modified UC-123B configuration, despite stripping the aircraft of unnecessary equipment, frequently had take-off weights approaching 60,000 pounds; loss of an engine immediately after take-off at these overweight conditions meant a certain crash unless weight was rapidly reduced by an emergency "dump" of the herbicide load. The installation of a large valve allowing the entire five tons of chemical to be dropped in only 30 seconds was a welcome improvement—but only when it worked. The crew of Captain Roy E. Smith, Major Henry K. Good, and Airman First Class Arthur H. Gack had a close brush with death on the day they lost an engine on take-off at Bien Hoa and the dump-valve failed to operate electrically. While the pilots struggled to keep the aircraft airborne, the fast-thinking flight mechanic grabbed a fire axe and forced the valve open. Meanwhile, ground crewmen watched in horror as the UC-123 disappeared into the trees off the end of the runway. Fortunately, the plane managed to gain flying speed as it staggered between the trees, and the pilots nursed the stricken plane back to an emergency landing. Captain Smith's crew transferred to a waiting spare plane whose engines had already been started, took off a second time, and caught up with the formation in time to complete the assigned mission. Not until return to Bien Hoa for debriefing did the realization of their near-crash catch up with them.[16]

As if they did not face enough threats to their safety, RANCH HAND crews were not immune to creating some problems on their own. At two- to four-week intervals all aircraft and TDY crew members were rotated from Da Nang to Bien Hoa, and were replaced by another TDY detachment from Bien Hoa. While ferrying between bases, crews usually took the over-water route just off the coast, and some of them delighted in diving down to "buzz" every fishing vessel and Navy ship they saw. In at least one case, the spray plane was just about to roar past a US Navy warship when the vessel's main batteries fired a salvo toward the nearby land; obviously the ship was on a fire-support mission. The shaken flight crew immediately returned to formation position, where they contritely remained for the rest of the flight.[17]

Some of the crews also took advantage of the ferry flights to "test" their issue M-16 rifles, and any other weapons they had managed to acquire, by firing them into the water. One aircraft commander, yielding to the pleas of his flight mechanic, descended to wave-top level to allow the young airman his chance to "shoot." After several minutes, the pilots decided that they could enjoy the action by making a series of S-turns, which would let them see the bullets kicking up spray as they hit the waves. The sergeant had not finished emptying his first clip of ammunition when the startled crew heard the familiar sound of bullets impacting on the aircraft, and learned about the unpredictability of bullets ricocheting from water. When the plane landed at Da Nang, two "hits" were quietly repaired without being entered on the maintenance records of the unit's hit summary sheet.[18]

A more legitimate hazard sometimes occurred due to the errant throwing aim of the flight mechanic. When ground fire was taken at low-level, the copilot would order "smoke-out," while the pilot notified the FAC and fighters with an appropriate radio call, for example, "Alpha three, automatic weapons fire on the right." The flight mechanic's job was to take one of the colored smoke grenades (usually red) hanging along the front of his armored box, pull the pin, and throw the grenade out one of the rear troop doors, which were secured open for this purpose. When done properly, the grenade provided a distinctly visible smoke mark about 300 meters downtrack from the enemy weapons position, so fighters could attack the site after the spray run was complete. If, however, the flight mechanic missed the open door, the spewing grenade could roll around the cargo-compartment floor, filling the aircraft with dense, colored smoke. The airflow pattern in the plane caused most of the smoke to exit through the open cockpit windows, forcing the nearly blinded pilots to abruptly pull up off target with colored smoke streaming from various opening in the fuselage. This maneuver was known as a "Smokey the Bear," and led more than one aircrew to experience one of those "moments of sheer, stark terror" that are a characteristic of flying.[19]

Despite such episodes of danger, the spray crews managed to maintain a high level of morale and sense of humor, although the latter often exceeded the bounds of good taste and military discipline. One Da Nang crew spent several days preparing a large streamer, made from cloth and two-by-fours, which they planned to tow across Da Nang on their return from a Laos mission; in large, bold letters the sign said: "Fuck Communism." Fortunately, when the crew extended the sign as a test while still over Laos, they discovered that it was upside down and that they could not pull it back into the aircraft because of the wind drag; the sign was cut loose, to float down somewhere over central Laos.[20]

The increased numbers of spray planes and larger spray formations in 1967 gave RANCH HAND another opportunity to show off. Most American servicemen transferred to and from South Vietnam were carried aboard civilian airliners under contract to the US government, and Bien Hoa airbase was a port of entry for arriving and departing American personnel. Almost every morning found several civilian airliners parked on the terminal ramp, their crews interested spectators to the surrounding scenes of a nation at war. The RANCH HAND pilots took as much pride in demonstrating precise formation spacing and movement during taxiing and engine run-up as they did during in-flight maneuvers. The early morning eight-ship mission, especially, gave the spray crews a chance to put on a show for the onlookers and, in particular, for the stewardesses on the airline crews, who were always ready with a cheerful wave and a bright smile—a momentary breath of "back home." To insure that everyone knew who was manning the lumbering spray aircraft, it became customary to fly a large flag with the RANCH HAND insignia from the top hatch of the lead aircraft until just before taking the runway. However, before long another flag appeared, this time flown by the last aircraft in eight-ship formations. Equally large, this flag was yellow, with large purple letters spelling out "Fuck Communism." After the latter phrase was sighted one morning by a senior officer, the 3d Wing commander ordered the offensive flag removed. It became legend among RANCH HAND veterans that the next morning, when the eight-shipper taxied out, "tail-end Charlie" was flying a large yellow flag that defiantly proclaimed "FUCK THE 3RD TFW COMMANDER."[21]

"Flying the flag" led to another incident of note at Da Nang Air Base. Captain Bill Borkowski lost one of the RANCH HAND flags out the top hatch and into the spinning propeller of his plane. Neither the flag nor engine survived the accident (which was probably reported as "combat damage"). The Da Nang aircrews immortalized the event at the next party by presenting Borkowski with a special award—a box of toothpicks and a mass of yellow, green, and brown strings (the colors of the RANCH HAND insignia on the flag).[22]

Once when a four-ship spray flight was planned into the always-dangerous A Shau Valley, the Da Nang fighter pilots tried out their own brand of humor on the RANCH HAND crews. Because of expected enemy resistance, a double force of fighters was scheduled, with half of them positioned to attack known "hot fire" areas just before the spray run began. As the herbicide aircraft approached the target area, the fighter pilots struck up a radio conversation preplanned for the benefit of the spray crews:

"The woods are full of troops!"

"Wow! Look at those tracers!"

"There are several fifty-cals in that bunker!"

"Joe, you get that quad-fifty on the left and I'll get the one on the edge of the woods!"

The fighter pilots' radio drama came to an abrupt end when a voice dryly asked, "Cowboy Lead, this is Cowboy Four. Do you suppose that our escort has that flight of MIG-21's in sight?"[23]

It was fortunate that the RANCH HAND crews could be so lighthearted since the demands on them were about to increase. In June approval was given to defoliate the northern half of the demilitarized zone. The Department of Defense also announced that 5 million gallons of herbicides had been purchased for $32 million in fiscal year 1967, which would end on 30 June (compared with $10 million spent on herbicides in fiscal year 1966), and revealed that it planned to increase purchases to $50 million for the next fiscal year, if the war continued.[24]

In the first six months of 1967, RANCH HAND had flown 3,207 sorties, dispensing nearly 2.1 million gallons of herbicides, while taking over 600 hits. In addition, the malathion aircraft dispensed nearly 200,000 gallons of insecticide. These records were achieved despite the loss of 756 sorties to weather and 155 due to battle damage that could not be repaired in time. For its efforts, the 12th Air Commando Squadron was awarded the Presidential Unit Citation for extraordinary heroism, the first of four such awards. During this period, the squadron also was awarded the Air Force Outstanding Unit Award (AFOUA) with "V" device for valor. This was the third award of this decoration for RANCH HAND, having previously earned two AFOUAs with "V" while part of the 309th Squadron.[25]

The heavier workload pushed the spray crews to the limit. Although all training was now concentrated at Hurlburt Field, Florida, the number of new crews was not keeping up with the demand. The loss of six crewmembers killed and several invalided home for wounds, in addition to normal rotations due to end of tour, forced the 315th Wing to seek pilots for the 12th Squadron. Each of the four airlift units was levied for two volunteers. With one exception, all were recently arrived copilot-qualified captains or lieutenants; the 19th Air Commando Squadron received permission to transfer a volunteer major, who was an instructor pilot. Although spray training and checkout usually took two months, in addition to the training already received at Hurlburt, the major's flight log revealed the urgent need of the herbicide squadron for crews:

last airlift mission - 23 July
first spray mission - 24 July

spray qualified - 3 August
lead qualified - 15 August
mountain qualified - 18 September
spray instructor pilot - 19 September

In the first 70 days in RANCH HAND, the major had only 8 nonflying days and accumulated over 200-hours flying time.[26]

Although the major's example reflected his previous eight months experience in Vietnam, and was not typical of the volunteers, all were fully utilized by the spray squadron. The need for extra pilots increased even as the volunteers arrived; on 21 July another aircraft and its entire crew were lost. This time the fatal target was in II Corps, 45 miles northeast of Pleiku. The Da Nang-based UC-123 was on a crop mission and had just crested a ridge-line; by the time the number two aircraft crossed the ridge, smoke was already rising from the burning wreckage on the downslope of the next valley. In addition to the four-man American crew, the Vietnamese observer, a VNAF noncommissioned officer, was lost.[27]

Tragedy stuck the spray squadron again in September. During an earlier spray mission, an aircraft had the control cables to one aileron* shot apart, nearly rolling the aircraft inverted while at low-level, and was forced to make an emergency landing at Nha Trang. By 4 September the aircraft had been repaired, and a volunteer crew caught a ride for Nha Trang aboard an airlift C-123 of the 19th Squadron to bring the spray plane back to Bien Hoa. Two days later the wreckage of the airlift aircraft was found near Bao Loc, its first scheduled stop. All aboard were dead, including the four hitchhikers from the 12th. Two of the RANCH HAND dead had nearly completed their tours in Vietnam and were preparing to leave for home.[28]

Perhaps the luckiest man in the defoliation squadron was Technical Sergeant Walter E. Sowles. Sowles was at Da Nang preparing to fly a mission on 21 July when he was ordered back to Bien Hoa; as the ranking flight mechanic he would be the new chief flight engineer, succeeding Master Sergeant Stanley Voshell, who was going home. The spare flight mechanic who took Sowles's place on the mission from Da Nang was killed. Six weeks later Sowles scheduled himself to go as part of the crew to recover the aircraft at Nha Trang. At the last minute, Sowles's assistant talked the chief engineer into letting him go to Nha Trang in his place. For the second time, Sowles missed a fatal mission.[29]

Despite their losses, RANCH HAND continued to fly sorties at a record pace, with 598 in July and 647 in September. In the biggest mission of the year, ten planes were deployed to Chu Lai to respray the DMZ on 8 September.

---

*The movable flight surface that causes roll around the longitudinal axis of the aircraft, thus providing lateral control.

Anticipating strong enemy reaction, the large spray formation was accompanied by an even larger number of fighters, while several HH-3 "Jolly Green Giant" rescue helicopters hovered nearby in expectation of downed aircraft; not a shot was heard during the run.[30]

Even during August, the lightest month of the quarter, 550 sorties were flown, although exceptionally heavy rains forced cancellation due to weather of 48.5 percent of the missions scheduled. In the meantime, 834th Air Division began studying RANCH HAND resources in light of a MACV forecast delivery requirement in fiscal year 1968 of 612,000 gallons of herbicide per month, and an increase in subsequent years to 864,000. To meet these delivery rates, MACV estimated that seven more aircraft and their supporting personnel would be needed in the spray squadron.[31]

The division study, published in September, found MACV's aircraft estimate totally inadequate. Instead of 7 additional aircraft, the 834th analysis called for a total of 34 herbicide aircraft by 1 July 1968 and recommended that crop destruction and mosquito control missions be assumed by the Vietnamese, possibly by converting VNAF-operated C-119 transports to spray configuration. The report probably reflected concern over the growing antiherbicide outcry in the United States, noting that one advantage in giving the VNAF these responsibilities would be "placement of a politically sensitive and post-war controversial mission under the full responsibility of the RVN." With the exception of the increase in aircraft, the recommendations apparently were not acted upon by Seventh Air Force, to whom the report was forwarded.[32]

The following month, a RAND Corporation evaluation of crop destruction was published that was highly critical of the program, calling crop destruction in Vietnam "dysfunctional" and "counter-productive"—responsible for arousing negative, antigovernment feelings among the Vietnamese farmers toward the Vietnamese and United States governments. Although the report apparently refuted critics' claims that the crop program had caused civilian starvation, it also concluded that the existing program did not provide significant benefit to the South Vietnamese government or significant harm to the Viet Cong.[33]

A companion statistical analysis of crop spraying in Vietnam, also produced by RAND, recommended discontinuing the crop program, despite admitted shortcomings in both data and methodology used in the study. Even in the areas of heaviest crop destruction by spraying (approximately 23 percent destroyed), the study found the effect on VC rations to be only a 5 percent reduction. On the other hand, the analysis indicated the civilian population carried "very nearly the full burden of the results of the crop destruction program."[34]

When both MACV and Seventh AIR FORCE took strong exception to the RAND studies, a civilian advisory group from CINCPAC Headquarters was sent to Vietnam to review 1967 crop destruction activities. Using captured enemy documents and an analysis of 622 crop sorties flown by RANCH HAND in 1967, the advisory group disagreed with the RAND findings, determining that crop destruction was a vital aspect of economic warfare and an "integral, essential and effective part of the total effort in South Vietnam." Contrary to the RAND reports, the CINCPAC review concluded that "the crop destruction program has had a significant adverse effect on VC/NVA food supply, logistical requirements, and combat effectiveness." Captured documents detailed specific instances, including assigning troops normally used for fighting to the task of raising food. Serious local food shortages among combat forces were reported; for example, the 95th NVA Regiment had to fast for one- to two-day periods several times due to lack of food. Not only did food shortages directly affect enemy forces physically, but resulting morale problems led to increased defections and to the physical exodus of people from enemy-controlled areas.[35]

The disparities between on-scene military studies and evaluations conducted by RAND led the Air Force chief of staff to order still another investigation of the crop program, this time by Seventh Air Force. Again the military study found the program to be carefully organized, tightly controlled, and very effective. The report noted that successful crop spraying projects had forced the NVA to alter their food production procedures from planting large cultivated plots to copying the "slash and burn" techniques of the Montagnard tribesmen and concealing crops along tree lines, on mountainsides, and in bombed-out structures. New NVA tactics had one unit move through an area, clear it, and move on; followed by a second unit that plowed and planted; while a third unit arrived later to harvest the crop—in effect, combat units on the move had to become part of the food production process. The Seventh Air Force study admitted that one of the goals of the crop destruction program was to force people to move away from VC-controlled areas, denying them "the people contact so essential to the guerrilla-type combat employed by the VC."[36]

The constant series of studies, evaluations, and reviews had little direct effect on the RANCH HAND crews, who kept on flying the assigned herbicide targets at a record pace. In November the MACV policy and procedure directive for herbicide operations was revised. The two major changes were limitation of crop destruction "to areas in I, II, and III Corps where food is scarce, and where denial of the food would create an operational burden on the enemy," and a warning to use "special care ... in planning and executing operations to prevent damage to rubber and fruit trees by herbicides." In a further effort to prevent damage to rubber trees, which were particularly sensitive to defoliants, a five-nautical-mile "no spray" zone was established in December around active rubber plantations, with a "White-only" spray zone extending out another five miles (White herbicide was not as susceptible to drift, due to its lower volatility). RANCH HAND routes to and from targets had to be planned to keep well clear of plantations, on the chance that one of the aircraft might have a "leaker"—a nozzle allowing the slow escape of herbicide.[37]

By the end of the year, the 12th Air Commando Squadron's 19 aircraft had flown 6,847 sorties, using 4,879,000 gallons of herbicides; defoliated were 1,226,823 acres in South Vietnam and 12,275 acres in Laos; crops destroyed totaled 148,418 acres. There was no doubt in anyone's mind that the next year would bring about even greater expansion of the chemical program. The ever-increasing desires of field commanders for herbicide operations and the cumbersome target approval system had created a huge backlog of work for the defoliation crews. A herbicide conference held shortly after the end of the year reported, "projects amounting to approximately half the area of South Vietnam have been authorized or are in the process of authorization." The 1967 cost to the 12th Commandos for their accomplishments was 1,016 hits, 2 UC-123s destroyed, and 15 men killed, in addition to a number of wounded.[38] As RANCH HAND celebrated the end of the old year, some of them must have wondered what price would be exacted in 1968.

New Planes and Old Tasks:
K Models and Airlift Duty

At the end of 1967, nearly 490,000 American servicemen were in South Vietnam. General Westmoreland had reported to the president, and to the National Press Club in Washington in November, that the war was being won—the tide had turned. An estimated 38,000 Viet Cong had deserted and surrendered during 1967. On the other hand, the cost of the war was approximately $2 billion per month, and growing, and US losses since 1961 were almost 16,000, with 9,353 in 1967 alone. In the United States, the antiwar movement had grown dramatically, and government spokesmen could not travel to any major American city without facing a hostile crowd of chanting demonstrators. Congress, too, began to question the unilateral decisions of the executive branch on Southeast Asia. The new year held little prospect of abatement in the clamor of domestic discontent.[1]

For RANCH HAND, 1968 was a year of contrasts. During the first five months, no crop destruction missions were scheduled because of a large backlog of high-priority defoliation missions and the unusually dry weather—Vietnamese agriculture was hit hard by the drought and there were few good crop targets available. Twice during the year spray aircraft were diverted to airlift duties, further hampering accomplishment of the herbicide mission, and in April the squadron started converting to the jet assisted K model UC-123 aircraft. As a result, for the first time since the program was established, acreage sprayed and herbicide sorties flown did not double the previous year's total, but instead fell by over 13 percent. More welcome was the dramatic reduction in hits on spray planes, down by nearly 28 percent.[2]

Part of the reduction in hits was due to the concentration on defoliation; crop targets normally were "hotter" targets, and exposure time usually longer than against single-pass defoliation targets, although there were exceptions to this rule of thumb. Another possible factor was, ironically, the greater number of targets presented to the enemy—instead of the 2- and 3-plane formations of past years, RANCH HAND missions now had 4 to 8, and sometimes even 12, spray planes, in addition to more accompanying fighters. Thus the enemy gunners, who previously could concentrate on only a few aircraft at a time, were distracted by larger numbers of herbicide planes, and also faced more escorting fighters and more effective escort tactics. Increasingly, RANCH HAND was not allowed to proceed with the mission if fighter cover was not available.[3]

In January 1968 the American Ambassador to Vietnam, Ellsworth Bunker, established a Herbicide Policy Review Committee to study the entire US/Vietnamese chemical program. This group was tasked to assess "the efficacy of herbicide operations in terms of military benefits to the Allied Forces ... as compared to economic costs and possible ecological effects." Besides the crop destruction and defoliation programs, the committee examined planning for refugee support, indemnification, and psychological warfare. It was assisted by four consulting scientists, three of whom were brought from the United States specifically for this purpose. While the committee did not recommend major policy changes in the program, it did suggest various actions to improve administrative control and management. Because of heavy defoliation in III Corps during 1966/67 (53 percent of the total area sprayed in 1966 and 66 percent in 1967), the reviewers recommended holding future defoliation there to "the minimum compatible with military requirements." The crop destruction program was criticized for failure to coordinate spraying efforts with other related activities, thereby missing the full benefits of the overall food denial program. The psywar and indemnification elements of the herbicide project were termed ineffective, and evidence was noted pointing to misuse of Vietnamese-managed indemnification funds by corrupt province and district officials. Stronger controls were recommended in both areas to improve the general public attitude toward the program and the central government.[4]

In the meantime, the 19-plane squadron continued defoliation operations throughout South Vietnam. Despite the temporary cessation of the crop mission, the herbicide unit flew 580 sorties in January and another 69 the first week of February, dispensing a total of 601,000 gallons of defoliant. Unexpectedly, only 30 hits were taken during this period, possibly because the enemy was laying low while preparing to launch an all-out offensive effort during the Tet holiday.[5]

On 21 January 1968, North Vietnamese Defense Minister General V Nguyen Giap, victor over the French at Dien Bien Phu 14 years earlier, began his offensive with a major assault on the Marine outpost of Khe Sanh in northwestern I Corps, the first in a series of attacks on the position that would last for nearly 2½ months. Allied leaders, aware of the buildup of NVA forces by Giap, were mesmerized by the parallels between Dien Bien Phu and the isolated, mountain-surrounded Marine base, but General Westmoreland was confident that the result at Khe Sanh would be different. Nine days later, while attention was focused on this northern bastion, North Vietnamese and Viet Cong forces made simultaneous attacks throughout South Vietnam against 36 of the 44 provincial capitals, 5 of the 6 autonomous cities, 64 district capitals, 23 airfields, and numerous other government controlled urban areas. This nationwide, coordinated offensive was particularly shocking to many Americans at home and in Vietnam due to widely quoted speeches by US government and military officials suggesting that the Allies were winning the war and the enemy was nearly beaten. This impression had been enhanced by inflated success reports by field forces and skewed reporting by the media. The shock was further intensified because it came only five days after the startling seizure of the American intelligence ship USS *Pueblo* by North Korea, both events seemingly revealing serious failures by American intelligence-gathering agencies and a US inability to cope with threats to its interests.[6]

The Tet Offensive meant a return to a mission RANCH HAND had not performed for several years, airlift. The month-long Tet attacks created an extraordinary demand for air transport to support beleaguered friendly forces throughout the country, while fighter units were totally occupied in providing close air support for Allied forces in contact with the enemy, and thus not available for RANCH HAND escort. In addition, Vietnamese herbicide handlers were unable (or unwilling) to report for work to refill the herbicide servicing system. On 5 February, in the midst of the initial Tet Offensive, the 12th Squadron was ordered to convert to an airlift role. Remaining on-board herbicide was emptied by the simple expedient of flying 13 ships against a nearby War Zone D target, the largest single spray formation to date—and proof that spray crews were not superstitious. The changeover was expected to take several days, but within 24 hours the RANCH HANDs had stripped their aircraft of herbicide tanks, spray booms, and plumbing, and reported themselves "ready to go." In a reversal of the pilot situation of the previous July, the 12th Squadron also sent 11 pilots on temporary duty to the other squadrons.[7]

Most spray crew members were minimally prepared for this new kind of flying, having received only brief airlift training in Florida on their way to Vietnam and no subsequent in-country practice. Nor did the squadron have loadmasters, normally a required member of an airlift flight crew. Nevertheless, RANCH HAND crews established an outstanding record; between 5 February and 20 March, 12th Air Commando planes flew 2,846 sorties, moving cargo and passengers at a rate comparable with more experienced sister squadrons. While the cargo haulers of the 315th Wing faced significant hazards during steep approaches and assault landings on short, unsurfaced, forward airstrips, the difference in mission hazards between spraying and airlift was reflected in the fact that no RANCH HAND aircraft were hit by enemy ground fire during the almost 3,000 airlift sorties; RANCH HAND's average for the previous 12 months of herbicide operations was approximately 1 hit every 6 sorties.[8]

On the ground, however, it was a different story. Bien Hoa, home base of the 12th Squadron, was a primary target in the Tet attacks, and was hit repeatedly with mortar, rocket, and ground attacks. On 28 February, during a rocket attack at 0200 hours, several 122-millimeter missiles landed in the RANCH HAND officers' barracks area, setting fires that completely destroyed four buildings and heavily damaged five others, including the community latrine. Although 33 officers lost everything but the clothes they wore, and 27 others salvaged only a few personal possessions, no RANCH HAND personnel were killed and only one officer was slightly wounded. The men of the unit housed directly across the street from the spray quarters were not as fortunate—one of their bunkers took a direct hit, killing 14 men.[9]

One of the luckiest members of the squadron was Sergeant Ed Frambie, temporarily detailed to the Security Police unit as an augmentee and assigned as a perimeter guard. Frambie had just stepped out of a jeep when he was suddenly knocked to the ground by a blow to the chest. A sniper, apparently firing from maximum range, had hit the young airman, but the force of the nearly spent bullet had been cushioned by a shirt pocket filled with a pair of sunglasses, a cigarette lighter, and several pencils, saving Frambie from anything more serious than a bad bruise and a scare. The bullet was found in the airman's fatigue pocket and was worn on a neck chain as a good luck charm for the rest of his tour.[10]

Some RANCH HAND personnel were convinced that the Vietnamese beer stand ("Bam-me-bam" stand) directly outside their compound was a good "early-warning" indicator of VC attacks on the base. Several airmen noted that if candles, rather than the regular lights, were used and there were few girls around, the base usually was hit. On the positive side, the Tet attacks benefited morale since several Red Cross girls found it too dangerous to return to Saigon and elected to spend some time as "guests" of the RANCH. A young lady of Norwegian lineage also reportedly enjoyed the hospitality of the spray officers, moving from one hooch to another over a period of two months.[11]

As the Tet Offensive ebbed away, RANCH HAND returned to its primary mission on 16 March, much to the relief of the crews, who had soon become bored of the routine of airlift duty. Through an all-out effort, the squadron flew 284 sorties and dispensed 220,000 gallons of herbicide in the last two weeks in March, despite having to reinstall spray systems on all aircraft. The credit for this record went to the long-suffering and seldom praised ground maintenance crews. Working without shelter on the open ramp in all kinds of weather, often by flashlight because other lights drew enemy fire, uncomplaining crew chiefs kept the spray planes flying in spite of the conditions.[12]

Although the Air Force had abandoned attempts to start forest fires after the failures of the previous year, in March 1968 nature proved a more effective arsonist. The drought in Southeast Asia in the first three months was the most severe in a quarter century, and major fires broke out in the forests of Vietnam, Malaya, Cambodia, and Thailand. One of the biggest fires was in the U Minh Forest, an insurgent stronghold on the southwest coast of Vietnam since the 1930s. Many sections of this large mangrove forest had been defoliated by RANCH HAND in attempts to expose enemy camps. When the initial fires broke out, dry vegetation and strong winds helped them spread rapidly. The explosion of a large VC ammunition dump and several new ignition points frustrated VC attempts to make firebreaks to contain the fires.[13]

Realizing the military value of the massive fire, MACV Headquarters directed Air Force FACs to use white phosphorous marking rockets and grenades to set more fires, while fighters added to the conflagration with bombs and napalm. Navy vessels also joined in with shellfire. Allied attacks not only started new fires, but interrupted VC attempts to control fires and to evacuate endangered supplies. The extent of VC losses was indicated when observers reported hundreds of secondary explosions in fire areas, occurring during one period at a rate of one every 20 minutes. Previously defoliated areas burned particularly well, although the weather deserved more credit than RANCH HAND. By the end of April, when the fire finally stopped spreading, approximately 80 percent of the 1,100-square mile forest had been destroyed, with heavy damage to VC forces in the area.[14]

In April the first UC-123s equipped with auxiliary jet engines arrived at Bien Hoa—the 12th Squadron was the last of the five units in the 315th Wing to get the improved aircraft. The new planes, designated "K" models, were reworked B models with a powerful J-85-17 jet engine on each wing outboard of the conventional engines, improved engine armor plating, a strengthened windshield to reduce shattering from hits, a larger spray pump, and a flowmeter to assure a constant chemical flow rate of three gallons per acre despite airspeed variations. Because of the extreme hazard associated with not being able to feather a propeller, the K models also were modified to use engine oil in the feathering system, rather than a separate oil supply. The jet engines provided a tremendous increase in safety on spray missions, particularly on mountain targets. Aircrews no longer had to fly target areas such as the A Shau Valley knowing the loss of an engine probably meant no escape. In return, the crews had to accept the disadvantages of the K model—the extra weight on the wings reduced maneuverability slightly and the high fuel consumption of the jet engines reduced combat range significantly.[15]

In practice the new models proved their worth. Full jet power was used on take-offs, almost eliminating the danger from one of the most hazardous phases of flight for the overloaded spray planes. This point was graphically demonstrated in August when a fully loaded UC-123K had a conventional engine explode just as the plane passed the end of the runway on take-off. For various reasons, cockpit confusion caused the remaining, undamaged conventional engine to be mistakenly feathered; however, the aircraft remained airborne and circumnavigated the airfield to a successful emergency landing on jet engines alone.[16]

To save fuel, once safely airborne the jets normally were shut down until arrival in the target area. During low-level runs, jets were run at 60 percent power so they would be immediately available if needed. Full power was used to climb away from the targets, thus reducing the always dangerous exposure time between treetops and 3,000-feet altitude. The jets were shut down once more during return to base to conserve fuel, unless needed because of a battle-damaged conventional engine. For landing the jets were run in idle, again to be available during this critical phase of flight. There was little doubt as to the worth of the modification; RANCH HAND commanders' end-of-tour reports for 1968, 1969, and 1970 all stated that several aircraft would have been lost while on target due to engine or propeller-dome hits if not equipped with the auxiliary jet engines.[17]

The arrival of the jet-equipped spray planes was publicly overshadowed by another development concerning the herbicide program. Even while spraying was being resumed in Vietnam, a vice-president of "Air America," the thinly disguised Central Intelligence Agency cover airline, revealed to the press that its aircraft had sprayed defoliants in Thailand, exposing Thai insurgents on the Isthmus of Kra. These operations, however, were not directly associated with the Vietnam project or the RANCH HAND unit. April also was the first full month of renewed spray missions in Vietnam, with 662 sorties dispensing over one-half million gallons of defoliant. Enemy gunners, apparently no longer concentrating on ground attacks, hit the spray planes 66 times.[18]

In May the NVA again launched a nationwide offensive against 109 cities and military installations, including 21 airfields. Bien Hoa once more was a target, and on 5 May rocket attacks at 0300 and 0600 hours were accompanied by a ground assault, which was beaten back with 192 enemy killed. The second rocket attack took place as the RANCH HAND crews boarded their aircraft, and several missiles exploded in the ramp area, damaging three aircraft. Colonel George Hench, Deputy Commander for Maintenance of the 315th Wing, was making an inspection visit to the squadron and had planned to fly as an observer on the Alpha lift with Major Ed Ridgeway. Hench was standing beside the aircraft when the rockets hit; he received shrapnel wounds in the shoulder and eventually was air evacuated from Vietnam. One other officer received minor injuries.[19]

Twice during the month RANCH HAND aircraft were on the runway for take-off when mortar rounds hit on or adjacent to the runway. Although no planes were damaged, considerable debate raged in the squadron as to whether it was best to attempt take off while the shells were still landing, or to abandon the aircraft and run to the nearest ditch until things quieted down. Agreement was never reached. Despite these assaults and frequent sleep-interrupting night attacks and false alarms, spray crews flew 750 sorties in May; however, the amount of herbicide dispensed—575,000 gallons—increased only slightly over April's figure. The disparity between sorties and herbicide was due to numerous airborne cancellations because of weather or lack of fighter support. Several times, fighters that had been assigned to RANCH HAND escort were diverted to support ground forces in contact with the enemy, forcing herbicide planes to return with unexpended loads since Seventh AIR FORCE directives now required fighter escort during spray missions. Another problem was that some missions were beyond the limits of the spray planes' combat range, forcing a stop for fuel at an intermediate base; thus each plane flew two sorties on these missions, but dispensed only one load of herbicide. These longer missions also forced the first lift to launch well before daylight, while the FAC had to wait for daylight to take off from his forward airstrip to check weather in the target area. This sequence frequently meant that spray crews were more than halfway to the target area before finding out that both the primary and alternate targets were weathered out, again causing the planes to return with loads intact.[20]

Some higher headquarters officials, not fully aware of the RANCH HAND program and oriented in their thinking to the "tonnage hauled" method of measurement of mission accomplishment in airlift, were disturbed by these "unproductive" sorties. The eventual solution was to order RANCH HAND to schedule a tertiary target—when other targets could not be sprayed, the aircraft resprayed the Rung Sat Special Zone. The result was an improved "mission effectiveness" rate on a headquarters wall chart, and a lot of expensive herbicide unnecessarily wasted.[21]

Modified UC-123s continued to arrive in the squadron in May, and a program was established to return B models to the United States for conversion. The trans-Pacific movements were made by regular ferry crews, rather than RANCH HAND crews as in the past. It was fortunate that the new aircraft were arriving faster than the old ones were departing, because the 12th Commandos lost another crew and aircraft to enemy fire in May. On the twenty-fourth, Lieutenant Colonel Emmet Rucker's crew was flying the number two aircraft in a six-ship Alpha lift against a heavily forested enemy base camp area target at the extreme southern tip of Vietnam (target number 4-20-3-67#2). The mission had taken heavy ground fire, including automatic weapons, and was just reaching the safety of the coast when number two's left engine exploded. The crews in the following aircraft watched in horror as the nacelle fuel tank was jettisoned from the burning engine and then the plane rolled over and crashed into the shallow South China Sea just off the shoreline, the tail of the aircraft sticking up out of the muddied waters. The remaining planes circled the site as a nearby patrol boat was summoned, but the crew had been killed instantly.[22]

The tragedy was compounded when an A-37 fighter escorting the Bravo lift at the same time was shot down during an initial pass, just as the spray planes descended to the start-spray point. The spray crews and the pilots of the A-37 unit (604th Air Commando Squadron [Fighter], known by its call sign, RAP) were particularly close since both were stationed at Bien Hoa. On 29 May, a joint service for the four airmen was held in the Bien Hoa Chapel.[23]

Again "Dame Fortune" had intervened to trade one man's life for another's. Staff Sergeant Billy D. Rhodes was scheduled as flight mechanic on Rucker's crew, while Sergeant Herbert E. Schmidt was assigned as duty driver for the day. Schmidt, however, had an appointment to have a tooth pulled in the afternoon. Since the Alpha lift would be back in time, and Schmidt then would have the rest of the day off to recover, he asked Rhodes to trade duty assignments. With the approval of the chief engineer, the trade was made, and Rhodes missed the fatal sortie.[24]

Despite the losses, by June the squadron had increased to 21 aircraft and maintenance was kept especially busy removing spray equipment from outgoing aircraft and installing it on new arrivals. On 13 June the first "all-jet" spray mission was flown against target number 3-2-1-66#1, near Ham Tan, using three UC-123Ks. Most of the time, however, the two models were intermixed; they were totally compatible, with the exception of the shorter range of the K models due to the higher fuel consumption. Even the range problem was partially solved in June as herbicide reservicing and refueling facilities were established at Nha Trang and Phu Cat. Now the squadron could fly a mission out of Bien Hoa or Da Nang into the central highlands, turn-around at the new facilities, and fly a second mission during the return. Due to the backlog of targets, this was a long overdue improvement.[25]

The 12th ACS nearly suffered another fatal flight on 16 June, this time along the Saigon River. The attack involved heavy suppression, with CBU planned along the right side of the spray track to help protect the six-ship spray formation with weapons effects and billowing white smoke; however, the smoke drifted onto the spray route and when the herbicide planes broke into the clear, they came under heavy fire. The number five aircraft took seven hits, mostly in the cockpit area. The flight engineer in the rear console box heard the copilot say that the pilot had been hit, and then the copilot began making gagging sounds. Thinking he was the only one alive, the flight engineer left his armored box and ran forward to the cockpit, hoping to keep the aircraft airborne. He found both men alive; the pilot had been struck by flying glass fragments and the copilot had been hit in his ceramic vest by a bullet that then glanced off and struck him in the throat-protective collar, a device developed as a result of the loss of Captain Davie the year before. The hard blow to the Adam's apple had rendered the copilot temporarily unable to speak. The life-saving vest, with the slug still stuck in the collar, was prominently displayed in the RANCH HAND personal equipment area, and the badly shaken crewmen were given several days to rest and recover in the more serene surroundings of Clark AFB in the Philippines.[26]

In June the squadron temporarily said good-bye to the still uncamouflaged Patches when the symbolic aircraft left the insecticide flight to return to the United States for modification as a K model. At the same time, a VNAF C-119 "gunship" squadron moved onto the west ramp with RANCH HAND. Together with an A-1 fighter refit program that occupied the spray squadron's only hanger, this further jammed an already overcrowded aircraft parking area, forcing senior officers to begin planning for a new facility to house the herbicide unit. Despite the problems on the ground, the squadron managed to fly 677 sorties, spraying 485,000 gallons of chemicals and collecting another 47 hits.[27]

The June hit total was well below the squadron average, but the potential for a large increase was nearly realized when the Da Nang detachment almost attacked one of the most hazardous targets in Vietnam. The A Shau Valley, along the Laotian border, was completely under enemy control, and head-quarters decided that it should be completely resprayed in June. Extra planes were sent north to give the detachment a six-ship formation. Intelligence reports identified 37-millimeter antiaircraft gun sites and heavy automatic weapons along the entire run on both sides. The RANCH HAND crews prepared to go, but for once they showed little enthusiasm and there were no jokes or humor at the morning briefing; the crew members seriously expected that no more than one of the six aircraft would make it back from the valley target. At the last minute, Seventh Air Force cancelled the mission; Major John Stile, the squadron flying safety officer, had called herbicide representatives at headquarters and finally convinced them of the extreme danger as opposed to the reduced importance of the target. The cancellation was not greeted with cheers, but the emotional relief among the airmen was obvious.[28]

As the crews found out in July, the recent low ratio of hits to sorties was not because the Viet Cong were not trying. On the second of the month, a 6-ship formation on a target near Ca Mau in IV Corps took 29 hits. Another July six-ship mission met a water-mounted enemy weapon. The target was a river bank and the formation was partway through the run when lead reported taking fire from a .50-caliber weapon on a boat in the river. Lead was hit; then, in order, numbers two and three reported being hit, as did four and five. As the crew of number six, closest to the river and most vulnerable, made themselves as small as possible in preparation for their share of enemy missiles, an escorting F-100 put a 500-pound bomb right into the middle of the boat, and the ground fire stopped. Missions like these added another 131 hits to the squadron accumulation in July, causing total recorded hits to exceed 3,000.[29]

The large amount of ground fire in IV Corps, in spite of heavy suppression tactics, forced Seventh Air Force to temporarily suspend defoliation operations in this area while the "high threat" to RANCH HAND was evaluated. The reduced availability of targets in the south was compensated for by transferring three aircraft north, increasing the Da Nang detachment to seven aircraft. The importance of RANCH HAND's work to friendly forces in the peninsular area, however, was underscored when "US Advisory personnel [in] IV Corps ... strongly petitioned for the resumption of defoliation efforts in the region." The Seventh Air Force reevaluation led to a change in heavy suppression tactics, placing emphasis on preventing the enemy from firing on the spray planes. This was a shift from the previous practice of saving ordnance for poststriking enemy positions revealed by the spray run. Eventually, missions to the southern corps area were resumed.[30]

Another milestone was passed in July 1968 when RANCH HAND sprayed its 4 millionth acre, but the aircrews took little time for formal celebration. During the month the squadron flew 631 sorties, spraying 412,000 gallons of defoliants. The totals would have been higher, except for frequent mission cancellations due to weather and several instances where missions were aborted because of friendly troops in the target area (precluding attacks by the fighters), mainly in I Corps. Another factor reducing spray sorties was the high rate of severe battle damage, particularly at Da Nang. For example, the Da Nang detachment attacked a new target southwest of Hoi An four times during July, with heavy damage each time. On the sixth of the month, 13 hits left only one aircraft in commission, and the second lift had to be cancelled. When the detachment returned to Hoi An a few days later, four of the five aircraft were damaged by 16 hits, and one of the pilots, Lieutenant Colonel Bryce C. Conner, earned his second Purple Heart. A third attack on the eighteenth was hit only eight times, but three planes were knocked out of commission. Heavy suppression by six escorting F-4 fighters from the 366th Tactical Fighter Wing on 21 July finally kept the enemy's heads down; the only fire taken was during descent to the spray-on point. Lead was hit once and number four took six hits. Unfortunately, even the use of protective CBU-2 had its cost. Shortly after completion of the final runs on the twenty-first, American Marines moved into the area. Not all of the ordnance used by the 366th fighters had gone off; when a Marine kicked an unexploded CBU-2 bomblet, he lost a leg.[31]

On 1 August 1968, the 315th Air Commando Wing was redesignated the 315th Special Operations Wing (SOW), a title that more clearly described the multitude of tasks assigned to this organization. The subordinate units, including the 12th, were also retitled as Special Operations Squadrons (SOS), but there was no change in the spray squadron's mission. Justification for continuation of the herbicide program was again provided to CINCPAC by another MACV report citing field commanders who, "without exception, state that herbicide operations have been extremely effective in assisting in the Allied combat effort."[32]

Because weather in northern South Vietnam was usually better than in the south during the late summer, on 18 August the Da Nang detachment was increased to 11 aircraft. The plan was to fly 18 sorties a day from Da Nang and only 6 from Bien Hoa, but nature was not cooperative. Only 5 sorties got on target the first day of expanded operations, 12 the second day, and 5 again on both the third and fourth days. By the time the weather improved, the detachment was being harassed by frequent enemy rocket attacks and an epidemic of flu among the aircrews. On 23 August a major VC rocket attack against Da Nang was coordinated with a ground assault against the city. Although the attacks were beaten back, Vietnamese personnel did not come to work on base for several days, severely curtailing a number of operations, including the herbicide storage and servicing facility. Spray crews also came under ground fire immediately after take-off from Da Nang—an unsettling experience. By the twenty-fifth, seven pilots and three navigators were grounded with the flu; there were not enough crew members to man all the aircraft. Even some of those who continued flying should not have done so—complications from the flu caused Lieutenant Colonel Larry Waitt, the squadron navigator, to hyperventilate in flight, and he was carried off the plane gasping for air.[33]

In the meantime, the aircraft left at Bien Hoa also faced nightly rocket and mortar attacks. When the VNAF bomb dump was hit on 22 August, an estimated 800 bombs blew up; the concussion tore doors loose all over the base and threw shrapnel into quarters and aircraft ramp areas two miles away. Later the same morning, four rounds landed next to the runway just as a RANCH HAND flight taxied into position for take-off. On the thirtieth a large napalm storage area on the north side of the base was hit and burned furiously. Overall, for the month of August, the two spray locations managed to launch 572 sorties, but sprayed only 367,000 gallons of herbicides.[34]

September was an even worse month for the spray crews—539 sorties put only 273,000 gallons of chemicals on target. More rocket attacks and heavy battle damage to aircraft at Da Nang reduced the number of planes the detachment could launch, and the situation was complicated on 4 September by the arrival of Typhoon "Bess." Even with sandbags on the wings and extra tie downs, one aircraft was damaged by being blown around in its revetment. Most affected by the storm were the maintenance personnel, who were housed in tents—the typhoon winds literally tore these flimsy shelters apart. Despite living in makeshift quarters in the operations building, maintenance crews had the planes ready to go when the typhoon abated four days later.[35]

Bad weather continued to plague the Da Nang detachment, and on 29 September it was decided to return six aircraft to Bien Hoa. To the consternation of RANCH HAND personnel, they were ordered to reconfigure these six aircraft and two others for airlift duty for an estimated 30 days. A critically large backlog of air cargo had developed, primarily due to the same bad weather that hindered spray operations, and 834th Air Division officers felt that the UC-123s could be more effectively used in an airlift role. The spray officers disagreed. Although the February airlift conversion obviously had been an emergency, the October change was regarded as unnecessary and disruptive to the squadron's primary mission. During the actual 45 days of airlift, the eight converted spray planes flew 1,141 sorties. One aircraft was heavily damaged when it landed gear-up at a forward airstrip. RANCH HAND commanders whose tours included this period were extremely critical of the airlift diversion and of the effect it had on spray operations.[36]

Criticism of a secondary airlift role for RANCH HAND seemed to have considerable validity. During the summer, Phase II airlift training for pilots destined for the spray squadron had been eliminated at Hurlbert AFB, and in October in-country airlift training for spray pilots also was stopped. This meant that in a very short time the 12th Squadron would no longer have any pilots even marginally trained for this mission. The changes in the training program made it appear that Air Force Headquarters did not intend for spray crews to augment the airlift force, but a clear directive to that effect was not forthcoming, and the issue remained confused.[37]

On the brighter side, at a press conference in Washington at the end of September, officials termed defoliation "a complete success" and reported it "unquestionably saved allied lives," while announcing that about 3,500 square miles of South Vietnam (approximately 5 percent of its area) had been defoliated thus far. On 15 October the spray squadron celebrated this testimonial to their work, and the second anniversary of the squadron, with a "RANCH-In" at Bien Hoa. Even the personnel from Da Nang flew in for the occasion, after their lifts were completed. Guest of honor was the new Seventh Air Force Commander, General George S. Brown. The herbicide squadron also invited Premier Ky, but the invitation was discreetly withdrawn when it was suggested that it might be interpreted as supportive of Ky in his power struggle with President Thieu. Traditionally RANCH HANDs did not allow speeches at their dining-ins, by the simple expedient of shouting speakers down with rude remarks and drenching them with whatever liquid was most handy. In deference to General Brown, however, the RANCH HAND Commander, Lieutenant Colonel Arthur F. McConnell, by threatening almost every penalty up to and including the firing squad, managed to convince the unruly squadron members to remain on their best behavior. Unfortunately, the general had been warned of the RANCH HAND tradition and, in the expectation of being shouted down, had not prepared any remarks. When called upon to speak, General Brown gave a less than inspiring talk as the spray crewmen quietly waited for the after-dinner toasts to begin.[38]

Even while toasting their anniversary, crew members knew they were about to return to the hazards of spraying the Ho Chi Minh Trail in Laos after a nine-month absence. On 17 October seven UC-123s staged through Pleiku for an attack on the trail just south of Attopeu. At Pleiku the crews briefed with pilots of the 6th SOS, who were to provide heavy suppression with six A-1 fighters. Normally the rules of engagement for A-1s prevented them from expending ordnance at the low level required by the spray planes, but an exception was made in this case by Seventh Air Force. Clearance for the mission had been arranged by the American Ambassador to Laos, William Sullivan, but only six herbicide planes were authorized to proceed over Laos; the seventh UC-123K took off as an airborne spare and orbited just short of the Laotian border during the mission.[39]

Despite the heavy suppression tactics of the fighter escorts, shortly after starting the run, the formation flew over an antiaircraft battery whose fire damaged all six aircraft. The flight also took intense small-arms fire from a NVA regular regiment camped along the road. Heaviest hit was Major Frank Moore's plane, which lost an engine and later had trouble extending landing gear. Number four's right engine quit just after landing at Pleiku and it had a two-foot hole in the right wing; three aircraft had flat tires from hits. One of the A-1 escorts also was hit and had to nurse his fighter back to base with a rough-running engine. Despite the damage, all herbicide aircraft made the complete spray run. Five of the most heavily damaged UC-123s were left at the central highlands base and the crew members piled on board the spare aircraft for return to Bien Hoa, and a party. The planes were later repaired and returned to their home base.[40]

In an attempt to reduce enemy ground fire, someone suggested dropping tear gas bombs ahead of the spray planes to blind enemy gunners. Of course this tactic forced the spray crews to wear protective masks during the run, a hindrance to communication and to aircraft control, in addition to being miserably uncomfortable. More importantly, the irritant gas failed in its purpose when a trial run in October on a target near Vung Tau still took hits; the scheme was quickly abandoned.[41]

On 31 October 1968, RANCH HAND returned to the An Xuyan target area where Lieutenant Colonel Rucker's crew was lost. The squadron had attempted this target only once since the fatal mission in May—a six-ship formation on 2 July again came under extremely intense ground fire and was hit 29 times, in spite of heavy suppression by escorting fighters. For the October return, even heavier suppression was planned, with ten F-100 fighters from the 90th Tactical Fighter Squadron at Bien Hoa striking preassigned targets just before the spray formation flew over the sites, and delivering heavy ordnance at minimum safe distance in front of the spray planes throughout the run. The tactic worked; no ground fire was reported and none of the planes were damaged.[42]

The continued arrival of K models and departure of B models left the 12th Squadron with only four unmodified aircraft by the end of October. To the great joy of the RANCH HANDs, one of the October arrivals was Patches, still without the mottled camouflage of the other aircraft, but proudly sporting the jet engines of a K model. (Rumor had it that an inordinate number of strings were pulled to insure that the beloved aircraft was not painted while undergoing modification.) Patches was temporarily returned to flying defoliation missions, and on 17 November, while leading a formation spraying a VC-controlled island off the delta (target 4-20-1-68), hit a fruit bat and sustained a broken nose. The distinctive silver plane, always the lead aircraft on herbicide missions, added several more hits to its substantial total before being returned to safer mosquito control duty.[43]

November also found the squadron involved in a highly classified mission into Laos, at the covert invitation of the Laotian government. The mission began when Lieutenant Colonel Phillip Larsen, OIC of the Da Nang detachment, and his targeting officer, First Lieutenant Lloyd West, were ordered to Udorn Air Base, Thailand, for a special briefing, where they learned the target was a large area of rice fields approximately 40 miles north of Vientiane, Laos, in the Nam Sane and Nam Pa Valleys. In civilian clothing, the officers boarded an Air America transport plane for a survey flight over the area. On 5 November the spray crewmen flew another aerial survey of the target, this time using an unmarked RANCH HAND aircraft. Noting the sparseness of crops in the designated area, the targeting officer assumed the mission was more a political gesture than a military necessity.[44]

On 11 November Colonel Larson returned to Udorn with four UC 123Ks. For the next four days the spray planes attacked various targets in Laos. Some friction developed between the Forward Air Controllers and the RANCH HAND navigators, however, with the FACs refusing spray clearance on some excellent crop targets and directing attacks on other targets that were not within the briefed area. During the eight lifts, the spray planes were hit four times. After the final mission, the detachment returned to Da Nang, where they put on a demonstration on arrival by trailing purple smoke from their tail-booms as they made an echelon fly-by and then tossed out drogue chutes on landing, in parody of fighter planes. Although the crews questioned the effectiveness of their mission to Laos, they enjoyed the almost stateside atmosphere of the base in Thailand; before leaving, they threw a party in the officers' club that left no doubt among the permanent party officers that RANCH HAND had been there.[45]

By December the squadron had increased to 25 aircraft, almost all K models. On the thirteenth the worth of the jet modification was proven once more on a target only 15 miles north of Bien Hoa. Just as the formation finished spraying and began climb-out, the lead aircraft came under intense automatic weapons fire. Almost immediately the aircraft started a hard roll to the left, which could be corrected only by full deflection of the control wheel by both pilots and full power on the left jet engine, with the right jet in idle. A check by the flight mechanic found that the left aileron was deflected full up and the control cable was severed. Eighteen hits in the forward section also had knocked out the nose steering hydraulic mechanism and the left main tire. After the crew determined they could keep the wings level by using full aileron trim, full right aileron, a large amount of right rudder, and differential power, they decided to attempt a landing at Bien Hoa. On touchdown, the crew discovered the normal braking system also was inoperative, but judicious use of emergency brakes and reverse power on the right engine kept the aircraft on the runway after a partial ground loop. The skill of the crew and the fact they were using a K model saved this sortie from a fatal conclusion, although the aircraft was so badly damaged that it was out of commission for 25 days. Realizing what the result would have been if the plane had been a B model, the squadron suspended further use of the few remaining unmodified aircraft for spray missions.[46]

On 20 December 1968, the Seventh Air Force commander personally decorated the squadron with the Presidential Unit Citation during change-of-command ceremonies in which Lieutenant Colonel McConnell was replaced as squadron commander by Lieutenant Colonel Rex K. Stoner. During the year RANCH HAND had flown 5,745 herbicide sorties, 280 mosquito control sorties, and 3,987 airlift sorties. Over 4.6 million gallons of herbicides had been used to clear lines of communication, reveal enemy base camps and staging areas, and limit enemy ambushes and assaults on friendly forces. Attacks on enemy food supplies also continued during 1968; however, the emphasis away from crop targets became evident as the number of sorties used on this mission dropped during the last half of 1968, from 15 percent of the total effort to 5 percent.[47]

The decrease in total herbicide sorties from the previous year was due partly to the diversions to airlift. Requests by field commanders for defoliation missions continued to increase. There was every indication that the herbicide program would remain a viable part of the war effort, with operations maintained at least at the 1968 rate. The annual cost to RANCH HAND had been one aircraft destroyed and three crewmen killed. The 733 hits during 1968 represented a significant decrease from the previous year, but Major General Gordon F. Blood's end-of tour report reminded officials that the increasing number and size of automatic weapons and antiaircraft guns in South Vietnam "will continue to increase the hazard of Ranch Hand operations."[48]

An unusually large crop target in an inland valley in II Corps is attacked by a RANCH HAND three-ship flight in September 1967. Photo courtesy of author.

A RANCH HAND ground crewman operating the Orange herbicide servicing system. His unconcern over any danger is indicated by the lack of specialized protective clothing. Photo courtesy of Lieutenant Colonel Arthur F. McConnell, Jr., USAF (Ret.).

126

Defoliation run over rolling scrub brush, near Highway 21 leading to Ban Me Thout, west of Dalat, Vietnam, 1967. Photo courtesy of Lieutenant Colonel Charles J. Meadow, USAF (Ret.).

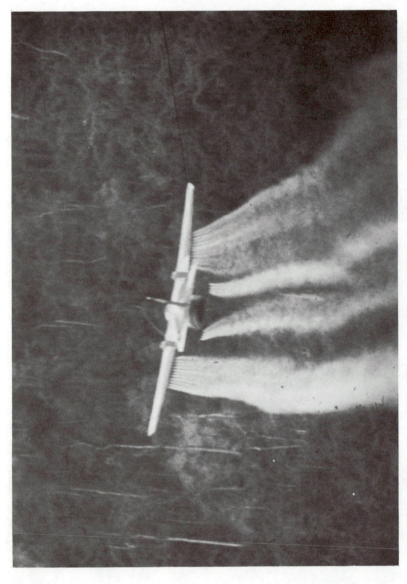

A UC-123 spray plane getting "deep" into its work on a target in Vietnam. The spray pattern from wing- and tail-booms is clearly visible, as are the dangerous bare tree trunks sticking up out of the heavy vegetation. Photo courtesy of Major Lloyd A. West, USAF.

The spray pilots took great pride in their precision formation, on target and at altitude. Clearly visible is the wing-boom on the camera aircraft. Photo courtesy of the author.

UC-123 RANCH HAND "Provider" over South Vietnam, 1967. Photo courtesy of Major John E. Brady, USAF (Ret.).

The contrast between defoliated and untouched cultivated fields is starkly obvious in this overhead view of a downed transport. Note especially the overspray across the road where the herbicide possibly was not turned off quite soon enough by one or two of the aircraft. Photo courtesy of the author.

Defoliated jungle area clearly exposes trails and pathways to aerial view and attack. Photo courtesy of Lieutenant Colonel Arthur F. McConnell, Jr., USAF (Ret.).

The effects of defoliants are clearly shown by this 1968 photo of the Rung Sat area between Saigon and the sea. The ruler edge of the spray pattern graphically demonstrates the precision with which the herbicide could be applied. Photo courtesy of Lieutenant Colonel Arthus F. McConnell, Jr., USAF (Ret.).

The excellent visibility provided in this multiple-sprayed jungle leaves little concealment for the enemy. The bomb craters indicate that airpower had already taken advantage of RANCH HAND's efforts. Photo courtesy of Lieutenant Colonel Arthur F. McConnell, Jr., USAF (Ret.).

RANCH HAND adopted the U.S. Forest Service poster as their own, with a slight modification in text. Photo courtesy of Major John E. Brady, USAF (Ret.).

Herbicide servicing area at Bien Hoa, South Vietnam. The 55-gallon drums scattered in the foreground are clearly marked with an orange stripe. The stains on the ground are likely the result of herbicide spills or leaks from the herbicide hydrant system. Photo courtesy of Lieutenant Colonel Arthur F. McConnell, Jr., USAF (Ret.).

Map 5: Reproduction of Department of Defense systems Analysis plots of mission coordinates for defoliation missions in South Vietnam between January 1965 and February 1971.

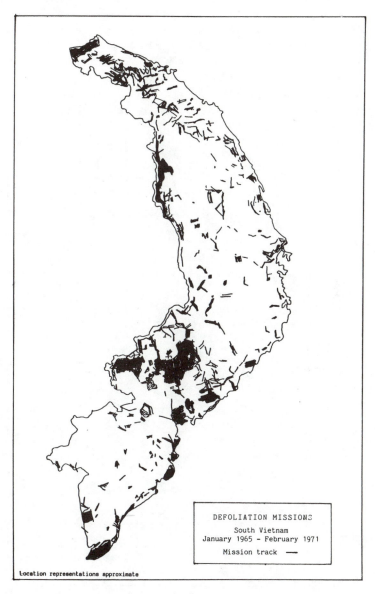

DEFOLIATION MISSIONS
South Vietnam
January 1965 - February 1971
Mission track ——

Location representations approximate

Source: U.S. Department of Defense, Assistance Secretary of Defense, System Analysis, *A Systems Analysis View of the Vietnam War:* vol. 5, *The Air War,* ed. Thomas C. Thayer (Washington, DC, 1975), 184–87.

Map 6: Reproduction of Department of Defense systems analysis plots of mission coordinates for crop destruction missions in South Vietnam Between January 1965 and February 1971.

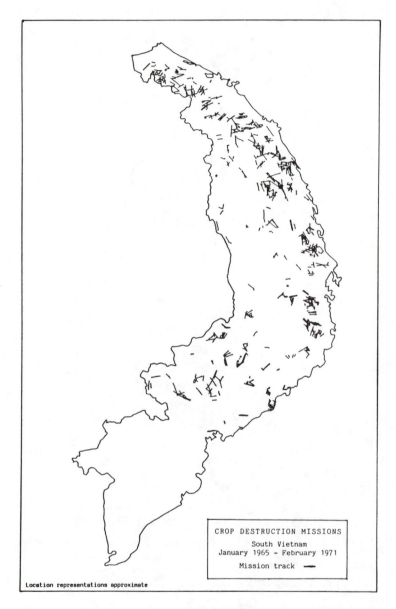

Location representations approximate

CROP DESTRUCTION MISSIONS
South Vietnam
January 1965 - February 1971
Mission track ➤

Source: U.S. Department of Defense, Assistance Secretary of Defense, Systems Analysis *A Systems Analysis View of the Vietnam War: 1965–1972,* vol. 5, *The Air War,* ed. Thomas C. thayer (Washington, D C , 1975), **184–87.**

138

11

The Final Years

Militarily 1968 had been a victory for the Allies in Vietnam as they defeated major VC/NVA offensives in February, May, and June, although additional American troops had to be rushed to Vietnam to bolster General Westmoreland's forces. Heavy losses were inflicted on the attackers by Allied ground units, aided by 840,117 USAF combat sorties during the year. By mid-year North Vietnam had agreed to begin peace talks in Paris aimed at ending the war, and the United States had begun a "Vietnamization" program, building up the South Vietnamese Armed Forces to assume a greater role in the security of their country, allowing the start of US combat troop withdrawal. Politically, however, the year was a disaster for the American administration. Soundly defeated in the Democratic primary in New Hampshire, facing a rising tide of criticism of the war, and embarrassed by the Pueblo incident, President Johnson ordered a halt to US bombing of the North and announced that he would not run for a second full term as president. A change of candidates did little to assuage voter discontent with the drawn-out conflict. Republican Richard Nixon defeated the Democratic nominee, Hubert Humphrey, in the presidential election in November, having pledged in his campaign to bring American troops home and to win an honorable peace, although he warned that the United States might first have to make a greater effort. To American fighting men stationed in Vietnam, the 1969 New Year's Day seemed little different from the previous year.[1]

Neither the change in administrations nor increased Vietnamization seemed likely to affect RANCH HAND, particularly since the VNAF had no equivalent unit with which to assume herbicide responsibilites. The departure of the last B model aircraft in January 1969 left the squadron only the safer K model UC-123s, and the programmed arrival of more modified aircraft from the United States implied an increasing role for herbicides in Vietnam.[2]

RANCH HAND's continuity seemed further confirmed by the occupancy of improved facilities at Bien Hoa. In January 1969, after two years of "making do" with marginal facilities on the west ramp, squadron operations and command sections moved into a new, air-conditioned building, designed especially for RANCH HAND. An adjoining facility was under construction for the maintenance section, as was a new spray aircraft parking ramp that included a special hydrant system for servicing herbicides. This new parking area was badly needed since Bien Hoa was crowded with 515 aircraft assigned to various base units—over one-fourth of the total aircraft stationed at the ten primary air bases in South Vietnam. Unfortunately, construction delays precluded completion of the ramp for almost a year, leaving the operations section and the aircraft parking area over two miles apart. The aircrews remained in substandard quarters, midway between the two sites.[3]

Parking space and housing were not the only problems the herbicide squadron faced. Virtually every RANCH HAND commander complained at one time or another that the UC-123, despite its splendid ability to absorb punishment and continue flying, was too slow and vulnerable to increasingly sophisticated enemy weaponry. If herbicide operations were to continue, a more efficient delivery system was needed. A hint of USAF research and development in this area occurred in January when F-4E "Phantom II" fighters, equipped with modified 370-gallon fuel drop-tanks, were used experimentally to spray several swaths in Laos. At 550-knots airspeed, the F-4Es covered a 100-foot-wide, 16-kilometer-long area in only 70 seconds; it was assumed that with this brief exposure time they would not need other fighter escort. During the tests, however, one F-4E spray plane was shot down by enemy ground fire—evidence that speed was not the total answer.[4]

In the meantime, RANCH HAND had to rely on the obsolescent twin-engine transports. In addition to continuing attacks throughout South Vietnam, on 17 January seven spray planes flew to Ubon, Thailand, to attack a special target in Laos the following day. The mission was uneventful, and the planes returned to Vietnam without being hit.[5]

By mid-February intelligence estimates pointed to another major attack on Bien Hoa. To prevent damage to spray aircraft and disruption of the mission, all in-commission aircraft were moved to Phan Rang Air Base on 22 February; a wise move since a four-hour mortar attack on Bien Hoa destroyed two US aircraft and damaged eight others the next day. Three days later, the "24 hour Battle of Bien Hoa" began. Two enemy battalions dug in just east of the base were attacked by units of the US 11th Armored Cavalry and RVN Marines, Rangers, and cavalry. Around-the-clock close air support was furnished by Army "Cobra" helicopters, USAF F-100s and F-4s, VNAF A-1Es, and numerous gunships. The Allied force drove off the enemy, which lost 141 dead and 50 captured.[6]

The spray aircraft remained at Phan Rang until 3 March, although the base lacked herbicide servicing facilities. This forced the first lift to take-off from Phan Rang, attack the first target, and then recover for refueling and reherbicide at Bien Hoa. After the second lift the spray planes again landed at Bien Hoa to reload herbicide before proceeding to Phan Rang for the night, a workable but inconvenient procedure that reduced time available for maintenance of the oft-repaired aircraft. Also taking part in the daily rotation was Patches. In December the silver UC-123 had gone to Taipei, Formosa, where an IRAN (Inspection and Repair As Necessary) contract facility had been established for the assault transports, and it returned to the RANCH on 1 February, resuming duty as the bug bird just in time to participate in the Phan Rang shuttle, since that base also did not have malathion servicing facilities.[7]

In addition to time lost on the Phan Rang rotation, weather continued to have a serious effect on spray operations—sortie losses varied from 12 percent in the best weather month to 52 percent in the worst. Battle damage in the first three months of 1969, however, was surprisingly light, with only 95 hits confirmed for the entire quarter. A total of 1,485 on-target sorties sprayed 1,237,535 gallons of herbicides, but the amount could have been higher—240 sorties were nonproductive air aborts.[8]

The low hit rate of the first quarter did not last long. When the 1969 Tet holiday offensive tapered off, enemy resistance to the spray planes increased, repeating a pattern established in previous years. An example occurred on the priority defoliation target at Truc Giang in the Delta, where a seven-ship RANCH HAND formation suffered heavy damage while attacking an enemy base camp area on 7 April. Three passes were scheduled over the target, each on a different heading. On the first pass, six of seven aircraft were hit by ground fire—two planes lost engines and returned to Bien Hoa. The five remaining aircraft reassembled and pressed the attack; on the second pass, all aircraft were hit again, and the formation was forced to break off the mission. Most seriously damaged was Major Jack Wolf's aircraft in the last position, which suffered wing damage and lost aileron control. Maintaining limited directional control by varying engine power settings, the damaged aircraft was flown to an unpaved airstrip at Ben Tre, where the crew found a C-130 transport blocking the runway. The spray pilots had too little control over their aircraft to wait for the larger plane to clear the field, so Major Wolf crash-landed the UC-123 in rice paddies to one side of the airstrip. The crew escaped injury, but the aircraft was damaged beyond repair.[9]

RANCH HAND uncomplainingly returned to the Truc Giang target six times, and received heavy battle damage each time. On the final attack, on 1 May, the spray planes began taking .50-caliber fire at 800 feet while on descent and all six aircraft received damage before the run even started, including loss of the rudder cable on the lead aircraft. All aircraft remained in formation and the entire run was completed, although damage prevented any of the planes from flying the second mission that day.[10]

One of the luckiest crewmembers on the final Truc Giang mission was Captain Ronald Mead, pilot of the number five aircraft. During the run Mead watched in amazement as a .50-caliber hole appeared in his instrument panel; later, on the ground, 14 holes were found in the aircraft, including one in the circuit-breaker panel above the pilot's head. Not until Mead's next mission two days later, however, did he discover that his clear helmet visor, which he left in the stowed position on his helmet during the Truc Giang mission, was shattered. Apparently the bullet that passed through the instrument panel hit the visor edge an inch from Mead's forehead, and then ricocheted into the circuit-breaker panel. In the excitement of the attack, the young officer had not been aware of his close call.[11]

The tail-end aircraft did not always take the most hits. Considerable debate took place among crew members as to which position was most vulnerable, and the flyers incessantly badgered scheduling officers to assign them to the position each thought most likely to take the most hits. The squadron hit board, which indicated each man's current total, was consulted as avidly as any stockbroker ever checked the progress of market quotations. The aim of VC gunners, however, was unpredictable. Only two days after the severe damage to the rear aircraft at Truc Giang, another RANCH HAND formation also took heavy fire. In this instance, the lead aircraft took all 24 hits. Although the pilot, Captain Larry Phillips, was wounded about halfway through the run, he continued the mission to the end of the target, refusing to relinquish the controls until the aircraft was safely at altitude. Phillips had a momento of the mission. The bullet that passed through his oxygen quantity gauge and wounded him struck the front of his armor vest and fell into the vest's front pocket.[12]

Heavy battle damage in April reduced the spray squadron to an average mission availability of only 12 aircraft, a figure that would have been even lower except for the outstanding efforts of maintenance crews. A shortage of spare parts forced maintenance personnel to use time-consuming expedients, such as cannibalizing fuel tanks from one aircraft to another in order to make one operational aircraft out of two out-of-commission planes. In one instance, the entire right wing of one aircraft was exchanged with another. Lack of parts grounded some aircraft for more than three months. Nevertheless, around-the-clock efforts in April resulted in a total of 806 sorties, an unusually high ratio of 65 sorties per plane. Neither the aircrews nor the maintenance men could sustain this effort, however, and total sorties during May and June dropped sharply.[13]

The heavy April workload helped keep the quarterly total at a respectable 1,427 herbicide sorties, dispensing nearly 1.2 million gallons of chemicals. Hits, however, were nearly five times the first quarter total—increasing to 437. More importantly, the majority of these hits were around the cockpit and engine areas, rather in the less critical cargo-compartment area as was previously the case. This was part of the cause for maintenance difficulties, since damaged components from these areas were nearly impossible to replace. For example, while the spray squadron commander was reporting new fuel tank "bladders were simply not available" (one of the most critical supply problems was replacement fuel cells), seven fuel tanks were punctured on a single mission.[14]

Increasingly effective enemy resistance may have been due partly to a lack of secure communications between operating units and controlling agencies. Senior RANCH HAND officers were convinced that many missions were compromised because of poor security. A few officers even questioned the reliability of some Vietnamese officials who were necessarily involved in the approval and coordination of the spray missions. So strong was this suspicion that in at least one case the responsible officer scheduled one target with headquarters while the crew actually planned for another nearby target to which the FAC and fighters could be easily diverted after they were airborne. These suspicions were reinforced by frequent discoveries of VC/NVA agents among Vietnamese civilians and military base personnel throughout South Vietnam, although no one directly associated with herbicide targeting or mission scheduling was arrested. Counterintelligence efforts during the war, however, apparently uncovered only the tip of the iceberg. Numerous enemy agents, including those privy to information at the highest levels of joint Vietnamese/US operations, revealed themselves after the fall of the Saigon government in 1975.[15]

Seventh Air Force, concerned about excessive RANCH HAND damage, had temporarily limited spray activities in IV Corps after the strong resistance met on the Delta targets in April. Then on 22 June a four-ship formation attacking a target at the opposite end of the country, in I Corps near Hoi An, was severely damaged. Because heavy ground fire had been encountered during April and May missions into this same target area, heavy suppression was scheduled in the form of prestrike with 1,500 rounds of artillery fire and over 40 1,000-pound bombs just before the spray run. In addition, eight fighters attacked the target with CBU only seconds ahead of the spray planes. In spite of this unusually heavy protective coverage, "the four aircraft took 62 hits, inflicting damage to engines, nacelle fuel tanks, landing gear, hydraulic systems, cockpit and cargo compartment." The number four aircraft had an engine shot out and lead had its windshield shattered. All three officers in the cockpit of the lead plane were wounded.[16]

Partially because of the Hoi An damage, Seventh Air Force began restricting RANCH HAND from certain targets due to "high threat." The spray squadron commander disagreed with this decision, noting that "100 feet altitude, 130 knots is high threat at any time in SVN." He argued that most damage came from only 4 of 60 current targets and that RANCH HAND knew the targets were "hot," but that pressing military needs made it worth the risk. The herbicide leader pointed out that despite enemy efforts, only one aircraft had been lost in 1969, calling this a "little price to pay for the military gains which were made as a direct result of these missions." Against the wishes of RANCH HAND, however, in August Seventh Air Force declared the entire I Corps region "high threat to herbicide" and the spray planes were briefly withdrawn from Da Nang.[17]

Maintenance problems received some indirect relief through the continuing addition of new aircraft to the squadron in mid-1969, while sortie requirements remained static. By the end of June, 29 UC-123Ks were assigned to the squadron, although not all were actually present. Some aircraft were en route from the United States, while others were undergoing IRAN at Taipei or corrosion control treatment at Kadena Air Base in Okinawa.[18]

RANCH HAND faced another crisis during the second quarter of 1969, when Cambodia once again charged that United States and Vietnamese aircraft had intruded over its territory, spraying chemicals on Kompong Cham Province (the so-called Fishhook area) and destroying 15,152 hectares (37,440 acres) of rubber plantations. According to Cambodian Ambassador to the United Nations Huot Sambath, most area residents suffered from diarrhea, colitis, and vomiting due to herbicide exposure, and local vegetation was badly damaged or destroyed. The US Department of State denied both the border violations and the claim that defoliants used in Vietnam could cause such symptoms. Although diplomatic relations between the United States and Cambodia had been severed in 1965, the United States asked permission to send an inspection team into the damaged area and the Cambodian government agreed. Four scientists visited the region in late June. An unofficial group of scientists later toured the same area in December. Both groups reported evidence of damage that they concluded could only have been caused by an overflight, deeming the chance that it was caused by herbicide drift from operations in adjacent Tay Ninh Province in Vietnam "highly unlikely."[19]

Investigations of the activities of the spray squadron during the period in question (mid-April to mid-May) also were conducted by the Department of Defense. The RANCH HAND commander, leader on one flight charged with violating Cambodian airspace, denied that the formation sprayed Cambodian territory, stating, "There was no way." He pointed out that

> Both ground and air photographs [of the Cambodian damage] showed fantastic results. Sections were "burned" along lines and perfect quadrangles were defoliated. We would have been delighted with such accuracy. In my view, it was done with ground equipment.... [20]

The RANCH HAND commander's statement was supported by findings that no US spray missions were flown in the area of the Dar and Prek Chlong plantations. To have defoliated even the minimum area claimed by the Cambodians, approximately 100 sorties would have had to have been flown by RANCH HAND. The official investigative report of October 1969 concluded the damage was caused by an unknown party. Egbert W. Pfeiffer, member of the unofficial December investigation, was not so circumspect, claiming that the area was "sprayed by a clandestine raid, presumably by Air America." Another member of the private group, Arthur H. Westing, long-time critic of the American herbicide program, reported as "fact" that 173,000 acres of Cambodia were "treated by the U.S. during the previous spring."[21]

While investigations of the Cambodian claims proceeded, the spray squadron continued trying to reduce the growing backlog of targets in Vietnam. On 7 July another milestone was passed when a six-ship defoliation mission took 37 hits from ground fire. RANCH HAND recorded hits now exceeded 4,000. There was little doubt that the total would grow, as 153 hits were added in July and 171 in August.[22]

Generally poor weather and the previously mentioned designation of all I Corps targets as high threat kept the number of sorties below 500 in August; the 424 productive sorties was the lowest monthly total in a year. The figure would have been even lower except for a record-setting three-day effort on 21-23 August when 66 sorties defoliated 35 square miles of forest. Scheduling officers took advantage of the recalled Da Nang aircraft to launch four 12-ship missions during this time.[23]

Even while the spray crews were struggling to overcome the weather and higher headquarters' restrictions, the American press was reporting that the herbicide program would be phased out within a year. Crewmembers downplayed the stories, refusing to believe that a successful weapon, in great demand by field commanders, would be terminated. Rumors of the project's demise were nothing new; similar reports had circulated almost continuously since the beginning. These stories, however, seemed to have more substance, especially after replacements were not provided for the departing administrative officer and squadron NCOIC. Both positions had to be manned on an additional duty basis by other personnel.[24]

Leadership of the squadron underwent a major change during the July-September quarter. Besides the losses noted above, both the commander's and operations officer's positions were filled by temporary incumbents during September. Other replaced personnel included: chief-standardization/evaluation section, chief-navigator section, chief-insecticide section, chief-training and scheduling section, chief targeting officer, safety officer, information officer, supply officer, and all flight commanders.[25]

The spray squadron also was hampered by a lack of experienced pilots. Even though senior officers at wing and division level were aware that "the situation in the defoliation squadron was somewhat different in that the experience, skill, and judgment requirements for copilots were considerably greater than in airlift," by late summer 65 percent of the pilots assigned to RANCH HAND were lieutenants, many newly graduated from the Undergraduate Pilot Training program. Trained only in high-altitude, electronically-assisted navigation and in jet aircraft, these young pilots were eager and capable, but hardly prepared for the demands of the RANCH HAND mission. Unlike their predecessors, the new graduates lacked operational flying experience of any kind, had never flown multiengine conventional aircraft, and were abysmally ignorant of the principles of low-level navigation and basic map reading.[26]

The shortage of senior pilots delayed in-country qualification of the new officers even more, and the squadron was forced to use "copilot-only" qualified personnel in the lead and deputy lead aircraft, instead of having fully qualified pilots in both seats in these critical formation positions as in the past. Careful selection of the best of the young officers for these assignments, together with extra training and rotation of the copilots through the bug bird program to gain additional experience, kept the problem from adversely affecting the primary mission, but it did make the missions more hazardous and put an additional workload on the more experienced pilots in the squadron.[27]

On 31 August RANCH HAND once more deployed five UC-123Ks to Udorn Air Base, Thailand, for a special mission. At the request of the commander of Military Region V in Laos, with the concurrence of the Laotian prime minister and the American embassy at Vientiane, the target was a group of enemy-held rice fields in central Laos. Twenty-eight sorties were flown from Thailand in a seven-day period, using Blue herbicide against the Laotian crop targets. During the mission, the five spray planes were hit 42 times by hostile fire. This operation was so politically sensitive that the unit historical report, classified "Confidential," gave no details of the event, other than to note the deployment to Thailand and remark that "higher headquarters prohibits the documentation of this mission in this report." Even the mission statistics were left out of the quarterly statistical analysis. With the furor over the Cambodian affair not yet died down, headquarters apparently was concerned over further unfavorable publicity should details of the Laotian operation become known.[28]

As the Laotian mission ended, Lieutenant Colonel Stoner relinquished command of the 12th SOS to return to the United States. Acting commander was Lieutenant Colonel Joseph M. Cesario, pending arrival of the new commander, Lieutenant Colonel Warren P. Fisher. Stoner had waged a bitter battle with Wing Headquarters over their numerous disapprovals and downgrading of decoration recommendations for spray crew members. Rumors of a "quota" system at wing level and belief that RANCH HAND mission hazards were disregarded by reviewing officers, prevalent in the spray squadron from its earliest days, seemed confirmed by the increasing number of rejections after March 1969. Thus, it was gratifying to Stoner that just before his departure the squadron was awarded the Vietnamese Presidential Unit Citation, in the form of the Vietnamese Cross for Gallantry with Palm, the first time an entire squadron was so honored.[29]

Seventh Air Force reopened most I Corps targets in September, and RANCH HAND, hoping to take advantage of better weather north of the fourteenth parallel, moved aircraft and crews back into Da Nang. In an attempt to reduce weather cancellations, targeting officers planned geographically separated primary and alternate targets. In spite of these efforts, September was one of the most unproductive months since the squadron was formed—only 246 herbicide sorties were flown. The drastic curtailment in missions was reflected in a similar reduction in hits; in-country missions were hit just 59 times.[30]

In November, shortly after it reached a peak of 33 assigned planes, the squadron was suddenly reduced to 14 aircraft and the excess planes were redistributed to airlift units or returned to the United States. RANCH HAND also lost the use of the herbicide reservicing facility at Nha Trang when the base was turned over completely to the VNAF; the herbicide pit at Phu Cat remained in operation. At the same time, in an attempt to decrease the amount of heavy damage to aircraft, spray tactics were changed to prohibit a second pass if ground fire was received on the first. Of greater effect on the defoliation mission was the decision of the Defense Department to restrict Orange herbicide to "areas remote from population." Continued use of White and Blue herbicides was permitted, but "large scale substitution of BLUE for ORANGE" was prohibited.[31]

Ordering reductions in the program was easier said than done. Allied troops were still in contact with the enemy, and commanders continued requesting defoliation missions to help protect their personnel and camps. Despite TACC's attempt to reduce the monthly mission maximum to 280, as ordered by MACV, scheduled herbicide sorties for the last three months of 1969 averaged 403. Overall, in its last full operational year, RANCH HAND flew 5,274 sorties, dispensing 4.3 million gallons of herbicides; the cost was 1,014 hits and a single aircraft destroyed. RANCH HAND's main effort in 1969 was on defoliation, with less than 5 percent of total sorties used for crop destruction. A major share of the crop missions (42 percent) took place in I Corps, primarily in Quang Nam and Quang Tin Provinces.[32]

On 1 January 1970, the 315th Special Operations Wing was redesignated as the 315th Tactical Airlift Wing (TAW). While the four airlift squadrons were also renamed, the 12th Squadron, in recognition of its unique mission, retained its Special Operations Squadron title. The RANCH HANDs enjoyed a holiday on the first of January because of a 24-hour truce, but a return to targets in IV Corps after the truce was over quickly reminded the crew members that enemy gunners were not on a holiday. A five-ship attack on the U Minh Forest took 14 hits and a three-ship defoliation run over a canal target counted 20 hits, with one aircraft making an emergency landing at Bien Tuy with an inoperative engine. In February a four-ship formation, also on a canal defoliation mission, took 31 hits; the number three aircraft lost complete electrical power, but safely returned to Bien Hoa with the rest of the formation. The casual attitude of the spray squadron toward this enemy fire was reflected by the unit historian—after documenting a list of missions with heavy damage in his quarterly report, he noted that spray planes had been hit on other missions too, but added that he did not list them specifically because "they totalled less than ten hits on any one mission." Apparently being hit less than ten times on a mission was too frequent an occurrence to warrant special attention. The 144 hits on 753 sorties during the January-March period brought the RANCH HAND total to 4,622.[33]

In April increased effort was placed on crop destruction. One of the most challenging missions of the quarter was flown on 10 April against enemy crop targets in the Song Be Valley in Quang Nhai Province. Using three extra aircraft especially deployed from Bien Hoa on the previous day, the Da Nang detachment put seven planes on target. Heavy enemy resistance was expected, and the formation was supported by four F-100 fighters, six "Huey" helicopter gunships, and ten "Cobra" helicopter gunships. Despite this impressive escort, the formation received continuous ground fire throughout the run. After about two minutes, Lieutenant Colonel Warren Fisher, in the lead aircraft, had his right engine shot out, forcing him to dump his remaining herbicide and make an emergency landing at Chu Lai. The other six aircraft stayed on target and completed the run, although all were hit. The flight took a total of 37 hits, including 12 on Fisher's plane, but no one was wounded. A week later a three-ship attack on a II Corps target added another 15 hits—equitably distributed 5 per plane—to the squadron's ever-growing total.[34]

In an attempt to reduce the amount of fire taken by the herbicide planes, heavy suppression with irritant gases was tried once more in early 1970. On 25 January a five-ship attack on the Rach Lang/Rach Duamoi Canal in IV Corps was preceded by "stun gas," but the lead aircraft still took 12 hits. On several other missions, CBU-30, a tear gas munition, was dropped along the target axis approximately ten minutes ahead of the spray run. This was followed by another flight of fighters dropping CBU-24 fragmentary bomblets 10 to 15 seconds ahead of the herbicide formation while they were on target. After a brief trial, however, the use of gas was again discontinued as ineffective.[35]

Another attempted response to increased ground fire involved better protection for the aircrews. New Air Force-designed armor protection for the flight engineer's position at the spray controls arrived to replace the locally made armored box. When this new plating proved unsatisfactory, the squadron reinstalled the original armored box and submitted a deficiency report to headquarters.[36]

Of greater effect on RANCH HAND operations was the decision of Secretary of Defense Melvin Laird in February to approve only $3 million of MACV's request for $27 million for herbicides in fiscal year 1971. Even at the existing reduced level of chemical consumption, this meant that the last of the herbicide would be gone by November 1970. Alternatives were to stretch the available supply by further reducing monthly consumption, or to complete current targets and then restrict remaining stock to emergency requirements only. MACV protested that the need for defoliation-provided surveillance and security was especially important now, with American units beginning to withdraw as part of the Vietnamization policy. If increased funding for additional herbicides could not be found, the Vietnam commander asked permission to save existing chemical stocks for priority targets only.[37]

CINCPAC agreed with the MACV position and recommended that RANCH HAND be reduced to the minimum number of aircraft needed to fly priority missions. On 31 March USAF Headquarters directed reduction of the spray squadron to eight aircraft—six herbicide and two insecticide—by the end of June. Less than three weeks later, on 15 April, all use of Orange herbicide was temporarily suspended by order of Deputy Defense Secretary David Packard, pending study of effects and new usage guidelines. Targets planned for Orange were rescheduled for the slower-acting White herbicide. This action drastically changed the herbicide supply situation in Vietnam, since most on-hand stock consisted of Orange. Only about 100,000 gallons of White herbicide was available for defoliation, less than enough for 30 days of operation even at the reduced consumption levels decreed on 31 March.[38]

A special problem created by suspension of Orange herbicide stemmed from the incompatibility of White and Blue; when intermixed they created a gummy precipitate that clogged pumps, valves, and nozzles. This problem normally was avoided by scheduling planes for at least three Orange sorties between changes of load from White to Blue, thus flushing the system since Orange was compatible with both. Otherwise, a time-consuming ground flushing process was required, which created large amounts of herbicide-contaminated water to be disposed of. Suspension of the use of Orange meant schedulers could not readily switch aircraft from defoliation (White herbicide) to crop destruction (Blue herbicide) or vice versa.[39]

Faced with both a rapidly dwindling supply of chemical and field commanders' continuing persistent calls for defoliation, CINCPAC asked the JCS to lift Orange herbicide restrictions as soon as possible, citing the drastic effect on the mission in Vietnam. While they awaited a higher headquarters decision, RANCH HAND consumed all the White at Bien Hoa and Da Nang and turned to the stock at Phu Cat, where three aircraft picked up the last White herbicide on 8 May. The following day the final RANCH HAND defoliation mission sprayed 2,500 gallons on a target near Bunard airfield, the last of 159 sorties that had dispensed nearly 150,000 gallons of herbicide during the quarter. Only limited quantities of Blue herbicide, the crop destruction chemical, were still available—but there were no mature crop targets at this time.[40]

Meanwhile US and Vietnamese forces were ordered into Cambodian territory in May 1970 to destroy major NVA supply dumps and troop staging facilities in the "Parrot's Beak" region. This invasion triggered a new wave of political unrest and violence on American college campuses, including the Kent State affair, where several protesters were killed or wounded during a confrontation with National Guardsmen. The US/Vietnamese incursion into Cambodia, however, gave RANCH HAND a new mission. On 9 May the squadron was ordered to prepare its herbicide aircraft to drop psywar leaflets and to serve as flare-ships for night illumination sorties. Since only one flare dispenser could be spared from the 56th Special Operations Wing at Nakhom Phanom Air Base, Thailand, to use as a model, RANCH HAND had to manufacture the remainder. Seventh Air Force anticipated that the removal of spray equipment and fabrication of flare dispensers would take 17 days. The 12th Squadron was ready for its first flare mission in six days. The flare sorties required the use of a loadmaster and "kickers" on the crew, neither of which the squadron had. This deficiency was solved by the loan of 5 loadmasters from the 315th TAW and 32 volunteer "kickers" from the squadron's enlisted men.[41]

Only six aircraft were available from Bien Hoa; the Da Nang detachment had been withdrawn on 26 April and four aircraft were transferred to TAC on 15 May. Using procedures developed by the 605th SOS for flare drops and by the 9th SOS for leaflet drops, RANCH HAND actively supported ground forces in Cambodia and Vietnam until the withdrawal from Cambodia left the squadron once more without a mission. The last leaflet and flare drops were made on 4 and 6 July, respectively. During its brief stint away from the chemical mission, the 12th Squadron dropped 2,271 illumination flares and 108.6 million leaflets, flying over 300 sorties.[42]

In the meantime, CINCPAC again asked that the temporary ban on the use of Orange herbicide be permanently resolved, noting that deactivation of the UC-123 squadron depended on the response. Despite a contrary recommendation by the Joint Chiefs of Staff, the Defense Department continued the herbicide restriction, leading on 13 June to a Seventh Air Force request for inactivation of the 12th Special Operations Squadron. Squadron personnel speculated that publicity concerning possible carcinogenic (cancer-producing) and teratogenic (fetus-deforming) properties of herbicide Orange, plus the furor aroused by the Cambodian invasion and the Kent State shooting deaths, made it impolitic for the government to change its original decision.[43]

Space at Bien Hoa was now at a premium. Closure of the airfield at Vung Tau under the American withdrawal program had caused an expansion of US Army and VNAF units at Bien Hoa, further crowding the already over-taxed base. On 28 June Seventh Air Force directed RANCH HAND to relocate to Phan Rang, home of the 315th Wing and its other squadrons, no later than 10 July. Four days later CINCPACAF approval to inactivate the squadron was received, but at MACV's request, the wing was required to "maintain a herbicide capability and continue the insecticide mission."[44]

In actual practice, RANCH HAND temporarily continued without change, except for relocation to Phan Rang and redesignation as "A" Flight of the 310th Tactical Airlift Squadron. While the 12th SOS was officially deactivated on 31 July, the administrative and maintenance functions remained separate from the 310th TAS until 26 September. Thus the flight was virtually a separate entity within the squadron until that date, recalling the 1965-66 period when RANCH HAND was an independent flight of the 309th Squadron.[45]

Even as the spray unit began moving to Phan Rang on 8-10 July, MACV ordered resumption of herbicide missions against crop targets in "Military Regions II and III" (formerly II Corps and III Corps). On 17 July COMUS-MACV reconfirmed that the crop program would be renewed, while fixed-wing defoliation sorties would remain on stand-by. RANCH HAND, however, faced two major problems before it could reinitiate anticrop warfare. First, rotation of experienced crew members and the lack of any spray missions for over two months meant that a spray retraining program had to be instituted. Second, the local province chief refused to permit storage of herbicides at Phan Rang Air Base, forcing spray aircraft to fly to one of three herbicide storage locations to load before each mission.[46]

The solution to the first problem was to establish a training area over a supposedly pacified zone just north of Nha Trang, and requalify all crew members in spray operations. Training flights began on 16 July, but after an aircraft was hit by ground fire, practice was moved to an over-water site. The new location was safer, but unrealistic; it did not prepare pilots for the terrain-following maneuvers required on crop destruction missions. The second problem was solved by scheduling spray missions two days apart; on the intervening days the planes were reloaded with herbicides. The limited number of spray missions made this solution inconvenient, but tolerable. When more sorties were required in a shorter time, the aircraft staged out of one of the herbicide bases for several days, rather than returning to Phan Rang.[47]

During RANCH HAND's two months of flare and leaflet drops, its aircraft had been hit by enemy ground fire only once—a single hit in the nose of an aircraft at 3,000 feet. Enemy antiaircraft skills had not declined during the spray planes' absence, however. On the first crop mission, on 20 July, the formation took 29 hits. Two days later, an attack on a crop target 20 miles west of Nha Trang received 46 hits. Major Dick Claxton's plane was heavily damaged and the major was wounded in the arm; an emergency landing was made at Nha Trang. As a result of this intense enemy resistance, tactics were changed to require crop missions to be flown using heavy suppression— normally CBU-24 or CBU-48 munitions—and the previous loose formation used on crop targets was changed to a close formation, to take advantage of the heavy suppression. The changes apparently were effective, since the remaining 54 sorties during the quarter took only 13 more hits.[48]

Although heavy suppression protected the spray planes, an increasing number of targets had to be cancelled because field commanders or Vietnamese officials would not grant clearance to use CBU in target areas. The US 23d Infantry Division, for example, established blanket denial covering their entire operational area. Even if clearance was received, the mission sometimes had to be scrubbed; on two occasions pre-mission survey flights were unable to find worthwhile crop anywhere in the target box. Aircrew members now were flying too seldom to maintain either interest or proficiency, and several asked for transfer to airlift units, where they would be kept busy. Although the unit was scheduled for 15 missions per month, only 5 were flown in October and again in November, with a single mission launched in December. This low utilization did not justify maintenance of six aircraft and 30 crewman, and the 834th Air Division recommended eliminating the herbicide mission entirely to better use the aircraft and crews elsewhere. Even battle damage had paled into insignificance; the 15 recorded hits in these three months were all .30-caliber projectiles, with damage limited to aircraft skin, except for 1 hit on a herbicide tank.[49]

The chronology of the unit historical report defiantly stated in the 1 December entry: "News releases for the past two months have indicated a complete shut down of all herbicide operations in SEA. RANCH HAND IS STILL IN OPERATIONS." Despite this bravado, the demise of the unit was only matter of time. In October COMUSMACV ordered consolidation of the remaining 1.6 million gallons of Orange herbicide in Vietnam, following instances of unauthorized use by the Army's Americal Division. On 4 December further shipments of Blue herbicide to Vietnam were cancelled by DOD, leaving RANCH HAND insufficient chemical stocks to complete even the targets already approved. Thus, it was no surprise when the White House announced on 26 December that the United States had decided on an "orderly, yet rapid phase-out" of the herbicide program. Meanwhile, the announcement said, there would be "strict conformance in Vietnam with policies governing the use of herbicides in the United States."[50]

Three days later the American Association for the Advancement of Science (AAAS) released a special committee's report that was highly critical of crop destruction in Vietnam. The committee's main finding was that the civilian populace, rather than the Viet Cong, bore the primary burden of the program. The study noted that the same conclusion had been reached earlier by Defense Department-sponsored studies, but had been disregarded by military leaders.[51]

RANCH HAND flew its last three sorties on 7 January 1971, exactly nine years to the day from the arrival of the first C-123 spray planes at Tan Son Nhut airport. The final herbicide mission was against a target in Ninh Thuan Province, not far from Phan Rang. On 28 January the JCS officially cancelled all further USAF crop destruction missions.[52] RANCH HAND crewmen would continue flying the two insecticide aircraft for several months more, but the project to save lives at the cost of vegetation was ended. Only the controversy over the US experiment in herbicidal warfare would go on. Like the other veterans of the war in Vietnam, the members of RANCH HAND, which the press called the most shot-at Air Force unit in South Vietnam, returned home—unwelcomed, unhonored, and unknown.

12

Critics of Herbicidal Warfare: Propaganda, Protest, and Investigations

From the beginning, the herbicide program in Vietnam aroused intense opposition throughout the world, partially as the product of an international movement dating from the 1890s against chemical warfare in general, partly because of scientific concerns for the environment as expressed in Rachel Carson's *Silent Spring,* but in a large measure as the result of propaganda aimed against any and all American intervention in Southeast Asia.[1] As the program in Vietnam grew, so did public outcry, particularly in the United States. Eventually, domestic political pressure helped lead the American government to renounce herbicidal warfare, despite objections from US military officials in South Vietnam who viewed it as necessary to troop security. Ironically, a military weapon specifically intended not to cause direct injury to living beings became the center of a controversy akin to that aroused by the most massive death-causing weapon, the nuclear bomb.

As already noted, intragovernmental discussions concerning the experimental and test phases of the herbicide project revolved at first around balancing potential military gains against the obvious "chemical warfare" propaganda advantage it would give to the North Vietnamese and their supporters. The results of the first tests appeared to favor the latter— "operational benefits of defoliant operations is assessed as only marginal." Colonel Serong, the senior Australian military representative in Saigon, commented that defoliation actually aided ambushers by removing foliage along the roads that could be used for cover by those ambushed. Although this statement was only one person's view, and an erroneous one at that, it was repeatedly quoted by later antiherbicide writers as proof of the uselessness of the project. Roger Hilsman, a constant critic, was one of those who made an

aerial inspection of initial test areas and pronounced them "not very impressive."
Hilsman reported:

> The leaves were gone, but the branches and trunks remained. Even if they had
> not, it was not leaves and trunks that guerrillas used for cover, but the curves
> in the road and the hills and valleys.[2]

These criticisms ignored the experimental nature of the initial efforts—
researchers were trying to determine what chemicals and what amounts would
be effective—and, in at least Hilsman's case, the observer was hardly qualified
to provide a worthwhile evaluation after only a brief glimpse from high above
the test site.[3]

The main issue in Washington was military utility versus political liability.
Defense Department officials generally emphasized the tactical and strategic
advantages of denying cover to the enemy as a vital aspect of a successful
guerrilla campaign. Later, they supported the food denial program primarily
because it would help separate active guerrillas from the general populace
upon whom they were dependent. Politically sensitive strategists, on the other
hand, focused on the negative aspects of the project that could be used by
enemy propagandists to rally world opinion and moral condemnation against
the United States for practicing, even peripherally, a particularly repugnant
type of warfare.[4]

A related question concerned the morality of a means of warfare that
placed a major burden on the civilian population, particularly since they often
appeared either apathetic toward the enemy or supportive of the side favored
by the United States. A constant theme of critics of the crop destruction
program was that differentiation between civilian and VC cultivations was
impossible. Nutritionist Jean Mayer cited historical evidence that wartime
food shortages also strike hardest at "the weakest element of the civilian
population"—children, child-bearing women, and the elderly—while effecting
the fighting men "last and least, if at all." Mayer concluded in 1967 that "from
a military viewpoint, the attempt to starve the Viet Cong can be expected to
have little or no effect."[5]

Defense Department-sponsored studies in 1967 came to the same conclusion. Through interviews with VC prisoners and with civilians from VC-
controlled areas, RAND Corporation researchers determined that, through
coercion, the Viet Cong frequently transferred the burden of deprivation to
local peasants. At the same time, because most crops destroyed were civilian
owned and cultivated, the indigenous population blamed the United States
and the Saigon government for their economic hardships. Local farmers knew
little of the purpose of spray operations in the larger sense, seeing only the
immediate damage to their personal property and their family's welfare by an

apparently indifferent central government and its allies. An indemnification program to compensate innocent and friendly victims of the chemical attacks often failed to provide relief where intended, and thus failed to counter the propaganda advantage the program gave the Viet Cong.[6]

The deciding factor in continuing the initial program, however, was President Kennedy's desire to strengthen the capacity of the United States to counter political instability brought on by guerrilla forces, interventions, and subversion in developing countries. Indeed, Kennedy reportedly had something of an obsession with counterinsurgency warfare in general. At the same time, the opposition of Hilsman and others was somewhat negated by the question of whether common plant-regulating agricultural compounds even fell within the body of proscribed materials associated with chemical warfare. Supporters of the program noted that the original concept of chemical warfare generally assumed the direct use of chemical weapons to cause injury or death to humans and animals, rather than plants. Beyond that, herbicide experimentation was only one very small aspect of Kennedy's expanded conventional counterinsurgency role for the United States armed forces, in place of the Eisenhower reliance on massive nuclear deterrence, thus attracting relatively little attention from those more concerned with the potential consequences of a nuclear exchange between the major powers.[7]

Naturally enough, the strongest initial antiherbicide reactions came from those targeted. Even before the arrival of the first C-123 spray planes in Vietnam in January 1962, local insurgent cadres were planning a propaganda campaign against the herbicide project, based on the effects of the 1961 tests. Villagers were warned that the defoliants were poisonous and were urged to flee the area "into the wind" as soon as spraying was observed. The NLF characterized the chemical attacks as a direct assault on the common people by the foreign-dominated Saigon government, rather than as a counter to the Viet Cong. The major international propaganda effort came from the Soviet Union, which charged that US "chemical warfare" was an "unprecedented action." The United States and South Vietnam were accused of "impairing [the] health of tens of thousands of people." North Vietnam was frequently more specific. An October 1962 Radio Hanoi English-language broadcast claimed that hundreds of people in two Ca Mau villages were severely affected. Radio Hanoi announced on 16 July 1963 that investigation by the "South Vietnam Liberation Red Cross Society" had determined that the United States had used "2,4-D and 2,4,5-T ... white arsenic alkali, alkali earth, calcic cyanamide, and metal arsenites ... [as well as] 2, 4 dinitropheno (DNP) and dinitro-orthocresol (DNC)" in Ben Tre and My Tho. The Hanoi broadcasts regularly reported that "poison sprays" were causing skin eruptions, hemorrhaging, paralysis, blindness, and even death among exposed animals and people. After a Kien Hoa defoliation mission, the Viet Cong asserted that nearly 500,000 people, the bulk of the province population, have been affected more or less seriously. 46,000 of them, mostly women, children, and old folks, are in a grave state.... hundred[s] of people seriously affected were sent to hospitals. Toxic chemicals exerted also a damaging effect on domestic animals. Hundreds of head of cattle were killed by eating poisoned grass. Thousands of others were effected. Tens of thousands of poultry, pigs and dogs died also.[8]

As the American herbicide program expanded, other Southeast Asian groups joined the VC and North Vietnamese in protesting what they termed chemical warfare. Prince Sihanouk of Cambodia provided a unique description in 1963 when he told the people of Peam Ror that the United States was using

a powder to destroy trees completely. When the powder falls on trees, it causes the leaves to fall to the ground, thus exposing the Viet Cong. Therefore, you citizens must take care *lest your hair also falls,* since even the leaves of the trees—which are more solid than our hair—cannot resist the powder.[9]

A year later Cambodia charged that eight United States attacks on six villages in this region (Prey Veng Province) killed 76 people. The Pathet Lao also claimed many people and oxen were poisoned in Cammon Province of Laos by a US plane spraying poisonous chemicals. Both the Soviet newspaper *Izvestia* and the press agency *Tass* echoed accusations that the United States Air Force was using "poison gas" and called for an international investigation of the use of poisonous substances against civilians.[10]

Claims that the United States was killing innocent people in Laos, Cambodia, and South Vietnam with toxic chemicals were regularly repeated, frequently in association with reports that the fatal substance was a yellow powder. According to *Voyennaya Mysl'* (Military Thought), a classified monthly organ of the Soviet Ministry of Defense, the number of South Vietnamese victims of chemical agents increased from 150,000 in 1965 to "several hundred thousand" in 1966. In 1968 "Neo Lao Hak Sat, a representative of the Party Central Committee," reported the death of 200 people in lower Laos as a result of toxic sprays in March and April. In most cases, independent investigators were not allowed to immediately confirm the harm to human beings and animals or to obtain samples of the "poisonous substances." Even when observers were permitted, it was usually well after the time of the incident, when definitive evidence was no longer available.[11]

In light of Cambodian charges in 1964 concerning the use of "poisonous yellow powder," it was significant that a 1968 Soviet article about chemical weapons listed dinitoorthocresol (Russian abbreviation, DNOK), "a yellow powder which is a derivative of nitrophenol," under the heading "toxic characteristics of some of the weed and pest killers being used in Vietnam," although American herbicides used in Vietnam were all liquids, not powders. This article also charged that "American aggressors" were "climbing the stairway of war escalation" while disregarding "morality, conscience and international law." Soviet propaganda peaked in 1971 when Engineer Major L. Nechayuk claimed that during a "perfidious operation . . . massive spraying killed all forms of life—plants, birds, animals, and even human beings." Nechayuk charged "the barbarians from the Pentagon" with launching "chemical warfare on the soil of Vietnam" in violation of the most elemental standards of human conduct and of accepted international law, citing the Geneva Protocol of 1925.[12]

Innovative twists occasionally surfaced amid the barrage of communist charges and stories. In 1966 an attempt to influence world Catholic opinion occurred when Joseph Mary Ho Hue Ba, "Catholic representative of the NLF," announced that United States' defoliants were killing newborn babies of Roman Catholic families. It was emphasized that these deaths were particularly reprehensible because they occurred before the babes could be baptized. Later, after initial US reports of 2,4,5-T herbicide-related teratogenic effects on laboratory animals, Hanoi compared the victims of herbicide toxicology to the survivors of the atomic bombings of Nagasaki and Hiroshima, claiming that both suffered the same genetic future of "miscarriages, congenital anomalies and frequent monstrosities." Cuban authorities provided visual propaganda by issuing a series of postage stamps labeled "Genocide in Vietnam." On the stamp depicting the results of chemical warfare, the bodies of dead and dying Vietnamese were shown lying on the ground, supposedly the result of an American chemical attack.[13]

Considerable censure of US policies also came from outside the Communist Bloc countries. The foremost British critic, Lord Russell, compared the use of napalm and herbicides in Southeast Asia to the illegal and immoral warfare of Germany and Japan in World War II, and sponsored an "international war crimes tribunal" to try various US officials *in absentia* on several charges, including "the use of poison chemicals against innocent victims." The defendants included President Lyndon Johnson, Secretary of State Dean Rusk, and Secretary of Defense Robert McNamara.[14]

It was announced that the trial would feature testimony only from people such as journalists, former servicemen, and victims from both North and South Vietnam; no "decision-makers" would be allowed to testify. Besides Lord Russell, the tribunal consisted of 16 prominent leftists, including Dr. Josue de Castro, former head of the United Nations Food and Agriculture Organization, ex-President Lazaro Cardenas of Mexico, French playwright Jean-Paul Sartre, French author Simone de Beauvoir, and Italian lawyer Lelio Basso, editor of the *International Socialist Journal*. Initially, the trial was to be held in either London or Paris, but government opposition in these capitals eventually caused it to convene in Stockholm after a delay of several months. In the interim period, Russell maintained media interest by repeatedly promising to produce "documentary evidence" of toxic chemical effects. When the panel finally met, however, the trial served merely as a reiteration of previous communist propaganda, and Russell's evidence proved to be no more than unsubstantiated statements by several Vietnamese and the diary of a North Vietnamese "doctor." The Royal Shakespeare Company in London took advantage of the notoriety of the subject by performing a play entitled "US," which featured "screams and allusions to napalm, gas, bullets, defoliation, and immolation."[15]

In Japan, Yoichi Fukushima, head of the Japanese Science Council's Agronomy Section, claimed that "appalling inhumane acts" had ruined over 3.8 million acres of land in Vietnam, while destroying more than 13,000 livestock and killing over 1,000 peasants. The Science Council, which included 70 senior Japanese scientists, protested the use of herbicides in war as "an abuse of the fruits of science." Mainland China's Foreign Ministry saw the chemical operations as evidence of the desperation of Western governments, commenting that "all decadent reactionary forces invariably resort to the most ruthless and despicable means in putting up a last-ditch struggle."[16]

This international reaction to the American herbicide program had little immediate impact on the decisions of the United States government; its primary effect was to refocus American scientific attention onto this particular aspect of the war effort. Although the main thrust of Rachael Carson's 1962 publication had been to arouse widespread apprehension over the biological and ecological results of indiscriminate use of pesticides, she also had warned of the unknown consequences of using weedkillers: "The full maturing of whatever seeds of malignancy have been sown by these chemicals is yet to come."[17] Written before the Vietnamese experiments, the author's comments concerned common domestic weedkillers used in the United States, but two of the chemicals she specifically singled out (2,4-D and 2,4,5-T) were primary ingredients in the military herbicides developed for the Asian conflict. Now, as the use of these herbicides expanded in 1965-66, so did the amount of critical literature from within American scientific circles.

Initial articles concerning the herbicide project were little more than informative, but limited, reports of the existence of the program, primarily appearing in major newspapers as part of the continuing coverage of the conflict in Vietnam and in professional military journals, such as *Army* and the *Armed Forces Chemical Journal*. An article in the former magazine in 1963 by Lieutenant Colonel Stanley D. Fair discussed both initial spray tests and operational evaluations, including descriptions of the chemicals used, the methods of application, and the general effectiveness of this tactic. A short discussion (six pages) of the use of herbicides also appeared in a controversial

1963 book by Wilfred G. Burchett which was very critical of the role of the United States in Vietnam and Laos.[18]

The first detailed reports of American chemical operations, however, did not appear in the popular press until 1965, paralleled by several stories describing damage to civilian crops as a result of USAF spraying. These stories caused the Federation of American Scientists to condemn "field testing" by the United States of "weapons of indiscriminate effect," noting that their use would hurt the United States in the long run, "even if military effectiveness in a specific situation can be demonstrated."[19]

The controversy expanded rapidly in 1966, with more descriptions of the herbicide project appearing regularly, both in newspapers and in such diverse publications as *Flying*, *Farm Chemicals*, and *Christian Century*. In January, 29 scientists and physicians from schools and institutions around Massachusetts issued a statement condemning the crop destruction program and urging the president to forbid the use of such weapons. Jean Mayer, of the School of Public Health at Harvard University, added his voice to the protest with a letter in *Science* in April in which he claimed that the entire food denial program would fail in its aim. In September President Johnson received a letter from the American Society of Plant Physiologists indicating their misgivings over the unknown factors involved in chemical herbicides, and he received a petition against chemical and biological weapons signed by over 5,000 scientists, including seven Nobel Prize winners. At their December meeting the American Association for the Advancement of Science passed a resolution establishing a Committee on the Consequences of Environmental Alteration to study the effects of chemical and biological agents.[20]

In an attempt to forestall independent investigations, the Defense Department contracted for a study by the Midwest Research Institute to supplement the various military agency reviews noted earlier. The resultant study, however, was merely a survey of available literature on herbicides, supplemented by interviews and telephone conversations with various experts; it lacked field evaluations and observations of actual effects in Vietnam. Even the literature review was of questionable value since the preponderance of material was related to herbicidal effects in temperate zones, having only tenuous applicability to the tropical vegetation of Southeast Asia. Overall, the 369-page study satisfied neither critics nor proponents of herbicidal warfare. An increasingly vocal group within the scientific community continued to demand an on-scene study of chemical effects and a halt to herbicide use until the study was satisfactorily completed.[21]

In another conciliatory move by the government, the Director of Defense Research and Engineering, John S. Foster, Jr., told the AAAS that "qualified scientists, both inside and outside our government, and in the governments of other nations, have judged that seriously adverse consequences will not occur." While admitting that questions of ecological impact "have not yet been answered definitively," Foster sought to placate the scientists by assuring them that the government would not continue use of herbicides if it was not confident of their safety.[22]

The AAAS was not assured. Its board proposed sending its own investigating team to Vietnam, but financial difficulties, and disputes over who would be on the team and what they would do, prevented positive action in 1967, and again in 1968. The December 1967 convention, in particular, was torn by dissidence, resignations, and interruptive tactics of radical activists supporting various causes. At the Dallas convention in 1968, the AAAS Board finally agreed to a compromise resolution to name a committee to prepare plans for a field study of both ecological risks and benefits. In the meantime, the Society for Social Responsibility in Science arranged to send two prominent scientists, Gordon H. Orians and Egbert W. Pfeiffer, on a 15-day inspection tour of Vietnam during March 1969. In their report, Orians and Pfeiffer urgently called for a major research effort to determine the long-term effects of herbicide use in Vietnam, specifically urging the AAAS to play a leadership role in setting up the organization.[23]

A study of far-reaching consequences for the herbicide issue also came to light in 1969. Five years earlier, in 1964, the National Cancer Institute of the Department of Health, Education, and Welfare had commissioned the Bionetic Research Laboratory of Bethesda, Maryland, to study the carcinogenic and teratogenic effects of several widely used chemical compounds. A preliminary report in 1966 indicated, among other results, that small amounts of 2,4-D and even smaller amounts of 2,4,5-T caused birth defects in laboratory rats and mice. This report apparently did not reach the Food and Drug Administration (FDA) until 1968, and was not seen by Agriculture or Defense Department officials until 1969, when part of the report was made public. The teratogenic results of the study were later verified by Dr. Jacqueline Verrett of the FDA, using chick embryos.[24]

When questioned about why the report was suppressed, a White House staffer reportedly claimed that release of the report would have helped the antiwar movement and added to international criticism of American chemical warfare. An FDA spokesman blamed pressure from chemical companies, particularly Dow Chemical, as the main cause.[25]

The Johnson and Nixon administrations were not alone in suppressing news of possible human-damaging effects of the defoliants. The Saigon government shut down *Tin Sang*, when that Vietnamese newspaper published reports of fetus deformations in Tan Hoi hamlet; three others were also closed down for "interfering with the war effort," after printing stories about deformed infants.[26]

The AAAS finally took the first step toward an independent study of herbicides in Vietnam in December 1969 when the board asked Dr. Matthew S. Meselson, Harvard microbial geneticist and long-time critic of herbicidal warfare, to form an investigative committee. Meselson's group, known as the Herbicide Assessment Committee (HAC) and directed by Dr. Arthur Westing, another foe of herbicide use in Vietnam, made extensive literature studies, interviewed numerous experts, and spent five weeks in South Vietnam during the summer of 1970. By the time the HAC arrived in Vietnam, however, the Department of Defense had banned the use of Orange herbicide. (Ironically, the domestic application of 2,4,5-T was not prohibited by other government agencies until a considerable time later.) The investigation was hampered because HAC members could not directly visit damaged areas due to lack of ground security, limiting them to aerial observation only in most areas of heavy spraying. Committee members also complained about the Defense Department's ill-considered decision not to give them access to records of previous spray mission coordinates. The government's argument that release of this information would compromise target locations was valid only if it was assumed that enemy forces in the sprayed areas did not know where they were.[27]

No one was surprised when the December 1970 HAC report to the AAAS convention found that the program had caused extensive and serious ecological damage to the countryside, and was extremely critical of the crop destruction program, terming it nearly a total failure. The central theme of the report was the need for more extensive investigation in Vietnam and for more research on the effects of herbicides in general. Considering the committee's obvious predisposition against herbicides, the unexpected aspect of the report was its failure to find supporting evidence of herbicide-caused adverse health effects among human beings, although, again, the need for further, more detailed research was emphasized. Nor were stories concerning injury to livestock confirmed. When Westing attempted to verify Montagnard descriptions of the fatal effects of herbicides on chickens by exposing laboratory chickens to all three military herbicides, none reacted as described.[28]

Not all of the scientific community agreed with the conclusions drawn. Several members of the AAAS pointed out that no consideration was given to military combat needs, and that ecological damage had not been weighed against the alternative of higher loss of Allied military lives if the forest cover had not been removed. There was also disagreement over the actual extent of permanent ecological damage.[29]

The question of applicability of the teratogenic tests was raised by one of the major manufacturers of the defoliants, Dow Chemical Company. During 1970 Dow laboratory tests indicated that herbicide-related laboratory fetus deformities could be linked to a trace contaminant in 2,4,5-T. This contaminant, 2,3,7,8-Tetrachlorodibenzo-p-dioxin (TCDD), more commonly known as dioxin, was a complicated chemical byproduct associated with high heat ranges during manufacture. Dow tests of the 2,4,5-T used in the Cancer Institute studies indicated as much as 27 parts per million dioxin contamination.

The chemical producer claimed these samples were from earlier batches of herbicide produced by other companies and that more stringent standards since then (Dow's current standard of manufacture was less than one part per million dioxin) had resulted in a "clean" herbicide, known as Orange II, which would not cause deformities. Critics countered that dioxin was such a deadly poison that any contaminant level was unacceptable.[30]

The real impact of the HAC report, however, took place even before it was presented to the AAAS convention. Furnished with advance notice of the report findings, the White House attempted to mitigate its effect by announcing three days before the AAAS meeting that President Nixon had directed the "orderly phase-out" of the entire herbicide program. This announcement did not satisfy critics, who questioned why the program was not terminated immediately since it seemed that the government at least partially accepted the HAC report. Herbicide supporters were equally unhappy since the White House action made it appear that the American government had bowed to pressure from the scientific community and a few individuals, and removed a weapon from the hands of its fighting men while they were still engaged in combat.[31]

The scientific community was not the only source of pressure on the US government to renounce the use of herbicides. Central to international criticism was the issue of whether defoliant use constituted a violation of international laws banning chemical/biological warfare. Although Senate refusal to ratify the 1925 Geneva Protocol had left the United States as one of the few nonsignatories among the world powers (see Chapter 1), the actions of the several administrations over the next 40 years indicated that the United States actually had accepted the terms of the protocol as binding in principle. In 1969 President Nixon renounced the use of chemical and biological weapons, except in defensive operations, and he asked the Senate to reconsider and approve the 1925 agreement as a further token of American sincerity.[32]

The problem, however, lay in interpretation of the language of the Geneva Protocol. Administration officials felt that tear gas and defoliants were not prohibited by the treaty. Testifying before the Senate Committee on Foreign Relations, Secretary of State William P. Rogers stated:

> Because we do not believe that the protocol imposes any obligations concerning the use of riot control agents and chemical herbicides, it would be both unnecessary and inappropriate for the United States to enter a reservation on this point.[33]

The General Assembly of the United Nations disagreed with the American view. A resolution adopted by the assembly on 16 December 1969 declared that the Geneva Protocol banned the wartime use of all toxic chemicals against animals and plants, in addition to man. The resolution passed by a vote of 80 to 3, with 36 abstensions; only Australia and Portugal joined the United States in voting against the measure. The United States, however, refused to acknowledge that interpretation of international law was an appropriate matter for General Assembly consideration. An unexpected ally in this argument was the Carnegie Endowment for International Peace, which claimed that the proper interpretive body should be the International Court of Justice.[34]

In the meantime, proponents of the herbicide ban based their arguments on the protocol phrase "and of all analogous liquids, materials or devices," which they insisted included such antiplant agents as defoliants and soil sterilizers. The opposing view was that since herbicides were not widely used nor was their military potential realized when the protocol was being drafted, it was therefore impossible for antiplant agents to fall within the restrictions of the agreement. The proherbicide faction also claimed these agents could not be included in the protocol because they were common agricultural chemicals, in routine use in the United States, Soviet Union, and scores of other countries to control weeds and other unwanted vegetation. The counterargument was that it was not how a chemical was used in peacetime that reflected its status in the protocol, but how it was used in war. Although the original treaty was largely a reaction to the horrors of poison gas warfare used during World War I, it was also obviously based on the "unnecessary suffering" principle of the law of war. Thus critics cited harm to people caused by destruction of food and suspected long-term health damage to exposed personnel as justification for inclusion of herbicides within the provisions of the Geneva Protocol.[35]

Superficially, the legalistic dispute appeared a moot point with the cessation of the herbicide program in 1971 and subsequent complete withdrawal of US forces from Vietnam. The underlying question of international interpretation and agreement on the use of chemical weapons, however, remained undecided. The Biological Weapons Convention, signed in 1971, seemed to indicate progress by separating the issues of biologial and chemical weapons; it also committed the participants to continuing negotiations toward banning chemical weapons entirely. In June 1974 President Nixon and General Secretary Brezhnev agreed to an "initiative" on chemical weapons to provide data to the long-standing Geneva Committee on Disarmament, leading to hope for an international agreement on the subject. The initiative was reaffirmed by President Gerald Ford and Brezhnev in November 1974, and bilateral meetings on chemical weapons began in 1976; however, after three years of talks, little substantive progress could be reported.[36]

In the meantime, debate over herbicide effects in Vietnam continued long after phase-out of RANCH HAND operations. Numerous books and articles kept the argument alive, although public interest ebbed over time. Wartime conditions and, subsequently, an unfriendly government in Saigon prevented actual on-scene investigation, leaving authors to rely on past incomplete data and speculation. Even the most carefully researched studies, moreover, were subject to misinterpretation or misreporting.

In 1970, while the AAAS Commission was preparing its report, Congress finally had ordered the independent study of herbicide effects that scientists had been demanding. Under Public Law 91-441, the Department of Defense was directed to contract with the National Academy of Sciences for an extensive investigation. The academy appointed a committee of 17 experts from six countries, chaired by Dr. Anton Lang of Michigan State University, a plant physiologist and world authority on plant hormones, and aided by the President of the National Scientific Council of South Vietnam, Le Van Thoi. After an exhaustive investigation, the committee made a report to Congress in 1974 that differed significantly from the pessimistic tone of earlier antiherbicide articles. In particular, the NAS Forestry Study Team disagreed with Arthur Westing and others on the loss of marketable timber in Vietnam, estimating loss at no more than 2 million cubic meters, versus the 45 million estimated by Westing.[37]

The NAS Committee also found no evidence to verify birth defects or other direct health damage to human beings, in spite of considerable effort in this area. In another point of disagreement, despite earlier claims of sterilized soil and permanent damage to agricultural lands caused by defoliant chemicals, Dr. Lang reported soils were capable of sustaining growth as soon as six weeks after spraying and that a year after spraying the effect on plant growth was "undetectable."[38]

Unfortunately, by the time the study's findings were made public their impact had been negated by an earlier, widely publicized fraudulent report of the results. A member of the academy, who disagreed with the study findings, had given the *New York Times* a "summary" of the report on 22 February, well before the actual study was released. According to later critics, the story the *Times* rushed into print, either through deliberate intent to misinform or accidental misunderstanding, "grossly misrepresented the findings of the scientific study group." The distortion was compounded because the story was fed to 362 newspapers subscribing to the *New York Times* News Service. Despite numerous protests, the *Times* did not correct the front-page headlined article for several months, and did not print a letter to the *Times* from Dr. Lang, the Committee Chairman, complaining about the inaccuracies. The *Times* later was criticized by the National News Council for its actions, and the Council of the National Academy of Sciences ordered the president of the academy to publish an apology to the study committee for the adverse effect on their report of the distorted article.[39]

The exposés of Watergate and the collapse of the Saigon government before the VC/NVA onslaught in 1975 pushed the herbicide issue into the backwater of history, but it did not sink wholly out of sight. When the Defense Department ordered suspension of the use of herbicide Orange in 1970, it created another dilemma—the problem of disposing of nearly 2.25 million gallons of the controversial chemical. After several military units illegally used some of the Vietnam-stored stocks of Orange during 1971, all herbicides in Vietnam were ordered moved in April 1972 to remote Johnston Island in the Pacific, pending disposal instructions (Project PACER IVY). In addition to the Johnston Island storage site, another 15,000 drums of Orange (860,000 gallons) lay in open storage at the Naval Construction Battalion Center at Gulfport, Mississippi. One of the problems facing disposal managers was that leaking or damaged barrels from Vietnam had been redrummed as "Orange," even though some were actually ancient barrels of high-dioxin-content Purple. Thus each of almost 25,000 55-gallon drums on Johnston Island would require individual testing for content before the chemical could be used, a further cost to be added to the Air Force's already large expenditure of nearly $400,000 per year to maintain the stored chemical. In any case, spreading stains on the ground among the long rows of aging, rusting drums at both sites indicated that a disposal decision soon had to be made.[40]

Initial plans to sell the herbicide back to producers for reprocessing met with widespread disinterest, and another scheme by private exporters to dilute the chemical and sell it to South America for agricultural use was rejected by the Environmental Protection Agency (EPA) and the State Department. State and EPA opposition also doomed proposals to incinerate the materials at Deer Park, Texas, and Sauget, Illinois, or to pour it into an empty, 2 ½-mile-deep well in Lea County, New Mexico. Another possible Air Force solution, to reprocess Orange herbicide to remove enough dioxin contamination to make the chemical commercially acceptable, also failed because the concentrated dioxin residues would create an even greater disposal problem.[41]

Eventually, the Air Force decided that high-temperature incineration at sea was the only way to dispose of this chemical albatross. Not until nearly three years later, however, after prolonged review by the EPA, was the necessary permit issued. In June 1977 the Dutch-owned incinerator ship *Vulcanus* loaded the herbicide from the Mississippi site and sailed for the Pacific. Under Project PACER HO, the Johnston Island stocks were processed by a civilian contractor and burned in a remote area of the Pacific Ocean by the *Vulcanus*. The last of the herbicide was destroyed on 3 September 1977—the final step in a weapons program first suggested some 35 years before, during the early days of World War II.[42] Contrary to the hopes of many government officials, however, destruction of the final stores of military herbicides did not end the controversy over its use, particularly as another apparent victim of herbicidal warfare emerged—the new victim, American veterans of the war in Southeast Asia.

13

Agent Orange: The Controversy Reborn

By the mid-1970s the herbicide topic should have been dead and buried—the RANCH HAND operation had been terminated, US forces had left Vietnam (although without winning the "honorable peace" pledged by Richard Nixon during his 1968 campaign), victorious North Vietnamese had closed the doors of Vietnam to the gaze of the outside world, and Americans had gladly turned their eyes away from the discordance of their longest war and the embarrassment of abandoned South Vietnam's final days. News media now focused on domestic disagreements and on new crises in Africa and the Middle East. The herbicide issue reemerged, however, when reports began to circulate concerning long-term genetic and mortality changes among American veterans of Vietnam. Increasing numbers of former servicemen were complaining to Veterans Administration (VA) medical officers of mysterious rashes, numbness in extremities, radical behavioral changes, various malignancies, decreased sexual drive, and unexplainable weakness. Especially disquieting were the stories of increased cancer rates among veterans and of unusually large numbers of severe birth deformities among children fathered by Vietnam returnees. In 1977 a VA employee in Chicago, Maude de Victor, brought this emerging pattern of similar claims to the attention of television newsmen. A subsequent CBS network program, "Agent Orange: Vietnam's Deadly Fog," roused a storm of publicity, a fresh wave of herbicide injury claims, and a number of lawsuits against herbicide manufacturing companies. Despite a lack of scientific data substantiating the veterans' claims—or even evidence documenting actual individual exposure—the issue soon achieved national prominence.[1]

The controversy led to the formation of several Vietnam veteran groups, including Agent Orange Victims International (AOVI), founded by Paul

Reutersham, a terminally ill former helicopter crew chief who blamed herbicide exposure for his colon cancer. Among the more vocal antiherbicide organizations were the National Veterans' Task Force on Agent Orange, National Association of Concerned Veterans, Vietnam Veterans of America, and the National Veterans Law Center. Blocked by the Feres decision of the Supreme Court, a 1950 ruling that the federal government could not be sued by military personnel for injuries suffered on active duty, even when resulting from recognized negligence, various veterans groups turned to individual suits against chemical manufacturers.[2]

The veterans also sought assistance from state legislatures, and eight states passed bills providing various degrees of support or relief for the supposed victims of herbicide poisoning. One of the most comprehensive programs was that of Texas. Through the efforts of the Brotherhood of Vietnam Veterans, an Austin-based organization, and several Texas state representatives, Texas House Bill 2129 was passed in 1981 directing the state health department to collect data on those who claimed contact with Orange herbicide and to conduct an epidemiological study of health problems reported by Texas veterans.[3]

Although the federal government initially denied US ground forces were near spray areas while defoliation took place, General Accounting Office (GAO) studies identified numerous instances of possible exposure of entire units of United States Marines. Documentation for Army personnel was less reliable due to inadequate record keeping. The comptroller general reported to Senator Charles Percy on 10 November 1979 that "DOD's contention that ground troops did not enter sprayed areas until 4 to 6 weeks afterward is inaccurate; the chances that ground troops were exposed to herbicide orange are higher than DOD previously acknowledged."[4]

The chances for widespread exposure appeared even more likely when the Comptroller General revealed 33 instances of emergency dumps of herbicide loads by RANCH HAND aircraft. Several of these emergencies occurred in the vicinity of major American airbases, and at altitudes where the chemical could have drifted over large areas, according to the comptroller general's report. Two years later Secretary of Health and Human Services Richard Schweiker announced that the actual number of identified emergency jettisons was 90, including 41 that were "directly over or near U.S. airbases and other military installations."[5]

What Schweiker and the comptroller general did not explain was that these emergencies almost always occurred either on take-off or while on target; thus, the 41 instances near US installations would almost always have involved low-altitude dumps off the end of runways at Bien Hoa, Tan Son Nhut, or Da Nang, areas in which few US servicemen were present. On-target jettisons were due to aircraft battle damage, which meant only that a higher than normal concentration of herbicide was released in a limited area of heavy enemy activity—again, an area where no US ground forces would be at the time. Failure of officials to clarify such reports to newsmen merely served to confuse an issue already blurred by conjecture and misinformation.

At the same time, the public could hardly be blamed for becoming concerned after reading some of the more sensational accounts by investigative reporters. Reutersham claimed to have flown through "clouds of Agent Orange" as an 18 year old in Vietnam, and reported the chemical so potent that "within two days [it] could topple a hardwood tree 150 feet tall." Another veteran describing his experiences remembered that "a tanker plane lumbered 600 feet above, spraying an umbrella of mist on the trees below—and into the helicopter onto [him]." A widow stated "Dioxins are what they sprayed in Vietnam. They make plants grow so fast they explode, so when it gets into humans, it must do much the same."[6] Even the respected *Eric Sevareid's Chronicle,* in a feature on Agent Orange, described it as a powerful herbicide whose *major component was dioxin*, a deadly poison.[7] The media seldom corrected or commented on these factual inaccuracies.

Story after story quoted veterans of Vietnam as saying that after the spray planes flew overhead the jungles were dripping with herbicide, or that they were "drenched" or "soaked" with the chemicals. These claims ignored the fact that at a dispersal rate of three gallons per acre (the maximum dispensing rate) the fluid coverage would amount to only 0.0529 teaspoon (or 4.232 drops) per square foot, assuming that all the herbicide and its fuel-oil carrier reached the surface. Scientists estimated, however, that only 6 percent of the herbicide actually reached the jungle floor in triple-layer-canopy forests, which would reduce the amount available to "soak" personnel to approximately one-fourth drop per square foot. Even the maximum rate would equate to only 2¾ drops in an area the size of a piece of typing paper—a rather sparse "drenching."[8]

Public sympathy and support for the supposed Agent Orange victims also were elicited by media stories and pictures of deformed children born to veterans. These malformations spanned a horrible catalog of twisted limbs, incomplete internal organs, malfunctioning body chemistry, and mental retardation. "The defects in our children are the proof we have our problems were caused by Agent Orange," stated Frank McCarthy, a 1965 veteran of Vietnam who replaced Reutersham as President of AOVI. *Rolling Stone* magazine announced "the effects of dioxin on humans have been *documented* by veterans." While such statements were obviously made by people who sincerely believed what they were saying, media repetition of these unsupported claims did not make them scientifically valid and may have diverted attention away from other possible causal factors. Almost unnoticed in the controversy were laboratory tests indicating that genetic damage in dioxin-exposed laboratory animals required exposure of the female in the species, not the male, due to the fact that male sperm production is continuous and exposure-damaged sperm would normally be cleared and replaced with healthy sperm in a matter of months. Conception of a defective fetus several years after male exposure would therefore be medically unlikely.[9]

In addition to the lack of certain data on the etiology of cancer, the problem of identifying the cause of the veterans' misfortunes was compounded by the presence of various other possible causal factors, for example, medications, illicit drug and medical narcotic use, exposure to various diseases in Southeast Asia, and even other toxic agents such as petroleum fumes, insecticides, napalm burn-off, and ordnance detonation smoke. In particular, the extent and frequency of drug abuse among American servicemen in Vietnam was widely known, especially among those of an age most likely to be initiating a family after their return from overseas, leading to speculation that a correlation might exist between veterans' genetic problems and previous drug use. A rare Southeast Asian bacteria, melioidosis, also was identified in a Dow Chemical Company medical study as having effects similar to some ailments blamed on Agent Orange.[10]

Even the publicity surrounding the growing controversy may have, in itself, generated some of the claims. Veterans with medical problems, or with children suffering from defects, were quick to identify their difficulties with the stories they read daily, although this sometimes led to inconsistencies. For example, a Florida veteran filed suit against the chemical companies, charging that defoliant exposure caused him to lose his teeth and father two children with birth defects. The claimant, however, served in Vietnam from 1970 to 1971, after the Defense Department suspended the use of Orange herbicide.[11]

The emergence of Agent Orange as an American cliché was confirmed when it served as a central plot device in the 5 March 1981 episode of a popular television comedy series, *Barney Miller*. A minor criminal arrested by Police Sergeant Wojohowitz was portrayed as a RANCH HAND veteran, who claimed to have liver damage, rashes, cancer, and other miscellaneous ailments as a result of exposure to the herbicide. The storyline further implied that 2,4,5-T exposure could be a contributing factor in the character's criminal activities. The television show had a parallel in real life a short time later when one of the coordinators for a national veterans' protest demanding research into the long-range effects of exposure to Agent Orange, Max Inglett, admitted attempting to commit armed robbery in 1972, but claimed he had no memory of the actual robbery due to "induced psychotic amnesia."[12]

Despite a continuing lack of verifiable evidence to support claims of medical problems due to herbicide exposure, in 1979 the Department of Defense bowed to pressure from veterans and their supporters and announced a long-range epidemiological study to identify possible effects of herbicide contamination. The study was slated to be under the control of the USAF School of Aerospace Medicine at Brooks AFB, Texas, and its subjects would be the approximately 1,200 surviving members of the RANCH HAND organization, the only group whose herbicide exposure could be accurately documented by type, time, and frequency. Simulated spray mission experiments also indicated that exposure levels for airmen on spray missions were as much as 1,000 times the maximum levels experienced by personnel on the ground in target areas. Thus, if health or genetic damage were a resultant of defoliant exposure, it could be expected to be most prevalent among the former aircrew members and the servicing personnel who handled the chemicals on a daily basis.[13]

Although some litigants and claimants hailed the RANCH HAND study as a step in the right direction, there were complaints concerning the limited spectrum of persons selected for evaluation, and protests that Air Force control of the project might lead to suppression of findings unfavorable to military interests. A special panel of the National Academy of Sciences and the National Research Council (NRC) criticized the USAF study protocol because of the limited size of the study group, the short time for which the study proposed to follow the health of the group (six years), and the credibility of conclusions, "given the temper of the times and the sense of diminishing public trust in the institutions of American society."[14]

While the size of the study group could not be changed—the RANCH HAND veterans were the only group whose exposure rate was documented at the time of original exposure, and their numbers were limited—in 1979 DOD again bowed to public and scientific pressure and agreed that the study would be conducted by an independent civilian organization with monitoring and review by scientists from outside the government, although supervision of the program would remain under the Surgeon General of the Air Force. The NRC's suggestion that the study extend over a period of 40 years was rejected, but the plan was expanded to a 20-year program, with comprehensive physical examinations at the first, third, fifth, tenth, fifteenth, and twentieth years. This concession was dependent on future congressional funding of the continuing investigation. In addition to extensive medical checkups, the program included morbidity (disease and birth defects) and mortality (death) studies.[15]

Since most of the subject airmen had retired or separated from the Air Force, a personal appeal to these men was made by the Air Force Surgeon General, Lieutenant General Paul W. Myers, through the RANCH HAND Vietnam Association, asking them to volunteer for the extensive physical and mental tests. Also selected from other volunteers was a control group, or clone group, approximating the former defoliators in age, background, physical attributes, etc., to be evaluated on a one-for-one basis for comparative purposes of morbidity. Another control group, on a five-to-one basis, would be used for the mortality study.[16]

Because much of the difficulty facing resolution of the herbicide problem was a result of the confusion surrounding attempts to determine scientifically exactly what the medical effects of dioxin exposure are on human beings, the

RANCH HAND study was not the only investigation initiated. By mid-1982, 36 government-sponsored research projects were underway, and at least 12 more projects were under consideration. In addition to the RANCH HAND evaluation, three other major studies were initiated: a mortality study of the general death rates and causes of death of Vietnam-era military personnel; a birth-defects study comparing 7,500 babies born with birth defects with 3,000 normal babies, to see if there was any relationship to parental service in Vietnam or exposure to 2,4-D/2,4,5-T herbicides; and a registry of workers in herbicide manufacturing plants, developed by the National Institute of Occupational Safety and Health, to compare their health status with that of Vietnam veterans. Agent Orange activists, however, were unwilling to wait for the results of these long-range studies and continued to press for courtroom resolution of their demands. Although litigants' expectations had been raised by private biopsies of a few individuals that found dioxin residues in fatty tissues, their hopes suffered a setback when reports from the first round of the RANCH HAND physical and neurological examinations indicated these high-exposure personnel had normal to below-normal mortality rates and were suffering no significantly higher rates of major health problems. An Australian government commission study also found nothing "untoward in the mortality rates being experienced by Vietnam veterans in Australia, nor does it find any evidence to support the allegations in respect of suicide or cancer."[17]

Studies of workers exposed to dioxins through industrial accidents seemed to further confirm a lack of significant increase in mortality rates. Of particular interest was research among 121 workers exposed during an autoclave rupture at the Monsanto Company plant in Nitro, West Virginia, in 1949. Although all workers were heavily exposed and developed immediate symptoms typical of dioxin contamination, including chloracne, "the mortality experience of these workers indicated no apparent excess of total mortality or of deaths due to malignant neoplasms or circulatory diseases." A study of 204 Dow Chemical Company employees engaged in 2,4,5-T manufacture during varying periods between 1950 and 1971, released in 1980, also found "no adverse effects ... with respect to occupational exposure to 2,4,5-T or its feedstock, 2,4,5-trichlorophenol."[18]

While other, more limited studies with smaller sample populations suggested some association between exposure and later development of various neoplasms, they did not document increases in herbicide- or TCDD-related deaths of children or adults, nor did these studies confirm any increases in congenital defects among children. An Air Force Environmental Laboratory report of 1978 noted that "reports published by North Vietnamese scientists provide insufficient data on which to draw contrary conclusions." A study of the largest industrial accident exposure in history, at Seveso, Italy, seemed to refute claims of human birth defects from even large concentrations of dioxin, finding no derangement of gestation, no fetal lethality, no gross malformations, no growth retardation at term, and no cytogenetic abnormalities as a result of the accident exposure. Further support for this conclusion came when a case-controlled study of birth defects in children in Australia indicated that Australian army veterans who could have been exposed to defoliants in Vietnam "suffered no increased risk of fathering children with birth defects."[19] When an identical finding was announced by the Center for Disease Control after the three-year study of birth defects in the United States, veterans groups denounced the research as "deliberately skewed because it was done by the government."[20]

One of the most important studies as far as Agent Orange claimants were concerned, however, was the congressionally mandated Veterans Administration investigation of the effect of herbicides on Vietnam veterans' health, which was still in the planning stages more than three years after Congress ordered the study. A $114,288 contract awarded to a team of University of California at Los Angeles scientists in May 1981 resulted only in a protocol that President Reagan's cabinet-level Agent Orange Working Group, overseer for all herbicide investigation programs, called inadequate. Veterans' groups criticized the delays as deliberate stalling, and charged the VA plan as nothing more than "a pile of garbage." The Veterans Administration, on the other hand, claimed their problems were a result of the agency having neither the doctors nor the technical expertise on its staff to do the extensive epidemiological study required.[21] The problem was further complicated by the lack of adequate documentation to confirm the kind and extent of exposure of claimants, providing little scientific basis for an accurate epidemiological study. Even if disability due to herbicide exposure could be scientifically confirmed, the length of time since possible contact in Southeast Asia, together with the widespread domestic use of various herbicides in agriculture, horticulture, forestry, and common household operations, were certain to make it difficult to determine the extent of harm resulting from service-connected exposure versus nonmilitary domestic exposure.

Pending formulation of the herbicide study, the Veterans Administration took steps to evaluate and record claims of veterans who reported herbicide exposure-related illnesses, even to the extent of offering free medical screening for all veterans who served in Vietnam. Veterans reporting to VA hospitals for treatment, however, became increasingly dissatisfied with the care they received for Agent Orange-related problems, claiming that tests were inadequate, doctors unsympathetic and untrained to look for herbicide symptoms, and records poorly maintained. General Accounting Office investigators agreed in part, calling the VA's computerized registry for herbicide incidents "so unreliable the system should be scrapped," and finding that many VA doctors were suspicious of veterans' complaints—several doctors indicated they believed the program "served only to pacify veterans who were exploiting the Agent Orange issue for personal gain."[22]

When the VA reported in 1982 that its long-delayed herbicide study would not provide results until at least 1988, the reaction from veterans' groups and congressmen was immediate and loud. One hundred members of the House of Representatives wrote the VA Administrator, Robert Nimmo, protesting the announcement. Yielding to congressional pressure, the VA agreed to turn control of the herbicide study over to the Center for Disease Control in Atlanta, Georgia, including the data already obtained from more than 95,000 Vietnam veterans given day-long physical screening. By late 1982, 14,236 claims had been filed for service-connected disabilities attributed to herbicide exposure. The VA, however, denied over 13,000 of these claims, with most of the remainder still under review.[23]

In the meantime, the issue of indemnification was further clouded by the actions of the Environmental Protection Agency in relation to cleanup of various toxic waste disposal sites around the United States. While veterans continued their protracted fight for mere official acknowledgment that a problem existed, they read of plans for the federal government to buy entire communities, such as Love Canal, New York, and Times Beach, Missouri, because of residual dioxin contamination from one of the manufacturers of 2,4,5-T. These identified waste sites also complicated the ability of the veterans to gain a sympathetic ear from lawmakers and the public, since the sites' measurable levels of dioxin frequently exceeded the most pessimistic claims of the veterans' lawsuits.[24]

Despite widespread scientific failure to find justification for the public concern over dioxin contamination and health hazards, by the 1980s several of the largest veterans' lawsuits had been combined into class-action suits on behalf of the thousands of servicemen who supposedly had been exposed to herbicides in Southeast Asia. These product-liability suits were being handled by some of the country's best environmental lawyers, including Victor J. Yannacone, Jr., who had successfully engineered the ban on DDT a score of years before, and potentially could led to the largest awards in legal history, totaling as much as $4.5 billion. Eventually the cases were combined into a single class-action suit and scheduled for what promised to be a lengthy trial before a federal district court. Unexpectedly, at the last minute the defendant chemical companies agreed to create a $180 million indemnification fund, without any admission of liability, in an out-of-court settlement. Apparently the companies felt that the legal costs and unfavorable publicity of a drawn-out court battle would be more expensive than the settlement, while the claimants' legal staff possibly were influenced by the increasing lack of scientific support for their position. Whatever the hopes of the contending parties, continued legal maneuvering both in and out of the courtroom promises to drag on for many years. The one certain result of the settlement has been that virtually no one is satisfied with the outcome, especially since it addressed neither the issue of extent of exposure nor the question of determination of actual injury.[25]

In any case, at the time of this analysis, the exact nature of dioxin's effect on humans, and that of other herbicide-associated chemicals, and the extent of actual exposure in Vietnam remain as unclear as they did a decade before. Despite the numerous ongoing scientific studies on all aspects of the effects of Agent Orange and its TCDD contaminant, public perception of the issues continues to be shaped by media presentation of a bitter controversy and the contentious statements of veterans, government officials, scientists, lawyers, and others. A recent study of the Agent Orange controversy found that it conformed to other environmental crisis "models" in which public and scientific concern were aroused by a potential threat to the "quality of life," placing "scientists, government officials, and individual citizens in adversary relationships." The study concluded that the Agent Orange question had "reached the crossroads of science and social concern," quoting Fred H. Tschirley, who said,

> Scientists may debate chemical hazards; legislators may evaluate them; administrative agencies may examine them; courts may adjudicate them. But ultimately the public must decide the critical issues.[26]

When dealing with such complex emotional issues, hinging on the use of science, the crucial question remains whether or not the public can ever hope to get an adequate degree of "truth" upon which to base a qualitative decision.

14

Epilogue

Even as the Vietnam veterans' "Agent Orange" claims were gaining public attention in the late 1970s, reports began appearing in the media concerning use of toxic agents by Soviet bloc forces against anti-communist insurgents in Laos, Kampuchea, and Afghanistan. Subsequently, the United States government denounced the USSR for sponsoring this "chemical warfare" use of various toxins, usually refered to as "Yellow Rain," thus coming full cycle since the accusations of the 1960s. The statement of Secretary of State George Schultz that

> the world cannot be silent in the face of such human suffering and cynical disregard for international law and agreements. The use of chemical and toxin weapons must be stopped.

was an echo of Soviet pronouncements a score of years before.[1]

There were significant differences this time, however. "Yellow Rain" toxins used by the communists appeared to be designed primarily to incapacitate human beings, while the focus of earlier accusations, American chemical herbicides, were intended to directly affect vegetation only.

Furthermore, the more recent accusations and evidence pointing to deliberate poisoning and killing of people with chemical weapons failed to arouse the storm of scientific protest and publicity that occurred in the case of American assaults on the Asian environment; there appeared no counterpart to the highly vocal groups of faculty, students, and scientists who played an antiwar role in the mid-1960s and then became so concerned over the ecological and social impact of chemical weapons in Southeast Asia, for example, the "Concerned Architects and Planners" of the University of California at Los

Angeles, the "Stanford Biology Study Group," or the numerous, and often repetitious articles of Arthur Westing and others. Comprehensive discussions of "Yellow Rain" usually were limited to a few scientific journals with little or no general circulation.[2]

One group, however, was well aware of the media effect of various chemical warfare reports—the RANCH HAND Vietnam Association. First formed in 1967 by several ex-defoliation crewmembers as a social organization to preserve the camaraderie of RANCH HAND veterans, association members became increasingly unhappy over what they saw as unsubstantiated attacks on their role in Southeast Asia. Several individuals actively campaigned to present the RANCH HAND side of the story: testifying before congressional committees, speaking before civic groups, and giving numerous newspaper interviews. As a group, RANCH HAND veterans questioned the conclusions drawn by some scientific investigative bodies, speculating that at least part of their concern for environmental protection was actually based on antiwar dissent or political disagreement. As military professionals, most former spray crewmen believed that herbicide use significantly improved battlefield conditions in favor of the Allies and reduced friendly casualties. When the defoliation program was cancelled by the Department of Defense, RANCH HAND veterans wondered whether American and Vietnamese lives were being sacrificed in Vietnam because of excessive and unwarranted concern over possible damage to the ecology.[3]

Not until the Agent Orange controversy arose, however, did the RANCH HAND veterans have a collective opportunity to demonstrate their willingness to help get at the truth of the issue. When the Department of Defense decided in 1978 to sponsor a scientific study of the health effects of herbicide exposure on a selected group of Vietnam veterans, the former spray unit members were the logical choice—not only did they have the highest exposure rate, but their periods and types of exposure were already documented. The Air Force Surgeon General's call for volunteers was met by an overwhelming response: of 1,206 eligible former RANCH HAND members, 1,174 participated at least partially in the first round of tests, and 1,045 men completed the entire examination. Preliminary results of the initial study did not verify that contact with the military herbicides used in Vietnam presented either significant health or genetic hazards.[4]

Further health testing will span the next decade or more, and most RANCH HAND veterans have indicated a willingness to continue to serve as guinea pigs until all necessary data has been accumulated to finally either verify or deny the actual health hazards of herbicide exposure. This willingness is not totally unselfish; the RANCH HAND veterans are vitally concerned with the final result, whatever the outcome. Herbicide opponents and claimants in the Agent Orange lawsuits, however, have not accepted either the protocol or the results of the RANCH HAND study, claiming that it is not composed of a valid sample of the exposed population. The surprise out-of-court settlement of the primary Agent Orange lawsuit only days before the case was scheduled to go to trial has satisfied neither side of the controversy, and has done nothing to place the truth before the public, although the possibility still exists that the case could be reopened.[5] In any event, the health and compensation issues are only a small part of the larger question of chemical weaponry and weapons utilization; it seems unlikely that any of these issues will be resolved to anyone's satisfaction in the near future, if ever.

The terrain of South Vietnam fit the five conditions "for the successful pursuit of guerrilla war" enumerated by the military theorist Karl von Clausewitz.[6] Faced with the need to counter these conditions, US military planners decided to use chemical defoliants, and, later, anticrop agents, against the Asian foliage. United States' experimentation with herbicide weapons had spanned nearly two decades; yet when RANCH HAND arrived in Vietnam, equipment was jury rigged, combat tactics undeveloped, and field testing incomplete. Since the chemicals selected were essentially weed-control products in common use in American agriculture, albeit at greater concentrations, apparently little, if any, additional toxicology evaluation was done. Standard precautions outlined in industrial manuals for routine handling were accepted as sufficient.

The 1980s are still too close to the war in Vietnam to allow dispassionate or complete historical assessment of the actions and motivations of the participants. Historical research remains bogged down in a tangled web of government security classification of source materials, self-justification, and complex emotional and personal biases. The Southeast Asian conflict was more than a simple confrontation between East and West, between democracy and communism. In the broadest sense, it was an attempt by a high-technology-reliant nation to counter a grass-roots guerrilla movement, substituting exotic weapons and massive firepower for manpower. The attack on the Asian landscape was only one facet of this application of modern science and industry to the solution of social and political problems.

Nor was RANCH HAND the sole effort the United States made to modify the landscape to overcome the natural terrain advantages of the enemy. In addition to the fixed-wing defoliators, more than 100 helicopters were, at one time or another, fitted with chemical spray equipment. Chemicals also were applied with hand sprayers, engine-driven pumps, and powerful airblasts from "Buffalo" turbines; delivery methods included backpacks, trucks, and boats. Furthermore, herbicides were just one of several weapons used specifically against the Asian countryside. The full story of environmental warfare in Southeast Asia, chemical and nonchemical, has yet to be told; when it is, the study must include everything that affected or altered the Asian scene—massive B-52 "Arclight" bombing, the side effects of "Rolling Thunder," great swaths through vegetation torn by "Rome Plows" and "Georgia Chains," damage caused by napalm and various types of CBU, the consequences of bomb cratering on agriculture and of shrapnel fragments embedded in trees on the timber industry, and the disruptive results of massive forced migration of people from rural regions to newly created urban sprawls.[7]

Beyond such a broad study of environmental warfare lies the need to investigate specifically how national policy concerning chemical weapons in Vietnam was shaped. Were clear-cut goals established? Was the program actually controlled by civilian leaders, or did it just feed on its own momentum while lost in the bureaucracy of America's most unpopular war? And if at least some phases of the chemical projects were successful, to what extent did political administrations bow to public and scientific pressure to terminate the program, even while American forces were still engaged and "worst-case" speculation remained unsubstantiated? Although the Communist regime in Vietnam has refused to allow disinterested scientific follow-up investigations of the physical or human environment in that country since 1975, reports of commercial pilots, satellite photos, and interviews with refugees indicate that the predicted "wasteland" of sterilized and polluted soil, popularized in scientific articles of the late 1960s, did not materialize. Indeed, repeated studies of Range C-52A at Eglin AFB, Florida, where frequent defoliation spray testing was carried out between 1962 and 1970, show little evidence of permanent damage to either wildlife or vegetation, although officials estimate that the test plot received as much as 30 times per acre the amount of herbicide Orange, and its predecessor, Purple, as was sprayed in Vietnam.[8]

As actually conducted, the crop destruction program now appears to have been counterproductive and, as predicted by many officials from the beginning, provided the Communist world with a telling argument against the presence of American forces in Vietnam. Despite some inconvenience to enemy forces, the burden of the program frequently came to bear on civilians, especially women and children and the very young and very old. This should not have been surprising. Food denial, and the subsequent suffering of the innocent, has been a tactic in warfare since early times. The ancient goal of siege warfare was to starve out an enemy too strong or well emplaced to conquer by direct attack. The German U-boat blockade of Great Britain in 1917 was partially intended for the same purpose, but on a broader scale. American and Vietnamese officials did attempt to reduce the effect of the crop destruction program on civilians by establishing refugee areas and camps for those who wished to leave VC-dominated regions which were under herbicide attack, in the same sense that truces during siege were offered to allow the exit of noncombatants from besieged areas. At the same time, there are strong indications, as suggested in Chapter 9, for example, that much indirect benefit of both the defoliation and food denial projects was lost because of failures in the adjunct psywar and indemnification programs; given the nature of South Vietnamese government, the latter program might never have succeeded in any event.[9]

On the other hand, the herbicide experiment in Vietnam proved successful in its primary purpose of reducing the concealing vegetation used by the enemy to mask his facilities, lines of march, and avenues of attack. Most field commanders were enthusiastic about the results of defoliation missions, and requests for additional sorties continued to arrive from the field until the program was cancelled. The reduction in enemy activity in defoliated areas was repeatedly documented.[10] While it is impossible to determine to what extent this saved lives, there can be no doubt that it did; however, the benefits of reduction in injury and death among American ground forces were overwhelmed by the controversies over environmental damage and possible indirect, long-term harm to human health.

In the past, many innovative weapons of war, initially regarded as "gimmicks," have become accepted parts of the national arsenal—airplanes, tanks, radar, night-scopes—and those who first used them are praised for their work. Others, like gas and "dum-dum" bullets, have been rejected by most nations. The special irony of the RANCH HAND herbicide program is that it was a technique that offered a way to blunt guerrilla and terrorist effectiveness without direct injury to enemy, ally, or innocent. It is not wholly absurd to suggest that if it had not been used, many persons would have criticized the Kennedy/Johnson administrations, the Air Force, or MACV for failing to utilize such a cheap and available weapon. Thus both its special strength and fatal weakness stemmed from its potential within the nuance-laden realm of counterinsurgency, where combat and justification exist in the shadows. Given the adverse publicity surrounding herbicidal warfare, it is unlikely that it will be used again by American forces, but this should not detract from honors due the 1,269 men of RANCH HAND who wrote a new and unique chapter in the history of air warfare.

Notes

SECURITY CLASSIFICATION AND SOURCE RESTRICTIONS

Most of the military source documents cited in this work were originally security classified, and many remain so. Where reference is made to a still classified document, it is with the specific permission of the Office of the Secretary of the Air Force, and does not indicate that the entire document has been declassified. In any event, no portion of this manuscript is classified. For simplicity of the notes and bibliography, no reference will usually be made to either the original or current security classification of the material. In addition, some of the respondents to my inquiries have specified that their original material (interviews, correspondence, or questionnaires) not be made publicly available until a later date; others have requested anonymity as the source for a particular item. I have respected these restrictions. Further, where an incident might prove embarrassing or detrimental to an individual, I have elected to omit details that would normally identify the specific person involved.

CITATION STYLE AND ABBREVIATIONS

In order to avoid a hopelessly large number of notes, I have normally collected the references necessary to a particular passage in a single note. Where a source applies to a larger body of material, it will be cited in the first applicable note, with a statement as to the extent of its further application. The full reference to each source will be used on first citation, with the exception of the following abbreviations:

Archives and Libraries

Classified Documents Section, Air University Library, Maxwell Air Force Base, Alabama, cited as AUL.

Lyndon Baines Johnson Presidential Library, Austin, Texas, cited as LBJ.

John F. Kennedy Presidential Library, Boston, Massachusetts, cited as JFK.

RANCH HAND Collection, Texas A&M University Archives, College Station, Texas (in process of formation), cited as TAMU. Unless otherwise stated, all questionnaires, interviews, and correspondence with former RANCH HAND personnel by the author, as well as all items referenced as "in File XXXX," are contained in this collection.

USAF Collection, Albert F. Simpson Historical Research Center of the United States Air Force, Maxwell Air Force Base, Alabama, cited as AFSHRC.

Major Government Agencies

United States Department of Agriculture, cited as USDA.

United States Department of the Air Force, cited as USAF. (In some instances specific documents use the acronym DAF as part of the title. In those citations I will retain the original title and acronym.)

United States Department of the Army, cited as USA.

United States Department of Defense, cited as DOD.

United States Department of the Navy, cited as USN.

United States Department of State, cited as DOS.

Other Military Agencies

Joint Chiefs of Staff (United States), cited as JCS.

Commander-in-Chief, Pacific, cited as CINCPAC.

Commander, United States Military Assistance Command, Vietnam, cited as COMUSMACV.

Pacific Air Forces, cited as PACAF.

Military Assistance Command, Vietnam, cited as MACV.

Fifth Air Force, cited as 5AF.

Seventh Air Force, cited as 7AF.

Thirteenth Air Force, cited as 13AF.

Documents and Document Series

American Embassy Telegram to the United States Department of State, cited as AmEmb, with the addition of the city name in which it was located and the telegram number; for example, AmEmb Saigon No. 215.

End-of-Tour Report, submitted by various commanders at the end of their tour of duty in Vietnam, cited as EOTR.

National Security File, Countries, Vietnam, cited as NSF-VN.

United States Department of State Outgoing Telegram, cited as DEPTEL.

Historical Reports of Military Organizations, in the Archives, Albert F. Simpson Historical Research Center, Maxwell Air Force Base, Alabama

(Organizational histories always reference the calendar period covered. Abbreviated references will contain the appropriate calendar period as part of the short title; for example, *TAC January-June 1962.*)

History of the Tactical Air Command, K417.01, cited as TAC.

CINCPAC Command History, K712.01, cited as *CINCPAC.*

Command History, Hq US Military Assistance Command, Vietnam, cited as *MACV.*

History of the Seventh/ Thirteenth Air Force, K744.01, cited as *7/13AF.*

History of the Thirteenth Air Force, K750.01, cited as *13AF.*

History of the USAF Special Air Warfare Center (TAC), K417.0731, cited as *SAWC.*

History of the 2d Air Division, K526.01, cited as *2AD.*

834th Air Division History, K-DIV-834-HI, cited as *834AD.*

History of the 315th Air Commando Wing, K-WG-315-HI, cited as *315° ACW.* Later titled as 315th Special Operations Wing (*315° SOW*) and 315th Tactical Airlift Wing (*315° TAW*).

315th Air Commando Group History, K-GP-A-CMDO-315-HI, cited as *315 ACG.*

Quarterly unit histories of the *12th Air Commando Squadron,* contained as appendices in appropriate *315 ACW,* cited as *12° ACS.* Later titled as 12th Special Operations Squadron (*12 SOS*).

309th Air Commando Squadron History, K-SQ-A-CMDO-309-HI, cited as *309 ACS.*

Quarterly unit histories of the *310th Tactical Airlift Squadron "A" Flight,* contained as appendices in appropriate *315 TAW,* cited as *310 TAS "A."*

Newspapers

New York Times, cited as *NYT.*

CHAPTER 1

1. ©TAF, Public Affairs Office, Westover Air Force Base, Massachusetts, "S.E.A. Vet to A.F. Museum," News Release, 1 July 1980; "RANCH HAND II Population Status as of September 1981," typed copy of USAF RANCH HAND Study Briefing Slide, briefing by Lieutenant Colonel George D. Lathrop [October 1981]. The number of actual hits taken by Patches is open to dispute, ranging from a conservative 567 to a wildly inflated 2,500. The news release quoted retired Major Jack Spey, President of the RANCH HAND Vietnam Association, as giving the figure of 1,000 hits on "362" when they "stopped counting" in 1966. The total identified living RANCH HAND members as of September 1981 was 1,204.

2. The code name RANCH HAND specifically referred to the C-123 herbicide spraying project. Herbicides were also applied by United States Army helicopters, ground blower systems (Buffalo turbines), and hand sprayers. In the early years, the Vietnamese Air Force flew some herbicide sorties, using both fixed-wing aircraft and helicopters. The code name for the overall herbicide program was TRAIL DUST. For a complete explanation of other code names and acronyms, see Appendix A.

3. "Agent Orange" was a media reference to the 50:50 herbicide mixture of 2,4-dichlorophenoxyacetate and 2,4,5-trichlorophenoxyacetate, used primarily for defoliation. See Appendix B. The herbicide was referred to in Vietnam simply as "Orange," a designation matching the orange stripe on the 55-gallon drums used to ship the chemical from the United States to Vietnam.

4. The term "Yellow Rain" is from Sterling Seagrave, *Yellow Rain: A Journey Through the Terror of Chemical Warfare* (New York, 1981).

5. Joseph B. Kelly, "Gas Warfare in International Law," *Military Review* 41 (March 1961), 30; Thucydides, *History of the Peloponnesian War,* 4 vols., trans. by C. Forester Smith

(New York, Loeb Classical Library, 1919-23), 1:401, 2:385; "Greeks 'Smoke Out' Foes," *NYT*, 21 March 1949, 3; "The Panmure Papers," 340-42, quoted in Clarence J. West, "The History of Poison Gases," *Science*, n.s., 49 (1919), 413-14 (quotation); Stockholm International Peace Research Institute (hereafter SIPRI), *The Problem of Chemical and Biological Warfare: A Study of the Historical, Technical, Military, Legal and Political Aspects of CBW, and Possible Disarmament Measures,* vol. 1: *The Rise of CB Weapons* (Stockholm, Sweden, 1971), 125-26 n. 1, 127.

6. SIPRI, *Rise,* 215, 217.

7. "Definition," in Arthur H. Westing and Malvern Lumsden, *Threat of Modern Warfare to Man and His Environment* (Paris, 1979), 10; Chester C. Starr, *A History of the Ancient World* (New York, 1965), 493.

8. Jacob D. Cox, *The March to the Sea* (New York, 1913), 36; James G. Randall and David Donald, *The Civil War and Reconstruction,* 2d ed. (Boston: D. C. Heath, 1961), 431 (quotation); US Department of War, *The War of the Rebellion: A Compilation of the Official Records of the Union and Confederate Armies,* 128 vols. (1880-1901), 37(2):301, 329.

9. Robert M. Utley, *Frontier Regulars* (paperback ed., Bloomington, IN, 1977), 3, 51-52, 412-13 n. 20; US Senate Document No. 331, 1614, cited in Tran Van Dinh, "Did the U.S. Stumble into the Vietnam War?" *Christian Century* 85 (1968), 755 (quotation).

10. B. W. Richardson, "Greek Fire," *Popular Science Review,* 3 (1864), 176; James B. Neilands, et al., *Harvest of Death: Chemical Warfare in Vietnam and Cambodia* (New York, 1972), 5.

11. West, 414-15; SIPRI, *Rise,* 29-31; Bo Holmberg, "Biological Aspects of Chemical and Biological Weapons," *Ambio: A Journal of the Human Environment* 4 (1975), 211. The French deny the charge of initiating gas warfare, claiming that they reacted to German violations of the Hague Agreements. Ethylbromacetate, a lachrymator, was over twice as toxic as chlorine, according to Augustin M. Prentiss, *Chemicals in War* (New York, 1937). The number of gas casualties is impossible to determine. Allied governments apparently avoided accurate compilation of gas-related casualties, even in secret government documents that were not made public until 1972. Robert Harris and Jeremy Paxman, *A Higher Form of Killing: The Secret Story of Chemical and Biological Warfare* (New York, 1982), 36-37. Casualties at Ypres might have been even higher but for the wind direction, which caused the line of chlorine cylinders facing the Canadian 1st Division, on the right of the French, to remain sealed. Only the cylinders between Steenstratte and Poelcappelle, fronting on the French, were in the right location for the gas to carry into the Allied lines.

12. SIPRI, *Rise,* 32-37, 42 (table 1.2a), 47 (table 1.3a), 51 (table 1.4a); *Army and Navy Register* (London), 29 May 1915, quoted in West, 414-15 (quotation).

13. SIPRI, *Rise,* 32-37; Holmberg, 211.

14. Erich von Ludendorff, *Ludendorff's Own Story,* 2 vols. (New York, 1919), 2:4-9; Cyril Falls, *The Great War: 1914-1918* (New York, 1961), 270.

15. William A. Ganoe, *The History of the United States Army,* rev. ed. (New York, 1942), 479, 495; SIPRI, *Rise,* 141-42.

16. William Beecher, "Chemicals vs. the Viet Cong: 'Right' or 'Wrong'?" *National Guardsman* 20(February 1966), 5; Part 5, Article 171, in DOS, *Papers Relating to the Foreign Relations of the United States: The Paris Peace Conference, 1919,* 13 vols. (1942–1947), 13:329 (quotation); "Treaty Relating to the Use of Submarines and Noxious Gases in Warfare," Article V, in DOS, *Conference on the Limitation of Armament: Washington, November 12, 1921-February 6, 1922* (1922), 1609; "The Limitation of Naval Armaments," *Congressional Digest* 8 (1929), 233.

17. SIPRI, *Rise,* 245, 274-77; "CBW Treaty," *Congressional Quarterly Almanac* 26 (1970), 444. The Geneva Protocol of 17 June 1925 and a list of the 98 signatory states, as of March 1971, is in Neilands, *Harvest,* Appendix I, 209-11.

18. SIPRI, *Rise,* 142; "The Spreading Offensive: Fighting Around Makale" (31 December 1935, 11), "Gas Bombs in Kworam" (17 March 1936, 15), "Italian Moves in Abyssinia" (20 March 1936, 13), "Italian Gas Warfare" (23 March 1936, 12), "The Northern Front: A Critical Phase" (4

April 1936, 14), "A Poison Gas Victory: Emperor's Protest" (1 July 1936, 16), *Times* (London); Edward J. Neil, "Gas Stopped Ethiopians," Associated Press dispatch, *Army, Navy, & Air Force Gazette* (3 September 1936), reprinted in "Use of Gas in Ethiopia-1936," Chemical Warfare School, Edgewood Arsenal, Maryland, 22 October 1936 (mimeographed), 3, 248.222-36D, AFSHRC.; Paul Murphy, "Gas in the Italo-Abyssinian Campaign," also reprinted in "Use of Gas in Ethiopia-1936," 7, above.

19. "Fight for San Sabastian" (19 August 1936, 10), "San Sabastian Warning" (8 September 1936, 12), "Madrid Again Bombed" (4 December 1936, 16), "Use of Poison Gas: A German Allegation" (7 July 1937, 15), *Times* (London); SIPRI, *Rise,* 146-52. Also see, Hugh Thomas, *The Spanish Civil War* (New York, 1961).

20. Eldon W. Downs and George F. Lemmer, "Origins of Aerial Crop Dusting," *Agricultural History* 39 (1965), 123, 125-26, 131; C. R. Neillie and J. S. Housen, "Fighting Insects with Airplanes," *National Geographic Magazine* 41 (1922), 333-34; USDA, "Airplane Dusting in Control of Malaria Mosquitoes," by W. V. King and D. L. Bradley, Circular 367 (April 1926), 1-4.

21. "Report on Comparative Tests of Chemical Bombs - E2R6 and 30-lb. M1 and Test of Airplane Spray," 1, 11, Langley Field, Virginia, 21 March-3 June 1932, 248.222-36D, AFSHRC; Letter, Office, Chief Chemical Warfare Service to Capt. Merrick G. Estabrook, A.C., 21 November 1932, and Memorandum for Acting Chief of the Air Corps from L/C J. E. Chany, Chief, Plans Division, "Military Requirements for Distribution of Chemical Agents by Airplane," 23 November 1932, in 145.93-270 (November 1932 to April 1936), AFSHRC.

22. Letter, To Commanding General, Headquarters 8th Corps Area, Fort Sam Houston, Texas, from Headquarters Fort Crockett, Texas, 20 December 1934, in 145.93-270, AFSHRC; "8th Ind. to AF 354.2 (5-15-35), HQ GHQ AF, Langley Field, Va, Mar 16, 1936 to the Adj. General, Washington, D.C.," in 145.93-270, AFSHRC; Memorandum, for Assistant Chief of Staff, G-4 (Attention Colonel Carlett), "Airplane Spray (Chemical)," 29 September 1937, in 145.93-265, AFSHRC.

23. Memorandum, "Airplane Spray (Chemical)."

24. Harris and Paxman, 53-54; "Technical Report on Visit to French Powder and Chemical Warfare Factories," September 1939, and "Notes on CW Preparedness of Enemy and Potential Enemy Countries," in the Papers of Lord Weir, Director General of Explosives (DXG) at the Ministry of Supply, 1939-41, Churchill College, Cambridge, England, and "Anglo-French Conversations on Chemical Warfare," Public Record Office, London, WO 193/740, both cited in ibid., 54-56.

25. SIPRI, *Rise,* 153-57, 304. Stocks of chemical warfare agents for selected belligerents in World War II are shown as: Germany, 70,000 tons; Japan, 7,500 tons; United Kingdom, 35,000 tons; United States, 135,000 tons. The United States figure alone is 20,000 tons more than the total of all chemical warfare agents used by participants in World War I. Storage of some of these materials as combat-ready supplies in the forward areas led to several incidents, the most serious of which occurred in the Italian port of Bari in December 1943. Following a German air attack, the American merchantman *SS John Harvey,* carrying 100 tons of mustard-gas bombs, blew up, sending a cloud of mustard gas over the harbor and nearby city. Nearly 1,000 servicemen and an equal number of civilians were killed or injured by the gas. The military regarded such incidents as a calculated risk necessary in order to have retaliatory weapons immediately available to the theater forces. See Glenn B. Infield, *Disaster at Bari* (New York, 1971).

26. Winston S. Churchill, *Their Finest Hour* (Boston, 1949), 34; Ivan N. Krylov, *Soviet Staff Officer,* trans. by Edward Fitzgerald (London, 1951), 142; Francis T. Miller, *History of World War II* (Philadelphia, 1945), 367.

27. Diderich H. Lund, "Revival of Northern Norway," *Geographical Journal* 109 (1947), 185-86, 193-94. Another interesting explanation of German reluctance to use chemical warfare is that of Harris and Paxman, 67, who state that because Hitler was wounded by mustard gas during World War I, he "was known to have a marked aversion to using chemical weapons."

28. US Congress, House Committee on Foreign Affairs, *Chemical-Biological Warfare: U. S. Policies and International Effects, Hearings before the Subcommittee on National Security Policy and Scientific Developments of the Committee on Foreign Affairs*, 91st Cong., 1st sess., 1969, 351 (quotation); "Lethbridge Report," in Public Record Office, London, WO 193/712.p 398-A, 19 February 1945, cited in Harris and Paxman, 148; Elaine Shepard, *The Doom Pussy* (New York, 1967), 233. Harris and Paxman claim that the plan for "soaking the island of Iwo Jima with poison gas" was approved by Nimitz.

29. David E. Lilienthal, *The Journals of David E. Lilienthal*, vol. 2: *The Atomic Energy Years, 1945-1950* (New York, 1964), 199; SIPRI, *Rise*, 298, 321. The president's decision against the use of gas was not an easy choice, and one that must have disturbed him when the early casualty figures became known. Losses from Iwo Jima alone were 17,252 Americans wounded and 5,931 killed. Casualty rates in the 4th and 5th Marine Divisions ran as high as 75 percent. Japanese losses were at least 21,305 killed and only 1,083 prisoners, most captured after the island was declared secured. It is difficult to believe that gas warfare would not have reduced the number of dead and wounded on both sides. See Samuel E. Morison, The *Two-Ocean War: A Short History of the United States Navy in the Second World War* (Boston, 1963), 524.

30. Louis F. Fieser, *The Scientific Method: A Personal Account of Unusual Projects in War and Peace* (New York, 1964), 25-33. Renewed interest in flammables as weapons in World War II (such as napalm) was only a rediscovery of what Callinicus the Syrian found in the early eighth century A.D., when he invented an inflammable liquid known as "Greek Fire." Callinicus's discovery was superseded by the use of gunpowder, although rediscovered in the fifteenth century by the defenders of Belgrade against the Turks. John B. S. Haldane, *Callinicus: A Defense of Chemical Warfare* (New York, 1925), 6. The postwar Strategic Bombing Survey indicated that "incendiary bombs, ton for ton, were found to have been between four and five times as destructive as high explosives" in attacks on German cities. Eugene M. Emme, ed., *The Impact of Air Power: National Security and World Politics* (Princeton, 1959), 277. See also, David Irving, *Destruction of Dresden* (London, 1963) and Wesley F. Craven and James L. Cate, eds., *The Army Air Forces in World War II*, vol. 5: *The Pacific: Matterhorn to Nagasaki, June 1944 to August 1945* (Chicago, 1953), 614-17.

31. Air Vice-Marshal W. S. Douglas (Deputy Chief of the Air Staff) to Air Marshal C. F. A. Portal, 20 June 1940, para. 10-11, and 4 July 1940, para. 6, reprinted in Charles K. Webster and Noble Frankland, *The Strategic Air Offensive Against Germany, 1939-1945*, 4 vols. (London, 1961), 4:116-17, 119.

32. Public Record Office, DEFE 2/1252, Report to the Chiefs of Staff Technical Warfare Committee, November 1945, and PREM 3/89, "Crop Destruction," a memo from Sir John Anderson to Winston Churchill, 9 March 1944, cited in Harris and Paxman, 107; Air Vice-Marshal W. S. Douglas (Deputy Chief of the Air Staff) to Air Marshal Sir Charles Portal, 24 July 1940, para. 8, and letter and enclosure from C. G. Vickers (Ministry of Economic Warfare) to Air Chief Marshal Sir Charles Portal, commenting on the Report of Committee of Operations Analysts, 3 April 1943, reprinted in Webster and Frankland, 4:122 (first quotation), 267-72 (second quotation). The report referenced was by a committee appointed by General Arnold to consider targets for the Anglo-American air offensive.

33. George W. Merck, "Peacetime Implications of Biological Warfare," in George Westinghouse Centennial Forum, *Science and Life in the World*, vol. 2 *Transportation—A Measurement of Civilization; Light, Life, and Man* (New York, 1946), 132-34; Sidney Shalett, "U.S. Was Prepared to Combat Axis in Poison-Germ Warfare," *NYT*, 4 January 1946, 13; Harris and Paxman, 127-28; Gale E. Peterson, "The Discovery and Development of 2,4-D," *Agricultural History*, 41 (1967), 246-47.

34. E. J. Kraus and John W. Mitchell, "Growth-Regulating Substances as Herbicides," *Botanical Gazette* 108 (March 1947), 301-2; Peterson, 247; Merck, "Peacetime Implications," 138-40.

35. Report of the Army Air Forces Board, AAF Tactical Center, Orlando, Florida, "Marking and Defoliation of Tropical Vegetation, Project No. 3690B470.6," 18 December 1944, 1 (quotations), 12, 38-43, 65-66, in 245.64, AFSHRC.

36. Charles E. Minarik, "Crops Division Defoliation Program," *First Defoliation Conference, Proceedings, July 1963* (n.p., January 1964), 21-22; Merck, "Peacetime Implications," 138 (first quotation); Hanson W. Baldwin, *Great Mistakes of the War* (New York, 1950), 104; Public Records Office, DEFE 2/1252, Report to the Chiefs of Staff Technical Warfare Committee, November 1945, quoted in Harris and Paxman, 108 (second quotation).

CHAPTER 2

1. SIPRI, *Rise,* 153 n., 305 n.; Harris and Paxman, 150-58; John W. Powell, "Japan's Biological Weapons, 1930-1945: A Hidden Chapter in History," *Bulletin of the Atomic Scientists* 37 (October 1981), 45-46.

2. Peterson, 248-50, 252: L. W. Kephart, "Chemical Weed Killers After the War," *Proceedings of the First Annual Meeting of the North Central States Weed Control Conference, 16-17 November 1944,* 79-80, 82; US Department of Commerce, Tariff Commission, "Synthetic Organic Chemicals: United States Production and Sales," 2d series, Report No. 159 (1946), 56.

3. "Discussion," *North Central States Weed Control Conference: Proceedings of the Second Annual Meeting (November 26-28, 1945),* 73-74; Merck, "Peacetime Implications," 141; Peterson, 252; E. M. Hildebrand, "War on Weeds," *Science* 103 (1946), 467-68.

4. O. B. Schreuder and W. N. Sullivan, "Spraying of DDT from Airplanes," *Air Surgeon's Bulletin* 2 (March 1945), 67; Letter, Hq FEAF, from CG FEAF to CG, 5th AF, 13th AF, FE Air Service Cmd, and CG, CRTC, Subject: "Malaria Control," 15 October 1944, and Report, Lt. Col. G. F. Baier III, to Air Surgeon, AAF, Subject: "Medical Report Fifth Air Force," 27 November 1943, both in "Narrative Report on DDT aircraft spraying for malaria control," in *Medical Support of Air Warfare in the South and Southwest Pacific, 7 December 1941-15 August 1945,* 6 vols., 2:293-94 (quotation), 4:278, 138.8-35, AFSHRC.

5. Schreuder and Sullivan, 67.

6. Report, 11th Malaria Control Unit, Sub: "Special Purpose of Aircraft Dusting," February 1944, 6:pt. II, 339, Annex 252; Letter, Hq 5th AF, from the Malariologist 5th AF to the Cmdg Gen FEAF, Sub: "Special Report on Aircraft Spraying of DDT," 28 July 1944, 6:pt. II, 341, Annex 317; Letter, Hq XI Corps, Office of the Surgeon, from the Malariologist to the Surgeon, 6th Army, Sub: "Airplane Spraying of DDT of Morotai Island," 27 September 1944, 6:pt. II, 341, Annex 254; all in *Medical Support of Air Warfare;* Schreuder and Sullivan, 68. L-4s sprayed at 5 to 25 feet and 60 mph, A-20s at 100 feet and 200 mph, B-25s at 200 feet and 200 mph, and C-47s at 50 feet and 150 mph.

7. Report, Hq 5th AF, Office of the Surgeon, from the Surgeon 5th AF to the President, AAF Board, Orlando, Florida, Sub: "Information to determine Event III of Para. 4j, AAF Board Project 3486B725," 30 April 1945, 6:pt. II, 343-45, and Air Evaluation Board, Southwest Pacific Area, Report of 10 May 1946, 1:1, both in *Medical Support of Air Warfare.* See also, Report, Hq USAFFE, by Earl S. Herald, 1st Lt., MC, Sub: "Outline of the Organization of a Special SWPA Aircraft Squadron to be used specifically for Aerial Spray Dispersal in a Permanent Malaria and Insect Control Program," January 1945, 6:pt. II, Annex 270, in ibid.

8. Special Activities of IX Troop Carrier Command (TCC) and Third Air Force, 5 November 1945-30 September 1946, Project X, and Letter, AAF to CAF, Subj: "DDT Spraying Projects," 6 September 1945, both referenced in "Military Aerial Spray Operations, 1946-1960," (undated typescript), 7, in K417.042-1, AFSHRC; AAF Ltr AFTAS-50, 11 December 1945; "DDT Spraying Projects," 1st Ind., Hq., Continental AF, 4 January 1945, in "Project DDT:

Spraying of DDT from Aircraft," 3-4, *History, IX Troop Carrier Command, 5 November 1945-31 March 1946,* vol. 6, part II, in 546.01, AFSHRC [hereafter *History, IX TCC].*

9. Special Order No. 62, Headquarters, Third Air Force, Greenville Army Air Base, South Carolina, 22 April 1946, and "Narrative;" both in "Project DDT," 10, *History, IX TCC,* vol. 6, part II; Letter, DDT Flight to 9 AF, subj: "Aerial Spraying Activities," 19 April 1949, and "Final Report of Aerial Spray Activities, Sq D, 313 AAF BU, 1946," both referenced in "Military Aerial Spray Operations," 10-11; US Department of War, "Spraying of DDT from Aircraft," Technical Bulletin MED 200, February 1946, in *History, IX TCC,* vol. 6, part II, Appendix 1.

10. Wesley R. Nowell, "Aerial Dissemination of Insecticides by the United States Air Force," *Proceedings, New Jersey Mosquito Extermination Association and American Mosquito Control Association* (9-12 March 1954), 85; "Final Report of Aerial Spray Activities Sq D 313 AAF BU, 1946," "Ltr, DDT Flight to 9 AF, subj: Aerial Spraying Activities, 19 Apr 49," in "Military Aerial Spray Operations," 11-12.

11. "Preliminary Report Aerial Spray Operations, DDT Flight, 1948," "Ltr, TNOOT-OI to TNOOT, subj: Review of Special Aerial Spray Flight Activities, 12 November 1952," "3d Ind, 9AF to ConAC, 3 May 49, to ltr, ConAC, subj: T/D, 15 Mar 49," "R&R, Air Surgeon to Air Installations Director, 7 Jun 49," "Aerial Spraying Operations, Special Aerial Spraying Unit Hq & Hq Sq TAC, 1950," in "Military Aerial Spray Operations," 12, 17-18.

12. Wesley R. Nowell, "The Entomological Program in the United States Air Force," *Proceedings, New Jersey,* 78; Nowell, "Aerial," 87-88; "Ltr, Surgeon 5AF to CG FEAF, subj: Aerial Spraying Requirements in Korea, 3 Mar 51," "Ltr, R. H. Morrish, USAF Installation, to Maj. F. McKay, SASF, 15 Jun 51," both in "Military Aerial Spray Operations," 19. The spray crews actually preferred to use the C-47 instead of the C-46; however, the former were in extremely short supply during the early days of the Korean conflict and the medical flight had to make do with C-46s.

13. Nowell, "Aerial," 87-89. See also, *1st Epidemiological Flight (Korea) History, September 1951-December 1960,* K-MED-1-HI; *4th Epidemiological Flight (Europe-North Africa) History, September 1951-June 1960,* K-MED-4-HI; *5th Epidemiological Flight (Korea) History, July 1952-June 1957,* K-MED-5-HI; *Air Surgeon's Office, Fifth Air Force History, May-December 1952,* K730.740; all in AFSHRC.

14. Annual Reports of Aerial Spraying Operations, SASF, cited in "Military Aerial Spray Operations," 23.

15. USDA, Economic Research Service, *Extent of Spraying and Dusting on Farms, 1958, With Comparisons,* Statistical Bulletin No. 314, (Washington, DC, 1962), 1; "Ltr, NATA to OSAF, 30 Jun 54," "Ltr, OSAF to Mr. Charles Parker, NATA, n.d.," cited in "Military Aerial Spray Operations," 12-13.

16. "Ltr, USAF Dir of Installations to Air Staff, subj: Proposed T/O&E for Special Aerial Spraying Unit, 11 May 51, with six comments," and appendices, in "Military Aerial Spray Operations," 21, 24-26.

17. William B. House, et al., *Assessment of Ecological Effects of Extensive or Repeated Use of Herbicides,* Final Report, 15 August-1 December 1967, MRI Project No. MRI-3103-B (Kansas City, 1967), 113; USN, Commander in Chief Pacific Scientific Advisory Group, "A Review of the Herbicide Program in South Vietnam," by William F. Warren, Scientific Advisory Group Working Paper No. 10-68, August 1968, 13, M-42294-1, AUL.

18. Daphane J. Osborne, "Defoliation and Defoliants," *Nature* (London) 219 (1968), 565; Mark A. Henniker, *Red Shadow Over Malaya* (Edinburgh, 1955), 180; Richard L. Clutterbuck, *Long, Long War: Counterinsurgency in Malaya and Vietnam* (New York, 1966), 160; Anthony Short, *The Communist Insurrection in Malaya, 1948-1960* (New York, 1975), 375 (quotation), 455-56.

19. SIPRI, *Rise,* 158; "Peiping Says US Uses Gas," *NYT,* 5 March 1951, 3; "The Attack on the Irrigation Dams in North Korea," *Air University Quarterly Review* 6 (1953-54), 40-43; Daily Diary entries for 3 March 1951 and 17 March 1951, General E. E. Partridge, "Diary of Korea,

1950-1951," in 168.7014-1, Vol. 3, AFSHRC; Testimony of Arthur W. Galston, in US Congress, *Chemical-Biological Warfare*. A comprehensive work dealing with the use of chemical weapons, published two years later, cited this unsubstantiated claim as "fact." See SIPRI, *Rise*, 163 n. 27.

20.   USAF, Occupational and Environmental Health Laboratory, "The Toxicology, Environmental Fate, and Human Risk of Herbicide Orange and Its Associated Dioxin," by Alvin W. Young, et al., Final Report, Report No. OEHL-TR-78-92 (San Antonio, 1978), 1-2; USAF, Wright Air Development Center, "Engineering Study on a Large Capacity Spray System Installation for Aircraft," (Wright-Patterson AFB, OH, 3 June 1952).

21.   USA, Chemical Corps, Biological Laboratories, "Defoliation Target Marking and Its Implications," by S. R. McLane and E. W. Dean, Camp Detrick, Maryland, June 1955, M-34185-14 no. 94, AUL; USA, Chemical Corps, Biological Laboratories, Fort Detrick, Maryland, "Vegetational Spray Tests in South Vietnam, Supplement," Project 4B11-01-004, by James W. Brown, April 1962, 28, 55, 61.

22.   Peterson, 252; USDA, Agricultural Research Service, *A Survey of Extent and Cost of Weed Control and Specific Weed Problems*, ARS 34-23-1 (Washington, DC, 1965), 2; John D. Howard, "Herbicides in Support of Counter-Insurgency Operations: A Cost-Effectiveness Study" (Naval Postgraduate School thesis, Monterey, CA, 1972), 9; House, 5-7.

23.   James W. Brown, "Summary Report, Vegetation Control, Camp Drum, 28 October 1959," in USA, "Spray Tests," 23, 27.

24.   Ibid., 23-29; USN, "A Review," 13.

25.   Oral History Interview with Carl W. Marshall, 9 October 1981, Fort Walton Beach, FL.

26.   Ibid.,; USA, "Spray Tests," 56.

CHAPTER 3

1.   Ellen J. Hammer, "Genesis of the First Indochinese War: 1946–1950," in *Vietnam: History, Documents, and Opinions on a Major World Crisis*, ed. Marvin E. Gettleman (New York, 1965), 63-86; Stephen Y. C. Pan and Daniel Lyons, *Vietnam Crisis* (New York, 1966), 20-30; DOS, Statement of Secretary of State Dean Acheson at Ministerial Level Meeting, Paris, France, 8 May 1950, *Department of State Bulletin* (22 May 1950), 821.

2.   Carl Berger, ed., *The United States Air Force in Southeast Asia* (Washington, DC, 1977), 8; "Background Information Kit on Vietnam, 24 June 1966, Assembled by Robert E. Kintner, Secretary to the Cabinet," Pt. II, 18, Confidential File, Box 71, National Defense 19/Countries 312 (Vietnam), White House Central Files, LBJ. South Vietnam was granted full independence on 4 June 1954 and the accords were not signed until 20 July 1954. For the complete Agreement on the Cessation of Hostilities in Vietnam, 20 July 1954, see Great Britain, Parliament, *Parliamentary Papers, 1953-54*, Vol. 31, Miscellaneous No. 20 (1954), Command Paper 9239, "Further Documents Relating to the Discussion of Indochina at the Geneva Conference," 27-38.

3.   "Final Declaration of the Geneva Conference (21 July 1954), in Gettleman, 153; "Information Kit," Pt. II, 19; Berger, 9. For the purpose of this work, the titles Republic of Vietnam, RVN, GVN, and South Vietnam will all be used interchangeably to describe the ruling political regime in Saigon. Terms for the Hanoi government will include the Democratic Republic of Vietnam, DRV, and North Vietnam. Vietnam will be used, in preference to Viet Nam, except when it appears in a quotation.

4.   "Information Kit," Pt. II, 20; Berger, 9; Great Britain, Parliament, *Parliamentary Papers*, 1961-62, Vol. 39, Vietnam No. 1 (1961), Command Paper 1551, "Eleventh Interim Report of the International Commission for Supervision and Control in Vietnam," and Vol. 19, Vietnam No. 1 (1962), Command Paper 1755, "Special Report of the International Commission for Supervision and Control in Vietnam."

5. Philippe Devillers, "Ngo Dinh Diem and the Struggle for Reunification in Vietnam," in Gettleman, 229; Press Conference by President John F. Kennedy, 23 March 1961, Washington, D.C.; Berger, 10-12. USAF, "Ranch Hand Herbicide Operations in SEA," 13 July 1971, prepared by Captain James R. Clary, M-38245-47a, AUL, incorrectly identifies CDTC as the Chemical Division Test Center.

6. "Memorandum for Colonel Trach, Chief, R&D ARVN, 25 July 1961," "Trip Report— South Vietnam, December 1961, by Dr. J. W. Brown," "Review and Evaluation, Tasks 2 and 20, October 1961," in USA, "Spray Tests," 15, 55, 57, 61.

7. Ibid., 55, 57.

8. Ibid., 15; Marshall Interview.

9. "Review and Evaluation, Tasks 2 and 20, October 1961," USA, "Spray Tests," 67.

10. "Vegetation Control Information, 24 February 1960," "Notes for Colonel Chilson, Tasks 2 & 20, 16 October 1961," "Review and Evaluation, Tasks 2 and 20, October 1961," in ibid., 10, 55, 62.

11. "September Progress Report, 1961," "Informal Progress Report, Task 20 (undated)," "Review and Evaluation, Tasks 2 and 20, October 1961," in ibid., 41, 52, 62-67.

12. Ibid., 41, 45-47, 69.

13. Ibid., 62-66.

14. "Notes for Colonel Chilson, Tasks 2 & 20, 16 October 1961," "Trip Report—South Vietnam, December 1961," in ibid., 56 (quotation), 59. The Taylor-Rostow mission visited Vietnam on 18-24 October 1961 to make an appraisal of the deteriorating situation there.

15. Ibid., 49, 59.

16. Ibid., 69.

17. George T. Adams, typescript describing RANCH HAND operations between 1961 and 1964, n.p., [August 1964], 1, in personal files of John R. Spey, Fort Walton Beach, Florida; Marshall Interview.

18. Ibid.; Message, AFOOP-TA 85477, USAF to TAC, 13 July 1961, in *TAC January-June 1962*, 1:645-46.

19. Berger, 11-12. Detachment 2A consisted of 151 personnel, 8 T-28 fighter-trainers, 4 SC-47 special transports, and 4 RB-26 reconnaissance bombers.

20. AmEmb Saigon No. 448, 7 October 1961, NSF-VN, Vol. I, Box 193-94, JFK. The Geneva Agreements prohibited the introduction into Vietnam of all types of arms, munitions, and materials of war, except as a one-for-one replacement for existing stocks that were used up, destroyed, or worn out. Replacements had to be similar in type and characteristics to the items replaced and had to be reported to and inspected by ICC teams.

21. Ibid.; Joint State/Defense Outgoing Telegram No. 556 to American Embassy Saigon, 7 November 1961, NSF-VN, Vol. II, Box 194-96, JFK; DEPTEL No. 582 to American Embassy Saigon, DEPTEL No. 427 to American Embassy Phnom Penh, 9 November 1961, NSF-VN, Vol. II, Box 194-96, JFK.

22. Adams, 2; Memorandum, Roswell L. Gilpatric, Deputy Secretary of Defense to the President, 21 November 1961, 2, National Security File, National Security Council, NSAM 115, Defoliant Operations, Vietnam, Box 332, JFK; Marshall Interview; Questionnaire No. 7498, Oleuse M. Leger, Jr., 22 October 1981.

23. Oral History Interview, John R. Spey, 2 September 1981, Fort Walton Beach, Florida, TAMU; USAF, Special Order No. TA-2618, Hq. Pope AFB and 464th Air Base Gp (TAC), 21 November 1961; Questionnaire No. 7423, John K. Hodgin, 23 November 1981; Adams, 3.

24. Spey Interview; Marshall Interview; Adams, 3; PACAF OPORD 224-61, 23 November 1961.

25. Spey Interview; Marshall Interview; Adams 4.

26. Spey Interview; Marshall Interview; Adams, 4-6.

27. Berger, 12-13; "Secretary of Defense Book for January Meeting - 14 January 1962," Talking Paper #2, K717.153-3, AFSHRC.

28. Marshall Interview. The first shipment of defoliation chemicals left the United States by sea on 13 December 1961.

29. Ibid.; Spey Interview.

30. "Memorandum for Record, Subject: Meeting with Mr. William Godel on 4 December 1961," 12 December 1961, in USA, "Spray Tests," 135.

31. Memorandum, Gilpatric to the President, 2-4; Memorandum, Secretary of State Dean Rusk for the President, 24 November 1961, NSF-VN, Vol. III, Box 194-96, JFK.

32. Message, PACAF to 5th AF, "Defoliant Project," 30/0134Z No. 61, in "Fifth Air Force in the Southeast Asia Crisis (A Sequel), 30 January 1962," prepared by Arthur C. O'Neill, K730.04-22, AFSHRC (hereafter cited as "Fifth AF").

33. Memorandum, Gilpatric to the President, 4; Berger, 12.

34. "Secretary of Defense Book," Talking Paper #2; "Ranch Hand" Map, in USA, "Spray Tests," 35, 68.

35. JCS 061853Z Jan 62, in CINCPAC 1962, 182; Message, PACAF to 13AF, 2d ADVON, PFOOC-S, 07/0126Z Jan 62, in "Fifth AF"; "Secretary of Defense Book," Talking Paper #2.

36. The results of French cutting and burning back of vegetation for 50 yards on either side of the road were still evident along Route 13 in the mid-1960s.

CHAPTER 4

1. Adams, 6. In addition to sources cited in specific notes, the information for this chapter came from interviews and correspondence with members of the original RANCH HAND organization: Earle H. Briggs, Jr., Edward H. Dabbert, Michael W. Devlin, John C. Hamilton, John K. Hodgin, Oleuse M. Leger, Jr., Carl Marshall, William F. Robinson, Jr., Marshall B. Rothermel, and John R. Spey.

2. Robert de T. Lawrence, "USAF Aids South Viet-Nam," Airman 6 (August 1962), 40; PACAF to 13AF, 2d ADVON, PFOCC-S 62-016, 070126Z Jan 62, in "Fifth Air Force." Security for the operations in South Vietnam was so strict that when an article in Airman magazine showed pictures of the tent quarters at Tan Son Nhut airport, the faces of personnel shown were blacked out with a bar so that they could not be recognized and they were not identified by name. Edison T. Blair, "The Air Commando," Airman 6 (September 1962), 19-23. The RANCH HAND villas in Saigon were passed from one group to another as the crews rotated. At least one lease was still running under the original signature as late as 1965.

3. Memorandum for Chief R&D Division (MAAG, VN), in USA, "Spray Tests," 79; "Secretary of Defense Book for January," Talking Paper #2; Adams, 7.

4. USA, "Spray Tests," 35-37, 78, 121, 133.

5. Ibid., 77-78.

6. COMUSMACV to CINCPAC, 231045Z Mar 62, para. 4(2), in ibid., 7 (quotation). After aerial inspection of defoliation efforts, both JCS Chairman General Lyman Lemnitzer and Assistant Secretary of State Roger Hilsman used the phrase "not impressive" to describe the results. COMUSTDC to SEC DEF, 300645Z Mar 62, in NSF-VN, Vol. VI, Box 194-96, JFK; Roger Hilsman, To Move a Nation: The Politics of Foreign Policy in the Administration of John F. Kennedy (Garden City, NY, 1967), 443. Part of the problem with initial defoliation efforts was that VNAF C-47 crews flew the spray tests at 1,000-feet altitude. "Secretary of Defense Book for January," Talking Paper #2.

7. Adams, 8; USA, "Spray Tests," 133. The exact cause of the crash was never determined. The first RANCH HAND casualties were Captain Fergus C. Groves II, instructor pilot; Captain Robert D. Larson, pilot; and Staff Sergeant Milo B. Coghill, flight engineer. The investigation

statement of then-Captain William F. Robinson, Jr., Acting Operations Officer, is in File 7687, item #1, TAMU.

8. Adams, 9.

9. Items for Discussion with the Secretary of Defense in the 23 July 1962 Meeting, Tab D, Item 1, "Defoliant Operations," K526.1511-6, AFSHRC. The United States reorganized its military structure in South Vietnam on 8 February 1962, changing the MAAG to the Military Assistance Command, Vietnam (MACV), under the command of General Paul D. Harkins, US Army. This change emphasized the increasing size and importance of United States military commitments in this area. In-country forces now totaled over 4,000, with another 1,400 due to arrive in March. "Information Kit," Pt. II, 22.

10. Information concerning the Delmore team study in this and subsequent paragraphs can be found in USA, Chemical Corps, "Review and Evaluation of ARPA/OSD 'Defoliation' Program. Research Phase: 15 July 1961-12 January 1962, Operational Phase: 13 January 1962-March 1962, in South Vietnam," by Fred J. Demore [15 July 1962]. General Delmore, who flew on many of the spray missions, was affectionately known to the RANCH HAND crews as "Uncle Fred."

11. Arturo F. Gonzales, Jr., "Defoliation—A Controversial U.S. Mission in Vietnam," Data 13 (October 1968), 12.

12. Memorandum for the President from Dean Rusk, 24 November 1961, NSF-VN, Vol. III, Box 194-96, JFK.

13. Jack Raymond, "Army Seeks Way to Strip Jungles," NYT, 6 June 1961, 11.

14. Robert Trumbull, "Saigon Builds Up for Drive on Foe," NYT, 1 January 1962, 1; "Defoliation Effort Delayed in Vietnam," NYT, 12 January 1962, 3.

15. Homer Bigart, "U.S. Spray Strips Foliage Hiding Vietnam Reds," NYT, 19 January 1962, 4; Bigart, "U.S. Shuns Harm to Vietnam Food," NYT, 26 January 1962, 2.

16. "Defoliation Effort," 3 (first quotation); Bigart, "Shuns," 2 (second quotation); Seymour M. Hersh, "Our Chemical War," New York Review of Books 10 (1968), 31.

17. USN, "A Review," 36. Some senior Air Force officers responsible for air transport units judged the efficiency of these organizations by tonnage carried—more tonnage meant more efficiency—a criteria that did not fit the RANCH HAND operation.

18. Various headgear for Air Commando personnel (USAF counterinsurgency personnel) was alternately approved and disapproved throughout the Vietnam War. The issue was not settled until the 1970s.

19. EOTR, Captain Eugene D. Stammer, 27 July 1964, in the personal papers of Earle H. Briggs, Jr., Pensacola, Florida. In defense of Captain Overman, many of the forward airfields in Vietnam were recognizable as such only if the pilot had seen it before, being no more than reasonably level, semi-cleared areas with little or no markings. Under marginal weather conditions the opportunity for error increased significantly. This was particularly true in the early years. Much of the checkout for new C-123 pilots in country involved having an experienced pilot show them the various fields and explain how to get to them. The almost total lack of effective electronic navigation aids forced crewmen to rely on pocket diaries with field notations such as "at the river bridge, turn into valley to the north, fly two minutes, and look for 1,800-foot north-south red dirt strip on small hill to the right, with star-shaped compound at south end. North end has 75-foot drop-off. Strong down-drafts and ground fire on final from north; approach from south, if possible." A crucial and immediate task for a new crewmen was to copy the entries in all the "old timers" field books he could get his hands on.

20. Message, PFOCC-S, 62-106, PACAF to TAC, 15 Mar 62, and Message, PFDOP, 62-1220-C, PACAF to USAF, 15 Mar 62, cited in TAC January-June 1962, 1:647; Oral History Interview of Lieutenant Colonel Benjamin Kraljev by Lieutenant Colonel R. L. Bowers, 29 January 1971, typed interview notes, n.p., K239.0512-778, AFSHRC.

21. Extract, Letter, PACAF to Concerned Agencies, Subject: Report of Staff Visit, PFDOP, 25 April 1962, in 13AF January-December 1962, 68; Messages, PFDOP 3055, PACAF to TAC, 25 Apr 62, and AFOOP-CO 82285, USAF to PACAF, 25 Apr 62; Daily Diary, DMLP, 30 Apr 62 and 3 May 62; in TAC January-June 1962, 1:648-49. A discrepancy in the amount of herbicide

remaining in Vietnam in April 1962 exists between various sources. The report of the PFDOP staff visit lists 112,000 gallons, while General Delmore's report lists 1,935 drums of Purple herbicide mixture (approximately 106,435 gallons) and 1,886 drums of Pink-Green herbicide mixture (approximately 103,730 gallons), in addition to 132 cartons of powder (100 pounds each, total 13,200 pounds) for mixing Blue herbicide. The Thirteenth Air Force staff members may have considered that only Purple and Blue were suitable for USAF missions.

22.   Message, AFOOP-CO 82285, USAF to PACAF, 25 Apr 62; Message, U-172, USAIRA Kabul to USAF, 29 May 62; Message, U-175, USAIRA Teheran to USAF, 20 May 62; Message, U-180, USAIRA Teheran to USAF, 30 May 62; all in *TAC January-June 1962*, 1:648-49; Downs and Lemmer, 133-34. Crew members on this historic flight were Captain William F. Robinson, mission commander; Captain Charles F. Hagerty, aircraft commander; Captain Lloyd H. Adkins, pilot; Second Lieutenant John K. Hodgin, navigator; and Technical Sergeant Leon Roe, flight engineer. The complete itinerary of this mission is contained in File 7687, item #2, TAMU.

23.   *TAC January-June 1962*, 1:650; USA, "Review and Evaluation of ARPA/OSD," 46-52.

24.   Extract, Letter, *13AF January-December 1962*, 69; *CINCPAC 1962*, 184.

25.   USAF, "Ranch Hand Operations in SEA," 13 July 1971, prepared by Captain James R. Clary, 7-8, K717.0413-20, AFSHRC (hereafter cited as "Ranch Hand in SEA"); Unsigned letter dated October 1962 [Memo for record, Col. Haygood, 6 October 1962], 1, catalogued Project Corona Harvest, #0216340, in K526.161-2, AFSHRC.

26.   "Defoliation and Ranch Hand in the Republic of South Vietnam," 1 July 1965, unsigned typescript, n.p., in K-GP-A-CMDO-315-SU-RE 1961-1965, AFSHRC; USAF, Pacific Air Forces, "Herbicide Operations in Southeast Asia, July 1961-June 1967," by Charles V. Collins, Project CHECO Report No. DETC-67-0020, 11 October 1967, 4-5, M-38245-47, AUL. Herbicides were effective throughout the year, but caused the greatest leaf fall when applied during the plant's active growing season. As long as the herbicide project was still in the experimental and testing phases, herbicide operations were usually suspended during the dry, nongrowing season.

27.   Record of the Fourth Secretary of Defense Conference, 21 March 1962, CINCPAC Ser. 00090, 1-3, and GENEVA 15 to CINCPAC, 3 PM, 9 July 1962 (quotation), cited in CINCPAC 1962, 185-86; Oral History Interview of Ambassador Frederick E. Nolting, Jr., by Major Richard B. Clement and Dr. James C. Hasdorff, 9 November 1971, typed transcript, 45-46, K239.0512-489, AFSHRC.

28.   COMUSMACV 211013Z Aug 62 and CINCPAC 212321Z Aug 62, cited in *CINCPAC 1962*, 186.

29.   Laszlo Hadik, Stanley W. Dziuban, and Susan Herbert, "Constraints on the Use of Weapons and Tactics in Counterinsurgency," Vol. 2, "Appendix A, Case Studies, June 1966," 13-21, cited in Eldon W. Downs and John H. Scrivner, "Defoliation Operations in Southeast Asia, A Special Report" (Aerospace Studies Institute, Air University, Special Report No. 70-16, Maxwell AFB, AL, March 1970), 5-6, K239.0370-16, AFSHRC; "Operational Data," COMUSMACV to CINCPAC, 161020Z Jan 67, cited in USAF, "Herbicide Operations," App. 1, 70; DEPTEL 402, State to Saigon, 4 October 1962, cited in USAF, "Ranch Hand in SEA," 40-41.

30.   Personal Narrative of Captain John R. Spey, 3 July 1965, 1-2, in K-GP-CMDO-315-SU-RE 1961-1965, AFSHRC; Adams, 14-25.

31.   Typescript of Radio Hanoi Broadcast in English to Europe and Asia, 14/1406Z October 1962, in the personal papers of Earle H. Briggs, Jr., Pensacola, Florida; Stanley D. Fair, "No Place to Hide: How Defoliants Expose the Viet Cong," *Army* 14 (September 1963), 55; Message, OIC to AIG 950, Subject: "Defoliation in Vietnam: Fact and Fantasy," 2 Apr 63, cited in *13AF January-June 1963*, 1:76; Memorandum, Col. Burris to Vice-President Lyndon B. Johnson, 12 March 1963, Vice-President Security File, Box 6, Col. Burris, Col. Burris, LBJ; Hilsman, 458.

32.   Joint State/Defense Outgoing Telegram No. 1055 to American Embassy Saigon, 7 May 1963, NSF-VN, Vol. X, Box 194-96, JFK; DOD, MACV, "Evaluation of Herbicide Operations in the Republic of Vietnam (September 1962-September 1963)," by Peter G. Olenchuk, et al., 10 October 1963, 35.

33. AmEmb Phnom Penh No. 875, 18 May 1963, NSF-VN, Vol. X, Box 196-98, JFK.

34. AmEmb Saigon No. 1042, 19 May 1963, NSF-VN, Vol. X, Box 196-98, JFK.

35. AmEmb Phnom Penh No. 875.

36. DOD, "Evaluation of Herbicide," 35.

37. Ibid., 6, 35; AmEmb Saigon No. 21, 3 July 1963, NSF-VN, Vol. XII, Box 196-98, JFK; Adams, 16-17; Report, Subject: Thirteenth Air Force Quarterly Review, 1300T, 30 June 1963, 7, in *13AF January-June 1963,* 1:76.

38. "The Pacific Air Forces," *Air Force and Space Digest,* 47 (September 1964), 103; Adams, 17; Downs and Lemmer, 134.

39. DOD, "Evaluation of Herbicide," 28, 30-31.

40. Adams, 17-18.

41. Ibid., 20-21; Personal Narrative, Spey, 2.

42. Draft Report, unsigned typescript, 1 June 1965, 2, in K-GP-A-CMDO-315-SU-RE 1961-1965, AFSHRC; Personal Narrative, Spey, 2.

43. EOTR, Stammer, 2; Adams, 18-19.

44. "Operational Data," cited in USAF, "Herbicide Operations," App. I, 70.

CHAPTER 5

1. "Talking Paper for the Chairman, JCS, for meeting with the President of the US, 9 January 1962, Subj.: Current US Military Actions in SVN," cited in *The Pentagon Papers: The Defense Department History of United States Decisionmaking on Vietnam,* 4 vols., Senator Gravel Edition (Boston, 1971), 1:658.

2. Berger, 28; Allan R. Millett, ed., *A Short History of the Vietnam War* (Bloomington, IN, 1978), 142.

3. Adams, 21-22.

4. Ibid., 22-23; Berger, 29.

5. Adams, 23; EOTR, Stammer, 2; "Defoliation and Ranch Hand," [5].

6. EOTR, Stammer, 2-3; "Defoliation and Ranch Hand," [5].

7. USN, "A Review," 5.

8. EOTR, Stammer, 3-4; "Defoliation and Ranch Hand," [5].

9. EOTR, Stammer, 3; Adams, 24-25.

10. EOTR, Stammer, 3; Adams, 26-27. For command and control purposes, South Vietnam was divided into four Corps Tactical Zones (CTZ), numbered I thru IV, north to south (I CTZ was pronounced "eye" corps), and the Capital Military District around Saigon. Zone boundaries were realigned in November 1963, with the main change being the III-IV CTZ boundary moved south of the Mekong River (see Map F). Use of the fast turnaround procedure was worthwhile only for targets within a short distance of the herbicide servicing facility. Constraints of FAC and fighter coordination and limited daylight spray hours usually precluded use of this procedure.

11. USAF, "Aircrew Procedures," Technical Manual T.O.1C-123B-1; Undated typescript, "Section H - Aerial Spray Missions," 3, Procedures Folder, TAMU; Adams, 26.

12. EOTR, Stammer, 3.

13. Adams, 27-28; AmEmb Saigon No. 161, 21 July 1964, sec. 5, 2, NSF-VN, Vol. 14, Box 6, LBJ.

14. US Mission to UN to Secretary of State No. 233, 28 July 1964, NSF-Cambodia, Vol. 2, Cables, Box 236, LBJ; AmEmb Phnom Penh No. 51, 29 July 1964, NSF-VN, Vol. 14, Box 6, LBJ; Sam P. Brewer, "U.S. Is Accused of Chemical War," NYT, 30 July 1964, 2.

15. AmEmb Phnom Penh No. 48, 29 July 1964, NSF-VN, Vol. 14, Box 6, LBJ.

16. AmEmb Saigon No. 245, 29 July 1964, NSF-VN, Vol. 14, Box 6, LBJ.

17. NYT, 19 June 1964, 2.

18. "Vietcong Is Accused," NYT, 30 July 1964, 2.

19. DEPTEL to Phnom Penh No. 250, 29 July 1964; DEPTEL to USUN, New York, No. 254, 31 July 1964; DEPTEL to Saigon Nos. 271 and 278, 28 July 1964; EPTEL to Saigon No. 287, 29 July 1964; all in NSF-VN, Vol. 14, Box 6, LBJ.

20. NYT, 15 August 1964, 2; "Dispatch from Pnompenh," NYT, 3 September 1964, 2; NYT, 12 September 1964, 3.

21. EOTR, Stammer, 4; "Defoliation and Ranch Hand," [5]; USAF, "Toxicology," I-14. The 315th Troop Carrier Group (Assault), activated at Tan Son Nhut airport on 8 December 1962, was a direct ancestor of the 315th Air Transport Group, organized 14 February 1942. K-WG-315-HI July-December 1966, 75, AFSHRC.

22. R. A. Darrow, K. R. Irish, and C. E. Minarik, "Herbicides Used in Southeast Asia," Technical Report SAOQ-TR-11078, Directorate of Air Force Aerospace Fuels, Kelly AFB, Texas, cited in USAF, "Toxicology," I-14; EOTR, Stammer, 4.

23. Air Force Developmental Aircraft, ARDC, April 1957, 83, 113, K243.04-4, AFSHRC; "Case History of the C-123 Airplane (26 April 1945-7 Sept. 1951)," prepared by Margaret C. Bagwell, March 1952, 2, 112, K202.1-50, AFSHRC.

24. Berger, 169; Questionnaire No. 7165, Howard F. Bowles, Jr., 18 October 1981.

25. Adams, 28; EOTR, Stammer, 4.

26. "Goldwater Poses New Asian Tactic," NYT, 25 May 1964, 1. For a brief description of the Fifth Air Force Special Study, see Chapter 2 above.

27. For detailed reviews of the Tonkin affair, see Joseph C. Goulden, Truth Is the First Casualty: The Gulf of Tonkin Affair—Inclusion and Reality (Chicago, 1969); Eugene G. Winchey, Tonkin Gulf (Garden City, NY, 1971); and Anthony Austin, The President's War: The Story of the Tonkin Gulf Resolution and How the Nation Was Trapped in Vietnam (Philadelphia, 1971).

28. Republic of Vietnam, Combat Development and Test Center, "The employment of helicopters in defoliation operations in the Republic of Vietnam," Special Report, by Lieutenant Colonel Stanley Fair, USA, and Captain Nouyen The Ton, ARVN (duplicate text, English/Vietnamese), Vietnam, 1964, 65, M-42008-4-C, AUL; USN, "A Review," 8; 2AD July-December 1964, 2:49.

29. DEPTEL to Saigon No. 1055, 7 May 1963, NSF-VN, Vol. X, Box 196-98, JFK; AmEmb Saigon No. 668, date illegible, No. 1249, 3 January 1964, and No. 1251, 3 January 1964 (quotation), all in NSF-VN, Vol. 4, Box 2, LBJ.

30. DEPTEL to Saigon No. 1056, 12 January 1964 (first quotation); AmEmb Saigon No. 1410, 28 January 1964, and No. 1543, 12 February 1964; Map, "Recommended Areas for Crop Destruction, Saigon 1543"; Memorandum, Michael V. Forrestal to Bundy, 2 March 1964; DEPTEL to Saigon, No. 1357, 3 March 1964 (second quotation); all in NSF-VN, Vol. 4, Box 2, LBJ.

31. DEPTEL to Saigon No. 1357, 3 March 1964, NSF-VN, Vol. 4, Box 2, LBJ; DEPTEL to Saigon No. 294, 29 July 1964 (quotations), NSF-VN, Vol. 14, Box 6, LBJ. The question of who spoke for the Vietnamese was frequently difficult to determine. President Diem was overthrown and assassinated in November 1963 by his Chief of Staff, General Duong Van Minh. Minh, in turn, was overthrown by Khanh, ARVN Commander in I Corps, in January 1964. Khanh was forced to resign and accept a post outside Vietnam as "ambassador-at-large" in late 1964. A series of additional changes followed. The instability of the Saigon government was due, in part, to the conflicting efforts of American officials, sometimes working at cross-purposes; in any event, confusion reigned throughout South Vietnam for much of the republic's existence. For an excellent discussion of RVN leadership problems, see Stanley Karnow, Vietnam: A History (New York, 1983), especially Chapters 9 and 10.

32. USN, "A Review," 8; 2AD July-December 1964, 2:49-51.

33. 12th Air Commando Squadron Briefing Form, undated typescript, personal papers of the author. The general procedures and tactics used for defoliaton and crop destruction missions outlined in this and following paragraphs are as described by numerous spray crewmembers

during conversations with the author during 1980-84, and as experienced by and taught by the author while serving with RANCH HAND.

34. "Defoliation and Ranch Hand," [6]; *2AD July-December 1964,* 2:49-51, 117.

35. "Defoliation and Ranch Hand," [6]; Personal Narrative, Spey, 6-7.

36. "Defoliation and Ranch Hand," [6]; *2AD July-December 1964,* 2:50.

37. MACV MilRep MAC J3 11727, 191057Z Oct. 64, in *2AD July-December 1964,* 2:50; "Defoliation and Ranch Hand," [6]; Downs and Scrivner, 10; Draft Report, 1965, 3.

38. EOTR, Stammer, 5. A hand-written entry on the original report indicates the arrival of the extra crews in January 1965. The entry is not dated.

39. CINCPAC to JCS, 192230Z July 64, NSF-VN, Vol. 14, Box 6, LBJ; Draft Report, 1965, 3.

CHAPTER 6

1. Lyndon Baines Johnson, *The Vantage Point: Perspectives of the Presidency, 1963-1969* (New York, 1971), 116-19; Millett, 143-45. The Gulf of Tonkin Resolution passed the Senate by a vote of 88 to 2, and the House by a unanimous vote, 416 to 0. In addition to source materials cited in specific notes, the material for this chapter came from interviews and correspondence with Ralph C. Dresser, Michael L. Shuppert, Harold R. Snell, Delmar B. (Pete) Spivey, and Verne D. Uhler, all members of the SASF during 1965.

2. John C. Donnell, Guy J. Pauker, and Joseph J. Zasloff, "Viet Cong Motivation and Morale: A Preliminary Report," RAND Memorandum RM-4507-ISA Mar 1965 (Santa Monica, CA, 1965), 38.

3. Leon Goure, "Some Impressions of the Effects of Military Operations on Viet Cong Behavior," RAND Memorandum RM-4517-ISA Mar 65 (Santa Monica, CA, 1965).

4. "Historical Data Requested by 315th A.C. Gp., 1 Jan. 65 - 8 Mar. 65," [1], in K-GP-A-CMDO-315-SU-RE, AFSHRC (hereafter "History January-March 1965"). The target numbering system used a four-part number in which the first number was the Corps area, the second number identified crop target (2) or defoliation target (20), the third number was the MACV sequence number, and the fourth number was the year of target approval. Thus, target 4-20-6-67 was a IV Corps defoliation target (near Phuc Vinh), with a sequence number of six, which was approved in 1967. For large recurring targets that were expected to last from one year to another, the first and last numbers were usually dropped, leaving only the type and sequence number, such as the referenced 20-32/33, meaning a recurring defoliation target with sequence numbers 32 and 33. If there was more than one target within the approved area, the number indicated this by adding the target number to the end of the sequence, that is, 4-20-6-67#3 would be the third target within the complex described previously. Questionnaire No. 7356, Henry K. Good, 7 March 1982.

5. "History January-March 1965," [2]; Message, COMUSMACV 301130Z Mar 65, in NSF-VN, Vol. 31, Box 15, LBJ. The Boi Loi plan was presented by Brigadier General Robert R. Rowland, Chief of the Air Force Advisory Group. Coordinates for the area in Universal Transverse Mercator Grid were Zone 48P, Square XT, and outlined by 440410, 475410, 475430, 483430, 510370, 530340, 547330, 525315, 520310, 505315.

6. Personal Narrative, Spey, 9; "History January-March 1965,"' [2]; Draft Report, 1965, 3. The latter source mistakenly reports only 22 hits during the operation and concludes that it proves the effectiveness of the fighter tactics used.

7. Personal Narrative, Spey, 9; *309 ACS January-June 1965,* 4-5; "History January-March 1965," [2]. Spey is particularly critical of safe haven destruction as economically impossible and undesirable, when not accompanied by occupation by permanent forces.

8. "History January-March 1965," [2]; "Historical Data Requested by 309th A.C.S., 8 Mar 66 - 30 Jun 65," [1], in K-GP-A-CMDO-315-SU-RE, AFSHRC (hereafter "History March-June 1965").

9. *309 ACS January-June 1965*, 1. A second C-123 transport squadron, the 19th ACS, was activated at Tan Son Nhut on 1 March 1965, under control of the 315th ACG.

10. Joint AmEmb Saigon/MACV/USOM No. 3004, 18 March 1965, NSF-VN, Vol. 31, Box 15, LBJ; "History March-June 1965," [1-2].

11. DEPTEL No. 1055, 3 May 1963.

12. DEPTEL No. 2039, 20 March 1965, No. 2048, 22 March 1965, No. 2053, 22 March 1965, No. 2084, 24 March 1965 (quotation), all in NSF-VN, Vol. 31, Box 15, LBJ; *NYT*, 23 March 1965, 46, and 25 March 1965, 43.

13. DEPTEL No. 2094, 25 March 1965, NSF-VN, Vol. 31, Box 15, LBJ.

14. AmEmb Saigon No. 3089, 25 March 1965, ibid.

15. AmEmb Saigon No. 3118, 27 March 1965, ibid.

16. DEPTEL No. 2110, 27 March 1965 and No. 2128, 30 March 1965, both in ibid.

17. MACV to NMCC, Telecom 250046Z, 25 April 1965, NSF-VN, Vol. 33, Box 16, LBJ; AmEmb Saigon No. 3275, 8 April 1965, NSF-VN, Vol. 32, Box 16, LBJ.

18. Intelligence and Reporting Subcommittee of the Interagency Vietnam Coordinating Committee, "Weekly Report: The Situation in South Vietnam," 28 April 1965, 6, in NSF-VN, Vol. 33, Memos, Box 16, LBJ.

19. "History March-June 1965," [2].

20. Ibid., [2-3]; Draft Report, 1965, 5-8 (quotations).

21. Draft Report, 1965, 5-7.

22. Ibid., 8-9.

23. Ibid., 9; "Comparision of Sorties Flown by RANCH HAND," COMUSMACV to CINCPAC, 161020Z Jan 67, cited in USAF, "Herbicide Operations," App. I, 71; "Ranch Hand Addition to 309th Historical Report," 31 December 1965, [1-2], in K-GP-A-CMDO-315-SU-RE, AFSHRC (hereafter "History July-December 1965"); DOD, MACV, "Herbicide Program Seminar," Hq MACV, Saigon, RVN, 28 January 1968, 38-39, 41, in CH-5-4, AFSHRC.

24. "Augmentation of Ranch Hand Aircraft," MAC J 311 to CINCPAC, No. 27672, 070745Z Aug 65, and "Redesignation of Spray Configured C-123," PACAF DOOT 38961, November 1965, cited in "History July-December 1965," [1-2]. Hurlbert Field, formerly Eglin Auxiliary #9 and subsequently Hurlbert AFB, became the training center for all crew members assigned to C-123s in Vietnam after mid-1964 when the 775th Troop Carrier Squadron (Medium) was transferred from Pope AFB with its 16 C-123s. In December 1965 the primary base unit, the 1st Air Commando Wing, was moved to England AFB, Louisiana, as a tactical organization. It was replaced by the 4410th Combat Crew Training Wing, with three squadrons—4408, 4409, and 4410. Hurlbert was crowded by addition of the 5th Reconnaissance Squadron and 317th Air Commando Squadron. Upgrade training for crew members required 29 C-123s by early 1966. Action was also being taken to transfer spray training to Hurlbert, and the Special Air Warfare Center recommended that all remaining Air Force C-123 resources in the United States be transferred to SWAC control. By May 1966 the 4408th CCTS was providing spray training for four to six pilots per month, although they had to use standard B model aircraft, pending receipt of spray-modified planes. Transition and spray training eventually moved again in July 1969 when the 4408th CCTS was moved to Lockborne AFB, Ohio. Hurlbert Field, however, is still considered the "home" of the Air Commandos, including RANCH HAND and the trash haulers. A memorial park with a display of commando aircraft was established at the entrance to the base in 1981. The RANCH HAND memorial to the comrades they lost in Southeast Asia was dedicated at this park during the RANCH HAND 20th reunion ceremonies in 1985. *SWAC*, Vols: Jan-Jun 1964, 2, 105; Jul-Dec 1965, 48-50, 105; Jul-Dec 1965, 16, 30, 40, 104; Jan-Jun 1966, 26-27, 29; Jul-Dec 1966, 16, 31; Attach. 1; Jul-Dec 1967, Attach. 19; Jan-Jun 1969, 5. The redesignation of the spray-modified aircraft to UC-123 was only part of an overall Air Force reevaluation of the assault transport in 1965. Because of its proven utility in Vietnam, the decision was made in October to upgrade its capabilities by the addition of two auxiliary jet engines, a version later designated as the K model C-123. Previous limited or test versions had included a J model, with wingtip jets, and the H and L models with wide-track gear and turbo-prop engines.

An early test model reportedly had jet engines only. Thus, the C-123 became the only aircraft that at one time or another was nonpowered, purely jet powered, purely conventional powered, turbo-prop powered, and combined conventional and jet powered. In the process the C-123 had no engines, two engines, or four engines, depending on the version. DAF, AFRDQPR, MR No. 1482(FS-1770/C-123B), 11 October 1965, revised 14 February 1969, *834AD July 1968-June 1970*, Vol. 2, Tab 54. See also, "Case History of the C-123 Airplane," K202.1-50, AFSHRC.

25. DOD, Directorate for Information Operations and Reports, "Herbs Tape" [February 1974]; USAF, "Herbicide Operations," App. I, 71; "History June-December 1965," [2]; USAF, "Ranch Hand in SEA," 12. Not all the F-100 personnel initially liked escort missions because of the long loiter times required, which sometimes stretched fuel reserves to the limits. One former commander of an F-100 squadron in Vietnam termed the missions "not too smart." Oral History Interview with Colonel Don D. Pittman by Major Samuel E. Riddlebarger, 13 February 1969, typed transcript, K239.0512-079, AFSHRC. Russell E. Mohney, who as a Major commanded the SASF during the last three months of 1965, was the first ex-RANCH HAND officer to be promoted to general officer.

26. USAF, "Ranch Hand in SEA," 21; USN, "A Review," 10; "History July-December 1965," [2]; Charles Mohr, "Defoliation Unit Lives Perilously," NYT, 20 December 1965, 3.

27. "History July-December 1965," [2-3]; Charles H. Hubbs, "Cowboy Zero One," [1967] typescript, [31], personal papers of Charles H. Hubbs, Camp Springs, Maryland.

28. Letter, 309th ACS to 315 ACG, 12 November 1965, in Hq USMACV Monthly Evaluation Report, November 1965, cited in USAF, "Herbicide Operations," 22.

29. "History July-December 1965," [3]; USAF, "Herbicide Operations," 22; USAF, Ranch Hand in SEA," 106.

30. USAF, "Herbicide Operations," App. I, 70-71; DOD, "Seminar," 8; W. B. Ennis, unpublished data, released by USDA to DOD for administrative use only, cited in House, "Assessment," 12; Mohr, "Defoliation," 3 (quotation). Considerable variance in the information for 1965 exists in the records. A secret message from COMUSMACV to CINCPAC in 1967 lists monthly sorties by RANCH HAND and has a total for 1965 of 696; however, the Herbicide Program Seminar at Hq MACV in January 1968 contains mission totals by type and Corps area for each year, and gives a grand total for 1965 of 897 sorties (p. 8). The latter figure appears more accurate. Crop destruction is listed in House (p. 15) as 49,637 acres, while AmEmb Saigon No. 3309, 12 March 1966, reports 27,300 hectares (67,460 acres); COMUSMACV, 161020Z Jan 67, gives 68,250 acres, and the "Herbicide Policy Review" (p. 4) lists 267 square kilometers (65,978 acres) destroyed. The COMUSMACV figure was selected as being the most compatible with the number of crop sorties flown (267) in 1965. (During the author's tour of duty, crop targets were estimated to cover 250 to 300 acres per sortie.) Defoliation data vary even more widely than the other two groups, from Butz's extremely low figure of 75,000 acres to House's (p. 15) 94,726 acres, the Herbicide Policy Review Committee's (p. 4) 630 square kilometers (155,674 acres), and COSMUSMACV's report of 655.2 square kilometers (161,900 acres). Again the largest figure is accepted as the most compatible with other data—630 sorties expended on defoliation at an estimated 300 acres per sortie. DOS, American Embassy Saigon, Herbicide Policy Review Committee, "Report on the Herbicide Policy Review," 28 August 1968, 4, in File 7110, Item #3, TAMU; J. S. Butz, Jr., "Tactical Airpower in 1965.... The Trial by Fire," *Air Force and Space Digest* 49 (March 1966), 42.

31. Quoted in USAF, "Herbicide Operations," xii-xiii.

32. Questionnaire No. 7423, John K. Hodgin, 23 November 1981; Hubbs, "Cowboy," [46]. Attempts to make the war a "spit and polish" affair were a periodic and highly resented activity of various commanders at major bases and higher headquarters. A high proportion of veterans interviewed expressed an intense dislike for the "chicken-shits" that attempted to enforce state-side standards in Vietnam. This was not restricted to the lower ranks. When TAC Headquarters prohibited wearing of the "Commando Hat" in January 1964 (Hq TAC DM Msg, 24 Jan 64), Brigadier General Gilbert L. Pritchard immediately protested to General Sweeny, TAC Commander, that the hat was needed for both protection and morale purposes. General Pritchard was

temporarily successful, although by 1967 the hat once more had been prohibited in Vietnam. *SAWC January-June 1964,* 197-98.

33. Hodgin Questionnaire.

34. Questionnaire No. 7731, Michael L. Shuppert, 18 October 1981; Questionnaire No. 7805, Verne D. Uhler, 23 October 1981.

35. Mohr, "Defoliation," 3. Captain Mitchell was well qualified to comment on the effect of ground fire, having been wounded early in 1965 when his instrument panel was shot up, hurling fragments into his face and arms. He was wounded again, after the interview, before completing his tour in Vietnam.

36. The "Order of the Punctured Provider" was a certificate given to crewmembers at the end of their tour which detailed the number of hits taken by aircraft they were on during their time in Vietnam. Although a crewmember was awarded his purple scarf as soon as he flew his first combat spray mission, he was still labeled an F.N.G. (Fucking New Guy) until he took his first hit from enemy ground fire. The record for the number of RANCH HAND missions without being hit is apparently held by then-Major James W. Umstead, who flew nearly 200 missions before finally getting his first hit. Oral History Tape No. 80-2, 10 October 1980, Tarpon Springs, Florida.

37. COMUSMACV to CINCPAC, 161020Z Jan [Jul?] 67, in USAF, "Herbicide Operations," App. I, 71.

CHAPTER 7

1. Berger, 40-44 (quotation); Millett, 145-46. In addition to the sources specifically cited below, the material for this chapter was drawn from interviews and correspondence with Howard F. Bowles, Jr., Andrew G. Burtyk, Ralph C. Dresser, Robert L. Harrison, Charles H. Hubbs, Donald D. McCulloch, Russell E. Mohney, Leonard J. Pochurek, Michael L. Shuppert, Harold R. Snell, Delmar B. Spivey, Lowell V. Thomas, and Verne D. Uhler, all members of the herbicide unit during 1966.

2. USAF, "Herbicide Operations," App. I, 71; Calvin J. Crochet, "A Special Report on Operation Pink Rose" (Air University, Air Command and Staff College, June 1970), 12, K239.032-5, AFSHRC; Top Secret Headquarters MACV Briefing for Major General C. E. Hutchins, cited in USAF, "Herbicide Operations," 24 (quotation).

3. Wesley Pruden, Jr., "Defoliating the Jungles in Vietnam," *National Observer* 5 (28 February 1966), 1.

4. Stewart Diamond, "'Most-Shot-At' Title May Go to Crews of Defoliation Unit," *Air Force Times,* 26 January 1966; Questionnaire No. 7884, Lowell V. Thomas, 22 February 1982. Thomas was a pilot and flight maintenance officer with the SASF, 309th ACS, in 1966.

5. Unit History, 12th ACS, in *315 ACW January-September 1967,* App. 106, 9.

6. The material on the early Laos missions discussed in this and the following paragraphs came primarily from: Oral History Interview of Colonel Ralph C. Dresser, USAF, by the author, 11 October 1980, Tarpon Springs, Florida; Questionnaire No. 7750, Delmar B. Spivey, 27 October 1981; Questionnaire No. 7104, Ralph C. Dresser, 18 October 1981; Thomas Questionnaire; and USAF, "Herbicide Operations," 22-24.

7. For details of Major Fisher's act in winning the Medal of Honor, see Donald K. Schneider, *Air Force Heroes in Vietnam,* USAF Southeast Asia Monograph Series, Vol. 7, Monograph 9 (Washington, DC, 1979), 2-8, 72.

8. Left- and right-seat pilots, respectively, were Captain Richard A. Peshkin and Captain Richard E. King. Despite numerous glass cuts, including in one eye, King was flying again within four weeks. Peshkin was known as the "Backfire King" because he reportedly never started an engine during the entire Pacific ferry trip without backfiring it, including blowing out a carburetor diaphragm on the start at Midway Island. Thomas Questionnaire.

9. Report, "Defoliant Operations in Laos," 1 January 1966, cited in USAF, "Herbicide Operations," 22-23. The report is apparently dated in error since the information cited includes data through the end of June 1966. The so-called "Buddhist Revolt" occurred when Premier Ky relieved the I Corps Commander, Major General Nguyen Chanh Thi, of his command on 10 March 1966. Thi refused to step down and was supported by most of the 1st ARVN Division and part of the 2d. Ky suppressed this revolt by his old rival by bringing in Vietnamese Marines and elite airborne troops, who were loyal to Ky. The brief rebellion was ended by 22 June and Thi was exiled by reassigning him to duty in the United States. The fighting between Vietnamese units, and subsequent purges of disloyal officers, severely weakened the capability of the ARVN to defend I Corps areas from incursion by North Vietnamese regulars a short time later. Francis J. West, Jr., *Small Unit Action in Vietnam, Summer 1966,* with an introduction by Brigadier General Edwin H. Simmons, USMC (Ret.) (New York, 1967, 1981), xiii. See also, Karnow, 445-50.

10. Interview with Captain Walter A. Marshaleck, Targeting Officer, August 1966-July 1967, by Captain Charles V. Collins, Project CHECO, 1967, and Folder, Project 3-20-2-66, 12th ACS Files, cited in USAF, "Herbicide Operations," 23-24. "Mac's Folly" may refer to Captain Donald D. McCulloch, a hard-luck pilot who not only sprayed the wrong area, but while in training caught the mumps and had to repeat the entire course. Questionnaire No. 7546, Donald D. McCulloch, 6 November 1981.

11. Questionnaire No. 7111, Russell E. Mohney, 9 November 1981.

12. Questionnaire No. 7394, Robert L. Harrison, 16 November 1981.

13. Mohney Questionnaire.

14. Hq USMACV Monthly Evaluation Reports, March, April, May 1966; Message, COMUSMACV to CINCPAC, Subj.: Herbicide Operations, 021105Z Apr 66.

15. Thomas Questionnaire; Spivey Questionnaire; Dresser Interview (quotation); Undated SASF Briefing Sheet, in File No. 7165, TAMU. In an interesting coincidence, the helicopter pilot who evacuated Lieutenant Clanton was a high school classmate. The two men had not seen each other since graduation and were not aware that the other was in Vietnam.

16. Interview with Lieutenant Colonel Robert Dennis by Captain Charles V. Collins, 1967, cited in USAF, "Herbicide Operations," 25-26.

17. Eric Pace, "Spray Killing of Enemy's Crops Stepped Up by U.S. in Vietnam," *NYT,* 26 July 1966, 2 (quotations); Marsheleck Interview, cited in USAF, "Herbicide Operations," 27.

18. Robert A. Shade, "Management of the Department of Defense Vietnam Herbicide Program" (M.S. thesis, George Washington University, 1969), 19-20, 32, 56-57; US Congress, Joint Committee on Defense Production, *Seventeenth Annual Report,* H. Rept. 1052, 90th Cong., 2d sess., 1968, 240 (quotation); "Vegetation Destruction in Vietnam Will Hamper Vegetation Control in the U.S.," *Chemical Engineering* (24 April 1967), 88. Shade's thesis provides a complete discussion of the herbicide procurement problems and the eventual solutions by the federal government and the chemical industry. The proposal to build government-owned herbicide plants had its precedent in the existing government-owned facilities for ammunition production.

19. Shade, 44-50; George R. Harvey and Jay D. Mann, "Picloram in Vietnam," Scientist and Citizen 10 (September 1968), 165-71. Tordon 101 was the registered tradename for a Dow Chemical Company product containing 4-amino-3,5,6-trichloropicolinic acid (picloram) and 2,4-D in a one-to-four ratio. The legal authority for control of production and distribution of material deemed necessary for national defense by the president is provided for in Title I, sec. 101, of the Defense Production Act of 1950 (Public Law 774, 81st Cong., 8 September 1950 [64 Stat. 798]).

20. "Spray Planes Shield Crippled Craft from Ground Fire," *Pacific Stars & Stripes,* undated clipping in File 7165, item #7, TAMU. The damaged plane was commanded by Major Leo J. Gagnon; the lead and number three aircraft were commanded by Major Ralph C. Dresser and Captain James R. Weaver.

21. Dresser Interview.

22. Ibid.

23. West, *Small Unit Action,* xiv; Bob Gassway, "Allied Divisions to Seal Viet Nam Neutral Zone," unidentified clipping of 26 September 1966, in brochure, A. L. Jones to Bill Moyers, Special Assistant to the President, 7 December 1966, White House Central File, Confidential File, ND 19/CO 312, PU 2-6, Box 71, LBJ; "Front-Line Units Urge Defoliation," *NYT,* 2 October 1966, 5; Message, COMUSMACV to CINCPAC, 270515Z August 1966, cited in USAF, "Herbicide Operations," 27.

24. Beecher, "U.S.," 2; "U.S. Denies It Defoliates Zone," *NYT,* 23 September 1966, 14; "U.S. Is Defoliating Near Buffer Zone," *NYT,* 24 September 1966, 2; "Westmoreland Submits A Defoliation Request," *NYT,* 27 September 1966, 3; "Front-Line Units"; Message, JCS to CINC-PAC, 192352Z December 1966, and Message, CINCPAC to COMUSMACV, 292041Z December 1966, cited in USAF, "Herbicide Operations," 27, 74.

25. Dresser Interview; Unit History, 12th ACS, July-December 1966, in *315 ACW 1966,* 24; USAF, Special Order G-256, Headquarters, Pacific Air Forces, Hickam AFB, Hawaii, 25 August 1966. Planning factors were provided in USAF, 7AF, Seventh Air Force Programmed Action Directive 67-7, 29 October 1966. Redesignation of the 315th ACG as the 315th ACW previously had taken place on 8 March 1966. *315 ACW 1966,* 75.

26. Dresser Interview; USN, "A Review," 39. Initially, only one-half of the storage trailers were joined to the hydrant system at Bien Hoa.

27. Marshaleck Interview, cited in USAF, "Herbicide Operations," 28.

28. Data for October 1966, 15, *7th AF Commander's Operations Command Book, July 1966-July 1967,* K740.197, AFSHRC (hereafter *7AF Book*).

29. Undated Commendation Letter, signed by Lieutenant Colonel Robert Dennis, 12th ACS, in File 7103, TAMU. Crewmembers who distinguished themselves on this mission were: lead aircraft, ten hits, Captains Robert H. Ikelman, Thomas E. Davis, Jr., Thomas E. Kluczynski, and Staff Sergeant Charles T. Davenport; number two aircraft, five hits, Captains Randal D. Custard and Howard F. Bowles, Jr., and Technical Sergeant Kingsbury P. Bragdon; number three aircraft, seven hits, Major Charles H. Hubbs, Captain Clyde W. Picht, and Staff Sergeant Willie C. Clark.

30. Data for October 1966, 15, *7AF Book*; "The Day 3 Flyers Cheated Death," *San Francisco Chronicle,* 1 November 1966, 2; clippings, File 7165, items #9 and #10 (quotations), TAMU. Crewmembers on the downed aircraft were Captains Thomas E. Davie and Joseph M. Daugherty, and Staff Sergeant Elijah R. Winstead. Both Captain Davie and Captain Kubley, the flight leader, would be killed in action within six months.

31. Data for November 1966, 15-16, *7AF Book.* Operational data varies between sources, but the *7AF Book* appears most accurate for this period. In November, for example, RANCH HAND sorties were reported to be 409 in the *7AF Book,* 407 in a Secret Message from COMUSMACV to CINCPAC (161020Z Jan [Jul?] 67), 463 total and 377 herbicide in the 12th ACS history in *315 ACW 1966,* and 396 in Appendix A, "RVN Herbicide Missions and Attrition Data," in USN, "A Review," A-1. The author did not have access to documents that would permit exact determination of which figures are correct.

32. Crochet, 2-12; Message, COMUSMACV to CINCPAC, April 1967, cited in *MACV 1967,* 2:876; USAF, PACAF, Hq 7AF, "Final Report: Operational Evaluation of Project Pink Rose," 5 May 1967 (quotations), K740.8051-2, AFSHRC. Crochet and other sources erroneously report 225 sorties and 255,000 gallons. The tanks on the UC-123 hold a maximum of 1,000 gallons each, indicating that one of the figures is in error. The final project report apparently gives the correct figure of 255 sorties, although it would be highly unusual for a large project to actually achieve 1,000 gallons per sortie launched due to incomplete spray-out caused by maintenance problems, weather, or battle damage.

33. Ibid.

34. Army Air Forces Board, "Marking and Defoliation," 65-66.

35. Oral History Interview of Charles H. Hubbs by the author, 10 October 1980, Tarpon Springs, Florida; Charles H. Hubbs, "Cowboy Zero One," typescript, 65-66, File No. 8015, TAMU. One of those "ducking" the RANCH departure from Saigon was the author, then serving

with the 19th Air Commando Squadron. Defoliation of the DMZ would again be authorized in 1967 as part of the project to create the "McNamara Line."

36.   Data for December 1966, 12, *7AF Book*; Message, COMUSMACV to CINCPAC, 161020Z Jan [Jul?] 67; House, "Assessment," 150; Unit History, 12th ACS, July-December 1966, in *315 ACW 1966*, 24-25; "Operation Ranch Hand," *Weeds, Trees, and Turf* 8 (March 1969), 21. Of the 18 authorized aircraft, 2 were en route to Vietnam and another 2 were undergoing modification in the United States. In personnel the squadron was 13 pilots and 2 navigators short of authorization. Sources for end-of-year data on sorties and hits reflect as wide a variance as the previously cited November data. The figures used appear to be most correct.

37.   Bowles Questionnaire; Questionnaire No. 7266, Robert Dennis, 12 December 1981; Questionnaire No. 7484, William C. Knothe, 2 February 1982. Almost every pilot of this period expressed the same dislike for the call sign change. Ironically, this change caused some critics of the herbicide program to become confused and to read evil symbolism into the "Hades" identification. For example, Thomas Whiteside erred in reporting: "The official code name for the program is Operation Hades, but a more friendly code name, Operation Ranch Hand, is commonly used." *Defoliation* (New York, 1970), 8. This is one of many errors in Whiteside's volume. John Lewallen also stated: "The herbicide campaign was publicly named Operation Ranch Hand, but was assigned a more appropriate code name, Operation Hades." *Ecology of Devastation: Indochina* (Baltimore, 1971), 65. The radio call sign was actually assigned by random from a list of approved names that could be easily recognized in radio communications; there was no significance to its assignment to a particular unit, and the names were frequently changed for the purpose of communications security.

CHAPTER 8

1.   In addition to specific sources referenced in individual notes, the descriptions of organizational authority, responsibilities, and procedures have been drawn primarily from: Downs and Scrivner, 17, 25; "Seminar," 37-51; USAF, "Herbicide Operations," 40-41; DOD, MACV, "Military Operations: Herbicide Operations," MACV Dir-525-1 and periodic revisions; EOTR, 24 January 1968-3 January 1969, Lieutenant Colonel Arthur F. McConnell, Jr., VI:A1-A2, M42193-390, AUL; EOTR, 11 September 1968-8 September 1969, Lieutenant Colonel Rex K. Stoner, Jr., 1-16, K740.131, AFSHRC; McConnell Interview; Dresser Interview; Brock, Dennis, Good, Gruenler, Mead, Mohney, Stoner, Waitt, West, and Willoughby Questionnaires; West, Diary, 19 February 1968-2 January 1969, copy in File 7845, item #1.

2.   Hubbs, "Cowboy Zero One," 75-76.

3.   Good Questionnaire; EOTR, August 1967-January 1969, Major General Gordon F. Blood, E-70, K740.131, AFSHRC.

4.   The restriction because of friendly units was to preclude accidental attack on them by the escorting fighters, rather than from any fear that the chemicals would harm human beings. Viet Cong stories about herbicide contamination causing sickness and death among animals and people were considered helpful by field commanders since they increased the disruptive effects of herbicide operations on enemy forces. On the other hand, the 2 percent dud rate for CBU munitions, another controversial weapon, made field forces leery of entering heavy suppression areas too soon after an attack.

5.   Pittman Oral History transcript; Oral History Interview of Major Fred N. Thompson by Major Samuel E. Riddlebarger, 2 June 1970, typed transcript, K239.0512-283, AFSHRC.

6.   A copy of a typical lift schedule for Bien Hoa is in File 7237, item #24. At times, a fourth aircraft could be accommodated on the herbicide reloading pits, which helped ease congestion.

7.   Bowles, Dresser, Harrison, Mohney, Picht, Spivey, and Thomas Questionnaires.

8.   Bowles, Good, Harrison, Knothe, Picht, Thomas, Topolosky, Waitt, and West Questionnaires; Hubbs, "Cowboy Zero One," 112-13. Numerous individuals who served at Bien Hoa

between 1967 and 1970 claim to have either initiated or helped with extra-legal procurement of materials to upgrade their quarters. If even half the claims made at RANCH HAND reunions were true, by 1970 the spray quarters would have been the envy of the Hilton Hotel chain. "Beach parties" at various small airstrips along the coast became more infrequent as the war intensified.

9. Dresser and Picht Questionnaires; Hubbs, "Cowboy Zero One," 118-20. "Hymns" are still heard at the annual reunions of RANCH HAND veterans, but more discreetly. Economics have changed the veterans' party weapons from champagne to beer.

10. Hubbs, "Cowboy Zero One," 113-14; Bowles Questionnaire.

11. Dresser, Knothe, Mohney, and Picht Questionnaires; EOTR, Stoner, 14-15.

12. Waitt Questionnaire; Dresser Interview.

13. Dresser Interview.

14. Shearon Questionnaire.

15. Knothe Questionnaire.

16. Spivey Questionnaire; Hubbs, "Cowboy Zero One," 21.

17. Hubbs, "Cowboy Zero One," 20; Knothe Questionnaire.

18. Dennis Questionnaire; Dresser Interview; Questionnaire No. 7718, John L. Scott, 9 November 1981 (quotation). In later years some officers asked to leave the squadron because the reduction in sorties after mid-1969 gave them too little flying time, with nothing else to do. Transfer to airlift meant less thrilling missions, but full occupation.

19. Bowles, Good, and Willoughby Questionnaires; McConnell Interview; Correspondence with Robert L. Dennis, 14 March 1982. In 1962-64 a captain commanded RANCH HAND; in 1968 a lieutenant colonel with several years in grade did not have enough rank to even be a flight commander. A roster of RANCH HANDs in the operations section as of 18 March 1968 is in File 7237, item #5. The rare crewmember who refused to fly spray missions could sometimes be forgiven. For instance, one officer stopped flying when notified that he had been passed-over for promotion, under the circumstances a bitter pill to swallow. Most passed-over personnel, however, continued to perform their duties loyally and effectively.

20. EOTR, Stoner, 10. RANCH HAND historical reports note high turnover in all positions, but especially in midlevel management. Flight examiners, flight commanders, and instructors frequently served only two or three months in these jobs before rotation home.

21. Ibid., 7-8; 12 SOS July-September 1969, 2-3. Pilots in the early days of RANCH HAND, even though low ranking, usually had 1,000 to 2,000 hours flying time, much of it in C-123 or similar aircraft. The 1969 newly graduated arrivals had approximately 400 hours total flying time (mostly from flying training), none of which was in large conventional aircraft. There was little hope that while in Vietnam any of them could accumulate the minimum 750 total hours required by regulation to upgrade to aircraft commander in the UC-123.

22. R. T. Holway, A. W. Morrill, and F. J. Santana, "Mosquito Control Activities of the U.S. Armed Forces in the Republic of Vietnam," in Proceedings and Papers of the Thirty-fifth Annual Conference of the California Mosquito Control Association and the Twenty-third Annual Meeting of the American Mosquito Control Association 35 (5-8 February 1967), 23, 28-29.

23. The account of the early tests and initial operational sorties is taken from interviews and correspondence with Carl W. Marshall, technical advisor on the tests, and Howard F. Bowles, Jr., who flew many of the sorties during the first six months of operation. The decision to convert part of the herbicide unit to insecticides was made almost exactly six years after the original decision to convert the Langley insecticide unit to herbicides. The UC-123 insecticide mission was only one aspect of a total preventive medicine program aimed at controlling malaria in Southeast Asia. Initial tests were planned for Thailand because part of the procedure required volunteers with flashlights to sit in the jungle all night long in order to make physical counts of mosquitoes, before and after the test sprayings—hardly a safe activity in South Vietnam in 1966.

24. "Exposure to Malaria 'Routine'," Pacific Stars & Stripes, undated 1967 clipping in File 7165, item #12.

25. "Commandos Draw Bead on VN Malaria Mosquito," *Seventh Air Force Times,* 31 March 1967.

26. Ibid,; EOTR, McConnell, II-3; *834AD October 1966-June 1967,* 157.

27. Pictures of "The Little Devil" and "Patches" are in the Photo and Slide Section, RANCH HAND Collection, TAMU.

28. "AF Air Commandos 'De-Bug' Vietnam," unidentified 1967 newspaper clipping in File 7165, item #13; "Psywar Pilots Pave Way for Sprayers," *Seventh Air Force News,* 7 June 1967, 4. The psywar leaflet dropped to convince people not to fire on insecticide aircraft was poorly proofread on at least one occasion; it featured a picture of a three-ship defoliation mission spraying a target. A copy of this leaflet in in File 7165, item #11.

29. EOTR, McConnell, III-1.

30. Ibid,; EOTR, Stoner, 3, 8, App. 1:1-5; Aircraft Records of C-123K, serial number 56-4362, AFSHRC; *12 ACS April-June 1968,* 11. Statistics for 1968-71 were compiled from the appropriate quarterly historical reports of the 12th ACS, 12th SOS, and 310th TAS "A" Flight.

31. *12 ACS January-March 1970,* 3, 9-10.

32. Ibid., 9-10.

33. *12 ACS April-June 1970,* 15-16.

34. *310 TAS "A" October-December 1970,* 6; Message, 7AF, 061047Z Dec 70. Although RANCH HAND became a part of the 310th TAS when it moved from Bien Hoa, it continued to file a separate historical report, independently of the squadron.

35. *310 TAS "A" January-March 1971,* 6; Questionnaire No. 7860, Thomas O. Williams III, 24 January 1982; *310 TAS April-June 1971,* v; Aircraft Records, 56-4362. Crewmembers on the fatal sortie were: Captain Charles M. Deas, pilot; First Lieutenant Richard W. O'Keefe, copilot; Lieutenant Colonel Daniel H. Tate, navigator; Master Sergeant Donald L. Dunn, flight engineer; and Technical Sergeant Clyde W. Hanson, flight engineer. The mission was Deas's final flight in Vietnam before returning home and he had arranged to have several other officers take pictures during his pass across the field. An accident investigation board found no evidence of enemy action as a causal factor, and judged pilot error as probable cause. Aircraft 56-4373 was one of the oldest planes in the squadron, having arrived in Vietnam in 1963.

CHAPTER 9

1. Major new US units added included the 4th and 25th Infantry Division, 11th Armored Cavalry Regiment, and 196th Light Infantry Brigade.

2. Field Enterprises, *1968 World Book Year Book* (Chicago, 1968), 266.

3. Message DM 42780, CINCPACAF to CINCPAC, subject: Status of Herbicide Report, 21 January 1967, quoted in *834 AD October 1966-June 1967,* 44.

4. Ibid.; Message 04714, COMUSMACV to CINCPAC, subject: Status of Herbicide, 8 February 1967 (quotations); USAF, "Toxicology," I-15, I-16.

5. *12 ACS January-September 1967,* Atch. 1; Knothe Questionnaire; Questionnaire No. 7774, James L. Tanner, 29 November 1981. Knothe was the pilot and Tanner the instructor pilot administering an evaluation ride on the number three aircraft. In addition to Kubley, the other crewmen who were lost on the lead aircraft were Major Lloyd F. Walker, Captain Harvey Mulhauser, Captain Howard L. Barden, and Airman First Class Ronald K. Miyazaki.

6. "U.S. Planes Defoliate Buffer Zone," *San Francisco Chronicle,* 7 February 1967; "U.S. Troops Begin Major Offensive," *NYT,* 7 February 1967; "U.S. Planes Defoliating Southern Half of DMZ," *Pacific Stars & Stripes,* 8 February 1967; West, *Small Unit Action,* xv (quotations).

7. *12 ACS January-September 1967,* Atchs. 3-5; *834 October 1966-June 1967,* 46, 156.

8. *12 ACS January-September 1967,* Atchs. 4-5; Dresser Interview; Questionnaire No. 7645, Clyde W. Picht, 28 October 1981. Captain Picht was evacuated home in February 1967,

after suffering a serious leg wound in January, his third wound in as many consecutive months. Captain Beakley survived numerous wounds in Vietnam, only to die in an automobile accident after returning to the United States.

9. *12 ACS January-September 1967,* 10; Good Questionnaire; Questionnaire No. 7853, Donald E. White, 28 October 1981.

10. *12 ACS January-September 1967,* Atchs. 6-8.

11. Ibid., 10; Dennis Questionnaire. The other crewmembers on Captain Davie's ill-fated mission were: Major Ralph E. Ragland, copilot, Captain Elmer A. Robinson, Jr., navigator, and Technical Sergeant Jacklin M. Boatwright, flight mechanic.

12. Tanner, Bowles, Dennis Questionnaires; Hubbs Interview. CBU hits were fairly common. Then-Captain Joseph M. Dougherty, who was shot down over the Iron Triangle in 1966, writes of sustaining "over 100 hits from CBU dropped by an escorting F-100" on one spray plane in a flight of three, while the other aircraft also took "numerous hits from the same source." "The Use of Herbicides in Southeast Asia and Its Criticisms" (Air War College Professional Study No. 4562, Air University, Maxwell AFB, AL, 1972), 6-7. Cluster Bomb Units were primarily an antipersonnel weapon, with the CBU dispensers on the fighters capable of ejecting several hundred small bomblets. RANCH HAND sorties usually used CBU-12, -24, or -30, all of which were spectacular and effective.

13. Dennis Questionnaire; Questionnaire No. 7861, David J. Willoughby, [10 November 1981].

14. Dennis Questionnaire; *834AD October 1966-June 1967,* 74-75 (quotation).

15. Questionnaire No. 7289, Robert J. Dyer, 30 October 1981; Questionnaire No. 7532, Winford D. Martin, Jr., 26 October 1981; Knothe and Dennis Questionnaires. A photograph of crew members holding an out-stretched bat in front of the damaged nose section of a UC-123 is in File 7356, item #16.

16. Dennis and Good Questionnaires.

17. Knother Questionnaire.

18. Anonymous by request.

19. Undated RANCH HAND briefing typescript [1967] in personal papers of the author, 3 [2]; Mohney Questionnaire; Questionnaire No. 7558, Charles J. Meadow, 23 November 1981. A phrase well known to flyers is that "flying consists of hours and hours of boredom, interrupted by moments of sheer, stark terror" (author unknown).

20. Spivey Questionnaire. Such signs were common in American-occupied areas in South Vietnam.

21. Flying the flag was usually reserved for the larger formations, but it sometimes was flown on three-shippers. There were several varieties of flags used, especially on "tail-end Charlie," at one time or another. A red flag with the same succinct message was spotted at Da Nang by General Westmoreland and several VIPs (Very Important Persons), and again RANCH HAND was told to get rid of it, this time without further reaction. Good Questionnaire. Such signs were neither uncommon in Vietnam nor unique to RANCH HAND.

22. Questionnaire No. 7726, Bernard F. Shearon, Jr., 18 November 1981.

23. Knothe Questionnaire.

24. "Summary of Important Events for Herbicide Operations in SEA," in USAF, "Herbicide Operations," 74; "Pentagon Triples Spending on Defoliation in Vietnam," *NYT,* 15 March 1967, 2.

25. COMUSMACV to CINCPAC, 161020Z Jan [Jul] 1967, cited in USAF, "Herbicide Operations," 71; *834AD October 1966-June 1967,* App. V, 157; Monthly Reports, January-June, *7AF Book*; EOTR, Brigadier General William G. Moore, Jr., Commander, 834th Air Division, 25 October 1966-11 November 1967, 24, K740.131, AFSHRC; USAF, Special Order GB-539, Headquarters, USAF, Washington, DC, 23 October 1968. AFOUAs cited were awarded under DAF Special Orders GB-313/65, GB-350/65, and BG-458/67 respectively. As previously noted, data for herbicides dispensed, sorties, and hits vary from one source to another. It is not possible

to determine which figures are correct, and the author has selected those sources that appear most correct.

26. Personal records and Air Force Form 5 in possession of the author.

27. White and Good Questionnaires; July 1967 Summaries, 11, *7AF Book*; USN, "A Review," A-3. The crew consisted of Lieutenant Colonel Everett E. Foster, Major Allen J. Sterns, Major Donald T. Steinbrunner, Staff Sergeant Irvin G. Weyandt, and Vietnamese Air Force Sergeant Le Tan Bo. Mission coordinates for the crash site were BS190240-BS340340. Sterns already had orders for his new assignment, flying C-97s in Germany.

28. RANCH HAND personnel lost were Captain William B. Mahone, Captain Virgil K. Kelly, Jr., Technical Sergeant Jacklin M. Boatwright, and Technical Sergeant Harold C. Cook. Both Mahone and Cook were due to rotate home. Cook, who helped design some of the spray crews' protective equipment, was the best scrounger in the squadron and decided to ride along to Nha Trang in the hopes of getting some more equipment for the crews before he left Vietnam. Pilot of the fatal aircraft was the 19th ACS Commander, and the author's former roommate in Saigon, Lieutenant Colonel Merle D. Turner.

29. Questionnaire No. 7747, Walter E. Sowles, 21 January 1982.

30. *12 ACS January-September 1967*, Atchs. 9-11.

31. Downs and Scrivner, 20-21.

32. USAF, 834th Air Division, "Ranch Hand Study FY's 68-69-70," 12 September 1967, 6-14, 15 (quotation), CH-4-12-13, AFSHRC; Downs and Scrivner, 22.

33. Russell Betts and Frank Denton, *An Evaluation of Chemical Crop Destruction in Vietnam*, Report No. RM-5446-1-ISA/ARPA (Santa Monica, CA, 1967), ix-xiii.

34. Anthony J. Russo, *A Statistical Analysis of the U.S. Crop Spraying Program in South Vietnam*, Memorandum RM-5450-1-ISA/ARPA (Santa Monica, CA, 1967), ix, 32. Russo is more notorious for his later role as "leaker" of the Pentagon Papers.

35. USN, CINCPAC Scientific Advisory Group, "Crop Destruction Operations in RVN During CY 1967," by William F. Warren, Lehman L. Henry, and Richard D. Johnston, Working Paper-20-67, 23 December 1967, 1-8, 9 (second quotation), 10, 11 (first quotation).

36. Downs and Scrivner, 18, 19 (quotation), 20.

37. Headquarters, Military Assistance Command, Vietnam, Directive Number 525-1, "Combat Operations, Herbicide Operations," 22 November 1967, reproduced in USN, "Crop Destruction," 30 (quotations), 31-36; DOD, "Herbicide Seminar," 51. The 1967 herbicide directive superseded a directive dated 15 February 1966.

38. *12 ACS October-December 1967*, 7; "Operation Ranch Hand," 22; USAF, "Herbicide Operations," 106; DOD, "Herbicide Seminar," 10 (quotation).

CHAPTER 10

1. Berger, 52; Millett, 147-48; Karnow, 488, 502-6; Field Enterprises, *1968*, 532-33.

2. After modest program increases during 1962-65, defoliation expanded rapidly in 1966 and 1967—by five times and nine times the 1965 area total, respectively. This annual doubling of acreage defoliated was planned to level off somewhat in 1968, with only a 28 percent increase over 1967 (to 7,700 square kilometers compared with 6,018). Acreage defoliated in 1968 actually totaled only 5,121 square kilometers, a 13 percent decrease. DOS, American Embassy, Saigon, "Report on the Herbicide Policy Review Committee," 28 August 1968, 3; US Congress, House, Subcommittee on Science, Research, and Development of the Committee on Science and Astronautics, "A Technology Assessment of the Vietnam Defoliant Matter: A Case History," prepared by Franklin P. Huddle (Washington, DC, 1969), 15 (Table 3).

3. The RANCH HAND experience in reducing enemy success rates by using larger formations and more escorts appears to parallel the success of the convoy pattern of naval vessels; thus far, however, there have been no official studies of this aspect of the herbicide mission. RANCH HAND crew members did not agree with later restrictions when fighters were not available, contending that intelligence estimates were so unreliable that they were never sure if the target was "hot" or "cold" until they actually attempted the run.

4. DOS, "Herbicide Policy Review," cover letter (first quotation), i-iii, iv (second quotation), 16, 24, 32. Bunker replaced Henry Cabot Lodge as ambassador on 1 May 1967.

5. *315 ACW January-March 1968,* 17; *12 ACS January-March 1968,* 7. The number of hits taken in the first quarter of 1968 is in dispute, with the 12th ACS history listing 30, while USN, "A Review," App. A, drawn from PACAF Headquarters official sources, lists only 19 in a summary broken down by monthly totals. Similarly, January sortie totals vary from 580 in squadron reports to 544 in the PACAF review. In any case, the number of hits was well below what was expected. No explanation is given for the reduction in enemy reaction, but it is probable that NVA/VC forces moving into position for the Tet Offensive avoided firing on Allied planes in order not to give themselves away and to save ammunition for the coming attacks.

6. Berger, 52, 56; Robert Pisor, *The End of the Line: The Siege of Khe Sanh* (New York, 1982), 115, 120-24, 126, 133-41; Dave R. Palmer, *Summons of the Trumpet: U.S.-Vietnam in Perspective* (San Rafael, CA, 1978), 69; Harry G. Summers, Jr., *On Strategy: A Critical Analysis of the Vietnam War* (Navato, CA, 1982), 154-55. See also, Don Oberdorfer, *Tet!* (Garden City, NY, 1971); Peter Braestrup, *Big Story: How the American Press & Television Reported and Interpreted the Crisis of Tet in Vietnam and Washington* (Garden City, NY, 1978); William C. Westmoreland, *A Soldier Reports* (Garden City, NY, 1976); Westmoreland, *Report on the War in Vietnam (as of 30 June 1968)* (Washington, DC, 1969).

7. Diary of then-Captain Donald T. Ayers, 19 November 1967-15 June 1968, file 7131, item #1; EOTR, Blood, part E, 69; *315 ACW January-March 1968,* vi, 5; EOTR, McConnell, 1-3; Arthur F. McConnell, Jr., "Recollections of a RANCH HAND Commander - 1968," San Juan Capistrano, California, 17 September 1982 (typescript), 4, TAMU; Questionnaire No. 6310, Robert H. Farris, 20 November 1981. Not only did Vietnamese base employees not report for work during the Tet Offensive, several casualties among enemy assault forces were later identified as base employees. This was not an unusual event during the war, and was one of the things that helped create an atmosphere of distrust and enmity among westerners toward the South Vietnamese.

8. EOTR, McConnell, 1-4; *315 ACW January-March 1968,* 17; *12 ACS January-March 1968,* 7; Ayers Diary. The PACAF committee's report indicates the dates of airlift duty as 8 February-17 March, M/G Blood's report shows 8 February-16 March, and the 12th ACS history has 5 February-20 March. Participants indicate the last spray mission was flown on the morning of 8 February, although 12th Squadron aircraft began flying mail runs several days earlier. Spray missions were not resumed until two missions on 16 March. RANCH HAND aircraft flew both spray and airlift until 20 March, when full spray operations were resumed. Flight Log Book, Donald L. Ayers, 22 November 1967- 17 October 1968, copy in File 7131, item #2; "Short Bursts" [Unofficial newspaper of the 3d TFW, Bien Hoa, Vietnam], Vol. 3, no. 49, 5 January [February] 1968, in File 7237, item #8.

9. *12 ACS January-March 1968,* 8; Meadow Questionnaire; Questionnaire No. 7871, Herbert A. Woodcock, Jr., 18 November 1981; Ayers Diary; McConnell, "Recollections," 3-4. Several spray aircraft were also damaged in the 28 February attack. The day following the attack, those who lost their clothing in the fires were allowed to get replacements from the base exchange and clothing sales store. Major Joe Meadow, who lived in the "field grade hooch" with the author, was one of those who lost everything, including his lucky Zippo lighter from the Korean War. Several days later, when bulldozers had cleared away all the rubble, Meadow was sitting on the blackened concrete foundation, idly sifting through some ashes in the grass, when he noticed a burned and slightly melted Zippo lighter—his "lucky" lighter—which he still carries. Victims of the attack still complain bitterly that the cruelest blow of all by the VC was the 122-millimeter

rocket that landed squarely on the cover of the community latrine's septic tank, with obvious results.

10. Martin Questionnaire. Each base unit was tasked to provide a number of enlisted personnel to assist the Security Police Squadron during periods of crisis. These "augmentees" to the base defense forces often served long hours in dangerous perimeter guard duty, in addition to their regular duties.

11. Farris Questionnaire; Questionnaire No. 7557, Ronald E. Mead, 30 January 1982; Questionnaire No. 7172, Harold K. Bramble, 22 October 1981.

12. West Diary; *315 ACW January-March 1968,* 17; EOTR, McConnell, II-4.

13. USDA, Forest Service, "Forest Fire As A Military Weapon: Final Report," by Craig C. Chandler and Jay R. Bentley, June 1970, App. A, M-37813-3, AUL.

14. Ibid.

15. West Diary; *12 ACS April-June 1968,* 11; USAF, Directorate of Maintenance Engineering, Modification Program Directive No. 1976 (FS-2159/UC-123K), 11 June 1968, in CH-4-14, AFSHRC; Willoughby Questionnaire; EOTR, Blood, E-70.

16. Willoughby Questionnaire; Conversation with Jack Spey, 10-11 October 1981, Fort Walton Beach, Florida.

17. Standard Ranch Operating Procedures, [December 1968], typescript, Procedures File, TAMU; EOTR, Stoner, 7.

18. *Le Monde* (French), 20 April 1968, cited in Neilands, *Harvest,* 128; *12 ACS April-June 1968,* 13.

19. Berger, 57; Willoughby and Woodcock Questionnaires; Questionnaire No. 7237, Bryce C. Connor, 25 March 1982; West Diary. Roger P. Fox, *Air Base Defense in the Republic of Vietnam, 1961-1973* (Washington, DC, 1979), 179, provides a computer printout of attacks on the ten primary USAF operating bases in Vietnam, including Bien Hoa. The 0600 hours attack (line number 097) lists no aircraft damage and no US wounded. In addition to the Wing DCM, Lieutenant Colonel Bryce Connor received the Purple Heart for injuries suffered during the attack; reports indicate there may have been others. This is not the only instance of RANCH HAND's presence at Bien Hoa being overlooked. When the Air Force Chief of Staff, General John P. McConnell, visited Bien Hoa in November 1968, his itinerary, prepared by the 3d Wing commander, did not include RANCH HAND. The 12th Squadron commander, however, "arranged" to be noticed by General McConnell, and made him aware of the spray unit. McConnell, "Recollections," 15-16.

20. Willoughby Questionnaire; West Diary; *12 ACS April-June 1968,* 14.

21. Questionnaire No. 7300, Arthur G. Ericson, 14 December 1981.

22. Questionnaire No. 7162, George T. Boone, 27 October 1981; West Diary; Woodcock Questionnaire; *12 ACS April-June 1968,* 10. Crewmembers lost were Lieutenant Colonel Emmet Rucker, Jr., Major James L. Shanks, and Sergeant Herbert E. Schmidt. The site of the crash was in the South China Sea approximately 1½ kilometers off the coast, at coordinates VQ 990480. A copy of the lift schedule for 24 May 1968 is in File 7237, item #24.

23. Willoughby and Woodcock Questionnaires. The downed fighter pilot was Second Lieutenant David H. Whitehall. A copy of the memorial service program is in the RANCH HAND Collection.

24. Questionnaire No. 7670, Billy D. Rhodes, 27 October 1981.

25. Willoughby and Woodcock Questionnaires; McConnell, "Recollections," 9.

26. Ericson and Willoughby Questionnaires; Questionnaire No. 7816, Lawrence L. Waitt, 1 November 1981.

27. Aircraft Records, 56-4362; *12 ACS April-June 1968,* 11, 15.

28. Ericson Questionnaire.

29. Willoughby and Ericson Questionnaires; EOTR, McConnell, III-2; *12 SOS July-September 1968,* Atch. 3-1, 8.

30. *12 SOS July-September 1968,* 8; Willoughby Questionnaire.

31. Woodcock Questionnaire; Michael D. Roberts, "Vietnam Weed Killer," undated

[August 1968] article in File 7644, item #7; *12 SOS July-September 1968,* Atch. 3-1; West Diary. The figure of 4 million acres was an estimate based on the number of sorties flown, rather than any real record of acreage sprayed. It was computed only for publicity purposes, so the wing commander could fly the "historic" mission. Conversation with Arthur F. McConnell, Jr., former RANCH HAND Commander, 5 October 1982, Round Rock, Texas.

32. *12 SOS July-September 1968,* 2; Message, COMUS to CINCPAC, "Effectiveness of Herbicide Operations," 30 August 1968, cited in CH-5-4-19, AFSHRC.

33. *12 SOS July-September 1968,* 9; West Diary.

34. Woodcock and Willoughby Questionnaires; *12 SOS July-September 1968,* Atch. 3-2.

35. *12 SOS July-September 1968,* atch. 3-3; West Diary.

36. EOTR, Blood, E-69; *12 SOS July-September 1968,* 2; 834AD 1968, 3:Tab I; EOTR, McConnell, Atch. A-1; EOTR, Stoner, 15; Questionnaire No. 7644, Robert S. Phillips, 20 October 1981.

37. EOTR, Stoner, 15.

38. "5 Pct. of S. Viet Defoliated; U.S. Calls It 100 Pct. Success," *Pacific Stars & Stripes,* 28 September 1968, 7; "Short Bursts" [newsletter of the 3d TFW, Bien Hoa AB, Vietnam], 16 October 1968, in File 7644, item #2; Woodcock and Mead Questionnaires; McConnell, "Recollections," 15.

39. Woodcock, Willoughby, and Boone Questionnaires; McConnell, "Recollections," 13.

40. Woodcock, Willoughby, and Boone Questionnaires; McConnell, "Recollections," 13-14.

41. Waitt Questionnaire.

42. Letter from Lieutenant Colonel William J. Becker, Commander, 90th Tactical Fighter Squadron, 11 November 1968, in McConnell, "Recollections," Atch. 4.

43. Woodcock, Waitt, and Willoughby Questionnaires. Woodcock dates Patches return as 13 November, while Willoughby cites 21 October. The latter is probably correct, while the former is likely the date the plane began flying missions again after reinstallation of the spray equipment.

44. West Diary; McConnell, "Recollections," 14; Letter, 12th SOS, "Crop Destruction, Laos," 16 November 1968, CH-5-4-20, AFSHRC, cited in Downs and Scrivner, 24.

45. West Diary; Letter, Major General Louis T. Seith, Deputy Commander, Seventh/ Thirteenth Air Force, Thailand, 22 November 1968, in McConnell, "Recollections," Atch. 3. A roster listing all the participants in the Laos mission is attached to General Seith's letter.

46. *12 SOS October-December 1968,* 2; Willoughby Questionnaire; "Well Done" Award Writeup from the *Air Force Flying Safety Magazine,* in File 7816, item #3; EOTR, Stoner, 6. Crew members were: Lieutenant Colonel Winthrop W. Wildman, pilot; Major Jack G. Womack, instructor pilot; Lieutenant Colonel Lawrence L. Waitt, navigator; and Staff Sergeant Richard L. Gage, flight engineer.

47. McConnell, "Recollections," 16; Woodcock Questionnaire; DOD, USMACV, "Year-End Review of Vietnam, 1968," CH-16-1-19, AFSHRC; USAF, "Herbicide Operations," 23, 74.

48. *12 SOS October-December 1968,* 11; EOTR, Blood, E-70 (quotation).

CHAPTER 11

1. Berger, 52-61. General Westmoreland was replaced as Commander of US forces in Vietnam by General Creighton W. Abrams on 11 June 1968.

2. EOTR, Stoner, 7; Willoughby Questionnaire; USAF, "Herbicide Operations," 75.

3. EOTR, Stoner, 11; "USAF Management Summery Southeast Asia," 3 January 1969, 39, cited in Fox, 61. Of the 1,956 aircraft assigned to the ten primary RVN bases, Bien Hoa had

515, including 75 VNAF, 220 USAF, and 220 USA aircraft of all types. A heavy flow of transient aircraft, both military and civilian, added to the congestion.

4. EOTR, Stoner, 7; USN, CINCPAC, "Minutes of the JTCG/CB Subcommittee Meeting on Defoliants/Anti-Crop Systems," 4-5 June 1970, CINCPAC Headquarters, Hawaii, 2, K717.03-139, AFSHRC (hereafter "Minutes JTCG/CB"); Telephone conversation, Richard D. Duckworth, 5 December 1981, College Station, Texas. See also, USAF, Tactical Air Command, "Category III Evaluation of the F-4/PAV-7/A Defoliant System," Final Report, March 1971, M-40586-2, 1970A no. 16T, AUL.

5. Mead Questionnaire.

6. *12 SOS January-March 1969,* 5; 3d Tactical Fighter Wing Daily Bulletin, 28 February 1969 (quotation), quoted in Willoughby Questionnaire.

7. *12 SOS January-March 1969,* 5; Questionnaire No. 7264, Denis DeLuchi, 14 November 1981; Willoughby Questionnaire.

8. "Project CHECO Southeast Asia Report: Impact of Darkness and Weather in Air Operations in SEA," 10 March 1969, D-114, K717.0413-55, AFSHRC; *12 SOS January-March 1969,* App. 1-1.

9. *12 SOS April-June 1969,* 4-5; EOTR, Stoner, 16. It was estimated that the aircraft, serial number 55-4570, would have taken nearly 15,000 man-hours to repair. Besides Major Wolf, other members of the crew were Captain William D. Claud, Lieutenant John F. Britton, Jr., and Staff Sergeant LeRoy Hill.

10. EOTR, Stoner, 16; Mead Questionnaire.

11. Mead Questionnaire.

12. Questionnaire No. 7373, Eric G. Gruenler, 4 February 1982.

13. EOTR, Stoner, 8, App. 1-3; *12 SOS April-June 1969,* 7.

14. EOTR, Stoner, 13, App. 1-3. Part of the problem could be laid to the supply policies of the host base deputy commander for materiel (DCM). Stoner reported that improved parts receipt occurred after a policy change initiated by the DCM's replacement in mid-1969.

15. EOTR, Stoner, 13-14; Fox, 33-36; Alan Dawson, "Saigon Regime Riddled with Viet Cong Before Its Fall," *Washington Star,* 9 September 1975, A3.

16. Memorandum for Record by Major Donald J. Maxwell, In-Country RPC, 5 October 1970, 2-3, K239.03032-6, AFSHRC; *12 SOS April-June 1969,* 5. The wounded officers were Lieutenant Colonel Vergene W. Ford, Major William R. Podluda, and Captain Harry W. Nehrig, Jr.

17. EOTR, Stoner, 5-6.

18. USAF, "Herbicide Operations," 75.

19. "Cambodia Prods U.N. on U.S. Defoliants," *Washington Post,* 5 June 1969, A18; *NYT,* 5 June 1969, 4; Thomas Whiteside, "A Reporter At Large: Defoliation," *New Yorker,* 7 February 1970, reprinted in US, Congress, Senate, Subcommittee on Energy, Natural Resources, and the Environment of the Committee on Commerce, *Effects of 2,4,5-T on Man and the Environment,* 91st Cong., 2d sess., 1970, 112-13 (quotation); Arthur H. Westing, "U.S. Food Destruction Program in South Vietnam," in Frank Browning and Dorothy Forman, eds., *The Wasted Nations* (New York, 1972), 24.

20. EOTR, Stoner, 6.

21. USAF, Seventh Air Force Report, "Investigation of Defoliation Damage to Cambodia," 13 October 1969, CH-41-2-19, AFSHRC; Egbert W. Pfeiffer, "Some Effects of Environmental Warfare on Agriculture in Indochina," *Agriculture and Environment* 2 (1975), 277 (first quotation); Westing, "Food Destruction," 24 (second quotation).

22. *12 SOS July-September 1969,* 5; EOTR, Stoner, app. 1-5.

23. *12 SOS July-September 1969,* 4.

24. John E. Woodruff, "U.S. Is Expected to End Task of Viet Defoliation," *Baltimore Sun,* 30 August 1969, copied in *12 SOS October-December 1969,* 24; *12 SOS July-September 1969,* 2.

25. *12 SOS July-September 1969,* 2.

26. EOTR, Colonel Gordon W. Lake, 21 March 1968-8 March 1969, 3 (quotation), K740.131, AFSHRC; *12 SOS July-September 1969*, 2-3.

27. *12 SOS July-September 1969*, 2-3; EOTR, Stoner, 7-8.

28. *7/13AF July-December 1969*, 35-37; *12 SOS July-September 1969*, 5, 9 n.8 (quotation); Questionnaire No. 7867, Richard E. Wolf, 26 October 1981.

29. *12 SOS July-September 1969*, 2, 7; EOTR, Stoner, 16. The award of the Cross of Gallantry, with palm, was for the period 15 April 1968 to 1 July 1969, and was personally presented to the 12th Squadron by the VNAF Commander, Major General Tran Van Mink.

30. *12 SOS July-September 1969*, 4-5, 12. This quarterly report erroneously labels the September statistics as the quarterly total, failing to include the information for July and August.

31. CINCPAC Message, 210740Z Oct 69; 7AF TACC Message, 230225Z Oct 69; 315 SOW Message, 100315Z Nov 69; CSAF Message, AFCAP, 131850Z Oct 69; *12 SOS October-December 1969*, 4-5, 7; JCS to CINCPAC, "Restriction on Use of Defoliants and Herbicides," 5 November 1969 (quotation), CHECO Microfilm Cartridge # S-225,064, AFSHRC.

32. *12 SOS October-December 1969*, 7; "Minutes JTCG/CB," 6. Data for 1969 were computed from historical reports of the 12th SOS and do not necessarily agree with other sources.

33. *12 SOS January-March 1970*, 10, 12-14; Berger, 346.

34. *12 SOS April-June 1970*, 9-10.

35. Note accompanying on-target tape recording #1, side 2, 25 January 1970 (quotation), File 7255, item #1, TAMU; *12 SOS January-March 1970*, 8.

36. *12 SOS January-March 1970*, 16.

37. *834AD July 1968-June 1970*, 1:7; CSAF to CINCPAC, "Herbicide Operations," 022006Z Feb 70; CINCPAC to CSAF, "Herbicide Operations," 060719Z Mar 70; cited in USAF, "Herbicide Operations," 24-25.

38. CSAF to CINCPAC/COMUSMACV, "Herbicide Operations," 312000Z Mar 70, and JCS to CINCPAC, "Restriction on Use of Herbicide Orange," 152135Z Apr 70, both cited in USAF, "Herbicide Operations," 24-25; 7AF TACC to 12SOS, 190405Z Apr 70, *12 SOS April-June 1970*, 10. The restriction transmitted to CINCPAC on 15 April was sent to Seventh AF on 17 April and reached the spray squadron on 19 April.

39. USAF, *Use of Herbicides*, Technical Manual, T.O. 42C-1-17, 22 November 1966, 3/4.

40. CINCPAC to JCS, "Restriction on Use of Herbicide Orange," 240335Z Apr 70, cited in CINCPAC to JCS, "Restriction on Use of Herbicide Orange," 280005Z May 70, K740.8051-3, AFSHRC; *12 SOS April-June 1970*, 9-11.

41. *12 SOS April-June 1970*, 11-12; Questionnaire No. 7332, Merlyn D. Fratt, 11 November 1981. For details and opinions of the Kent State affair, see Joseph Kelner, *The Kent State Coverup* (New York, 1980), James A. Michener, *Kent State: What Happened and Why* (Greenwich, CT, 1971), and Richard W. Whitney, *The Kent State Massacre* (Charlottevillle, NY, 1975).

42. *12 SOS April-June 1970*, 6-7, 11-14; 7AF to 315 TAW, "Herbicide Operations," 191100Z Apr 70; *310 TAS "A" July-September 1970*, 1; *315 TAW April-June 1970*, 1:18-19, 26.

43. CINCPAC to JCS, "Restriction on Use of Herbicide Orange," 280005Z May 70; 7AF to CINCPAC, 130700Z Jun 70; *310 TAS "A" July-September 1970*, 3. Former National Security Advisor Henry Kissinger later testified that "the Nixon administration overruled the military and stopped spraying the herbicide Agent Orange in South Vietnam because it was seeking support for a chemical weapons ban." "Nixon Ban on Agent Orange Claimed," *Austin American-Statesman*, 16 November 1983, A8.

44. *834AD July 1968-June 1970*, 1:7; 7AF to 315 TAW, 281000Z Jun 70; COMUSMACV to 7AF, 170709Z Jul 70; *310 TAS "A" July-September 1970*, 3 (quotation), 4.

45. *310 TAS "A" July-September 1970*, vi, 1-4; Questionnaire No. 7630, Michael J. Parr, 14 December 1981.

46. Fratt Questionnaire; COMUSMACV to 7AF, 170709Z Jul 70; Correspondence with Thomas O. Williams III, 9 February 1982; Questionnaire No. 7860, Thomas O. Williams III, 24 January 1982; *310 TAS "A" July-September 1970*, 2, 7.

47. *310 TAS "A" July-September 1970*, 7, 8, 27.

48. *12 SOS April-June 1970,* 14; *310 TAS "A" July-September 1970,* 7-9; Williams Questionnaire. Claxton was another crew member who reportedly owed his life to the ceramic vest developed for RANCH HAND.

49. Questionnaire No. 7759, John A. Stipatich, 12 October 1981; Interview of Major Robert Markham, Targeting Officer, 310th TAS, by Captain James R. Clary, Phan Rang AB, 22 May 1971, cited in USAF, "Herbicide Operations," 30-31; *834AD January-June 1971,* 2:Tab 15; *310 TAS "A" October-December 1970,* 6, 21.

50. *310 TAS "A" October-December 1970,* iv (first quotation); COMUSMACV to 7AF, "Herbicide Operations," 170515Z Oct 70; SAAMA (Kelly AFB, TX) to 7AF, "Herbicide Operations," 042145Z Dec 70, cited in USAF, "Herbicide Operations," 31; Ralph Blumenthal, "U.S. Says Unit in Vietnam Used Banned Defoliant," *NYT,* 24 October 1970, 3; "Effects of Herbicides," *Congressional Quarterly Almanac* 26 (1970), 495 (second and third quotations). Although the American Division received the most publicity, records indicate that 29 non-fixed-wing herbicide missions took place after April 1970, all involving base perimeter defoliation. A total of 5,749 gallons of Orange herbicide was dispensed on these missions. None of these violations involved RANCH HAND. DOD, Directorate for Information Operations and Reports, "Herbs Tape," [February 1974], Binh Dinh, Phu Yen, Khanh Hoa, Ninh Thuan, and Cam Ranh Province reports.

51. Phillip M. Boffey, "Herbicides in Vietnam: AAAS Study Finds Widespread Devastation," *Science* 171 (1971), 43-45.

52. *310 TAS January-March 1971,* 1-3; *834AD January-June 1971,* Tab 16.

CHAPTER 12

1. Rachel Carson, *Silent Spring* (Greenwich, CT, 1962).

2. Hadik, Dziuban, and Herbert, 2:10, cited in Downs and Scrivner, 4 (first and second quotations); Gonzales, 15; Hersh, "Our Chemical War," 32; Hilsman, 443 (third and fourth quotations).

3. Hilsman's inspection of results was limited to a brief view from an aircraft flying over the sprayed area. He had little recent experience at low-level flight over Asian jungles upon which to base an accurate evaluation of whether herbicides had improved air-to-ground visibility. Expert evaluators later reported significant improvement in both horizontal and vertical visibility following application of proper concentrations of military herbicides, opinions supported by field forces that entered defoliated areas. House, et al., 113-15. If Colonel Serong's line of reasoning was correct, Allied forces should have been planting bushes and trees along ambush-prone roads.

4. Press conference by Presidential Science Advisor Donald F. Hornig, cited in Lewallen, 82; Ngo Vinh Long, "Leaf Abscission?" *Bulletin of Concerned Asian Scholars* 2 (October 1967), 54; Memorandum for the President from Roswell Gilpatric, 21 November 1961, NSF, National Security Council, NSAM 115, Defoliant Operations, Vietnam, Box 332, JFK; Memorandum for the President from Dean Rusk, 24 November 1961, NSF-VN, Vol. III, Box 194-96, JFK; Memorandum for Mr. McGeorge Bundy from William H. Brubeck, 22 September 1962, Presidential Office File, Countries, Vietnam, Security, 1962, JFK; Hersh, "Our Chemical War," 33.

5. Deborah Shapley, "Herbicides: DOD Study of Viet Use Damns with Faint Praise," *Science* 177 (1972), 777; Jean Mayer, "Starvation as a Weapon: Herbicides in Vietnam, I," *Scientist and Citizen* 9 (August-September 1967), 119 (second quotation), 121 (first and third quotations).

6. Betts and Denton, viii-33; Russo, vi-ix, 30-32; L. Craig Johnstone, "Ecocide and the Geneva Protocol," *Foreign Affairs* 49 (1971), 715; Terri Aaronson, "A Tour of Vietnam," *Environment* 13 (March 1971), 43; DOD, Assistant Secretary of Defense, Systems Analysis, *A Systems Analysis View of the Vietnam War: 1965-1972,* Vol. 5: *The Air War,* Thomas C. Thayer,

ed., Final Report, 18 February 1975, 169-70. Despite military denials of the validity of the RAND conclusions, additional reviews in 1968 and 1969 again highlighted problems in the indemnification and psychological warfare programs (see Chapter 10).

7.   Geoffrey Warner, "The United States and Vietnam 1945-65, Part II: 1954-65," *International Affairs* 48 (1972), 599, n. 32; Johnstone, 716-18; Theodore C. Sorensen, *Kennedy* (New York, 1965), 632-33.

8.   Bigart, "U.S.," 2 (first quotation); Seymour M. Hersh, *Chemical and Biological Warfare: America's Hidden Arsenal* (Indianapolis, 1968), 154 (second quotation); *NYT,* 9 April 1963, 12 (third quotation); Extracts from Hanoi NVA broadcasts in English to Europe and Asia, 1235 GMT, 7 December 1962 (fifth quotation), and 0533 GMT, 16 July 1963 (fourth quotation), cited in USN, "A Review," C-3, C-5; Undated Viet Cong report (sixth quotation), quoted in ibid., C-2.

9.   Speech delivered by Prince Sihanouk, 21 May 1963, Peam Ror, Banam District, Prey Veng Province, excerpt quoted in USN, "A Review," C-7 (emphasis in original).

10.   Brewer, 2; "Bombing Is Protested," *NYT,* 19 June 1964, 5; "Washington Rebuts Poison Gas Charge," *NYT,* 11 March 1963, 4; Hersh, *Chemical,* 145.

11.   Major General S. Azar'yev, "Employment of Chemical Weapons in South Vietnam by the American Interventionists," *Voyennaya Mysl'* 8 (August 1968), translated in *Foreign Press Digest* 0019/70 (30 March 1970), 92 (quotations); Kathleen Teltsch, "U.S. Urges Inquiry on Poison Charge," *NYT,* 15 August 1964, 2; id., "U.S. Says Cambodia Blocks U.N. Efforts," *NYT,* 12 September 1964, 1.

12.   Azar'yev, 90 (first and second quotations), 92 (third quotation); L. Nechayuk, "Weapons of 'Civilized' [sic] Barbarians," *Soviet Military Review* 8 (1971), 52 (fourth-sixth quotations), 53.

13.   "Hanoi Says U.S. Chemicals Kill South Vietnam Infants," *NYT,* 11 April 1966, 2; "Hanoi Sees Birth Defects," *NYT,* 30 December 1970, 8 (first quotation); "Issued by Cuba," *NYT,* 9 December 1966, 4 (second quotation).

14.   "Vietnam Policy Protested," letter from Bertrand Russell, 28 March 1963, *NYT,* 8 April 1963, 46; "Sartre on Panel to 'Try' U.S. Leaders," *NYT,* 3 August 1966, 2. Lord Russell was somewhat less than neutral, for example, in a 1963 letter to the *New York Times,* he suggested that "Communism is no longer a menace and that the real threat to world peace comes from the West's efforts to check Communist aggression." Editorial, "Lord Russell's Letter," *NYT,* 8 April 1963, 46. See also, "Is Communism a Menace?—Russell's Answer," *NYT Magazine,* 7 April 1963, 35.

15.   "Sartre," 2; "Russell 'War Crimes Trial' May Not Be Held in Paris," *NYT,* 8 October 1966, 2; Dana A. Schmidt, "Genocide is Laid to U.S. at 'Trial'," *NYT,* 8 May 1967, 8; "Russell Defends War Crimes Trial," *NYT,* 6 October 1966, 46; "An Anti-U.S. Play Opens In London," *NYT,* 15 October 1966, 32.

16.   Fukushima quoted in Carnegie Endowment for International Peace, *The Control of Chemical and Biological Weapons* (New York, 1971), 40; "Japanese Scientists Score U.S.," *NYT,* 8 October 1966, 3.

17.   Carson, 201.

18.   Fair, 54-55; Wilfred G. Burchett, *Furtive War: The United States in Vietnam and Laos* (New York, 1963), 60-65. One of the earliest articles to appear on the herbicide mission was in the 27 November issue of *Newsweek,* which mentioned the use of chemicals to kill crops in enemy-held areas. "Vietnam: Buildup," *Newsweek* 58 (27 November 1961), 40.

19.   *NYT,* 28 March 1965, 4; 21, 25, 27, 31 December 1965, 1, 12, 24, 20, respectively; Bernard B. Fall, "This Isn't Munich, It's Spain: A Vietnam Album," *Ramparts* 4 (September 1965), 24; John Cookson and Judith Nottingham, *A Survey of Chemical and Biological Warfare* (New York, 1969), 41-42 (quotations).

20.   "29 Scientists Score Use of Chemicals on Viet Cong Crops," *NYT,* 17 January 1966, 4; Letter, *Science* 154 (1966), 856; "22 Scientists Bid Johnson Bar Chemical Weapons in Vietnam," *NYT* 20 September 1966, 1, 3; Arthur W. Galston, "Warfare with Herbicides in Vietnam," in John Harte and Robert H. Socolow, eds., *Patient Earth* (New York: Holt, 1971), 141; AAAS Council Resolution of 30 December 1966, *Science* 155 (1967), 856.

21.   Galston, "Warfare," 140; Fred H. Tschirley, "Review: Ecological Effects of Extensive

or Repeated Use of Herbicides," *Ecology* 49 (1968), 1211-12; Frank E. Egler, "Review: Status of Knowledge on Herbicide and Ecology," *Ecology* 49 (1968), 1212-15; Sheldon Novick, "The Vietnam Herbicide Experiment," *Scientist and Citizen* 10 (January-February 1968), 20-21.

22. Foster to AAAS, 29 September 1967, quoted in Cookson and Nottingham, 47-48.

23. Cookson and Nottingham, 48; "Defoliation: AAAS Study Delayed by Resignations from Committee," *Science* 159 (1968), 857; James Spaulding, "Spraying Leaf Killers in Vietnam: US Scientists Plan a Full Study," *Milwaukee Journal,* 12 January 1969, sec. 5, 3; Orians and Pfeiffer, "Mission to Vietnam, Part 1," *Scientific Research* 4 (9 June 1969), 22; id., "Mission to Vietnam, Part 2," *Scientific Research* 4 (23 June 1969), 26-27, 29-30.

24. Lewallen, 115; Whiteside, "A Reporter," 114-15. See also, US, Office of Science and Technology, "Report of 2,4,5-T: A Report of the Panel on Herbicides of the President's Science Advisory Committee," by Colin M. MacLeod, John D. Baldeschwieler, Nyle C. Brady, Emmanuel Farber, Paul Kotin, Brian MacMahon, Norton Nelson, L. Dale Newsom, John W. Tukey, James G. Wilson, Edward J. Burger, Jr., and David Pimental (Washington, DC, 1971), 3, 8, 38.

25. Lewallen, 115-16.

26. *New York Post,* 4 November 1969, 4; Ralph Blumenthal, "U.S. Shows Signs of Concern Over Effect in Vietnam of 9-Year Defoliation Program," *NYT,* 14 March 1970, 14.

27. Aaronson, 34, 43; Boffey, 44, 46-47. Most domestic use of compounds containing 2,4,5-T was not banned until 1979, nine years after DOD's action. The claims of independence and objectivity for the "outside" scientific study groups, as opposed to the supposedly biased government-sponsored investigations, were questionable because of the inclusion of extremely antiwar individuals. Probably the best example is that of Arthur Westing, professor of botany at Putney, Vermont, and author of many widely quoted antiherbicide articles, who was a member of the AAAS Herbicide Study Team. At the initial briefing at the Fort Detrick Plant Science Laboratories, Westing's opening comment to the briefing officers was "I am the enemy," and he further stated that in his opinion the committee's job was to go "all out to prevent the use of herbicides in Vietnam." In a letter to the editors of *Science,* Roy M. Sachs, of the Department of Environmental Horticulture, University of California at Davis, pointed out that Westing was one of the private group of scientists who made a four-day "intensive field investigation" of reported herbicide damage in Cambodia in December 1969 (see Chapter 11). This committee reported that they "could find no evidence of Viet Cong activity in Cambodia; nor did our repeated conversations with Cambodians and Europeans living along the border suggest any such activity," even though the Cambodian leader, Prince Sihanouk, had admitted the presence of Communist forces in Cambodia as early as 1967. Five months later, the incursion into Cambodia revealed large amounts of military supplies and a large permanent underground military headquarters at Chuo and Minot, where the Westing party had spent two of their four days of field investigations. Roy M. Sachs, "Vietnam: AAAS Herbicide Study," *Science* 170 (1970), 1034-36 (quotations); Westing, Pfeiffer, J. Laveri, and L. Matasso, "Report on Herbicidal Damage by the United States in Southeastern Cambodia," 31 October 1969, in Whiteside, *Defoliation,* App., 117-132. Other scientists, including MIT biologist Ethan Signer and Yale biologist Arthur W. Galston, also were criticized in letters to *Science* for apparently accepting or repeating North Vietnamese propaganda efforts at face value. Letters, *Science* 173 (1971), 379. The misinformation supplied by VC and North Vietnamese propagandists continued after the war as American defoliation was blamed for postwar agricultural failures. Commenting on these charges, Trong Nhu Tang, one of the founders of the NLF and Justice Minister in the new government after the 1975 North Vietnamese victory until he fled to Paris in 1979, admitted to reporters that defoliation damage in South Vietnam had been "exaggerated." Al Santori, "Why Viet Cong Flee," *Parade,* 11 July 1982, 7 (quotation).

28. Aaronson, 35-37; Boffey, 43.

29. Boffey, 43-44.

30. US Office of Science and Technology, "Report," 16, 48; Jerry M. Flint, "Dow Aides Deny Herbicides Risk," *NYT,* 18 March 1970, 72. Critics claimed that later studies found birth defects in laboratory animals treated with dioxin or with "extremely pure" 2,4,5-T. Stanford

Biology Study Group, "A Legacy of Our Presence: The Destruction of Indochina," Stanford, California, [c.1970], pamphlet, 5.

31. Aaronson, 34, 42; "Effects of Herbicides," 495 (quotation).

32. D. M. MacArthur, "Treaties and the Use of Military Chemicals," *Ordnance* 50 (1966), 466; Carnegie, *Control,* 125-26 (quotation); "CBW Treaty," 444; DOS, "Geneva Protocol on Gases and Bacteriological Warfare Resubmitted to the Senate," *Department of State Bulletin* 63 (7 September 1970), 273-75; Charles H. Bay, "The Other Gas Crisis—Chemical Weapons: Part II," *Parameters* 9 (December 1979), 7 n.6; "Statement by President Richard M. Nixon," *Congressional Quarterly Almanac* 25 (1969), 797.

33. "Hearings before the House Foreign Affairs Subcommittee on National Security Policy and Scientific Development, November and December, 1969," *Congressional Quarterly Almanac* 25 (1969), 797; DOS, "Department Urges Senate Approval of Geneva Protocol on Poisonous Gases and Biological Warfare," *Department of State Bulletin* 64 (29 March 1971), 457 (quotation). The riot control agent referred to was a highly effective tear gas, CS-2, which was widely used in Vietnam as a combat weapon against underground tunnel and bunker complexes. Between 1965 and 1969, 13.7 million pounds of CS-2 was expended in South Vietnam.

34. "CBW Treaty," 444; DOS, Statement of the United States Ambassador to the United Nations James F. Leonard, 10 December 1969, and Text of Resolutions, "Chemical and Biological Methods of Warfare," *Department of State Bulletin* 62 (26 January 1970), 96; Carnegie, *Control,* 28, 109.

35. Ann Van Wynen Thomas and A. J. Thomas, Jr., *Legal Limits on the Use of Chemical and Biological Weapons* (Dallas, 1970), 75 (quotation); Carnegie, *Control,* 14; Jozef Goldblat, "Are Tear Gas and Herbicides Permitted Weapons?" *Bulletin of the Atomic Scientists* 26 (April 1970), 16; SIPRI, *The Problem of Chemical and Biological Warfare,* vol. 4: *CB Disarmament Negotiations, 1920-1970* (New York, 1971), 241; Phillip A. Karber, "The Nixon Policy on CBW," *Bulletin of the Atomic Scientists* 28 (January 1972), 25; Johnstone, 716.

36. Article IX, "Convention on the Prohibition of the Development, Production and Stockpiling of Bacteriological (Biological) and Toxic Weapons and on Their Destruction," signed at Washington, London, and Moscow, 10 April 1972, cited in Charles H. Bay, "The Other Gas Crisis—Chemical Weapons: Part I," *Parameters* 9 (September 1979), 72-73, 79 n.5.

37. Public Law 91-441, Section 501(c), 84 Stat. 913; National Academy of Sciences, National Research Council, Committee on the Effects of Herbicides in Vietnam, *The Effects of Herbicides in South Vietnam, Part A — Summary and Conclusions* (Washington, DC, 1974), xxi-xxiv; J. S. Bethel, K. J. Turnbull, David Briggs, and Jose Flores, "Military Defoliation of Vietnam Forests," *American Forests* 81 (January 1975), 30. Westing, the AAAS Herbicide Assessment Committee's forestry expert during their five weeks in Vietnam, reportedly did not inspect the hardwood forests from the ground or air, and instead compiled his report from published materials. Boffey, 46.

38. "Report Actually Refuted Most Defoliation Scare Stories," *AIM* (Accuracy In Media) *Report* 3 (March 1974), 1-2; "Vietnam Still Fertile," United Press International report reprinted in *American Forestry* 81 (January 1975), 30.

39. *"Report Actually Refuted,"* 1 (quotation), 2-3; Bethel, et al., 59-60.

40. T. J. Thomas, D. P. Brown, J. Harrington, T. Stanford, L. Taft, and B. W. Vigon, "Land Based Environmental Monitoring at Johnston Island - Disposal of Herbicide Orange," Final Report, Contract No. F08635-76-D-0168, USAF OEHL Report TR-78-87 (Columbus, OH, September 1978), I:1; USAF, "Toxicology," II-1.

41. USAF, "Toxicology," II-1, II-2; Deborah Shapley, "Herbicides: Agent Orange Stockpile May Go to the South Americans," *Science* 180 (1973), 43-44; James Rowen, "Dumping 'Agent Orange'," *New Republic* 166 (January-June 1972), 10-11.

42. Thomas, et al., "Environmental Monitoring," I:2; USAF, "Toxicology," II-2, II-3, II-5. The eventual number of drums of herbicide destroyed included 15,480 from Gulfport, Mississippi, and 24,795 from Johnston Island.

CHAPTER 13

1. "Agent Orange: Vietnam's Deadly Fog," Television Documentary, WBBM-TV, Chicago, Illinois, 12 March 1978, transcript; Jon Franklin and Alan Doelp, "Vietnam Veterans' Fear, Rage Focus on 'Deadly Fog'," *Baltimore Evening Sun,* 20 February 1980, 1.

2. Franklin and Doelp, 1; Marlene Cimons, "Veterans Gaining Ground In Agent Orange Struggle," *Los Angeles Times,* 27 December 1979, 12; "Lawyers Pool Information In Agent Orange Lawsuit," *Santa Rosa* (California) *Register,* 23 September 1980, 1. Various suits were brought against one or more of the following companies: Dow Chemical, Monsanto, Hercules, Diamond-Shamrock, Thompson-Hayward, Uniroyal Merchandising, Hooker Chemical, Hoffman-Taft Ansul, Northwest Industries, North American Phillips, and Riverdale Chemical. Consolidated suits asked for creation of a trust fund of as much as $40 billion to be set up to compensate the victims of herbicide exposure and their families. In September 1980, more than 100 lawyers representing Agent Orange litigants met in Chicago to pool information and coordinate their efforts.

3. "War Vets in Agent Orange Fight," *Bryan-College Station* (Texas) *Eagle,* 15 March 1981, 3A (hereafter *BCS Eagle*); Anne Keegan, "Agent Orange," *BCS Eagle,* 15 March 1981, 1A; Wendy Watriss, "Agent Orange," *Texas Observer,* 73 (25 September 1981), 8. A report of findings of the preliminary round of tests indicated no significant difference in cell or sperm damage between exposed and nonexposed Texas veterans, although evaluators cautioned that many more tests needed to be made before final conclusions could be drawn. "Herbicide Effect Unsettled," *Austin American-Statesman,* 27 March 1984, B2.

4. US, General Accounting Office, Report by the Comptroller General of the United States, "U.S. Ground Troops in South Vietnam Were In Areas Sprayed With Herbicide Orange," 16 November 1979, coverpage, 8 (quotation) (hereafter GAO Report). In-country prohibitions against US ground forces in the spray areas were not to protect them against exposure to the herbicides, which were then considered harmless to human beings, but to avoid accidental bombing or machine gunning of friendly forces by the spray planes' escorting fighters in the event ground fire was received. The primary exposure possibility identified by the GAO report was Marine units encamped within "drift" distance of herbicide runs. The report concluded that "troops' actual exposure or the degree of exposure to the herbicide cannot be documented from available records." Ibid., 8. The reader can form his or her own opinion as to the amount of herbicide drift after viewing some of the damage photographs in this book. In the author's experience, even as little as 50 feet too much lateral spacing between formation aircraft would leave stripes of undefoliated trees in the target area. Any appreciable drift should have compensated for these variances in spacing; since it did not, the inescapable conclusion is that any drift that occurred was limited and insignificant.

5. GAO Report, 7; Press Conference on Agent Orange, 23 September 1981, Washington, D.C., by Richard S. Schweiker, quoted in *BCS Eagle,* 24 September 1981, 4A. Spray organizations did not attempt to conceal these emergency jettisons or their locations. All jettisons were routinely reported in normal incident and flying safety reports, in addition to their regular annotation on herbicide spray charts.

6. "Veteran Who Battled Defoliant Dies," *Los Angeles Times,* 17 December 1978, 16 (first quotation); "Ailing Veteran Blames Army Herbicide," *Washington Post,* 2 December 1979, A31 (second quotation); Anne Keegan, "Agent Orange," *BCS Eagle,* 17 May 1982, 5A (third quotation). Tales of newly sprayed trees toppling and of plants exploding indicated a total lack of comprehension of the process through which systemic herbicides were effective, but they attracted media headlines.

7. "Eric Sevareid's Chronicle," Televison News Documentary, KTVH, Houston, Texas, 20 June 1982. TCDD is a trace contaminant caused by the 2,4,5-T manufacturing process, not a component. Savareid, however, was not the only layman to mistakenly identify this minute product as a primary component of the herbicide.

8. "Debunking the Myth of Agent Orange," *Santa Rosa* (California) *Register,* 13 June 1981, D14. Calculations are based on 1 teaspoon equaling 1/6 fluid ounce or 80 drops. The estimation that only 6 percent of the spray reached the jungle floor was reported in DOD, Assistant Secretary for Health Affairs, "Department of Defense (DOD) Herbicide Orange Status Report," Press Release (mimeographed), [September 1980], 2. For toxicology data on the various herbicides, see Appendix B.

9. Patrick Yack, "Herbicides in Vietnam Leave a Legacy of Fear," (Jacksonville) *Florida Times-Union,* 9 September 1979, A1 (first quotation); Diane Ripley, "Agent Orange: What It Is and Does," *Rolling Stone,* 4 March 1982, (second quotation); Margot Hornblower, "A Sinister Drama of Agent Orange Opens in Congress," *Washington Post,* 27 June 1979, A4; Franklin and Doelp, "Dangers of Dioxin Are Proven, But Not Vietnam Vet's Charges," *Baltimore Evening Sun,* 21 February 1980, A4.

10. "Bacteria Blamed for Ailments," *BCS Eagle,* 6 February 1982, 9A.

11. Barbara Pusch, "Local Veteran Files Agent Orange Damage Suit," *Fort Walton Beach* (Florida) *Playground Daily News,* 25 April 1981, 1. The possibility that the widespread publicity might lead to specious claims has its precedent in postwar claims following the American Civil War, among others; however, this determination will be a matter for the courts.

12. "Barney Miller" Television Series, ABC Television Network, broadcast of 5 March 1981; Rod Speer, "Viet Vets Mobilizing for Protests on July 4," *Santa Rosa* (California) *Register,* 27 June 1982, A3.

13. "Herbicide's Effect On Airmen Study Topic," *Midland* (Michigan) *Daily News,* 5 June 1979, 1; *Air Force Times,* 18 June 1979, 4; DOD, "Status Report," 5-7.

14. "From Academy Reports: To Study Effects of Agent Orange on Health ...," *News Report* (National Academy of Science) 30 (July 1980), 5.

15. Len Famiglietti, "AF Bows to Criticism, Won't Do Orange Study," *Air Force Times,* 26 May 1980, 26; "'Outside' Scientists Monitor Agent Orange Study," *Air Force Times,* 6 October 1980, 9; USAF, Reprint of Testimony of Lieutenant General Paul W. Myers, Air Force Surgeon General, to the Subcommittee on Medical Facilities and Benefits of the House Veterans Affairs Committee, 16 September 1980, in AFRP 190-2, October 1980, 37-39; Len Famiglietti, "Agent Orange: Physical Exams to Begin This Fall," *Air Force Times,* 4 May 1981, 2. The Louis Harris Company was selected to conduct initial interviews with all volunteer participants. The contract to perform the physical and psychological examinations was awarded to the Kelsey-Seybold Clinic of Houston, Texas, which would be closely monitored by the Epidemiology Division of the USAF School of Aerospace Medicine and personally supervised by the division chief, Colonel (Dr.) George D. Lathrop.

16. USAF, Typescript of speech given before the Annual Reunion of the RANCH HAND Vietnam Association by Lieutenant General (Dr.) Paul W. Myers, Surgeon General, USAF, Tarpon Springs, Florida, 11 October 1980, in File 8003, TAMU; Famiglietti, "Physical Exams," 2. Of the 1,269 identified RANCH HANDS, as of September 1981, 234 were still on active duty and 65 were in the Air Force Reserve or Air National Guard. "RANCH HAND II," Briefing Slide. The RANCH HAND Vietnam Association was formed in 1967, with headquarters in Fort Walton Beach, Florida. All former members of RANCH HAND units are automatically members, and the organization holds an annual reunion in October.

17. Pete Earley, "Delay On VA Study Of Agent Orange May Be Extended," *Austin American-Statesman,* 8 August 1982, C4; "Agent Orange Data Compiled," ibid.; Pete Earley, "Death Rate of Defoliant Crews Called Normal," *Austin American-Statesman,* 1 December 1982, A8; USAF, School of Aerospace Medicine, Epidemiology Division, "An Epidemiologic Investigation of Health Effects in Air Force Personnel Following Exposure to Herbicides: Baseline Mortality Study Results," 30 June 1983, by George D. Lathrop, et al., ii; idem., "An Epidemiologic Investigation of Health Effects in Air Force Personnel Following Exposure to Herbicides: Baseline Morbidity Study Results," 24 February 1984, by George D. Lathrop, et al., XIX-4 - XIX-9; "Australian Report Clears Defoliant," *Austin American-Statesman,* 23 August 1985, A10 (quotation).

18. Judith A. Zack and Raymond R. Suskind, "The Mortality Experience of Workers Exposed to Tetrachlorodibenzodioxin in a Trichlorophenol Process Accident," *Journal of Occupational Medicine* 22 (January 1980), 11-12 (first quotation); M. G. Ott, B. B. Holder, and R. D. Olson, "A Mortality Analysis of Employees Engaged in the Manufacture of 2,4,5-Trichlorophenoxyacetic Acid," *Journal of Occupational Medicine* 22 (January 1980), 47 (second quotation). The 29-year Nitro study is the longest study of TCDD effects, and represents the largest group investigated through long-term follow-up.

19. Zack and Suskind, 12; USAF, "Toxicology," v-31 (first quotation); G. Reggiani, "Acute Human Exposure to TCDD in Seveso, Italy," *Journal of Toxicology and Environmental Health* 6 (January 1980), 40-43; "Few Birth Defects Related to Defoliant, Study Shows," *Daily Texan*, 25 August 1983, 11 (second quotation). See also, Report to the Minister for Veterans' Affairs, "Case-Control Study of Congenital Anomalies and Vietnam Service (Birth Defects Study): Report," by J. W. Donovan, Michael A. Adena, Glen Rose, and Diana Battistutta (Canberra, Australia, January 1983). Incidents in which human beings have been exposed to possible dixoin contamination include: Dow Chemical plant in Midland, Michigan (1937 and 1964); Monsanto plant in Nitro, West Virginia (1949); Badischer Anilin & Soda-Fabrik factory at Ludwigshafen am Rhein, West Germany (1953); 2,4,5-trichlorophenol plant near Grenoble, France (1956); Philips Duphar factory in Amsterdam, the Netherlands (1963); 2,4,5-T plant near Prague, Czechoslovakia (1965-69); Coalite and Chemical plant in Derbyshire, England (1968); waste oil sludge contamination of numerous sites near St. Louis, Missouri, from a plant near Verona, Missouri (1971); and a ICMESA factory explosion in Lombardy, Italy (1977).

20. Charles Seabrook, Agent Orange Birth Perils Discredited," *Austin American-Statesman*, 17 August 1984, A1.

21. Earley, "Delay," C4;. The VA study was mandated by the Veterans Health Program Extension and Improvement Act of 1979, Public Law 96-151.

22. Jerry Harkavy, "VA Offering Free Medical Tests for Agent Orange," *Houston Chronicle*, 16 December 1981, 2; "Vets Say Health Shunned," *BCS Eagle*, 28 March 1981, 11A; "Agent Orange Exams Are Called Inadequate," *Austin American-Statesman*, 26 October 1982, A3 (quotations).

23. "Agent Orange Research Pressured Out of VA Jurisdiction," *Austin American-Statesman*, 15 October 1982, A4.

24. Robert Reinhold, "Times Beach Buyout Leaves Clean-up Questions Unanswered," *Austin American-Statesman*, 27 February 1983, C1. Orange herbicide used in Vietnam had a mean dixoin level of 1.98 parts per million (ppm), although individual lots may have varied from 0.02 to 15 ppm, and Dow Chemical Company claimed that later production of Orange II was quality controlled to less than 1 ppm. Such concentrations were then diluted and dispensed over the countryside at a maximum rate of approximately three gallons per acre, for a total estimated quantity of 368 pounds of TCDD for all of Vietnam during the ten year period. Existing concentrations of TCDD at Times Beach have been accurately measured at levels of nearly 300 parts per billion (ppb), and the Minker and Stout sites, also in Missouri, have concentrations of up to 740 ppb. At one trailer park 40 miles southwest of St. Louis, Missouri, dioxin levels as high as 1,100 ppb were found. In contrast to the 368 pounds of TCDD dispensed over Vietnam, a single toxic dump site in the United States, the Hyde Park dump near Niagara, New York, reportedly contains a full ton of dioxin, together with some 80,000 tons of other hazardous chemicals dumped by the Hooker Chemical Corporation, infamous for the Love Canal site. USAF, "Toxicology," I-25, I-28; Robert Rickles and Harold Holzer, "Agent Orange," *Rolling Stone*, (4 March 1982), 11; "Dioxin Peril in Missouri Unexpected," *Austin American-Statesman*, 14 May 1983, A7.

25. "Dioxin Threats Rated Low on List of Problem Chemicals," *Austin American-Statesman*, 10 December 1983, A5; *Midland* (Michigan) *Daily News*, 26 April 1979, 1; *Santa Rosa* (California) *Register*, 31 December 1980, 1; "Agent Orange Lawsuit," *Washington Post*, 15 October 1979, A20; "Jungle Suits," *Wall Street Journal*, 5 January 1981, 9; "Agent Orange Suits Given OK," *Washington Star*, 30 December 1980, A5; "Agent Orange Class Action Thrown

Out," *BCS Eagle,* 27 November 1980, 10C; "Agent Orange Pact Gets Tentative Okay from Federal Judge," *Austin American-Statesman,* 26 September 1984, A4; "Agent Orange Victims Handed Pay Setback," *Austin American-Statesman,* 29 May 1985, A7.

26. Alvin L. Young, "Agent Orange at the Crossroads of Science and Social Concern" (Student Research Report No. 2750-81, Air Command and Staff College, Air University, Maxwell AFB, AL, May 1981), 5-11, 55 (first and second quotations), 57 (fourth quotation), 58 (third and fifth quotations). The final quotation is from Fred H. Tschirley, ed., "Scientific Dispute Resolution Conference on 2,4,5-T" (Richmond, IL, 1979), cited in ibid.

CHAPTER 14

1. Statement of Richard Burt, Director of the Bureau of Politico-Military Affairs, before the Subcommittee on Arms Control, Oceans, International Operations, and Environment of the Senate Foreign Relations Committee, 10 November 1981, reprinted in DOS, Bureau of Public Affairs, "Use of Chemical Weapons in Asia," Current Policy No. 342, November 1981 (first and second quotations); Barbara Rehm, "U.S. Accuses Soviets of Afghan Toxin Use," Austin American-Statesman, 30 November 1982, A9 (third quotation). See also, Seagrave, *Yellow Rain.*

2. The brief flurry of charges in Congress and the few scientific journal articles caused little reaction in the media, perhaps because of limited press access to the areas where the events took place, and perhaps because few Americans are interested in areas such as Laos, Kampuchea, and Afghanistan.

3. In 1975 it was proposed to the RANCH HAND Association's Board of Directors that a letter be sent to the president and to all members of Congress addressing "the events leading up to the fall of South Vietnam and US commitments to foreign countries." Most efforts to present the RANCH HAND side of the story to the press, however, were on an individual basis, with the President of the Association, Jack Spey, one of the most active speakers. "RANCH HAND Newsletter," June 1975 (typescript), Newsletter File, TAMU.

4. Letter, Lieutenant General Max B. Bralliar, Surgeon General, USAF, to Jack Spey, 25 March 1983, reprinted in "RANCH HAND Newsletter," 1 September 1983 (typescript), Newsletter File, TAMU; USAF, Epidemiology Division, USAF School of Aerospace Medicine, "An Epidemiologic Investigation of Health Effects in Air Force Personnel Following Exposure to Herbicides: Baseline Mortality Study Results," 30 June 1983, by George D. Lathrop, et al., ii; USAF, Epidemiology Division, USAF School of Aerospace Medicine, "An Epidemiologic Investigation of Health Effects in Air Force Personnel Following Exposure to Herbicides: Baseline Morbidity Study Results," 24 February 1984, by George D. Lathrop, et al., II-5, V-4. The study protocol estimated that only 39 percent of the entire RANCH HAND population would volunteer and complete the physical portion of the study; better than 86 percent did.

5. Reportedly, the chemical companies settled the Agent Orange case out of court because the settlement was no larger than the potential trial legal fees and the cost of the resultant bad publicity, while the plaintiffs' lawyers settled due to the continuing lack of scientific verification of complaintants' claims. Another defense factor might have been the fear that open hearings might also expose material indicating that chemical executives were aware of potential personnel risks well before the outcry of the mid-1960s. Some veterans, on the other hand, felt that their lawyers had sold them out in order to speed up collection of their legal fees. In any case, the settlement did nothing to resolve the quesstions of damage or liability, and potential appeals or other suits could still reopen the issue to public view. Editorial, *Austin American-Statesman,* 9 May 1984, A12; "Dioxin Puts Dow on the Spot," *Time* 121 (2 May 1983), 62; "Warnings on Agent Orange Indicated in Company Files," *Austin American-Statesman,* 4 February 1985, A4; "Veterans to Oppose Agent Orange Pact," *Austin American-Statesman,* 8 August 1984, A9; "Houston Lawyer Rebuked," *Houston Post,* 9 January 1985, 8A.

6. Peter Paret and John W. Shy, *Guerrillas of the 1960's* (New York, 1962), 13. The conditions for successful guerrilla war were: (1) it must be fought in the interior of the country, (2) the countryside must be irregular, difficult, and inaccessible, (3) the conflict must extend over a large area, (4) the outcome must not depend on a single battle, and (5) the national character must support the guerrilla effort.

7. Not all the programs cited were deliberately intended to affect the environment—"Rolling Thunder" was a highly controlled attack against very specific installations in North Vietnam—but some of the side-effects of these programs perhaps had more long-range effects than an intentional assault on the terrain. For example, the massive cratering by bombs and artillery could have long-term impacts on both agriculture and disease-carrying insect populations in South Vietnam.

8. Letter summarizing experimental studies on Range C-52A, Plant Sciences Laboratory, Fort Detrick, Maryland, 20 November 1970; USAF, Air Force Armament Laboratory, "Animal Survey Studies of Test Area C-52A Eglin AFB Reservation, Florida," April 1972, Technical Report AFATL-TR-72-72, M-42025, AUL; Jim Chitwood, "Target: Range C-52A," *Pensacola* (Florida) *News-Journal*, 1 February 1981, 1-2. Many of the statements of scientists and government officials, both pro and con the herbicide issue, seem to have been based on personal proclivities, rather than well-founded investigation.

9. Mayer, "Starvation," 116-21; Milton Leitenberg, "America in Vietnam: Statistics of a War," *Survival* (Institute for Strategic Studies, London) 14 (1972), 271; DOS, "Herbicide Policy Review," 26-27, 32 34. Both corruption among some local officials and lack of security in areas of high damage apparently prevented development of an adequate compensation program for herbicide damage to "friendly" agriculture. The frequent changes of government in South Vietnam, as first one general and then another took charge, also contributed to what policy evaluators termed "administrative irregularities" and "irregular practices." DOS, "Herbicide Policy Review," 32, 34.

10. DOD, MACV, "Evaluation of the Defoliation Program," October 1968, Tabs B-C, E-J; USN, "A Review," 51-58.

APPENDIX A Glossary of Terms and Abbreviations

AAAS	American Association for the Advancement of Science
AAF	Army Air Forces
ABG	Air Base Group
ACG	Air Commando Group
ACS	Air Commando Squadron
ACW	Air Commando Wing
ADVON	Advanced Echelon
AFB	Air Force Base
AFOUA	Air Force Outstanding Unit Award
AGILE	Project to field-test various herbicides in South Vietnam during 1961
ALCC	Airlift Control Center
AOC	Air Operations Center (Vietnamese)
AOVI	Agent Orange Victims International
ARPA	Advanced Research Projects Agency
ARVN	Army of the Republic of Vietnam (South Vietnamese Army)
CBU	Cluster Bomb Unit
CCTS	Combat Crew Training Squadron
CCTW	Combat Crew Training Wing
CDTC	Combat Development and Test Center
CHECO	Contemporary Historical Examination of Current Operations
CIA	Central Intelligence Agency
CINCPAC	Commander-in-Chief, Pacific
CINCPACAF	Commander-in-Chief, Pacific Air Forces

COMUSMACV	Commander, United States Military Assistance Command, Vietnam
CTZ	Corps Tactical Zone (later called Military Region)
DASC	Direct Air Support Center
DET	Detachment
DDT	Dichloro-diphenyl-trichloroethane
DMZ	Demilitarized Zone
DNOK	Russian abbreviation for Dinituorthocresol
DOD	Department of Defense
DRV	Democratic Republic of Vietnam (North Vietnam)
EPA	Environmental Protection Agency
FAC	Forward Air Controller
FARMGATE	Operation to provide American aviation support to South Vietnamese forces, beginning in 1961
FDA	Food and Drug Administration
FEAF	Far East Air Forces
GAO	General Accounting Office
GCI	Ground Controlled Intercept
GVN	Government of Vietnam (South Vietnam)
HAC	Herbicide Assessment Committee of the American Association for the Advancement of Science
HIDAL	Helicopter Insecticide Dispersal Apparatus, Liquid
ICC	International Control Commission
IRAN	Inspection and Repair As Necessary
JCS	Joint Chiefs of Staff
JGS	Joint General Staff (South Vietnamese)
MAAG	Military Assistance Advisory Group
MACV	Military Assistance Command, Vietnam
MULE TRAIN	Operation to provide airlift support to South Vietnam by American-flown transport aircraft, beginning in 1961
NAS	National Academy of Sciences
NCOIC	Noncommissioned Officer-in-Charge
NLF	National Liberation Front (*Mat-Tran dan-toc giaiphone*)
NRC	National Research Council
NVA	North Vietnamese Army
OIC	Officer-in-Charge
PACAF	Pacific Air Forces
PCS	Permanent Change of Station
Polwar	Political Warfare
Psywar	Psychological Warfare

RANCH HAND	USAF herbicide operation in Southeast Asia, beginning in 1961
RVN	Republic of Vietnam (South Vietnam)
R&D	Research and Development
R&R	Rest and Recuperation
SAAMA	San Antonio Air Material Area
SASF	Special Aerial Spray Flight
SAWC	Special Air Warfare Center
SOS	Special Operations Squadron
SOW	Special Operations Wing
TAC AF TRANS- RON PROV 1	Tactical Air Force Transport Squadron, Provisional One
TAC	Tactical Air Command
TACAN	Tactical Air Navigation System
TACC	Tactical Air Control Center
TAPS	Tactical Air Positioning System (British)
TAS	Tactical Airlift Squadron
TAW	Tactical Airlift Wing
TCDD	Tetrachlorodibenzo-p-dioxin
TCG	Troop Carrier Group
TDY	Temporary Duty
TFW	Tactical Fighter Wing
TRAIL DUST	Overall herbicide program in Vietnam, 1961-1971
USAID	United States Agency for International Development
USAF	United States Air Force
USIS	United States Information Service
VA	Veterans Administration
VC	Viet Cong
VNAF	Vietnamese Air Force (South Vietnam)
2,4-D	2,4-Dichlorophenoxyacetate
2,4,5-T	2,4,5-Trichlorophenoxyacetate

APPENDIX B   Military Herbicides

GENERAL DESCRIPTION

Systemic herbicide defoliation acts much like normal seasonal defoliation, by causing leaf fall through reduction of the production of the hormone *auxin* in leaf blades. This causes an abscission layer of large, weak cells to form at the base of the leaf stalk (petiole), and leaf fall occurs. Other damaging effects of herbicide application include interference with respiration and photosynthesis and conversion of stored carbohydrates to soluble sugars. Two of the major herbicides used in Vietnam, Orange and White, were hormone-mimicking compounds that were particularly effective against dicotyledonous plants. In restricted concentrations, these herbicides are highly selective, making them agriculturally useful for retarding the growth of broad-leafed weeds and for the defoliation of crops such as cotton, so that mechanical pickers may be more efficiently used. At the concentration levels used in Southeast Asia, however, these herbicides were deliberately nonselective to insure maximum and prolonged effect on a broad range of jungle vegetation.[1]

The third major herbicide used in Vietnam was a dessicating compound, code named Blue, which was more effective against monocotyledonous plants. Herbicide Blue, a contact agent, was used primarily to attack grasses and food crops such as rice, although it could be used as a defoliant during the dry season. Both Blue and White were water-based herbicides; thus, their effectiveness was easily reduced when diluted or washed off by rains within 12 hours of application. Orange herbicide was the preferred agent during the rainy season because it was oil soluble. In addition, the oily base of this herbicide helped the chemical to penetrate waxy leaf surfaces faster than the

225

water-based herbicides. The higher volatility of Orange, compared with White, increased canopy penetration in heavy vegetation, making it the choice for general jungle defoliation. White herbicide was required in areas where drift had to be minimized, such as the vicinity of rubber plantations, and was an alternative to Orange under other circumstances.

All agents were most effective while vegetation was in the rapid growth stage, but could be used year-round in Southeast Asia because of the nearly continuous growth cycle. Maximum damage to crops, such as rice, occurred when the agents were applied prior to maturity or grain (fruit) formation stage. Tuber crops, such as sweet potatoes, were ideally sprayed during root-forming stages.

The primary purpose of the defoliating agents was to increase visibility by causing the leaves to fall off. Most vegetation was only temporarily damaged, although repeated applications in the same area, without allowing opportunity for the plants to recover, could result in plant loss. In addition, some susceptible species, such as mangroves (in particular, *Rhizophora* and *Ceriops*, both Rhizophoraceae), suffered high mortality rates after only one application. Young plants were more likely to incur significant injury than mature vegetation, for example, investigation of accidental sprayings of several rubber plantations indicated that rubber trees (*Hevea brasiliensis*) more than seven years old usually recovered after initial leaf drop, while younger trees might not survive.[2]

At the combat application rate of three gallons per acre (1,000 gallons of herbicide mixture in an area 300 feet wide and 14 kilometers long), horizontal visibility in jungle target areas improved from an average of 30 percent to an average of 75 percent, and vertical visibility increased from 40 to 80 percent, in 1963 evaluations. A survey of field commanders of all services in mid-1968 concluded that defoliation with the improved A/A 45Y-1 system was providing a "60 to 90 percent improvement in vertical visibility and a 50 to 70 percent improvement in horizontal visibility."[3]

The objectives of the crop destruction program were to deny local food supplies to the enemy, force diversion of enemy manpower to food transportation and production, and weaken enemy morale. An indirect result of the program was the movement of noncombatants from the attacked areas, reducing the workforce available to the enemy. If sprayed just before maturation, rice, cereals, and broad-leafed crops had a high rate of mortality. Although Blue herbicide was the preferred anticrop chemical, White and Orange also were effective, but to a lesser degree.[4] Thus, any crops in areas undergoing defoliation also were damaged. Compensation to civilians for inadvertent losses was provided for in the crop destruction project, but the indemnification program was difficult to administer and usually proved to be one of the weakest links of the project.[5]

PRIMARY CHEMICALS

Cacodylic Acid
(Hydroxydimethylarsine Oxide)

Structural Formula

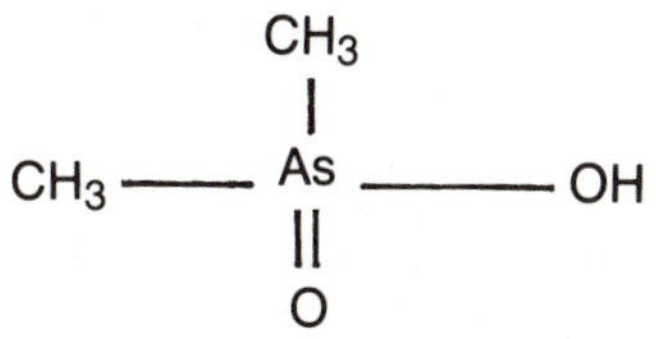

$$CH_3 \underset{\underset{O}{\overset{\|}{}}}{\overset{\overset{CH_3}{|}}{As}} OH$$

Toxicological Properties

Cacodylic acid[6] was reported to have an acute oral LD_{50}* toxicity to young male and female albino rats of 830 milligrams per kilogram (mg/kg) and some subacute toxicity evidence at 226 mg/kg. Dermal and ocular testing indicated that the chemical compound was essentially nonirritating when accidentally applied.

Trade Names

Cacodylic acid was manufactured under several names, including Phytar 138, Rad-E-Cate, Chexmate, and Bolls-Eye cotton defoliant. The military mixture was refered to as Phytar 160 and, later, Phytar 560G.

Picloram
(4-Amino-3,5,6-Trichloropicolinic Acid)

Structural Formula

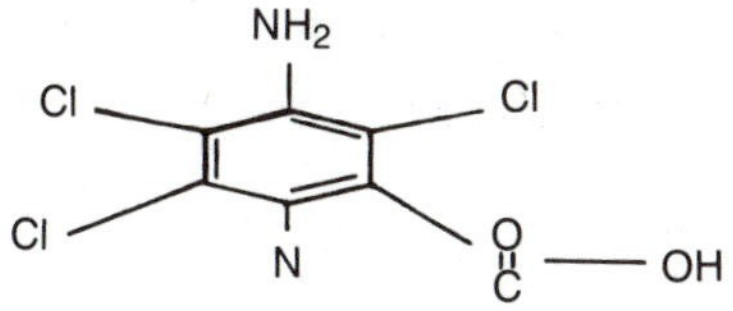

Toxicological Properties

Picloram[7] was reported to have a low-order toxicity to fish and wildlife, with acute LD_{50} levels ranging from 8,200 mg/kg for rats to greater than 750 mg/kg for cattle. Mild skin irritation was noted, with moderate eye irritation which healed rapidly with no corneal injury likely. Inhalation of dusts was cited as somewhat irritating, but not likely to cause illness.

---

*The ingestion level at which 50 percent mortality can be expected.

Trade Names

In combination with 2,4-D, picloram was manufactured under the general trade name of Tordon. The military mixture was known specifically as Tordon 101.

2, 4-D
(2,4-Dichlorophenoxyacetic Acid)

Structural Formula (n-butyl ester)

$O-CH_2-CO-O-(CH_2)_3-CH_3$

Cl —— Cl

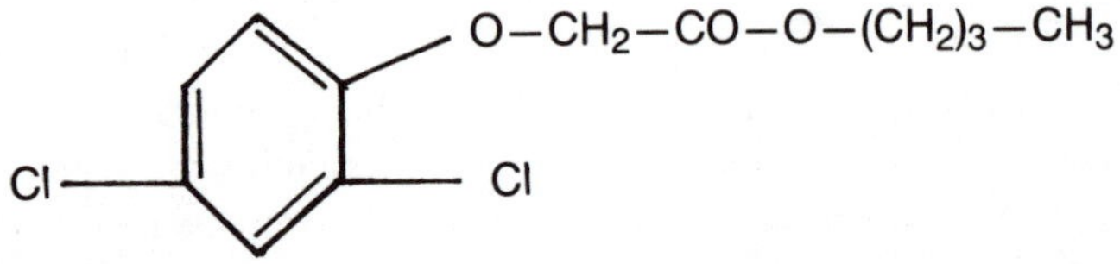

Toxicological Properties

The acute oral LD_{50} toxicity of 2,4-D[8] for rats, rabbits, and guinea pigs ranges from 300 to 1,000 mg/kg. It is reported not harmful to wildlife under use conditions. Some formulations are reported to cause skin irritation. Inhalation toxicity is considered minimal. Pure 2,4-D was reported to have caused slight mortality for fingerling bream and largemouth bass at 100 parts per million (ppm).

Trade Names

The chemical compound 2,4-D, often in combination with picloram or 2,4,5-T, was manufactured under various formulations, including Weedone, Esteron, Weedar, and Dacamine.

2,4,5-T
(2,4,5-Trichlorophenoxyacetic Acid)

Structural Formula (n-butyl ester)

$O-CH_2-CO-O-(CH_2)_3-CH_3$

Cl

Cl

Cl

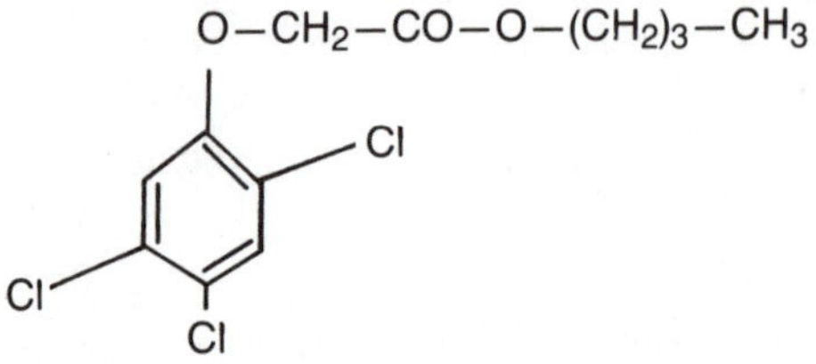

Toxicological Properties

At recommended use rate of 0.5 to 16 pounds per acre, the hazard of 2,4,5-T[9] to wildlife was reported negligible, with an acute LD_{50} of 300 mg/kg for rats and 100 mg/kg for dogs. No significant increase in tumors occurred when 2,4,5-T was fed to mice for 18 months at 21.5 mg/kg/day.

Trade Names

Manufacture names of 2,4,5-T formulations included Weedone, Weedar, Esteron, and various brands of "brush-killers."

HERBICIDE FORMULATIONS USED IN SOUTHEAST ASIA

Blue Herbicide (1961-64)

Early Blue herbicide was a powdered cacodylic acid with 65 percent active ingredient, 30 percent sodium chloride, 3 percent sulfates, and 2 percent water. Mixed in the field with water at the rate of 2.9 pounds of powder per gallon, 5,200 gallons of the formulation was reportedly used in Vietnam. This mixture contained organic arsenic and traces of inorganic arsenic.

Blue Herbicide (1965-71)

Blue herbicide, the preferred anticrop chemical, was a soluble combination of 4.7 percent cacodylic acid, 26.4 percent sodium cacodylate, 5.5 percent sodium chloride, mixed with 3.4 percent surfactant, 0.5 percent antifoam agent, and 59.5 percent water. This formulation contained 3.1 pounds of active ingredient per gallon. The mixture contained no dioxin, but did have 15.4 percent organic arsenic and traces of inorganic arsenic.

Green Herbicide (1962-64)

Green herbicide, an oil-soluble formulation consisting wholly of n-butyl 2,4,5-T, contained 8.16 pounds active ingredient per gallon. Estimated dioxin (2,3,7,8-tetrachloradibenzo-*p*-dioxin) concentration was 65.6 ppm. Use of Green was very limited—only 8,208 gallons was procured.

Orange Herbicide (1965-69)

Orange herbicide was soluble in diesel fuel and organic solvents. The formulation contained 49.49 percent *n*-butyl ester of 2,4-D, 0.13 percent free acid of 2,4-D, 48.75 percent of n-butyl ester of 2,4,5-T, 1.0 percent free acid of 2,4,5-T, and 0.62 percent inert ingredients. The solution contained 8.62 pounds of active ingredient (4.21 of 2,4-D and 4.41 of 2,4,5-T) per gallon. The mean dioxin concentration has been estimated at 1.98 ppm. Estimated procurement of herbicide Orange was 11.8 million gallons.

Orange Herbicide (1968-69)

An Orange herbicide formulation produced during 1968-69 by one company, known as Orange II, varied slightly from previous Orange herbicide in that the isocytl ester of 2,4,5-T replaced the n-butyl ester of 2,4,5-T in the mixture. Proportions remained approximately the same, but improved quality controls on manufacturing temperatures reportedly reduced the mean dioxin levels to below 1.0 ppm. Approximately 950,000 gallons gallons of Orange II was shipped to Vietnam in 1968-69.

Pink Herbicide (1962-64)

Pink herbicide was another oil-soluble herbicide, consisting of 60 percent n-butyl 2,3,5-T and 40 percent isobutyl 2,4,5-T, with 8.16 pounds active ingredients per gallon. Dioxin concentration was estimated at 65.6 ppm average, and procurement was 122,792 gallons.

Purple Herbicide (1962-64)

Purple herbicide was soluble in diesel fuel and organic solvents, and consisted of 50 percent n-butyl ester of 2,4-D, 30 percent n-butyl ester of 2,4,5-T, and 20 percent isobutyl ester of 2,4,5-T. The mixture contained 8.6 pounds of active ingredient per gallon. The mean dioxin concentration has been estimated at 32.8 ppm. Procurement of Purple was 145,000 gallons.

White Herbicide (1965-71)

White herbicide, a water soluble liquid, consisted of 10.2 percent triiso-propanoliamine salt of 4-amino 3,4,6-trichoropicolinic acid (picloram), 39.6 percent triisopropanolamine salt of 2,4-D, and 50.2 percent inert ingredients, mostly triisopropanolamine solvent. The herbicide contained 2.54 pounds of active ingredient per gallon. Procurement of White herbicide was approximately 5.6 million gallons. The mixture contained no dioxin.

Other Herbicides (1961-62)

Other chemicals evaluated as herbicides during tests in Vietnam in 1962 included Dinoxol, Trinoxol, Diquat, and minute amounts of 16 other chemicals. Soil-applied herbicides also were reported to have been evaluated, including Bromacil, Tandex, Monuron, and Dalapon.

HERBICIDE EXPENDITURES IN SOUTHEAST ASIA (1962-71)

By Chemical and Type Mission

Available records indicate 90 percent of all Orange herbicide used between 1965 and 1971 was for defoliation, while 8 percent was expended on crop targets and 2 percent on base perimeters, lines of communication, waterways, etc. Ninety-nine percent of White herbicide was used for defoliation, with the remainder used on base perimeters. Crop destruction missions used 49 percent of the Blue herbicide, with the other 51 percent used for defoliation or perimeter grass control. The pre-1965 percentages are estimated to be approximately the same for the equivalent chemicals.

TABLE 1: Estimated Herbicide Expenditure By Year and Total Gallons

1962	17,171	49,240
1963	74,760	
1964	281,607	218,510
1965	664,657	
1966	2,535,788	2,600,000
1967	5,123,353	4,879,000
1968	5,089,010	4,639,900
1969	4,558,817	4,265,800
1970	758,966	854,600
1971	10,039	1,900

Sources: First column calculated from SIPRI, Ecological, Table 3.2; Second column calculated from RANCH HAND unit historical reports in the Albert F. Simpson Historical Research Center. Blanks indicate data missing or not included.

TABLE 2: Estimated Area Treated by Year and Acreage

1962		5,681	5,724		13,614
1963		24,947	24,920		21,568
1964		93,842	93,869		78,894
1965	75,501	221,559	221,552	72,327	229,920
1966	608,106	842,764	845,263	847,496	742,857
1967	1,570,114	1,707,738	1,707,784	1,599,903	1,375,241
1968	1,365,479	1,330,836	1,696,337	802,380	1,325,685
1969	1,365,754		1,519,606		1,218,800
1970	294,925		252,989		244,171
1971	1,259		3,346		633

Sources: First column, NAS Report, reprinted in USAF, "Toxicology," Table 4; second column, calculated from USA, Chemical Corps, Biological Laboratories, "Information Manual for Vegetation Control in Southeast Asia," by K. R. Irish, R. A. Darrow, and C. E. Minarik, 1969; third column, calculated from SIPRI, Ecological, Table 3.2; fourth column, calculated from USN, "A Review," App. A, Table 2; fifth column, calculated from RANCH HAND unit reports in the Albert F. Simpson Historical Research Center. Blanks indicate data missing or not included.

================

APPENDIX NOTES

1. Except as otherwise noted, all material in this appendix is from: USAF, San Antonio Air Materiel Area, *Technical Manual: Use of Herbicides,* T.O. 42C-1-17, 22 November 1966, 1-4; USAF, "Toxicology," Chap. I; USN, "A Review," Apps. A,B; and SIPRI, *Ecological Consequences of the Second Indochina War* (Stockholm, Sweden, 1976), 24-29.

2. Orians and Pfeiffer, "Part I," 23.

3. MACCOC7, "Evaluation of the Defoliation Program," 12 October 1968, Letter of Transmittal, 1, in DOD, Military Assistance Command, Vietnam, "Report, AC of S, J3 to Chief of Staff, Subject: Evaluation of the Defoliation Program," 12 October 1968.

4. White herbicide normally was not programmed against food-growing areas because of the longer persistence of picloram due to its slower rate of microbial decomposition, but even White herbicide apparently did not harm plant growth by the next crop season.

5. DOS, "Herbicide Policy Review," 31-34.

6. Nguyen Khac Vien, ed., *Chemical Warfare* (Hanoi, 1971), foldout chart; Herbicide Handbook Committee, *Herbicide Handbook of the Weed Science Society of America,* 3d ed. (Champaign, IL, 1974), 80-82.

7. Nguyen, foldout chart; Herbicide Handbook, 302-5.

8. Nguyen, foldout chart; Herbicide Handbook, 116-21.

9. Nguyen, foldout chart; Herbicide Handbook, 375-78.

APPENDIX C

RANCH HAND
Honors

As Special Aerial Spray Flight, 309th Air Commando Squadron:

Air Force Outstanding Unit Award, with V Device for Valor,
8 March 1965-30 April 1965.
Air Force Outstanding Unit Award, with V Device for Valor,
30 June 1965-9 July 1965.

As 12th Air Commando Squadron/12th Special Operations Squadron:

Presidential Unit Citation,
21 August 1966-30 June 1967.
Air Force Outstanding Unit Award, with V Device for Valor,
15 October 1966-30 April 1967.
Republic of Vietnam Gallantry Cross, with Palm,
15 October 1966-31 July 1967.
Presidential Unit Citation,
21 January 1968-12 May 1968.
Republic of Vietnam Gallantry Cross, with Palm,
1 May 1968-1 July 1969.
Presidential Unit Citation,
15 May 1968-15 April 1969.
Republic of Vietnam Gallantry Cross, with Palm,
1 June 1969-1 June 1970.
Presidential Unit Citation,
1 April 1970-30 June 1970.

Sources

CONTACT WITH PARTICIPANTS

Much of the detailed information in this study came from interviews with, correspondence with, and questionnaire responses by the participants, verified by official correspondence, personal papers, classified memoranda, diaries, intelligence reports, mission reports, and so on. The following are lists with dates of the author's contacts with participants.

Conversations and Oral History Interviews

Arthur, James H., Technical Sergeant, USAF(Ret.). Oral History Interview, Tarpon Springs, Florida, 10 October 1980.

Brady, John E., Major, USAF(Ret.). Oral History Interview, Tarpon Springs, Florida, 10 October 1980.

Dresser, Ralph C., Colonel, USAF. Oral History Interview, Tarpon Springs, Florida, 11 October 1980.

Duckworth, Richard D., Colonel, USAF(Ret.). Telephone Conversation, College Station, Texas, 5 December 1981.

Hubbs, Charles H., Lieutenant Colonel, USAF(Ret.). Oral History Interview, Tarpon Springs, Florida, 10 October 1980.

Luke, Harold W., Major, USAF(Ret.). Oral History Interview, Tarpon Springs, Florida, 10 October 1980.

Marshall, Carl W., Lieutenant Colonel, USAF(Ret.). Oral History Interview, Fort Walton Beach, Florida, 10 October 1981.

McConnell, Arthur F., Jr., Lieutenant Colonel, USAF(Ret.). Oral History Interview, Fort Walton Beach, Florida, 10-11 October 1981. Conversation, Round Rock, Texas, 5 October 1982.

Meadow, Charles J., Lieutenant Colonel, USAF(Ret.). Conversation, College Station, Texas, 25 November 1981.

Spey, John R., Major, USAF(Ret.). Oral History Interview, Fort Walton Beach, Florida, 2 September 1981.

Umstead, James W., Lieutenant Colonel, USAF(Ret.). Oral History Interview, Tarpon Springs, Florida, 10 October 1980.

Questionnaires and Correspondence

Aldrich, William B., Major, USAF(Ret.). Questionnaire No. 7118, 28 October 1981.

Ayers, Donald T., Colonel, USAF. Correspondence, 3 March 1982.

Boone, George T., Colonel, USAF(Ret.). Questionnaire No. 7162, 27 October 1981.

Bowles, Howard F., former Captain, USAF. Questionnaire No. 7165, 18 October 1981 and 6 February 1982. Correspondence, 29 January 1982.

Boyer, Joe C., Colonel, USAF(Ret.). Questionnaire No. 7167, 10 October 1981.

Bramble, Harold K., Sr., Colonel, USAF. Questionnaire No. 7172, 22 October 1981.

Brennecke, Harold J., Colonel, USAF(Ret.). Questionnaire No. 7173, 26 January 1982.

Briggs, Earle H., Technical Sergeant, USAF(Ret.). Questionnaire No. 7174, 26 January 1982.

Brock, Eugene B., Colonel, USAF. Questionnaire No. 7176, 9 November 1981.

Bugg, Richard D., Master Sergeant, USAF(Ret.). Questionnaire No. 7187, 30 October 1981.

Burtyk, Andrew G., Master Sergeant, USAF(Ret.). Questionnaire No. 7190, 15 October 1981.

Chandler, Wayne R., Lieutenant Colonel, USAF. Questionnaire No. 7211, 23 October 1981.

Claud, William D., former Captain, USAF. Questionnaire No. 7885, 22 February 1983.

Connor, Bryce C., Lieutenant Colonel, USAF(Ret.). Questionnaire No. 7237, 25 March 1982.

Crocker, Aubrey N., Senior Master Sergeant, USAF(Ret.). Questionnaire No. 7249, 18 November 1981.

Cusenbary, Charles L., Colonel, USAF(Ret.). Questionnaire No. 7252, 22 October 1981.

Dabbert, Edward H., Technical Sergeant, USAF(Ret.). Questionnaire No. 7254, 18 November 1981.

Dallas, Burnie R., Jr., Chief Master Sergeant, USAF(Ret.). Questionnaire No. 7255, 26 January 1982. Correspondence, 13 December 1981.

Deluchi, Denis A., Major, USAF(Ret.). Questionnaire No. 7264, 14 November 1981.

Dennis, Robert, Lieutenant Colonel, USAF(Ret.). Questionnaire No. 7266, 12 December 1981. Correspondence, 14 March 1982, 4 April 1982.

Devlin, Michael W., former Major, USAF. Questionnaire No. 7268, 28 October 1981.

Downs, James J., Colonel, USAF. Questionnaire No. 7280, 5 November 1981.

Dresser, Ralph C., Colonel, USAF. Questionnaire No. 7104, 18 October 1982. Correspondence, 20 March 1982.

Dyer, Robert J., Lieutenant Colonel, USAF(Ret.). Questionnare No. 7289, 30 October 1981.

Ericson, Arthur G., Lieutenant Colonel, USAF. Questionnaire No. 7300, 14 December 1981.

Farris, Robert H., Lieutenant Colonel, USAF(Ret.). Questionnaire No. 7310, 20 November 1981.

Fratt, Merlyn D., Lieutenant Colonel, USAF(Ret.). Questionnaire No. 7332, 11 November 1981.

Frimpter, Donald J., former Staff Sergeant, USAF. Questionnaire No. 7333, 5 November 1981.

Gagnon, Leo J., Jr., Colonel, USAF(Ret.). Questionnaire No. 7342, 30 October 1981.

Gerlach, Daniel D., Master Sergeant, USAF. Questionnaire No. 7349, 1 November 1981.

Good, Henry K., Lieutenant Colonel, USAF(Ret.). Questionnaire No. 7356, 7 March 1982 and 14 May 1982.

Gorman, Millard D., Master Sergeant, USAF(Ret.). Questionnaire No. 7358, 3 February 1982.

Gray, James E., Technical Sergeant, USAF(Ret.). Questionnaire No. 7361, 23 October 1981.

Gresham, Berlin J., Senior Master Sergeant, USAF. Questionnaire No. 7368, 23 November 1981.

Gross, William T., Master Sergeant, USAF(Ret.). Questionnaire No. 7372, 7 November 1981.

Gruenler, Eric G., Lieutenant Colonel, USAF(Ret.). Questionnaire No. 7373, 4 February 1982.

Hamilton, John C., Master Sergeant, USAF(Ret.). Questionnaire No. 7380, 1 February 1982.

Hanson, Paul R., Colonel, USAF(Ret.), Questonnaire No. 7387, 20 October 1981.

Harrison, Robert L., Master Sergeant, USAF(Ret.). Questionnaire No. 7394, 16 November 1981.

Hassertt, Robert W., Technical Sergeant, USAF(Ret.). Questionnaire No. 7396, 12 November 1981.

Hejde, Daniel I., Colonel, USAF. Questionnaire No. 7407, 17 November 1981.

Hodgin, John K., Major, USAF(Ret.). Questionnaire No. 7423, 23 November 1981.

Hopper, Marion W., Staff Sergeant, USAF(Ret.). Questionnaire No. 7427, 20 October 1981.

Horn, David R., Lieutenant Colonel, USAF(Ret.). Questionnaire No. 7428, 18 October 1981.

Hubbs, Charles H., Lieutenant Colonel, USAF(Ret.). Questionnaire No. 7103, 12 August 1981 and 22 October 1981.

Hutchinson, Merle D., Senior Master Sergeant, USAF(Ret.). Questionnaire No. 7444, 12 November 1981.

Jefferson, William H., Major, USAF(Ret.). Questionnaire No. 7453, 15 November 1981.

Kibodeaux, Andy, Major, USAF(Ret.). Questionnaire No. 7473, 10 February 1982.

Knight, Wallace S., Technical Sergeant, USAF(Ret.). Questionnaire No. 7483, 14 January 1982.

Knothe, William C., Lieutenant Colonel, USAF(Ret.). Questionnaire No. 7484, 2 February 1982.

Larson, Frank W., Lieutenant Colonel, USAF. Questionnaire No. 7496, 6 February 1982.

Leger, Oleuse M., Jr., Master Sergeant, USAF(Ret.). Questionnaire No. 7498, 22 October 1981.

Luke, Harold W., Major, USAF(Ret.). Questionnaire No. 7108, 15 October 1981.

Mahan, Wiley H., Captain, USAF. Questionnaire No. 7519, 4 November 1981.

Mantler, Robert C., Technical Sergeant, USAF(Ret.). Questionnaire No. 7521, 24 October 1981.

Marshall, Robert E., former Major, USAF. Questionnaire No. 7528, 25 October 1981.

Martin, Winford D., Jr., Master Sergeant, USAF. Questionnaire No. 7532, 28 October 1981.

McCarthy, James R., Brigadier General, USAF(Ret.). Questionnaire No. 7542, 21 October 1981.

McConnell, Arthur F., Jr., Lieutenant Colonel, USAF(Ret.). Questionnaire No. 7110, 25 December 1981.

McCullough, Donald D., Major, USAF(Ret.). Questionnaire No. 7546, 6 November 1981.

McGee, Edward A., Major, USAF(Ret.). Questionnaire No. 7552, 1 February 1982.

Mead, Ronald E., Lieutenant Colonel, USAF. Questionnaire No. 7557, 30 January 1982.

Meadow, Charles J., Lieutenant Colonel, USAF(Ret.). Questionnaire No. 7558, 23 November 1981.

Meekins, Roger P., Lieutenant Colonel, USAF(Ret.). Questionnaire No. 7561, 15 November 1981.

Milam, George B., Senior Master Sergeant, USAF(Ret.). Questionnaire No. 7570, 15 January 1982.

Mohney, Russell E., Major General, USAF. Questionnaire No. 7111, 9 November 1981 and 17 March 1982.

Mullinax, John C., Technical Sergeant, USAF(Ret.). Questionnaire No. 7595, 20 October 1981.

Nolan, Jimmy, Chief Master Sergeant, USAF. Questionnaire No. 7611, 3 January 1982.

Nolan, William C., Master Sergeant, USAF(Ret.). Questionnaire No. 7612, 6 November 1981.

Oba, Robert N., Master Sergeant, USAF(Ret.). Questionnaire No. 7617, 25 October 1981.

Parr, Michael J., Major, USAF. Questionnaire No. 7630, 14 December 1981.

Phillips, Robert S., Colonel, USAF(Ret.). Questionnaire No. 7644, 20 October 1981.

Picht, Clyde W., Lieutenant Colonel, USAF(Ret.). Questionnaire No. 7645, 28 October 1981.

Pochurek, L. James, Lieutenant Colonel, USAF(Ret.). Questionnaire No. 7113, 20 April 1982.

Price, Charles W., Technical Sergeant, USAF(Ret.). Questionnaire No. 7657, 30 October 1981.

Reese, Arthur G., Master Sergeant, USAF(Ret.). Questionnaire No. 7666, 12 October 1981.

Rhodes, Billy D., Technical Sergeant, USAF(Ret.). Questionnaire No. 7670, 27 October 1981.

Richmond, John P., Lieutenant Colonel, USAF(Ret.). Questionnaire No. 7672, 20 November 1981.

Robertson, Eugene S., Technical Sergeant, USAF(Ret.). Questionnaire No. 7681, 20 October 1981.

Robinson, William F., Lieutenant Colonel, USAF(Ret.). Questionnaire No. 7687, 15 January 1982.

Rothermel, Marshall B., Senior Master Sergeant, USAF(Ret.). Questionnaire No. 7698, 7 December 1981.

Scott, John L., Major, USAF(Ret.). Questionnaire No. 7718, 9 November 1981.

Shearon, Bernard F., Jr., Major, USAF. Questionnaire No. 7726, 18 November 1981.

Shuppert, Michael L., Staff Sergeant, USAF. Questionnaire No. 7731, 18 October 1981.

Smith, Elwood L., Technical Sergeant, USAF(Ret.). Questionnaire No. 7736, 24 January 1982.

Snell, Harold R., former Staff Sergeant, USAF. Questionnaire No. 7744, 1 November 1981.

Sowles, Walter E., Master Sergeant, USAF(Ret.). Questionnaire No. 7747, 21 January 1982.

Spey, John R., Major, USAF(Ret.). Questionnaire No. 7101, 24 July 1981 and 22 December 1981.

Spivey, Delmar B., Lieutenant Colonel, USAF(Ret.). Questionnaire No. 7750, 27 October 1981.

Stihl, John T., Brigadier General, USAF. Questionnaire No. 7757, 19 October 1981.

Stipatich, John H., former Captain, USAF. Questionnaire No. 7759, 12 October 1981.

Stoner, Rex K., Jr., Lieutenant Colonel, USAF(Ret.). Questionnaire No. 7762, 27 October 1981.

Tanner, James L., Colonel, USAF(Ret.). Questionnaire No. 7774, 29 November 1981.

Thomas, Lowell V., Lieutenant Colonel, USAF. Questionnaire No. 7884, 22 February 1982.

Thompson, Joseph W., Master Sergeant, USAF(Ret.). Questionnaire No. 7785, 28 October 1981.

Topolosky, Michael J., Jr., Lieutenant Colonel, USAF(Ret.). Questionnaire No. 7793, 25 October 1981.

Tremaine, Alan D., Technical Sergeant, USAF(Ret.). Questionnaire No. 7798, 20 January 1982.

Uhler, Verne D., Master Sergeant, USAF(Ret.). Questionnaire No. 7805, 23 October 1981.

Waitt, Lawrence L., Lieutenant Colonel, USAF(Ret.). Questionnaire No. 7816, 1 November 1981.

Walker, Ralph L., Technical Sergeant, USAF(Ret.). Questionnaire No. 7820, 10 November 1981.

Watson, Ray E., Technical Sergeant, USAF(Ret.). Questionnaire No. 7828, 29 January 1982.

West, Lloyd A., Major, USAF. Questionnaire No. 7845, 10 December 1981, 9 February 1982, and 10 April 1982.

White, Donald E., Technical Sergeant, USAF(Ret.). Questionnaire No. 7853, 26 October 1981 and 17 March 1982.

Wildman, Winthrop W., Colonel, USAF(Ret.). Questionnaire No. 7858, 6 January 1982.

Williams, Thomas O., III, Colonel, USAF. Questionnaire No. 7860, 24 January 1982.

Willoughby, David J., Colonel, USAF(Ret.). Questionnaire No. 7861, 10 November 1981.

Wilson, Woodrow, Jr., Major, USAF. Questionnaire No. 7862, 9 January 1982.

Wolf, Richard E., Master Sergeant, USAF. Questionnaire No. 7867, 26 October 1981.

Woodcock, Herbert A., Jr., Lieutenant Colonel, USAF(Ret.). Questionnaire No. 7871, 18 November 1981.

Unpublished Diaries and Recollections

Ayers, Donald T., Colonel, USAF(Ret.). Diary of then-Captain Ayers, 19 November 1967-15 June 1968. In File 7131, item #1, RANCH HAND Archives, Texas A&M University.

———. Flight Log Book, 22 November 1967-17 October 1968. In File 7131, item #2, RANCH HAND Archives, Texas A&M University.

Hubbs, Charles H., Lieutenant Colonel, USAF(Ret.). "Cowboy Zero One." n.p. [1967]. Typescript. In the personal papers of Charles H. Hubbs, Camp Springs, Maryland.

McConnell, Arthur F., Jr., Lieutenant Colonel, USAF(Ret.). "Recollections of a RANCH HAND Commander - 1968." San Juan Capistrano, California, 17 September 1982. Typescript. In File 6016, RANCH HAND Archives, Texas A&M University.

West, Lloyd A., Major, USAF. Diary of then-Second Lieutenant West, 19 February 1968-2 January 1969. In File 7845, item #1, RANCH HAND Archives, Texas A&M University.

ARCHIVAL COLLECTIONS AND DOCUMENTS

Document and file titles beginning with numerals are listed in numerical order following the alphabetical listing in each section. The same scheme is followed when there is an internal mix of numbers and letters. All titles cited are preserved as on the original document or file.

Lyndon Baines Johnson Presidential Library, Austin, Texas

National Security File, Countries, Cambodia, Vol. 2, Cables, Box 236.

National Security File, Countries, Vietnam, Vol. 4, Box 2; Vol. 14, Box 6; Vol. 31, Box 15; Vols. 32-33, Box 16.

Vice-President Security File, Box 6, Col. Burris, Col. Burris.

White House Central File, Confidential File, National Defense 19/Countries 312 (Vietnam), Box 71.

John Fitzgerald Kennedy Presidential Library, Boston, Massachusetts

National Security File, National Security Council, NSAM 115, Defoliant Operations, Vietnam, Box 322.

Presidential Office File, Countries, Vietnam, Security, 1962.

White House Central File, National Security File, Countries, Vietnam, Vols. I, II, III, VI, X, Box 194-96; Vols. X, XII, Box 196-98.

Albert F. Simpson Historical Research Center of the United States Air Force, Maxwell Air Force Base, Alabama

Aircraft Records of C-123K, serial number 56-4362.

Air Force Developmental Aircraft. ARDC. April 1957. K243.04-4.

Air Surgeon's Office, Fifth Air Force History, May-December 1952. K730.740.

Blood, Gordon F. End-of-Tour Report, August 1967-January 1969. K740.131.

"Case History of the C-123 Airplane (26 April 1945-7 Sept. 1951)." Prepared by Margaret C. Bagwell. March 1952. K202.1-50.

CINCPAC Command History, 1962. K712.01.

CINCPAC to JCS, "Restriction on Use of Herbicide Orange," 280005Z May 70. K740.8051-3.

Command History, Hq US Military Assistance Command, Vietnam, 1967.

"Defoliation and Ranch Hand in the Republic of South Vietnam." 1 July 1965. Unsigned typescript, n.p. In K-GP-A-CMDO-315-SU-RE 1961-1965.

Department of Defense. Military Assistance Command, Vietnam. "Herbicide Program Seminar." Hq, MACV, Saigon, RVN, 28 January 1968. CH-5-4.

———. USMACV. "Year-End Review of Vietnam, 1968." CH-16-1-19.

Draft Report. Unsigned typescript, 1 June 1965. In K-GP-A-CMDO-315-SU-RE 1961-1965.

"Fifth Air Force in the Southeast Asia Crisis (A Sequel), 30 January 1962." Prepared by Arthur C. O'Neill. K730.04-22.

"Historical Data Requested by 315th A.C. Gp., 1 Jan. 65-8 Mar. 65." In K-GP-A-CMDO-315-SU-RE.

"Historical Data Requested by 309th A.C.S., 8 Mar 65-30 Jun 65." In K-GP-A-CMDO-315-SU-RE.

History, IX Troop Carrier Command, 5 November 1945-31 March 1946. Vol. 6. 546.01.

History of the Seventh/Thirteenth Air Force, 1969. K744.01.

History of the Tactical Air Command, January-June 1962. K417.01.

History of the Thirteenth Air Force. January-December 1962. January-June 1963. K750.01.

History of the USAF Special Air Warfare Center (TAC). January-June 1964. July-December 1964. July-December 1965. January-June 1966. July-December 1966. July-December 1967. January-June 1969. K417.0731.

History of the 2d Air Division, July-December 1964. K526.01.

History of the 315th Air Commando Wing. 1966. January-September 1967. January-March 1968. April-June 1970. K-WG-315-HI.

"Items for Discussion with the Secretary of Defense in the 23 July 1962 Meeting." K526.1511-6.

JCS to CINCPAC. "Restrictions on Use of Defoliants and Herbicides." 5 November 1969. CHECO Microfilm Cartridge # S-225,064.

Lake, Gordon W. End-of-Tour Report, 21 March 1968-8 March 1969. K740.131.

Letter. Office, Chief Chemical Warfare Service to Captain Merrick G. Estabrook, A.C. 21 November 1932. In 145.93-270 (November 1932 to April 1936).

Letter. To Commanding General, Headquarters 8th Corps Area, Fort Sam Houston, Texas, from Headquarters Fort Crockett, Texas. 20 December 1934. In 145.93-270 (November 1932 to April 1936).

Medical Support of Air Warfare in the South and Southwest Pacific, 7 December 1941-15 August 1945. 6 vols. 138.8-35.

Memorandum for Acting Chief of the Air Corps from L/C J. E. Chany, Chief, Plans Division. "Military Requirements for Distribution of Chemical Agents by Airplane." 23 November 1932. In 145.93-270 (November 1932 to April 1936).

Memorandum, for Assistant Chief of Staff, G-4 (Attention Colonel Carlett). "Airplane Spray (Chemical)." 29 September 1937. In 145.93-265.

Memorandum for Record by Major Donald J. Maxwell, In-Country RPC. 5 October 1970. K239.03032-6.

Message. COMUS to CINCPAC. "Effectiveness of Herbicide Operations." 30 August 1968. In CH-5-4-19.

"Military Aerial Spray Operations 1946-1960." By John I. Lumpkin and Mary J. Konopnicki. Undated typescript. K417.042-1.

Moore, William G., Jr. End-of-Tour Report. 25 October 1966-11 November 1967. K740.131.

Oral History Interview of Lieutenant Colonel Benjamin Kraljev by Lieutenant Colonel R. L. Bowers. 29 January 1971. Typed interview notes, n.p. K239.0512-778.

Oral History Interview of Ambassador Frederick E. Nolting, Jr., by Major Richard B. Clement and Dr. James C. Hasdorff. 9 November 1971. Typed transcript. K239.0512-489.

Oral History Interview with Colonel Don D. Pittman by Major Samuel E. Riddlebarger. 13 February 1969. Typed transcript. K239.0512-079.

Oral History Interview of Major Fred N. Thompson by Major Samuel E. Riddlebarger. 2 June 1970. Typed transcript. K239.0512-283.

Partridge, General E. E. "Diary of Korea, 1950-1951." In 168.7014-1, Vol. 3.

Personal Narrative of Captain John R. Spey. 3 July 1965. In K-GP-A-CMDO-315-SU-RE 1961-1965.

"Project CHECO Southeast Asia Report: Impact of Darkness and Weather in Air Operations in SEA." 10 March 1969. K717.0413-55.

"Ranch Hand Addition to 309th Historical Report." 31 December 1965. In K-GP-A-CMDO-315-SU-RE 1961-1965.

Report of the Army Air Forces Board, AAF Tactical Center, Orlando, Florida. "Marking and Defoliation of Tropical Vegetation, Project No. 3690B470.6." 18 December 1944. In 245.64.

"Report on Comparative Tests of Chemical Bombs - E2R6 and 30-lb. M1 and Test of Airplane Spray." Langley Field, Virginia. 21 March-3 June 1932. 248.222-36D.

"Secretary of Defense Book for January Meeting - 14 January 1962." K717.153-3.

Stoner, Rex K., Jr. End-of-Tour Report. 11 September 1968-8 September 1969. K740.131.

United States Air Force. Directorate of Maintenance Engineering. Modification Program Directive No. 1976 (FS-2159/UC-123K). 11 June 1968. CH-4-14.

———. PACAF. Headquarters, Seventh Air Force. "Final Report: Operational Evaluation of Project Pink Rose." 5 May 1967. K740.8051-2.

———. Seventh Air Force Report. "Investigation of Defoliation Damage to Cambodia." 13 October 1969. CH-41-2-19.

———. 834th Air Division. "Ranch Hand Study FY's 68-69-70." 12 September 1967. CH-4-12-13.

United States Department of War. "Spraying of DDT from Aircraft." Technical Bulletin MED 200. February 1946. In 546.01, Vol. 6, Pt. 2, App. 1.

United States Navy. CINCPAC. "Minutes of the JTCG/CB Subcommittee Meeting on Defoliants/Anti-Crop Systems." 4-5 June 1970. CINCPAC Headquarters, Hawaii. K717.03-139.

Unsigned letter dated October 1962 [Memo for Record, Col. Haygood, 6 October 1962]. Catalogued Project Cornoa Harvest, #0216340. K526.161-2.

"Use of Gas in Ethiopia-1936." Chemical Warfare School, Edgewood Arsenal, Maryland. 22 October 1936. Mimeographed. 248.222-36D.

1st Epidemiological Flight (Korea) History, September 1951-December 1960. K-MED-1-HI.

4th Epidemiological Flight (Europe-North Africa) History, September 1951-June 1960. K-MED-4-HI.

5th Epidemiological Flight (Korea) History, July 1952-June 1957. K-MED-5-HI.

7th AF Commander's Operations Command Book, July 1966-July 1967. K740.197.

"8th Ind. to AF 354.2 (5-15-35), HQ GHQ AF, Langley Field, VA, Mar 16, 1936 to the Adj. General, Washington, D.C." In 145.93-270 (November 1932 to April 1936).

309th Air Commando Squadron History January-June 1965. K-SQ-A-CMDO-309-HI.

315th Air Commando Group History. K-GP-CMDO-315-HI.

834th Air Division History. October 1966-June 1967. July 1968-June 1970. 1968. January -June 1971. K-DIV-834-HI.

GOVERNMENT DOCUMENTS

Australia. Report to the Minister for Veterans' Affairs. "Case-Control Study of Congenital Anomalies and Vietnam Service (Birth Defects Study): Report." By J. W. Donovan, Michael A. Adena, Glen Rose, and Diana Battistutta. Canberra, January 1983.

Great Britain. Parliament. *Parliamentary Papers, 1953-54.* Vol. 31, Miscellaneous No. 20 (1954), Command Paper 9239, "Further Documents Relating to the Discussion of Indochina at the Geneva Conference."

———. Parliament. *Parliamentary Papers, 1961-62.* Vol. 39, Vietnam No. 1 (1961), Command Paper 1551, "Eleventh Interim Report of the International Commission for Supervision and Control in Vietnam."

———. Parliament. *Parliamentary Papers, 1961-62.* Vol. 19, Vietnam No. 1 (1962), Command Paper 1755, "Special Report of the International Commission for Supervision and Control in Vietnam."

McConnell, Arthur F.,Jr. End-of-Tour Report. 24 January 1968-3 January 1969. M-42193-390, Classified Documents Section, Air University Library, Maxwell Air Force Base, Alabama.

Republic of Vietnam. Combat Development and Test Center. "The Employment of Helicopters in Defoliation Operations in the Republic of Vietnam." Special Report. By Lieutenant Colonel Stanley Fair, United States Army, and Captain Nouyen The Ton, Army of the Republic of Vietnam. Duplicate text, English/Vietnamese. 1964.

United States Congress. House. Committee on Foreign Affairs. *Chemical-Biological Warfare: U. S. Policies and International Effects, Hearings before the Subcommittee on National Security Policy and Scientific Developments of the Committee on Foreign Affairs.* 91st Cong., 1st sess., 1969.

———. House. Subcommittee on Science, Research, and Development of the Committee on Science and Astronautics. "A Technology Assessment of the Vietnam Defoliant Matter: A Case History." Prepared by Franklin P. Huddle, Science Policy Research Division, Legislative Reference Service, Library of Congress. Washington, DC, 1969.

———. Joint Committee on Defense Production. *Seventeenth Annual Report.* H. Rept. 1052, 90th Cong., 2d sess., 1968.

———. Senate. Committee on Commerce. Subcommittee on Energy, Natural Resources, and the Environment. *Effects of 2,4,5-T on Man and the Environment.* Serial 91-60. 91st Cong., 2d sess., 1970.

United States Department of Agriculture. "Airplane Dusting in Control of Malaria Mosquitoes." By W. V. King and D. L. Bradley. Circular 367. April 1926.

———. Agricultural Research Service. *A Survey of Extent and Cost of Weed Control and Specific Weed Problems.* ARS 42-23-1. Washington, DC, 1965.

———. Economic Research Service. *Extent of Spraying and Dusting on Farms, 1958 with Comparisions.* By Paul E. Strickler and William C. Hinson. Statistical Bulletin No. 314. Washington, DC, May 1962.

———. Forest Service. "Forest Fire as a Military Weapon: Final Report." By Craig C. Chandler and Jay R. Bentley. June 1970.

United States Department of the Air Force. Reprint of Testimony of Lieutenant General Paul W. Meyers, Air Force Surgeon General, to the Subcommittee on Medical Facilities and Benefits of the House Veterans Affairs Committee, 16 September 1980. In AFRP 190-2, October 1980, 37-39.

———. "Aircrew Procedures." Technical Manual T.O. 1C-123B-1.

———. Special Order GB-539, Headquarters USAF, Washington, DC, 23 October 1968.

———. Typescript of speech by Lt. Gen. (Dr.) Paul W. Meyers, Air Force Surgeon General, before the Annual Reunion of the RANCH HAND Vietnam Association, Tarpon Springs, Florida. 11 October 1980.

———. "Use of Herbicides." Technical Manual T.O. 42C-1-17. 22 November 1966.

———. Air Force Armament Laboratory. "Animal Survey Studies of Test Area C-52A Eglin AFB Reservation, Florida." Technical Report AFATL-TR-72-72. April 1972.

———. Occupational and Environmental Health Laboratory. "The Toxicology, Environmental Fate, and Human Risk of Herbicide Orange and Its Associated Dioxin." By Alvin W. Young, John A. Calcagni, Charles E. Thalken, and James W. Tremblay. Final Report, Report No. OEHL-TR-78-92. 1978.

———. Pacific Air Forces. "Herbicide Operations in Southeast Asia, July 1961-June 1967." By Charles V. Collins. Project CHECO Report No. DTEC-67-0020. 11 October 1967.

———. OPORD 224-61. 23 November 1961.

———. Special Order G-256, Headquarters, Pacific Air Forces, Hickam AFB, Hawaii, 25 August 1966.

———. Directorate of Operations Analysis. "Ranch Hand Herbicide Operations in SEA." Prepared by Captain James R. Clary. 13 July 1971.

———. Public Affairs Office, Westover AFB, MA. "S.E.A. Vet to A.F. Museum." News Release. 1 July 1980.

———. San Antonio Air Materiel Area. *Technical Manual: Use of Herbicides.* T.O. 42C-1-17. 22 November 1966.

———. School of Aerospace Medicine. Epidemiology Division. "An Epidemiologic Investigation of Health Effects in Air Force Personnel Following Exposure to Herbicides: Baseline Morbidity Study Results." By Colonel George D. Lathrop, Colonel Patricia M. Moynahan, Dr. Richard A. Albanese, and Lieutenant Colonel William H. Wolfe. 24 February 1984.

———. School of Aerospace Medicine. Epidemiology Division. "An Epidemiologic Investigation of Health Effects in Air Force Personnel Following Exposure to Herbicides: Baseline Mortality Study Results." By Colonel George D. Lathrop, Colonel Patricia M. Moynahan, Dr. Richard A. Albanese, and Lieutenant Colonel William H. Wolfe. 30 June 1983.

———. Seventh Air Force. "Seventh Air Force Programmed Action Directive 67-7." 29 October 1966.

―――. Tactical Air Command. "Category III Evaluation of the F-4/PAU-7/A Defoliant System." Final Report. March 1971.

―――. Tactical Air Command. Special Order No. TA-2618, Headquarters Pope AFB and 464th Air Base Group (TAC), 21 November 1961.

―――. Wright Air Development Center. "Engineering Study on a Large Capacity Spray System Installation for Aircraft." 3 June 1952.

United States Department of the Army. Chemical Corps. "Review and Evaluation of ARPA/OSD 'Defoliation' Program. Research Phase: 15 July 1961-12 January 1962, Operational Phase: 13 January 1962-March 1962 in South Vietnam." By Fred J. Delmore. [15 July 1962].

―――. Chemical Corps. Biological Laboratories. "Defoliation Target Marking and Its Implications." By S. R. McLane and E. W. Dean. Camp Detrick, Maryland. June 1955.

―――. Chemical Corps. Biological Laboratories. "Information Manual for Vegetation Control in Southeast Asia." By K. R. Irish, R. A. Darrow, and C. E. Minarik. 1969.

―――. Chemical Corps. Biological Laboratories. "Vegetational Spray Tests in South Vietnam, Supplement." Project 4B11-01-004. By James W. Brown. April 1962.

―――. Office of the Chief of Engineers. Engineer Strategic Studies Group. *Herbicides and Military Operations.* 3 vols. Washington, DC, 1972.

United States Department of Commerce. Tariff Commission. "Synthetic Chemicals: United States Production and Sales." 2d Series. Report No. 159. 1946.

United States Department of Defense. Assistant Secretary of Defense, Health Affairs. "Department of Defense (DOD) Herbicide Orange Status Report." Press Release [September 1980]. Mimeographed.

―――. Assistant Secretary of Defense, Systems Analysis. *A Systems Analysis View of the Vietnam War: 1965-1972.* Vol. 5: *The Air War.* Ed. by Thomas C. Thayer. Final Report. 18 February 1975.

―――. Directorate for Information and Reports. "Herbs Tape." [February 1974].

―――. Military Assistance Command, Vietnam. "Evaluation of Herbicide Operations in the Republic of Vietnam (September 1962-September 1963)." By Peter G. Olenchuk, Robert T. Burke, Oran K. Henderson, and Wayne E. Davis. 10 October 1963.

——. Military Assistance Command, Vietnam. "Military Operations: Herbicide Operations (U)." Report No. MACV Dir-525-1, 12 August 1969.

——. Military Assistance Command, Vietnam. "Report, AC of S, J3 to Chief of Staff, Subject: Evaluation of the Defoliation Program." 12 October 1968.

United States Department of the Navy. Commander-in-Chief Pacific Scientific Advisory Group. "Crop Destruction Operations in RVN During CY 1967." By William F. Warren, Lehman L. Henry, and Richard D. Johnston. Report No. Working Paper-20-67. 23 December 1967.

——. Commander-in-Chief Pacific Scientific Advisory Group. "A Review of the Herbicide Program in South Vietnam." By William F. Warren. Scientific Advisory Group Working Paper No. 10-68. August 1968.

United States Department of State. *Conference on the Limitation of Armament: Washington, November 12, 1921 - February 6, 1922.* Washington, DC, 1922.

——. "Department Urges Senate Approval of Geneva Protocol on Poisonous Gases and Biological Warfare." *Department of State Bulletin* 64 (29 March 1971), 455-59.

——. "Geneva Protocol on Gases and Bacteriological Warfare Resubmitted to the Senate." *Department of State Bulletin* 63 (7 September 1970), 273-75.

——. *Papers Relating to the Foreign Relations of the United States: The Paris Peace Conference, 1919.* 13 vols. Washington, DC, 1942-47.

——. Statement of Secretary of State Dean Acheson at Paris Ministerial Meeting. *Department of State Bulletin* 43 (22 May 1950), 821.

——. Statement of the United States Ambassador to the United Nations James F. Leonard, 10 December 1969, and Text of Resolutions. "Chemical and Biological Methods of Warfare." *Department of State Bulletin* 62 (26 January 1970), 95-99.

——. American Embassy, Saigon. Herbicide Policy Review Committee. "Report on the Herbicide Policy Review." 28 August 1968.

——. Bureau of Public Affairs. Statement of Richard Burt, Director of the Bureau of Politico-Military Affairs, before the Subcommittee on Arms Control, Oceans, International Operations, and Environment of the Senate Foreign Relations Committee, 10 November 1981. Reprinted in "Use of Chemical Weapons in Asia." *Current Policy* 342 (November 1981).

United States Department of War. *The War of the Rebellion: A Compilation of the Official Records of the Union and Confederate Armies.* 128 vols. Washington, DC, 1880-1901.

United States General Accounting Office. Report by the Comptroller General of the United States. "U.S. Ground Troops in South Vietnam Were in Areas Sprayed with Herbicide Orange." Report to the Permanent Subcommittee on Investigations, Committee on Governmental Affairs, US Senate, 16 November 1979.

United States Office of Science and Technology. "Report of 2,4,5-T: A Report of the Panel on Herbicides of the President's Science Advisory Committee." By Colin M. Macleod, John D. Baldeschweiler, Nyle C. Brady, Emmanuel Farber, Paul Kotin, Brian MacMahon, Norton Nelson, L. Dale Newsom, John W. Tukey, James G. Wilson, Edward J. Burger, Jr., and David Pimental. Washington, DC, 1971.

United States. Public Law 91-441. Section 501(c). 84 Stat. 913.

BOOKS

Austin, Anthony. *The President's War: The Story of the Tonkin Gulf Resolution and How the Nation Was Trapped in Vietnam.* Philadelphia, 1971.

Baldwin, Hanson W. *Great Mistakes of the War.* New York, 1950.

Berger, Carl, ed. *The United States Air Force in Southeast Asia.* Washington, DC, 1977.

Braestrup, Peter. *Big Story: How the American Press & Television Reported and Interpreted the Crisis of Tet in Vietnam and Washington.* Garden City, NY, 1978.

Browning, Frank, and Dorothy Forman, eds. *The Wasted Nations.* New York, 1972.

Burchett, Wilfred G. *Furtive War: The United States in Vietnam and Laos.* New York, 1963.

Carnegie Endowment for International Peace. *The Control of Chemical and Biological Weapons.* New York, 1971.

Carson, Rachel. *Silent Spring.* Greenwich, CT, 1962.

Churchill, Winston S. *Their Finest Hour.* Boston, 1949.

Clutterbuck, Richard L. *Long, Long War: Counterinsurgency in Malaya and Vietnam.* New York, 1966.

Cookson, John, and Judith Nottingham. *A Survey of Chemical and Biological Warfare.* New York, 1969.

Cox, Jacob D. *The March to the Sea.* New York, 1913.

Craven, Wesley F., and James L. Cate, eds. *The Army Air Forces in World War II.* Vol. 5: *The Pacific: Matterhorn to Nagasaki, June 1944 to August 1945.* Chicago, 1953.

Emme, Eugene M., ed. *The Impact of Airpower.* Princeton, 1959.

Falls, Cyril. *The Great War: 1914-1918.* New York, 1961.

Field Enterprises. *1968 World Book Year Book.* Chicago, 1968.

Fieser, Louis F. *The Scientific Method: A Personal Account of Unusual Projects in War and Peace.* New York, 1964.

Fox, Roger P. *Air Base Defense in the Republic of Vietnam, 1961-1973.* Washington, DC, 1979.

Ganoe, William A. *The History of the United States Army.* Rev. ed. New York, 1942.

George Westinghouse Centennial Forum. *Science and Life in the World.* Vol. 2: *Transportation—A Measurement of Civilization; Light, Life, and Man.* New York, 1946.

Gettleman, Marvin E., ed. *Vietnam: History, Documents, and Opinions on a Major World Crisis.* New York, 1965.

Goulden, Joseph C. *Truth Is the First Casualty: The Gulf of Tonkin Affair—Inclusion and Reality.* Chicago, 1969.

Haldane, John B. S. *Callinicus: A Defense of Chemical Warfare.* New York, 1925.

Harris, Robert, and Jeremy Paxman. *A Higher Form of Killing: The Secret Story of Chemical and Biological Warfare.* New York, 1982.

Harte, John, and Robert H. Socolow. *Patient Earth.* New York, 1971.

Henniker, Mark C. A. *Red Shadow Over Malaya.* Edinburgh, 1955.

Herbicide Handbook Committee. *Herbicide Handbook of the Weed Science Society of America.* 3d ed. Champaign, IL, 1974.

Hersh, Seymour M. *Chemical and Biological Warfare: America's Hidden Arsenal.* Indianapolis, 1968.

Hilsman, Roger. *To Move a Nation: The Politics of Foreign Policy in the Administration of John F. Kennedy.* Garden City, NY, 1967.

Infield, Glenn B. *Disaster at Bari.* New York, 1971.

Irving, David. *Destruction of Dresden.* London, 1963.

Johnson, Lyndon Baines. *The Vantage Point: Perspectives of the Presidency, 1963-1969.* New York, 1971.

Karnow, Stanley. *Vietnam: A History.* New York, 1983.

Kelner, Joseph. *The Kent State Coverup.* New York,1980.

Krylov, Ivan Nikititch. *Soviet Staff Officer.* Trans. by Edward Fitzgerald. London, 1951.

Lewallen, John. *Ecology of Devastation: Indochina.* Baltimore, 1971.

Lilienthal, David E. *The Journals of David E. Lilienthal.* Vol. 2: *The Atomic Energy Years, 1945-1950.* New York, 1964.

Ludendorff, Erich von. *Ludendorff's Own Story.* 2 vols. New York, 1919.

Michener, James A. *Kent State: What Happened and Why.* Greenwich, CT, 1971.

Miller, Francis T. *History of World War II.* Philadelphia, 1945.

Millett, Allan R., ed. *A Short History of the Vietnam War.* Foreword by Major General Edward G. Lansdale, USAF(Ret.). Bloomington, IN, 1978.

Morison, Samuel E. *The Two-Ocean War: A Short History of the United States Navy in the Second World War.* Boston, 1963.

National Academy of Sciences. National Research Council. Committee on the Effects of Herbicides in Vietnam, Division of Biological Sciences, Assembly of Life Sciences. *The Effects of Herbicides in South Vietnam, Part A — Summary and Conclusions.* Washington, DC, 1974.

Neilands, James B., Gordon H. Orians, Egbert W. Pfeiffer, Alje Vennema, and Arthur H. Westing. *Harvest of Death: Chemical Warfare in Vietnam and Cambodia.* New York, 1972.

Nguyen Khac Vien, ed. *Chemical Warfare.* Hanoi, 1971.

Oberdorfer, Don. *Tet!* Garden City, NY, 1971.

Palmer, Dave Richard. *Summons of the Trumpet: U.S.-Vietnam in Perspective.* San Rafael, CA, 1978.

Pan, Stephen Y. C., and Daniel Lyons. *Vietnam Crisis.* New York, 1966.

Paret, Peter, and John W. Shy. *Guerrillas of the 1960s.* New York, 1962.

The Pentagon Papers: The Defense Department History of United States Decision-making on Vietnam. 4 vols. The Senator Gravel Edition. Boston, 1971.

Pisor, Robert. *The End of the Line: The Seige of Khe Sanh.* New York, 1982.

Prentiss, Augustin M. *Chemicals in War.* New York, 1937.

Randall, James G., and David Donald. *The Civil War and Reconstruction.* 2d ed. Boston, 1961.

Schneider, Donald K. *Air Force Heoroes in Vietnam.* USAF Southeast Asia Monograph Series, Vol. 7, Monograph 9. Washington, DC, 1979.

Seagrave, Sterling. *Yellow Rain: A Journey Through the Terror of Chemical Warfare.* New York, 1981.

Shepard, Elaine. *The Doom Pussy.* New York, 1967.

Short, Anthony. *The Communist Insurrection in Malaya, 1948-1960.* New York, 1975.

Sorenson, Theodore C. *Kennedy.* New York, 1965.

Starr, Chester C. *A History of the Ancient World.* New York, 1965.

Stockholm International Peace Research Institute. *Ecological Consequences of the Second Indochina War.* Stockholm, Sweden, 1976.

————. *The Problem of Chemical and Biological Warfare: A Study of the Historical, Technical, Military, Legal and Political Aspects of CBW, and Possible Disarmament Measures.* Vol.1: *The Rise of CB Weapons.* Stockholm, Sweden, 1971. Vol. 4: *CB Disarmament Negotiations, 1920-1970.* New York, 1971.

Summers, Harry G., Jr. *On Strategy: A Critical Analysis of the Vietnam War.* Navato, CA, 1982.

Thomas, Ann Van Wynen, and A. J. Thomas. *Legal Limits on the Use of Chemical and Biological Weapons.* Dallas, 1970.

Thomas, Hugh. *The Spanish Civil War.* New York, 1961.

Thucydides. *History of the Peloponnesian War.* 4 vols. Trans. by C. Forester Smith. Leob Classical Library. New York, 1919-1923.

Utley, Robert M. *Frontier Regulars.* Paperback ed. Bloomington, 1977.

Webster, Charles K., and Noble Frankland, eds. *The Strategic Air Offensive Against Germany, 1939-1945.* 4 vols. London, 1961.

West, Francis J., Jr. *Small Unit Action in Vietnam, Summer 1966.* With an introduction by Brigadier General Edwin H. Simmons, USMC(Ret.). New York, 1967, 1981.

Westing, Arthur H., and Malvern Lumsden. *Threat of Modern Warfare to Man and His Environment.* Paris, France, 1979.

Westmoreland, William C. *A Soldier Reports.* Garden City, NY, 1976.

————. *Report on the War in Vietnam (as of 30 June 1968).* Washington, DC, 1969.

Whiteside, Thomas. *Defoliation.* New York, 1970.

Whitney, Richard W. *The Kent State Massacre.* Charlotteville, NY, 1975.

Winchey, Eugene G. *Tonkin Gulf.* Garden City, NY, 1971.

PUBLISHED REPORTS

Betts, Russell, and Frank Denton. *An Evaluation of Chemical Crop Destruction in Vietnam.* Report No. RM-5446-1-ISA/ARPA. Santa Monica, CA, 1967.

Donnell, John C., Guy J. Pauker, and Joseph J. Zasloff. "Viet Cong Motivation and Morale: A Preliminary Report." RAND Memorandum RM-4507-ISA, March 1965. Santa Monica, CA, 1965.

Goure, Leon. "Some Impressions of the Effects of Military Operations on Viet Cong Behavior." RAND Memorandum RM-4517-ISA, March 1965. Santa Monica, CA, 1965.

House, William B., Louis H. Goodson, Howard M. Gadberry, and Kenneth W. Dockter. *Assessment of Ecological Effects of Extensive or Repeated Use of Herbicides.* Final Report, 15 August-1 December 1967. MRI Project No. MRI-3103-B. Kansas City, 1967.

Russo, Anthony J. *A Statistical Analysis of the U.S. Crop Spraying Program in South Vietnam.* Report No. RM-5450-1-ISA. Santa Monica, CA, 1967.

Thomas, T. J., D. P. Brown, J. Harrington, T. Stanford, L. Taft, and B. W. Vigon. "Land Based Environmental Monitoring at Johnston Island - Disposal of Herbicide Orange." Final Report. Contract No. FO8635-76-D-0168. USAF OEHL Report TR-78-87. Columbus, OH, September 1978.

ARTICLES AND ESSAYS IN PERIODICALS AND BOOKS

AAAS Council. Resolution of 30 December 1966. *Science* 155 (1967), 856.

Aaronson, Terri. "A Tour of Vietnam." *Environment* 13 (March 1971), 34-43.

"The Attack on the Irrigation Dams in North Korea." *Air University Quarterly Review* 6 (1953-54), 40-61.

Azar'yev, S., Major General. "Employment of Chemical Weapons in South Vietnam by the American Interventionists." *Voyennaya Mysl' (Military Thought)* 8 (August 1968), translated in *Foreign Press Digest* 0019/70 (30 March 1970), 88-92.

Bay, Charles H. "The Other Gas Crisis—Chemical Weapons: Part I." "The Other Gas Crisis—Chemical Weapons: Part II." *Parameters* 9 (September 1979), 70-80; 9 (December 1979), 65-78.

Beecher, William. "Chemicals vs. the Viet Cong: 'Right' or 'Wrong'?" *National Guardsman* 20 (February 1966), 2-6.

Bethel, J. S., K. J. Turnbull, David Briggs, and Jose Flores. "Military Defoliation of Vietnam Forests." *American Forests* 81 (January 1975), 26.

Blair, Edison T. "The Air Commando." *Airman* 6 (September 1962), 19-23.

Boffey, Phillip M. "Herbicides in Vietnam: AAAS Study Finds Widespread Devastation." *Science* 171 (1971), 43-47.

Butz, J. S., Jr. "Tactical Airpower in 1965 ... The Trial by Fire." *Air Force and Space Digest* 49 (March 1966), 35-42.

"CBW Treaty." *Congressional Quarterly Almanac* 26 (1970), 444-46.

"Defoliation: AAAS Study Delayed by Resignations from Committee." *Science* 159 (1968), 857.

Devillers, Philippe. "Ngo Dinh Diem and the Struggle for Reunification in Vietnam." *In Vietnam: History, Documents, and Opinions on a Major World Crisis,* 210-34. Edited by Marvin E. Gettleman. New York, 1965, 210-34.

"Dioxin Puts Dow on the Spot." *Time* 121 (2 May 1983), 62.

"Discussion." *North Central States Weed Control Conference: Proceedings of the Second Annual Meeting (November 26-28, 1945).*

Downs, Eldon W., and George F. Lemmer. "Origins of Aerial Crop Dusting." *Agricultural History* 39 (1965), 123-35.

"Effects of Herbicides." *Congressional Quarterly Almanac* 26 (1970), 495.

Egler, Frank E. "Review - Herbicides and Vegetation Management -Vietnam and Defoliation." *Ecology* 49 (1968), 1212-15.

Fair, Stanley. "No Place to Hide: How Defoliants Expose the Viet Cong." *Army* 14 (September 1963), 54-55.

Fall, Bernard B. "This Isn't Munich, It's Spain: A Vietnam Album." *Ramparts* 4 (September 1965), 23-29.

"From Academy Reports: To Study Effects of Agent Orange on Health. . . ." *News Report* [National Academy of Science] 3 (July 1980), 5.

Galston, Arthur W. "Warfare with Herbicides in Vietnam." In *Patient Earth,* 136-50. Edited by John Harte and Robert H. Socolow. New York, 1971.

Goldblat, Jozef. "Are Tear Gas and Herbicides Permitted Weapons?" *Bulletin of the Atomic Scientists* 26 (April 1970), 13-16. Reprinted in Congressional Record 116:20567-69. 91st Cong., 2d sess., 1970.

Gonzalez, Arturo F., Jr. "Defoliation—A Controversial U.S. Mission in Vietnam." *Data* 13 (October 1968), 12-15.

Hammer, Ellen J. "Genesis of the First Indochinese War: 1946-1950." In *Vietnam: History, Documents, and Opinions on a Major World Crisis,* 63-86. Edited by Marvin E. Gettleman. New York, 1965.

Harvey, George R., and Jay D. Mann. "Picloram in Vietnam." *Scientist and Citizen* 10 (September 1968), 165-71.

"Hearings before the House Foreign Affairs Subcommittee on National Security Policy and Scientific Development, November and December, 1969." *Congressional Quarterly Almanac* 25 (1969), 797.

Hersh, Seymour M. "Our Chemical War." *New York Review of Books* 10 (1968), 31-36. Reprinted in *Congressional Record* 115:5480-83. 91st Cong., 1st sess., 6 March 1969.

Hildebrand, E. M. "War on Weeds." *Science* 103 (1946), 465-68.

Holmberg, Bo. "Biological Aspects of Chemical and Biological Weapons." *Ambio: A Journal of the Human Environment* 4 (1975), 211-15.

Holway, Richard T., A. W. Morrill, and F. J. Santana. "Mosquito Control Activities of the U.S. Armed Forces in the Republic of Vietnam." *Proceedings and Papers of the Thirty-fifth Annual Conference of the California Mosquito Control Association and the Twenty-third Annual Meeting of the American Mosquito Control Association* 35 (5-8 February 1967), 23-29.

Johnstone, L. Craig. "Ecocide and the Geneva Protocol." *Foreign Affairs* 49 (1971), 711-20. Reprinted in *Congressional Record* 117:28550-52. 92d Cong., 1st sess., 1971.

Karber, Phillip A. "The Nixon Policy on CBW." *Bulletin of the Atomic Scientists* 28 (January 1972), 22-27.

Kelly, Joseph B. "Gas Warfare in International Law." *Military Review* 41 (March 1961), 30-42.

Kephart, L. W. "Chemical Weed Killers After the War." *Proceedings of the First Annual Meeting of the North Central States Weed Control Conference 16-17 November 1944,* 79-82.

Kraus, E. J., and John W. Mitchell. "Growth-Regulating Substances as Herbicides." *Botanical Gazette* 108 (March 1947), 301-49.

Lawrence, Robert de T. "USAF Aids South Viet-Nam." *Airman* 6 (August 1962), 38-41.

Leitenberg, Milton. "America in Vietnam: Statistics of a War." *Survival* (Institute for Strategic Studies, London) 14 (1972), 268-74.

Letter. *Science* 154 (1966), 284.

"The Limitation of Naval Armaments." *Congressional Digest* 8 (1929), 233.

Lund, Diderich H. "Revival of Northern Norway." *Geographical Journal* 109 (1947), 185-97.

MacArthur, D. M. "Treaties and the Use of Military Chemicals." *Ordnance* 50 (1966), 464-66.

Mayer, Jean. "Starvation as a Weapon: Herbicides in Vietnam, I." *Scientist and Citizen* 9 (August-September 1967), 115-21.

Merck, George W. "Peacetime Implications of Biological Warfare." In *Science and Life in the World.* The George Westinghouse Centennial Forum. 3 Vols. Vol. 2: *Transportation—A measurement of Civilization; Light, Life, and Man,* 129-46. New York, 1946.

Minarik, Charles E. "Crops Division Defoliation Program." *First Defoliation Conference, Proceedings, July 1963* (January 1964), 21-22.

Murphy, Paul. "Gas in the Italo-Abyssinian Campaign." *Army, Navy, and Air Force Gazette,* 3 September 1936. Reprinted in 248.222-36D, Albert F. Simpson Historical Research Center.

Nechayuk, L. "Weapons of 'Civilised' Barbarians." *Soviet Military Review* 8 (1971), 52-54.

Neillie, C. R., and J. S. Housen. "Fighting Insects with Airplanes." *National Geographic Magazine* 41 (1922), 333-34.

Ngo Vinh Long. "Leaf Abscission?" *Bulletin of the Concerned Asian Scholars* 2 (October 1969), 54.

Novick, Sheldon. "The Vietnam Herbicide Experiment." *Scientist and Citizen* 10 (January-February 1968), 20-21.

Nowell, Wesley R. "Aerial Dissemination of Insecticides by the United States Air Force." *Proceedings, New Jersey Mosquito Extermination Association and American Mosquito Control Association* (9-12 March 1954), 82-92.

———. "The Entomological Program in the United States Air Force." *Proceedings, New Jersey Mosquito Extermination Association and American Mosquito Control Association* (9-12 March 1954), 76-82.

"Operation Ranch Hand." *Weeds, Trees, and Turf* 8 (March 1969), 20-22.

Orians, Gordon H., and Egbert W. Pfeiffer. "Mission to Vietnam, Part 1." "Mission to Vietnam, Part 2." *Scientific Research* 4 (9 June 1969), 22; 4 (23 June 1969), 26.

Osborne, Daphne J. "Defoliation and Defoliants." *Nature* (London) 219 (1968), 564-67.

Ott, M. G., B. B. Holder, and R. D. Olson. "A Mortality Analysis of Employees Engaged in the Manufacture of 2,3,5-trichlorophenoxy acetic acid." *Journal of Occupational Medicine* 22 (January 1980), 47-50.

"The Pacific Air Forces." *Air Force and Space Digest* 47 (September 1964), 100-3.

Peterson, Gale E. "The Discovery and Development of 2,4-D." *Agricultural History* 41 (1967), 243-53.

Pfeiffer, Egbert W. "Some Effects of Environmental Warfare on Agriculture in Indochina." *Agriculture & Environment* 2 (1975), 271-81.

Powell, John W. "Japan's Biological Weapons, 1930-1945: A Hidden Chapter in History." *Bulletin of the Atomic Scientists* 37 (October 1981), 44-52.

Pruden, Wesley, Jr. "Defoliating the Jungles in Vietnam." *National Observer* 5 (28 February 1966), 1.

Reggiani, G. "Acute Human Exposure to TCDD in Seveso, Italy." *Journal of Toxicology and Environmental Health* 6 (January 1980), 27-43.

"Report Actually Refuted Most Defoliation Scare Stories." *AIM* [Accuracy In Media] *Report* 3 (March 1974), 1-2.

Richardson, B. W. "Greek Fire." *Popular Science Review* 3 (1964), 176.

Rickles, Robert, and Harold Holzer. "Agent Orange." *Rolling Stone* (4 March 1982), 11.

Ripley, Diane. "Agent Orange: What It Is and Does." *Rolling Stone* (4 March 1982), 13.

Rowen, James. "Dumping 'Agent Orange'." *New Republic* 166 (January-June 1972), 10-11.

Santori, Al. "Why Viet Cong Flee." *Parade* (11 July 1982), 4-7.

Schreuder, O. B., and W. N. Sullivan. "Spraying of DDT from Airplanes." *Air Surgeon's Bulletin* 2 (March 1945), 67-68.

Shapley, Deborah. "Herbicides: Agent Orange Stockpile May Go to the South Americans." *Science* 180 (1973), 43-45.

––––––. "Herbicides: DOD Study of Viet Use Damns with Faint Praise." *Science* 177 (1972), 776-79.

"Statement by President Richard M. Nixon." *Congressional Quarterly Almanac* 25 (1969), 797.

Tran Van Dinh. "Did the U.S. Stumble into the Vietnam War?" *Christian Century* 85 (1968), 755.

Tschirley, Fred H. "Review Ecological Effects of Extensive or Repeated Use of Herbicides." *Ecology* 49 (1968), 1211-12.

––––––. , ed. "Scientific Dispute Resolution Conference on 2,4,5-T." Richmond, IL, 1979. Cited in Alvin L. Young, "Agent Orange at the Crossroads of Science and Social Concern." Air University, Air Command and Staff College, Student Report No. 2570-81, Maxwell AFB, AL, 1981.

"Vegetation Destruction in Vietnam Will Hamper Vegetation Control in the U.S." *Chemical Engineering* (24 April 1967), 88.

"Vietnam: Buildup." *Newsweek* 58 (27 November 1961), 40.

"Vietnam Still Fertile." United Press International report. Reprinted in *American Forestry* 81 (January 1975), 30.

Warner, Geoffrey. "The United States and Vietnam 1945-65, Part II: 1954-65." *International Affairs* 48 (1972), 593-615.

Watriss, Wendy. "Agent Orange." *Texas Observer* 73 (25 September 1981), 1, 8-13.

West, Clarence J. "The History of Poison Gases." *Science* 49 (1919), 412-17.

Westing, Arthur H. "Ecocide in Indochina." *Natural History* 80 (March 1971), 56-61.

————. "U.S. Food Destruction Program in South Vietnam." In *The Wasted Nations*, 21-25. Edited by Frank Browning and Dorothy Forman. New York, 1972. Also in New York Times, 12 July 1971, 27.

Whiteside, Thomas. "A Reporter At Large: Defoliation." *New Yorker,* 7 February 1970, 34.

Zack, Judith A., and Raymond D. Suskind. "The Mortality Experience of Workers Exposed to Tetrachlorodibenzodioxin in a Trichlorophenol Process Accident." *Journal of Occupational Medicine* 22 (Jan 1980), 11-14.

NEWSPAPER ARTICLES

"AF Air Commandos 'De-Bug' Vietnam." Unidentified 1967 newspaper clipping in File 7165, item #13, RANCH HAND Collection, Texas A&M University Archives, College Station, Texas.

"Agent Orange Class Action Thrown Out." *Bryan-College Station* (Texas) *Eagle,* 27 November 1980, 10C.

"Agent Orange Data Compiled." *Austin American-Statesman,* 8 August 1982, C4.

"Agent Orange Exams Are Called Inadequate." *Austin American-Statesman,* 27 February 1983, C1.

"Agent Orange Lawsuit." *Washington Post,* 15 October 1979, A20.

"Agent Orange Pact Gets Tentative Okay from Federal Judge." *Austin American-Statesman,* 26 September 1984, A4.

"Agent Orange Research Pressured Out of VA Jurisdiction." *Austin American-Statesman,* 15 October 1982, A4.

"Agent Orange Suits Given OK." *Washington Star,* 30 December 1980, A5.

"Agent Orange Victims Handed Pay Setback." *Austin American-Statesman,* 29 May 1985, A7.

"Ailing Veteran Blames Army Herbicide." *Washington Post,* 2 December 1979, A31.

"An Anti-U.S. Play Opens In London." *New York Times,* 15 October 1966, 32.

"Australian Report Clears Defoliant." *Austin American-Statesman,* 23 August 1985, A10.

"Bacteria Blamed for Ailments." *Bryan-College Station* (Texas) *Eagle,* 6 February 1982, 9A.

Beecher, William. "U.S. Will Step Up Defoliation Missions in Vietnam." *New York Times,* 10 September 1966, 2.

Bigart, Homer. "U.S. Shuns Harm to Vietnam Food." *New York Times,* 16 January 1962, 2.

———. "U.S. Spray Strips Foliage Hiding Vietnam Reds." *New York Times,* 19 January 1962, 4.

Blumenthal, Ralph. "U.S. Says Unit in Vietnam Used Banned Defoliant." *New York Times,* 24 October 1970, 3.

———. "U.S. Shows Signs of Concern Over Effect in Vietnam of 9-Year Defoliation Program." *New York Times,* 14 March 1970, 14.

"Bombing Is Protested." *New York Times,* 19 June 1964, 5.

Brewer, Sam P. "U.S. Is Accused of Chemical War." *New York Times,* 30 July 1964, 2.

"Cambodia Prods U.N. on U.S. Defoliants." *Washington Post,* 4 June 1969, A18.

Chitwood, Jim. "Target: Range C-52A." *Pensacola* (Florida) *News-Journal,* 1 February 1981, 1-2.

Cimons, Marlene. "Veterans Gaining Ground in Agent Orange Struggle." *Los Angeles Times,* 27 December 1979, 12.

"Commandos Draw Bead on VN Malaria Mosquito." *Seventh Air Force Times,* 31 March 1967, 3.

Dawson, Alan. "Saigon Regime Riddled with Viet Cong Before Its Fall." *Washington Star,* 9 September 1975, A3.

"The Day 3 Flyers Cheated Death." *San Francisco Chronicle,* 1 November 1966, 2.

"Debunking the Myth of Agent Orange." *Santa Rosa* (California) *Register,* 13 June 1981, D14.

"Defoliation Effort Delayed in Vietnam." *New York Times,* 12 January 1962, 3.

Diamond, Stewart. "'Most-Shot-At' Title May Go to Crews of Defoliation Unit." *Air Force Times,* 26 January 1966, 4.

"Dioxin Peril in Missouri Unexpected." *Austin American-Statesman,* 14 May 1983, A7.

"Dioxin Threats Rated Low on List of Problem Chemicals." *Austin American-Statesman,* 10 December 1983, A5.

"Dispatch from Phnompenh." *New York Times,* 3 September 1964, 2.

Earley, Pete. "Death Rate of Defoliant Crews Called Normal." *Austin American-Statesman,* 1 December 1982, A8.

————. "Delay on VA Study of Agent Orange May Be Extended." *Austin American-Statesman,* 8 August 1982, C4.

Editorial, "Deal Appears Fair on Agent Orange." *Austin American-Statesman,* 9 May 1984, A12.

Editorial, "Lord Russell's Letter." *New York Times,* 8 April 1963, 46.

"Exposure to Malaria 'Routine'." *Pacific Stars & Stripes.* Undated clipping in File 7165, item #12, RANCH HAND Collection, Texas A&M University Archives, College Station, Texas.

Famiglietti, Len. "Agent Orange: Physical Exams to Begin This Fall." *Air Force Times,* 4 May 1981, 2.

————. "AF Bows to Criticism, Won't Do Orange Study." *Air Force Times,* 26 May 1980, 26.

"Few Birth Defects Related to Defoliant, Study Shows." *Daily Texan* (University of Texas), 25 August 1983, 11.

"Fight for San Sebastian." *Times* (London), 19 August 1936, 10.

Flint, Jerry M. "Dow Aides Deny Herbicides Risk." *New York Times,* 18 March 1970, 72.

Franklin, Jon, and Alan Doelp. "Dangers of Dioxin Are Proven, But Not Vietnam Vet's Charges." *Baltimore Evening Sun,* 21 February 1980, A4.

———. "Vietnam Veterans' Fear, Rage Focus on 'Deadly Fog'." *Baltimore Evening Sun,* 20 February 1980, 1.

"Front-Line Units Urge Defoliation." *New York Times,* 2 October 1966, 5.

"Gas Bombs In Kworam." *Times* (London), 17 March 1936, 15.

"Goldwater Poses New Asian Tactic." *New York Times,* 25 May 1964, 1.

"Greeks 'Smoke Out' Foes." *New York Times,* 21 March 1949, 3.

"Hanoi Says U.S. Chemicals Kill South Vietnam Infants." *New York Times,* 11 April 1966, 2.

"Hanoi Sees Birth Defects." *New York Times,* 30 December 1970, 8.

Harkavy, Jerry. "VA Offering Free Medical Tests for Agent Orange." *Houston Chronicle,* 16 December 1981, 2.

"Herbicide Effect Unsettled." *Austin American-Statesman,* 27 March 1984, B2.

"Herbicide's Effect on Airman Study Topic." *Midland* (Michigan) *Daily News,* 5 June 1970, 1.

Hornblower, Margot. "A Sinister Drama of Agent Orange Opens in Congress." *Washington Post,* 27 June 1979, A4.

"Houston Lawyer Rebuked." *Houston Post,* 9 January 1985, 8A.

"Issued by Cuba." *New York Times,* 9 December 1966, 4.

"Italian Gas Warfare." *Times* (London), 23 March 1936, 12.

"Italian Moves in Abyssinia." *Times* (London), 20 March 1936, 13.

"Japanese Scientists Score U.S." *New York Times,* 8 October 1966, 3.

"Jungle Suits." *Wall Street Journal,* 5 January 1981, 9.

Keegan, Anne. "Agent Orange." *Bryan-College Station* (Texas) *Eagle,* 15 March 1981, 1A.

———. "Agent Orange." *Bryan-College Station* (Texas) *Eagle,* 17 May 1982, 5A.

"Lawyers Pool Information in Agent Orange Lawsuit." *Santa Rosa* (California) *Register,* 23 September 1980, 1.

"Madrid Again Bombed." *Times* (London), 4 December 1936, 16.

Mohr, Charles. "Defoliation Unit Lives Perilously." *New York Times,* 20 December 1965, 3.

"Nixon Ban on Agent Orange Claimed." *Austin American-Statesman,* 16 November 1983, A8.

"The Northern Front: A Critical Phase." *Times* (London), 4 April 1936, 14.

"'Outside' Scientists Monitor Agent Orange Study." *Air Force Times,* 6 October 1980, 9.

Pace, Eric. "Spray Killing of Enemy's Crops Stepped Up by U.S. in Vietnam." *New York Times,* 26 July 1966, 2.

"Peiping Says US Uses Gas." *New York Times,* 5 March 1961, 3.

"Pentagon Triples Spending on Defoliation in Vietnam." *New York Times,* 15 March 1967, 2.

"A Poison Gas Victory: Emperor's Protest." *Times* (London), 1 July 1936, 16.

Press Conference on Agent Orange, 23 September 1981, Washington, D.C., by Richard S. Schweiker. Quoted in *Bryan-College Station* (Texas) *Eagle,* 24 September 1981, 4A.

"Psywar Pilots Pave Way for Sprayers." *Seventh Air Force News,* 7 June 1967, 4.

Pusch, Barbara. "Local Veteran Files Agent Orange Damage Suit." *Fort Walton Beach* (Florida) *Playground Daily News,* 25 April 1981, 1.

Raymond, Jack. "Army Seeks Way to Strip Jungles." *New York Times,* 6 June 1961, 11.

Rehm, Barbara. "U.S. Accuses Soviets of Afghan Toxin Use." *Austin American-Statesman,* 30 November 1982, A9.

Reinhold, Robert. "Times Beach Buyout Leaves Clean-up Questions Unanswered." *Austin American-Statesman,* 27 February 1983, C1.

"Russell Defends War Crimes Trial." *New York Times,* 6 October 1966, 46.

"Russell 'War Crimes Trial' May Not Be Held in Paris." *New York Times,* 8 October 1966, 2.

"San Sebastian Warning." *Times* (London), 8 September 1936, 12.

"Sartre on Panel to 'Try' U.S. Leaders." *New York Times,* 3 August 1966, 2.

Schmidt, Dana A. "Genocide Is Laid to U.S. at 'Trial'." *New York Times,* 8 May 1967, 8.

Seabrook, Charles. "Agent Orange Birth Perils Discredited." *Austin American-Statesman,* 17 August 1984, A1.

Shorlett, Sidney. "U.S. Was Prepared to Combat Axis in Poison-Germ Warfare." *New York Times,* 4 January 1946, 13.

Spaulding, James. "Spraying Leaf Killers in Vietnam: US Scientists Plan a Full Study." *Milwaukee Journal,* 12 January 1969, 5.

Speer, Rod. "Viet Vets Mobilizing for Protests on July 4." *Santa Rosa* (California) *Register,* 27 June 1982, A3.

"Spray Planes Shield Crippled Craft from Ground Fire." *Pacific Stars & Stripes.* Undated clipping in File 7165, item #7, RANCH HAND Collection, Texas A&M University Archives, College Station, Texas.

"The Spreading Offensive: Fighting Around Makale." *Times* (London), 31 December 1935, 11.

Teltsch, Kathleen. "U.S. Says Cambodia Blocks U.N. Efforts." *New York Times,* 12 Sepember 1964, 1.

———. "U.S. Urges Inquiry on Poison Charge." *New York Times,* 15 May 1964, 2.

Trumbull, Robert. "Saigon Builds Up for Drive on Foe." *New York Times,* 1 January 1962, 1.

"U.S. Denies It Defoliates Zone." *New York Times,* 23 September 1966, 14.

"U.S. Is Defoliating Near Buffer Zone." *New York Times,* 24 September 1966, 2.

"U.S. Planes Defoliate Buffer Zone." *San Francisco Chronicle,* 7 February 1967, A14.

"U.S. Planes Defoliating Southern Half of DMZ." *Pacific Stars & Stripes,* 8 February 1967, 2.

"U.S. Troops Begin Major Offensive." *New York Times,* 7 February 1967, 12.

"Use of Poison Gas: A German Allegation." *Times* (London), 7 July 1937, 15.

"Veteran Who Battled Defoliant Dies." *Los Angeles Times,* 17 December 1978, 16.

"Veterans to Oppose Agent Orange Pact." *Austin American-Statesman,* 8 August 1984, A9.

"Vets Say Health Shunned." *Bryan-College Station* (Texas) *Eagle,* 28 March 81, 11A.

"Viet Cong Is Accused." *New York Times,* 30 July 1964, 2.

"Vietnam Policy Protested." Letter from Bertrand Russell, 28 March 1963. *New York Times,* 8 April 1963, 46.

"War Vets in Agent Orange Fight." *Bryan-College Station* (Texas) *Eagle,* 15 March 1981, 3A.

"Warnings on Agent Orange Indicated in Company Files." *Austin American-Statesman,* 4 February 1985, A4.

"Washington Rebuts Poison Gas Charge." *New York Times,* 11 March 1963, 4.

"Westmoreland Submits A Defoliation Request." *New York Times,* 27 September 1966, 3.

Woodruff, John E. "U.S. Is Expected to End Task of Viet Defoliation." *Baltimore Sun,* 30 August 1969, 24.

Yack, Patrick. "Herbicides in Vietnam Leave a Legacy of Fear." (Jacksonville) *Florida Times-Union,* 9 September 1979, A1.

"5 Pct. of S. Viet Defoliated; U.S. Calls It 100 Pct. Success." *Pacific Stars & Stripes,* 28 September 1968, 7.

"22 Scientists Bid Johnson Bar Chemical Weapons in Vietnam." *New York Times,* 20 September 1966, 1.

"29 Scientists Score Use of Chemicals on Viet Cong Crops." *New York Times,* 17 January 1966, 4.

TELEVISION PROGRAMS

"Agent Orange: Vietnam's Deadly Fog." Television Documentary. WBBM-TV, Chicago, Illinois, 12 March 1978. Transcript.

"Barney Miller." Television Series. ABC Television Network. Broadcast of 5 March 1981.

"Eric Sevareid's Chronicle." Television News Documentary. KTVH, Houston, Texas, 20 June 1982.

UNPUBLISHED MATERIALS

Crochet, Calvin J. "A Special Report on Operation Pink Rose." Air University, Air Command and Staff College, Maxwell AFB, Alabama, June 1970.

Dougherty, Joseph M. "The Use of Herbicides in Southeast Asia and Its Criticism." Air University, Air War College, Professional Study No. 4562, Maxwell AFB, Alabama, 1972.

Downs, Eldon W., and John H. Scrivner. "Defoliation Operations in Southeast Asia, A Special Report." Air University, Aerospace Studies Institute, Special Report No. 70-16, Maxwell AFB, Alabama, March 1970.

Howard, John D. "Herbicides in Support of Counter-Insurgency Operations: A Cost-Effectiveness Study." Naval Postgraduate School Thesis, Monterey, California, 1972.

Shade, Robert A. "Management of the Department of Defense Vietnam Herbicide Program." M.S. thesis, George Washington University, 1969.

Young, Alvin L. "Agent Orange at the Crossroads of Science and Social Concern." Air University, Air Command and Staff College, Student Research Report No. 2750-81, Maxwell AFB, Alabama, 1981.

MISCELLANEOUS MATERIALS

Adams, George T. Typescript describing RANCH HAND operations between 1961 and 1964. n.p. [August 1964]. In personal files of JohnoR. Spey, Fort Walton Beach, Florida.

Cecil, Paul F. Personal Records Group and Air Force Form 5. In possession of the author, Round Rock, Texas.

Letter, Lieutenant General Max B. Bralliar, Surgeon General, USAF, to Jack Spey, 25 March 1983. Reprinted in "RANCH HAND Newsletter," 1 September 1983 (typescript). Newletter File, RANCH HAND Collection, Texas A&M University Archives, College Station, Texas.

"RANCH HAND Newsletter," June 1975. Newsletter File, RANCH HAND Collection, Texas A&M University Archives, College Station, Texas.

"RANCH HAND II Population Status as of September 1981." Typed copy of USAF RANCH HAND Study Briefing Slide. Briefing by Lieutenant Colonel George D. Lathrop. [October 1981].

Stammer, Eugene D. End-of-Tour Report, 27 July 1964. In the personal papers of Earle H. Briggs, Jr., Pensacola, Florida.

Stanford Biology Study Group. "A Legacy of Our Presence: The Destruction of Indochina." Pamphlet. Stanford, California., [c.1970].

Typescript of Radio Hanoi Broadcast in English to Europe and Asia, 14/1406Z October 1962. In the personal papers of Earle H. Briggs, Jr., Pensacola, Florida.

12th Air Commando Squadron Briefing Form. Undated typescript. In the personal papers of the author, Round Rock, Texas.

Index

About the Author

Paul Frederick Cecil is currently Senior Research Historian for the Texas State Historical Association, Austin, Texas, and an Associate Editor in charge of automated data processing for the *Handbook of Texas*, the definitive work on Texana. A native of Hutchinson, Kansas, he became an adopted Texan when he retired as a Lieutenant Colonel in 1974 after more than 20 years with the United States Air Force. His service career included nearly 6,000 hours flying time, 26 awards and decorations, and 1,068 combat missions in Vietnam, including duty as a RANCH HAND instructor pilot. After leaving the Air Force, he earned three degrees, including a Ph.D. from Texas A&M University where he began his research on *Herbicidal Warfare*. A military historian, he also is an active baseball and football official at the high school and college level, including the Southwest Conference. Besides memberships in numerous professional historical and military organizations, he is currently historian and archivist for the RANCH HAND Vietnam Association.